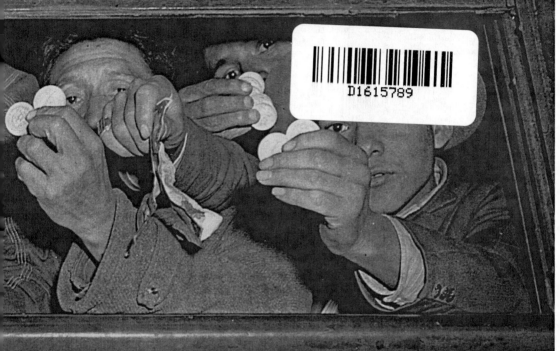

BRACEROS

Migrant Citizens and Transnational Subjects
in the Postwar United States and Mexico

DEBORAH COHEN

Designed by and set in Whitman with Archive Antiqua Extra Condensed and Viper
Nora by Rebecca Evans. The paper in this book meets the guidelines for permanence
and durability of the Committee on Production Guidelines for Book Longevity of the
Council on Library Resources. The University of North Carolina Press has been a
member of the Green Press Initiative since 2003.

Parts of this book have been reprinted with permission from the following articles:
"Masculinité et visibilité sociale: le spectacle de l'Etat dans la construction de la nation
mexicaine," *Clio: histoire, femmes, et societé* 12 (2000): 163–76; "Caught in the Middle:
The Mexican State's Relationship with the United States and Its Own Citizen-Workers,
1942–1958," *Journal of American Ethnic History* 20, no. 3 (2001): 110–32; "Masculinity
and Social Visibility: State Spectacle in the Construction of the Mexican Nation,"
Estudios Interdisciplinarios de América Latina y el Caribe 16, no. 1 (2005): 119–32;
and "From Peasant to Worker: Migration, Masculinity, and the Making of Mexican
Workers in the US," *International Labor and Working Class History* 69 (2006): 81–103.

Library of Congress Cataloging-in-Publication Data
Cohen, Deborah, 1968–
Braceros: migrant citizens and transnational subjects in the postwar United States
and Mexico / Deborah Cohen.
     p. cm.
"Published in association with the William P. Clements Center for Southwest Studies,
Southern Methodist University."
Includes bibliographical references and index.
ISBN 978-0-8078-3359-9 (cloth: alk. paper)
ISBN 978-1-4696-0974-4 (pbk.: alk. paper)
1. Migrant agricultural laborers—United States—History—20th century. 2. Mexicans—
United States—History—20th century. 3. Migrant labor—Government policy—United
States—History—20th century. 4. Transnationalism. 5. United States—Emigration and
immigration—Social aspects. 6. Mexico—Emigration and immigration—Social aspects.
7. United States—Foreign economic relations—Mexico. 8. Mexico—Foreign economic
relations—United States. I. Title.
HD1525.C62 2010   331.5'44097309045—dc22   2010029264

cloth   15 14 13 12 11   5 4 3 2 1
paper 17 16 15 14 13   5 4 3 2 1

Yeah, in the fields they would sing. . . . Thirty, forty,
or fifty. . . . Life was hard, very hard, and beautiful.
—ISMAEL DÍAZ DE LEÓN, ex-bracero

Well, the term "bracero" . . . it is a word of distinction,
for me it is a word of great pride. I would like that word
to go down in history.—JUAN LOZA, ex-bracero

Contents

     A section of photographs appears after p. 198.

BRACEROS

Places of interest in California and Mexico

Introduction

"I lived with many other men, in a barracks," Álvaro García told me as he snipped a customer's hair. He was, as always, holding court in the local barbershop he owned in a small village in the central part of the Mexican state of Durango. "I had never done that—lived with other men before—only with my family." The barbershop served as a central meeting place for the *pueblo* elders and thus was where I spent most afternoons during my fieldwork. It was the summer of 1995. Don Álvaro, then in his late sixties, recounted his tale to the audience of several men seated with me on a low wooden bench or poised in the doorway, all of whom nodded in agreement.[1] This man of a complicated geography and social positioning was blessed with salt-and-pepper hair and an engaging smile, which he flashed at unexpected moments. "I remember lying in bed at night," he continued, "right before the lights went out, and listening . . . After we had been there awhile, after we had gotten paid and bought radios, you'd hear lots of music. . . . You'd hear television, a phonograph, too; men bought these things. I brought back a radio that used batteries . . . a small one. Someone who went before me brought back one that required electricity when we didn't have electricity. . . . I liked that radio. . . . Only braceros had them. They were progress."[2]

Don Álvaro had gone north as part of the bracero program, the unofficial name for the series of agreements between Mexico and the United States that began in 1942, during World War II, and lasted till 1964. The program brought Mexican men to the United States for temporary work in agricultural fields and then sent them home again.[3] In our many conversations, don Álvaro taught me much about what it meant to be a bracero. He spoke of modern technological innovations and the progress that he sought. Between long days in the field and nights in crowded barracks, don Álvaro learned to cut hair and started to practice this trade. On his return, he used the money he had saved to buy a few more head of cattle, invest in his land, and open the community's first barbershop. By the time I met him, he owned a tractor and more land, which he and hired laborers worked a few mornings a week. The barbershop was doing a brisk, if often unpaid, business. Though far from wealthy, don Álvaro was now one of the *pueblo*'s most influential men. He had left his country a poor farmer and returned to become a small business owner and prominent local citizen.

Don Álvaro's upward mobility was not unique, for the bracero program yielded economic benefits for many of its nearly 2 million participants.[4] Indeed, his economic betterment was understood as a by-product of the modernization that the program was designed to extend to all braceros: an individual modernization figured as key to Mexico's national transformation. The story that don Álvaro recounts also has a deep U.S. resonance. It parallels a grand narrative of opportunity, progress, and self-refashioning that newly arrived immigrants have been told and which some have later recited about the promise of their new nation. While this narrative shaped public expectations for the program, its actual history is not a simple account of progress. Rather, the bracero program spurred a broad and complicated remaking of the relationships between citizen and nation, state and world, which did not mirror the trajectory from premodern to modern that U.S. and Mexican program architects imagined for the Mexican men who would travel northward. Stories such as don Álvaro's speak to this dissonance between expectations held by principal parties and the actual transformations that these actors would undergo.

These expectations, and the struggles to realize them, are a window onto the profound transformations that occurred. The bracero program involved negotiations between many influential parties, such as Mexican and U.S. government officials, growers, and labor activists. Yet those actors ostensibly lowest on the economic ladder—the labor migrants themselves who traveled from communities in Mexico to U.S. agricultural fields and back—also shaped the program. When a man (the program excluded women) applied to migrate, he began a crossing that would bring him into contact with not only various Mexican state representatives but also other critical program actors in the United States: domestic farmworkers, the leaders and rank and file of agricultural labor unions, growers and their foremen, tavern owners, and Catholic priests.

This is not a story of braceros' transformations alone, however. The interactions, negotiations, and struggles between such critical actors produced a particular transnational system and space. *Transnational*, as used here, connotes a mutually constitutive process, not a relationship that merely extends its roots or ties beyond the nation.[5] Nor am I suggesting that braceros were the only transnational actors. Although many—in particular, state agents, growers, and U.S. domestic farmworkers—appear to be securely and fully positioned within a single national context, the positions and subjectivities of *all* these actors were nevertheless negotiated vis-à-vis ideologies, experiences, social categories, and practices that mapped this transnational world.

Yet migrants were the ones who came to be seen as transnational. Examining the process through which braceros became transnational shows the complexity of this transnational world and how this system operated at its center and its seams. This privileging of braceros' transformations, then, problematizes the conventional ways and arenas in which the effects of migration and relations between nations have been seen. Even though the bracero program formally ended virtually fifty years ago, the U.S.-Mexican economy remains predicated on labor migration built around ties and knowledge from this earlier period. Today's migrants are courted by U.S. growers (and a host of other businesses) even as they are objects of derision and nationalist fears and the vexed focus of state policymakers and labor organizers.[6] The ways braceros inhabited political and social borders between, beyond, and in relation to the nation reveal how these nation-states and their attendant actors were mutually constituted, largely through a language of the modern.

This transnational world—which I talk about as the border—and those actors most associated with it—the braceros—became the focus for nationalist, often xenophobic, anxieties, because many of the actors involved were deeply invested in a worldview for which the transnational constituted a dire threat. Core to this worldview was the belief in, and accompanying narrative of, progress and opportunity. Its privileged agent was the citizen of one sovereign nation-state that engaged in fraternal—that is, equal—relations with other sovereign nation-states. The promise of progress lay at the heart of *the modern*, the then broadly accepted term for the ideological package that figured progress, democracy, and technological and scientific advancement as unquestionable goals. Modernization theory, the theory of how nations and peoples achieved the modern, defeated eugenicist models of national development that strictly correlated the modern with the whiteness of a nation's citizenry. While modernization theory never explicitly denied, a priori, the ability to achieve the modern or reap its benefits to any nation or people, the "modern" (like the "nonmodern" or its variants, the "traditional" or "primitive") carried lingering overtones from earlier eugenicist models; whiteness and maleness were still the standard, with the "nonmodern" associated with the feminine and nonwhite. Understandings of the modern not only shaped U.S. and Mexican expectations for the program and the scope of government policies; they also acted as fodder for the profound transformations—full of fits, starts, and dead ends—that program participants would undergo. The modern anchored entrenched alliances between some program actors (U.S. growers and the state; and the U.S. and Mexican states), framed the questioning and realignment of others (braceros and the Mexican state), and severed the hopes of solidarity between still others (braceros and domestic farmworkers). While all stakeholders were transformed through the program, braceros alone came to be seen as problematically and perpetually transnational. Analyzing the social world framed by the modern and produced in the negotiation of these multiple relationships makes vivid issues of national identity, exploitation, the rise of consumer cultures, development, and gendered class and race formation.

I am not suggesting that the program's importance comes from the modernization of bracero workers—others before me have noted this unintended result for earlier migrations.[7] Nor am I implying that this was the first moment in which U.S. foreign policy promoted the modernization of those countries deemed backward and primitive, for a related logic undergirded policies from the Monroe Doctrine to the then-reigning Good Neighbor Policy. Nor was this the only time that the Mexican government recognized migration's modernizing possibilities: a policy in the mid-1870s offered land to southern European immigrants, seen as white and more advanced than rural Mexicans, and in the 1920s and 1930s bureaucrats again used land offers, this time to lure U.S.-resident Mexicans and their U.S.-acquired skills back home. These migration policies courted those *already* modern; in the bracero program, by contrast, those deemed *ready* for modernization were to be sent to the quintessential place of the modern (the United States), transformed, and returned home. That is, the program not only had modernization as an explicit goal rather than an incidental outcome, which *both* state signatories supported; this modernization was built around human transformation through migration. As we will see, the program that coincided with the heyday of the nation-state as a global organizing principle would produce not just national but transnational actors.

Migrants were the intended objects of transformation, yet all involved were transformed. Braceros, however, would disproportionately bear the costs of this system. Leaving their homes as peasants, members of communal landholding projects (*ejidatarios*), sons of revolutionary soldiers, urban factory laborers, paid farmhands, and Mexicans, they came into contact with growers, foremen, priests, domestic farmhands, and U.S. and Mexican state agents, and returned as transnational subjects and part of a larger transnational world.[8] By transnational subject, I refer to a particular kind of political and social person with ties to, claims on, or self-understanding beyond the nation.[9] Such sociopolitical persons recognize themselves as participants in multiple national communities, albeit not equally or in the same way, as well as in a community that transcends the nation. This occurs despite the fact that national communities do not always recognize such persons as unambiguously national or transnational. In short, a transnational subject is both national *and* supranational, simultaneously exceeding or misaligned with these affective political bodies.

While braceros are key in making this transnational world visible, it would be a mistake to presume that they always started as fully national subjects. The nation was not the only, or even the strongest, imagined community in play for men who sought to migrate. Often their vibrant connections were familial, local, sometimes regional, and even transnational, as many already had work experience and family north of the border. Part of migrants' transformation, as we will see, was into national subjects. Their often fragile national connections were due, in part, to the timing of the program, which began during an explicit moment of Mexican nation building. The program's first year, 1942, was only two and a half decades distant from the Mexican Revolution (1910–17), which had torn apart the principal state institutions and devastated poor communities in many parts of the country.[10] It had wrenched the president, state officials, and former oligarchs from elite positions, as those who demonstrated military prowess and bravery established a new state structure. Because these new elites were linked to different industries, regions of the country, and competing revolutionary factions with distinct priorities, the revolutionary state's orientation changed.

Crucial in this reorientation was who could exert pressure on the state and make demands for national inclusion. Since the revolution was animated by calls for land, liberty, and better living conditions, and was carried forward through the efforts of peasants and the poor, officials were beholden to this mobilized constituency, even as they sought to bring these citizens into the national sphere in a way that diminished their organization and power. To ground the nation-state project designed in the revolution's aftermath, bureaucrats used a collectivist language that contrasted, at times explicitly, with the often individualist rhetoric of the United States. In short, Mexican officials sought to make citizens national in a particular mold.

Fundamental to making braceros national was making them modern. President Manuel Ávila Camacho (1940–46) and officials, like the earlier Mexican elites and government agents who had faulted peasants for the country's backwardness, imagined the national benefits to be reaped from transforming the country's poor rural men into modern national subjects and tasked the bracero program with their modernization.[11] Mexican bureaucrats contended—and the California legislature later agreed—that in the United States braceros would learn modern farming techniques and absorb its work ethic.[12] Armed with such knowledge and a pot of money from the program's mandated saving plan, these now-modernized men would put this knowledge into practice and change unproductive Mexican land into modernized farms. As we will see, the conditions under which braceros labored too often challenged any depiction of the United States as modern, or the program as a vehicle for modernization. Still, these unmodern conditions did not shake the faith of Mexican or U.S. state actors in this work as modernizing or in the rewards that a democratic capitalist modernization would yield, which braceros would come to share.[13] The modern, then, undergirded the transnational world that the program tapped into and fostered.

The negotiation of this world involved complex interactions between braceros and the array of program principals. Braceros sought respect for their work and for themselves in the United States despite facing a priori obstacles that denied it to them. They demanded the national belonging promised by the Mexican state both in its revolutionary agenda and at men's induction into the program. In so doing, braceros simultaneously became U.S. racially marked aliens, Mexican citizens, workers, and transnational subjects as they moved and interacted within and between U.S. and Mexican national spaces.[14]

A broadly cultural approach to questions of state-to-state relations, the political economy of labor migration, and the intensification of large-scale corporate agriculture shows these issues to be rooted in and connected to current concerns over globalizations and transnational politics. By focusing on actors and processes at the state, federal, and global level while prioritizing braceros' transformations, we see the economic practices that various

Mexican officials sought to instill in migrants, along with the kinds of attachments deemed essential to transform braceros into proper citizens. At the same time, large agriculturalists petitioned for support from the U.S. government, solidifying a state-grower alliance. This alliance shaped the program's diplomatic context and the resulting relationship between Mexico and the United States. Struggles over such multiple and often competing agendas and political projects, which every significant protagonist brought to the program, shaped the ensuing transformations.

This struggle over competing projects produced a specifically transnational subjectivity, along with a transnational space from which braceros tried to and did assert claims on each state. Here I draw on three senses of the prefix *trans-*: *trans-* as going beyond, which denaturalizes the nation; *trans-* as relational, made in the in-between; and *trans-* as change, as in the subject position formed and in play between nations and through crossing borders. Although the framework through which braceros were both made protagonists of Mexico and excluded from the status of the modern in the United States was seemingly nation based, it too was transnational. It depended on the ideological borders between Mexico and the United States, borders which, like the nation-states themselves, were mutually constituted. In short, the nation-state is a transnationally, not just nationally, contingent and ongoing project.

The modern, then, was the ultimate border that braceros had to cross. Men's attempts to cross it produced new, distinctly bracero subjectivities, which were set in dialogue with state functionaries, local officials, and community and family members and fostered different claims on the nation. Thus, the process of becoming foreigners in one country and new kinds of citizens vis-à-vis the other made them transnational subjects: tied to these nation-states and yet not fully or uncomplicatedly of either. For the United States, Mexico, and the braceros themselves, the program put into play questions of who was modern, what the modern looked like, and who could make these determinations. In short, through relationships with other program stakeholders, braceros became simultaneously national, alien, transnational, and modern, a process with important implications on nation-state formation.

Examining the migration between the central swath of Durango and the Imperial Valley in California (always the state ranked either first or second in the number of braceros used) helps elucidate the tensions between the local, regional, national, and transnational so central to the metamorphosis of braceros and of the transnational world emerging from the program. The valley is an important site not just because of the sheer numbers of braceros who worked there (in the first half of 1956, for example, 10 percent of California's total bracero allotment worked in Imperial County alone, and in the subsequent year almost 80 percent of the county's seasonal farm laborers were braceros). Its importance also stems from the fact that the very agricultural practices and labor regimes used in the valley (first with proletarianized domestic agricultural workers and then with braceros) helped make California the nation's preeminent agricultural state.[15] Seemingly national actors, such as domestic farmhands, were made transnational through these regimes, and growers turned into elites through their success at exploiting transnational markets. The same processes that (re)shaped braceros as transnational subjects were strategically taken up and used by these migrants and domestic farmworkers to advocate for the rewards and privileges they believed they were due. California, imagined as hypermodern at home and abroad, brought together the investment that migrants, domestic farmworkers, growers, and the U.S. and Mexican governments had in the program.[16] The Imperial Valley clearly reveals the economic, political, and social processes and practices at work in the bracero program and the subsequent realignment now termed globalization.

Durango also stands out for several reasons. First, the people of this state, and northern Mexico in general, were seen as more "European looking" (i.e., whiter and less indigenous) and more endowed with European racial characteristics than those in other parts of the country. That is, they were the sort of people whom the Mexican state imagined as most ready for modernization and in whom it was most willing to invest energy to modernize.[17] Second, the region had already been the locus of twentieth-century development projects, in particular, large-scale cotton growing and textile manufacture, akin to those the Mexican government would subsequently urge for the rest of the country.[18] Third, the Laguna, a region comprising northeastern Durango and southwestern Coahuila, was the principal site of this seed-to-fabric production system, which gave rise to decades of workers' and peasants' protests for better working conditions. Thus, Laguna workers had participated in the same type of labor regimes as would braceros, and some braceros had even labored in these fields and factories. Fourth, the area had an earlier and more complete history of integration into a U.S. sphere of influence than other regions of Mexico. Therefore, many of these men were already familiar with the labor projects and attendant social relations and commodities that all braceros would experience in the United States. In short, the Mexican government saw Durango's people as more ready to be modernized. Though these men had rebelled against the kind of worker discipline that braceros would encounter in Southern California, the area itself was already structured in ways similar to those the government hoped the bracero program would bring.[19] Moreover, later in the century many economic and social arrangements affecting the area would come to dominate the entire country as well as the United States and beyond. These social and spatial arrangements affected, and were affected by, the program, and they in turn shaped and were used by migrants as the latter (like other program stakeholders) became transnational subjects.

When I began this project I was taken aback that a program so intuitively antimodern could have been expected to modernize these men. Braceros, after all, came to do the agricultural stoop labor that was, in the United States, considered quintessentially backward. How could anyone have believed that World War II's Axis powers could be defeated through men's stoop labor, as then-contemporary Mexican newspapers alleged? Furthermore, how could U.S. and Mexican government actors have been sincere in their framing of the program? I assumed that this seemingly preposterous notion was merely a cover and a tool to lend legitimacy. Researchers since have condemned the program as abusive and exploitative, and I initially greeted contemporary articles, ads, and government announcements in local Durango newspapers with skepticism.

Nevertheless, I plugged along in my research, noting the consistency in framing. Day after day I sat in Durango's main library, my power cord stretched across the room and the laps of other researchers to reach the only outlet. There I encountered local and national newspaper articles trumpeting the country's modernization, alongside ads for everything from household appliances to clothes to furniture to makeup sold by a cast of family characters that would have been at home in any U.S. newspaper of the time. In the ads, the husband, wife, and two children were smartly dressed and set in a well-appointed living room, bedroom, or kitchen, with hairstyles and clothes pulled from *Leave It to Beaver* reruns. Homes depicted in the newspapers did not reflect the ones that I saw even five decades later. Rather, these ads and articles captured the broad sentiment behind the possibilities of Mexico's coming modernization. This same high spirit was conveyed in yellowed documents in Durango's cramped state archive and in more spacious rooms in national archives in Mexico City and Washington. In many ways, it was akin to what Manuel Gamio, a famous Mexican anthropologist turned government official, had noted in the 1920s and 1930s, when he saw manual labor as a valuable opportunity—a sort of classroom where a host of modern skills and attitudes might be learned. Gamio's hopefulness was everywhere.

I even found this energy and spirit in former braceros' recollections of the program. I had expected memories of racism and discrimination, yet that was not what I found. Or, more to the point, it was not what the men wanted to talk about. Instead, they described a range of mostly positive experiences. Still, I was skeptical. I assumed that, seeing my "white" female face, hearing my fluent but accented Spanish, knowing my national affiliation, they would present me with stories they thought I wanted to hear. I presumed that they were trying to make their experiences more palatable to my ears and to appear strong and in command of their past to theirs.

Yet men did mention negative and contentious incidents. They told me of having to work under extreme conditions, of not getting the food, salaries, or living conditions they had been promised; about who had cheated them—not only U.S. government representatives and growers (as I expected) but also Mexican officials (in the United States and Mexico) and the Mexican American foremen with whom they interacted so closely—and what they had done to rectify these situations. They recounted confrontations with local police in the United States, the U.S. Border Patrol, and Mexican officials at home and at the border. They talked about being threatened, cheated, and harassed when they returned to Mexico, and about the comical (at least at five decades' distance) incidents that occurred due to their lack of English. For many, these moments were mentioned in passing, almost as if they took this treatment for granted, as par for their life's course. What, I wondered, was going on?

One afternoon when I was returning from the archives, something clicked. The language of opportunity, progress, and modernization that I was reading about every day was not a cover—both governments' policies drew on it, as did newspaper ads and articles, the writings of Manuel Gamio and the U.S. farm labor activist and scholar Ernesto Galarza, and the stories of former migrants. I realized that it was part of the wider logic of that moment, a logic structured around the desire for the modern. In recognizing the influence of the language and logic of the period, I do not seek to get inside the heads of the multitudes of U.S. and Mexican officials, growers, foremen, labor leaders, domestic farmworkers, and Catholic priests active in the program (if that were even possible) or portray their often competing visions and agendas as a single coordinated (state) project. Rather, there was a general convergence concerning economic goals and the explicit methods formulated to accomplish them.[20] That is, there was a broad worldview or ideology, a commonsense, then in play that this array of disparate actors supported.[21] The modern constituted that commonsense.

This worldview was not just held by supporters but also by the program's many opponents, who prized the possibilities of the modern and decried the exploitative and unsanitary conditions in which braceros were forced to live in the United States, and the long hours they were forced to work. Abused by growers, maltreated or neglected by state officials, and humiliated by racial discrimination, these men were victims, contended the critics. Though on the face of it program detractors held a radically different perspective, notions of exploitation, like those of progress, encompassed the expectation of a linear path toward the modern. In short, this exploitation-versus-opportunity frame was used by stakeholders and the larger public to debate the merits of program, and it continues to be used today.[22] While I do not dismiss the extreme abuse some braceros experienced, the lack of analysis of this frame has not only obscured braceros' actions to fight such abuse but also concealed the global restructuring then under way, some of which braceros furthered.

This modernist framing was visible in everything I read, yet historians do not rely only on the visible surface of things. What is absent from documents—what cannot be said—is often just as critical to a particular historical moment as what is present.[23] This is especially true for illiterate or marginally literate historical protagonists or those without ties to modes of communication or the governmental bureaucracy. Reading the silences, reading against the grain, reading what is missing from a historical conversation—these are now understood as fundamental to the historian's craft, and challenges I have taken seriously.

Who were these men? Why did they want to migrate? How did they understand the complexities of their journeys northward? How, in turn, did their complex experiences shape understandings of themselves, Mexico, the United States, and the transnational world of the program? The world I construct here, with its particular social and spatial arrangements, draws for evidence on my almost four years of ethnographic fieldwork spread out across two Durango *pueblos*, the city of Durango, and the Chicago neighborhood home to The Eatery, a restaurant (like most in the city) with a large Mexican immigrant workforce, and my analysis of a range of other primary and secondary historical sources (government documents, newspapers, songs, rituals, papers of U.S. and Mexican activists, testimonies written by growers, as well as research by political scientists, economists, and historians). I also conducted more than thirty interviews with former braceros (and several Mexican state officials) to answer these questions.

When I first met Álvaro García, the barbershop owner whose story opens this chapter, and others residents of the small Durango town of Santa Angélica, they asked me what I was doing in there, even though they knew I was friends with a lawyer whose family lived in the *pueblo* and owned a small general store. After all, I was not family to anyone, and Santa Angélica is far off the tourist path. I told them about my research on the bracero program and that neither the Mexican nor U.S. governments had adequately recognized the value of their labor. The Mexican government, I said, denied both the extent and importance of migration, while in the United States, Mexican migration was framed in terms of illegality and the loss of jobs for U.S. workers. I said I wanted to publicize the contributions that they, as former braceros, had made to the economic, social, political, and cultural lives of both countries.

As people learned of my project, my presence alone would shift the barbershop conversations to recollections of journeys or memories associated with migration. Men would talk among themselves about these experiences, while I sat and listened. I avoided asking specific questions or guiding the conversation, although frequently I requested additional explanation. Still, the resulting discussion would move in a direction more of their making than of mine and in ways that I could never have predicted. I was able to interact with the men over a long period of time and to develop deeper friendships with many. This also gave me access to other events in the *pueblo*.

These open-ended barbershop conversations contrast starkly with the interviews I conducted in San Andrés, the other Durango community I studied. Again, I entered the community through a contact (in this case, Roberto, a colleague at the Instituto de Investigaciones Históricas [Institute for Historical Research] of the Universidad Juárez del Estado de Durango [Juárez University of the State of Durango]), where I was affiliated. During my fieldwork in 1995–96, I stayed at his in-laws' house there. In their late seventies and unable to maneuver the *pueblo*'s unpaved streets, they asked a neighbor, Guillermo, to help me. This young married man spent his mornings baking bread and pastries and his afternoons escorting me around the village.

Strolling the rocky streets of San Andrés during my first visit, Roberto and I came across a group of older men hanging out on a street corner. We walked over and Roberto introduced me, saying that I was interested in talking to men who had been braceros. I chatted with each of them individually for a few minutes and jotted down their names. I told them that I would return the following week and asked if I could talk to them at greater length. One man on the corner that afternoon was Mauricio Herrera, then almost completely blind, who had first migrated during the mid-forties. During a subsequent conversation at his house he mimicked the bodily motion required to pick cotton, which I describe in chapter 5 as I analyze how this arduous work contributed to the creation of a transnational subjectivity. I also met Antonio Ramírez and Luis Camarena, both in their mid-seventies. Don Antonio, a musician, told me that he had been asked to play the guitar and sing at a prison while abroad. Don Luis, who had a broad and now deeply wrinkled face, talked about his troubles with Mexican border guards when he returned. As I elaborate in chapter 7, my conversation with him focused on these incidents, so fundamental to his understanding of the program.

San Andrés had no singular meeting place akin to Santa Angélica's barbershop, so Guillermo and I went from house to house to talk to former braceros. During my second visit, we compiled a basic list of all the residents who had migrated during the program—about forty—and sought to interview each in his home. At the start of these interviews I gave the same vague synopsis of why I was there and tried to let the men just talk about their experiences. Yet the act of interviewing individual men in their homes a single time, with family members roaming about, meant that I asked more direct questions and obtained information that was different from what I gained in Santa Angélica. Whereas the barbershop generated extensive conversations about the braceros' various experiences, to which I usually remained peripheral, here the men talked only to me . . . or rather, to Guillermo, since the conversation was largely directed at him as they knew him and I was an unmarried woman. These in-home interviews focused on details about the program and the work routine: how much money they had made, when they went and with whom, which crops they hoped to or hated to pick. With a few notable exceptions, which I attribute to the deeper relationship some had with Guillermo, men were less forthcoming with stories not directly connected with work, such as how they spent their time outside of work or the moments of confusion they faced.

At first I was disappointed by what these men were telling me. Their precise details did not draw me in as much as the lengthy barbershop conversations did. Plus, because I spoke with them only once, I did not get to know them as I did the men of the barbershop. However, as I later reflected on how each group of men portrayed their experiences and what each considered important, I realized that their portrayals, alongside my other documentary, textual, and ethnographic evidence, revealed the nuances of a transnational world and of braceros as its critical constituents.

I did not recognize the complexity of this transnational world until I returned to Chicago and poured over my fieldnotes and documents. Former braceros expressed satisfaction at having had the chance to work in the United States and refused to see themselves as victims or martyrs. They portrayed themselves instead as actors: they fought for their rights (however this term is defined) and made their world, an attitude captured with equal clarity in the archival materials. Document after historical document showed the strategies that men used to push their grievances and the lengths to which they went to have disputes favorably resolved. Labeled passive and docile by U.S. agriculturalists (and even Mexican American foremen), braceros demanded that Mexican consular officials, U.S. state employees, and growers take them and their demands seriously. Moreover, the attitude of ex-braceros when describing experiences suggests that they saw their participation as important—not just in own lives, but in the resulting economic and social configuration of Mexico and the United States. They wanted recognition for their important contribution. In the end, I began to see their words and my analysis of literary texts, state records, newspaper articles, letters from union activists, and the like, as a window on social hierarchies and relationships at work within both the United States and Mexico, and on a world comprised of experiences unique and momentous, and dull and monotonous. This book has been shaped by the ways migrants depicted and understood their experiences, the program, and its legacies, and their refusal to be seen as victims.

Braceros' interactions with other critical program actors—such as growers, the leaders and rank and file of U.S. labor unions, religious leaders, and state actors from both countries—shaped a particular social world. The first of this book's three parts, "Producing Transnational Subjects," exposes the transnational connections and ideological underpinnings of all principal actors involved in the program—bureaucrats for the two governments, the U.S. growers, and the braceros. These shaped the expectations of individuals and groups and formed the foundation of the program itself. Chapter 1, "Agriculture, State Expectations, and the Configuration of Citizenship," analyzes the expectations that U.S. and Mexican government actors had for the program. Understandings of the modern, grounded in prior transnational economic, social, and political relationships and the realignments then under way, configured these expectations. Key ideological components embraced by state agents undergirded the very design and mission of the program, a mission communicated to the men who sought to migrate as well as to larger domestic audiences. Chapter 2, "Narrating Class and Nation: Agribusiness and the Construction of Grower Narratives," turns to growers' expectations for the program and about their farmhands, domestic and foreign. These expectations were conditioned by the long-standing narrative of the small, family farmer as bulwark of Jeffersonian democracy, a narrative recast as one about modern businessmen and selectively used during the program to coincide with the importance that the entire nation saw in all things modern. This dual narrative and its necessary juggling show the transnational grounding of seemingly nation-based claims, which enabled the formation of elite growers as a class. Chapter 3, "Manhood, the Lure of Migration, and Contestations of the Modern," explores the hopes of aspiring and actual migrants, specifically, the masculinist desire to be modern and its imagined benefits. This desire was a site of braceros' negotiation with the Mexican government over the gendered form for the nation's modern citizen. Various actors each saw something at stake in the program and sought to shape it correspondingly, drawing on a specific set of nationally and transnationally resonant symbols.

Part 2, "Bracero Agency and Emergent Subjectivities," examines the emergence of a particular transnational subjectivity that occurred as migrants struggled to realize their migration expectations. Chapter 4, "Rites of Movement, Technologies of Power: Making Migrants Modern from Home to the Border," analyzes the bracero selection process as a set of moments in which men recognized, engaged, accommodated, and resisted state demands that they act like the backward rural men they were supposed to be. It was one point in their state-imagined transformation from backward to modern. The next chapter, "With Hunched Back and on Bended Knee: Race, Work, and the Modern North of the Border," uses men's living, working, and leisure conditions to analyze how these challenged what men understood to be the purpose of the program and how men rebutted those challenges. The gendering and realignment of certain connections, such as class and nation, came to the forefront, while more localized others retreated to the background. Chapter 6, "Strikes against Solidarity: Containing Domestic Farmworkers' Agency," picks up on the previous chapter's engagement with class. Domestic farmworkers refused to align themselves with braceros as a class but instead retrenched around national difference, itself racialized. Given the preemptive closing off of this potential bracero–domestic farmworker alliance, we can understand why other possible bracero claims, such as that on the nation, became more salient. This leads to the next chapter, "Border of Belonging, Border of Foreignness: Patriarchy, the Modern, and Making Transnational Mexicanness." Men went to great lengths to claim their place in the Mexican nation, anchored in their newly acquired position as modern subjects. Braceros' encounters with Mexican border guards and others, such as family and friends, once they returned home reveal the realms that men sought to modernize and for which they sought recognition as modern citizens, as well as those spaces off limits from this modernizing transformation—the domestic. Men struggled to accomplish their own particular goals for the program, struggles that opened up certain alignments and closed off others in ways that brought about a transnational subjectivity.

Part 3, "The Convergence of Elite Alliances," shows the impact of braceros' emergent subjectivities, how men's actions and demands on both governments and nations strained and reconfigured elite alliances. Its sole chapter, "Tipping the Negotiating Hand: State-to-State Struggle and the Impact of Migrant Agency," suggests how bracero demands and transformations affected the wider terrain of the program, the relationship between the United States and Mexico, and larger global political, economic, and social arrangement. While program rules were officially dictated by governments and elite actors in ways that set the context for braceros' struggles, braceros' actions also constrained the hands of state actors and forced them to take braceros' needs seriously, even as the actions also show the limits on braceros' agency. Taken together, we see the formation of this transnational world.

The book ends by revisiting the opportunity-versus-exploitation dichotomy, strains of which repeatedly emerged throughout the program and which I have suggested figure our understanding of braceros' actions, demands, and claims on the governments and nations in question and formed the context for their transformation into transnational subjects. This dichotomy not only structures the current U.S. debate over migration and the push to militarize the border but is a particular response to our general distrust of the transnational subject. That is, the continued demand for unhyphenated "Americans," whose fealty to a single nation is without question, is part of a longer historical unease with this kind of subject, the lingering specter in a nation whose foundational fiction is of immigrants without prior affective (or political) ties. In looking at the legacies of the program and logics of immigration, we can begin to understand how, despite talk of transnationalism, globalization, and the irrelevance of the border, the transnational subject is still highly suspect. This suspicion, and ways of fighting it, is a constituent part of the transnational world in which we now live.

Part I Producing Transnational Subjects

Agriculture, State Expectations, and the Configuration of Citizenship

At four o'clock one morning in August 1942, a mere eight days after the Mexican government announced its intent to support the world war against fascism by sending men to work in the United States, hopeful migrants congregated in lines that wound around the Ministry of Labor building. Only six thousand spots were available for the entire country, yet more than ten thousand men converged on the capital.[1] Over the next twenty-two years, more than 4.5 million work contracts were awarded in what one newspaper called an "important experiment in planned migration."[2] Why would so many men wait hours, days even, for the chance to do stoop labor in U.S. fields? Why did the Mexican and U.S. governments, whose relationship had been stormy since the Mexican Revolution (1910–17), partner in this experiment, allocating public monies and resources for this movement of men? What did each of these state actors expect to gain from such an investment? I tackle these questions in this chapter. Understanding the rationale behind state actions, together with the growers' and migrants' expectations I explore in the subsequent two chapters, reveals what was at stake in the program and how it came to be imagined as an opportunity.

Shifting Diplomatic Relations

Not long after the United States entered World War II, U.S. growers predicted a labor shortage as many farmhands marched off to war or found higher-paying jobs at manufacturing plants. California growers were especially nervous that a scarcity of workers would energize a new round of union organizing, which they had fought since the early 1900s; they hoped to send agents south of the border to recruit farmhands, as they had during World War I. Social reformers, union activists, and federal employees of the proworker Farm Security Administration (FSA) challenged growers' gloomy assessment. They argued that the supposed shortage resulted instead from a mismatch between where jobs were concentrated and where laborers were located, pointing, too, to insufficient pay for these jobs. This contention was supported by U.S. Labor Secretary Henry Wallace's announcement that there were 1.6 million surplus U.S. farmworkers.[3] Yet as thousands exited stoop labor jobs, the specter of food shortages and crops rotting in the fields pushed U.S. officials to approach their southern counterparts about the possible importation of laborers.[4] Resistant at first, Mexican President Manuel Ávila Camacho (1940–46) agreed to negotiate once he realized the possibilities the program offered. Not only would braceros be Mexico's contribution to the war effort; the program also enabled his administration to reframe the independent northward exodus of hundreds of men to Mexico's domestic and diplomatic benefit. Even years later, Mexican Senator Pedro de Alba would portray braceros' contribution as sustaining "morale on [Mexico's] home front" and deserving of its "gratitude and that of foreigners."[5]

Ultimately, Mexico allowed men over the age of eighteen join the program. The bilateral agreement guaranteed that those chosen would meet physical standards for farmwork, live in sanitary housing, have access to medical care, have paid roundtrip transportation (guaranteed under Mexican law), and be paid the prevailing wage for the crop they picked (guarantees not accorded to U.S. domestic farmworkers).[6] Furthermore, these men could not be used as strikebreakers or to influence labor disputes in any way. Negotiators rejected a U.S. proposal to allow wives and children to accompany migrant husbands, fearing that it would encourage permanent emigration. While U.S. authorities would control the number of contracts, Mexican officials formulated domestic requirements: men had to have experience in agriculture and be currently unemployed;[7] members of landholding collectives (ejidos) were barred, although many found ways around this restriction.[8] When bureaucrats studied the issue in the late 1940s, they concluded that during the early phase of the program "approximately 45 percent of those who lined up to be recruited [already] had work" in jobs that "had nothing to do with agricultural activities."[9] This pattern, even stronger in a 1950 study, would contradict the government's anticipated benefits.[10] Though many would evade requirements, formalizing these measures enabled Mexican authorities to juggle domestic needs and constraints—in particular, to quell the anticipated uproar from plantation owners in northern Mexico (hacendados) who worried about losing field hands to higher-paying U.S. jobs.[11] Officials, sharing these concerns, charged the Ministry of Labor and Social Welfare with guaranteeing that the program did not disrupt agricultural production, especially in the north.[12]

The program had three unofficial phases, each with different conditions: 1942–47 (World War II), 1948–51 (interim), and 1951–64 (Korean War and beyond). During the first phase, men were recruited under a bilateral agreement that operated initially under the auspices of the 1917 Immigration Law and then Public Law 45. The U.S. government was the braceros' employer of record and intermediated between U.S. growers and the Mexican government. This measure was intended to preempt problems that earlier migrants had faced, and it was a stipulation on which Mexico would not waiver. The second phase operated under a series of U.S. executive orders rather than an international agreement, as Mexican officials refused to sign another accord until certain changes were made. Migrants, still coming, worked directly for growers without U.S. governmental oversight; not surprisingly, the number of complaints increased dramatically. The third phase began with the Korean War and a tightening U.S. labor market; it brought the U.S. government back to the negotiating table and allowed Mexico to reimpose certain conditions: in particular, that the U.S. government stand in as the braceros' official employer. Each phase also had different contract lengths. In the first phase, men signed up for six-month contracts, but during the second phase (when competition for jobs was at its peak and growers wielded more power) contracts only lasted for forty-five days. With so little time, braceros often barely earned enough to warrant the trip, even with a bountiful harvest. Toward the end growers attempted to quell complaints and delay the program's impending demise by sanctioning contracts of up to eighteen months. Because the United States had initiated the program, the Mexican government entered first-round negotiations with leverage and achieved some of its demands, many of which promoted its overarching program goal: the return of a labor force with capital and new agricultural knowledge.

This initial leverage would be undercut over the term of the program by constraints and pressures at home. Birthrates, life expectancies, and literacy levels were increasing, improving the quality of life for Mexican citizens.[13] These improvements, driven by new state programs, brought about a growth in the number of working-age people and placed stresses on an agricultural system unable to feed a growing population.[14] In the early 1940s, Luis Fernández del Campo, director of the Ministry of Labor's Social Security Office, conducted a study to learn why the braceros wanted to migrate. He found that of the 303,054 braceros who migrated between 1942 and 1945, roughly 72 percent went for better salaries, 14 percent went for personal reasons, and 12 percent went in search of adventure; just under 2 percent sought the new knowledge that was the program's public rationale.[15] A later survey of 303 braceros found that almost 85 percent came for economic reasons and less than 1 percent were motivated to "learn new techniques."[16] In addition, greater state presence—in increased numbers of schools, enforcement of school attendance, public works projects, institution of formal holidays, and newly instituted radio programs—had given citizens a government to hold responsible for their as-yet-unrealized expectations. The demand for bracero spots called attention to these expectations and to the inadequacy of state programs. Many men, facing stiff competition for bracero contracts, slipped across the border, undermining the very entity charged with their protection. With a resolute belief in the program's benefits, officials reasoned that its formalized provisions, however weak, still protected migrants; moreover, by the 1950s, their remittances comprised the country's third-largest source of hard currency and a fundament for Mexico's economy and the state's modernization projects, just as international financing of development projects was decreasing dramatically.[17]

However, not everyone was convinced of the program's advantages. Among its critics was the Catholic Church, which feared exposing its largely poor constituency to the Protestant faith. Also against the program were Mexican unions and people concerned about economic redistribution. Some critics had initially supported the program, but as newspapers exposed the abuses that braceros faced, former supporters called for the program to be replaced with public works projects.[18] Many in the United States also called for its termination. The poverty and maltreatment of farmworkers gained notoriety through mass strikes in the late 1940s and later through Edward R. Murrow's 1960 exposé, *Harvest of Shame*. By the early 1960s, growers hoping to stave off the program's termination consented to stronger protections and monitoring, even as they and their legislative advocates championed its numerous benefits for individual braceros and for Mexico.[19]

In the end, a program billed as crucial to U.S. wartime labor needs supplied a mere 5 to 10 percent of all farm laborers during World War II.[20] Compare this figure to 1959, when during peacetime braceros constituted almost a quarter of the U.S. agricultural workforce.[21] At the same moment, U.S. small farmers were being "driven off the land by mechanization" and "the lack of opportunities to improve their farms," claimed Robert Handschin, secretary of the pro–small farmer National Farmers' Union.[22] These changes, along with an expanded use of bracero (and undocumented) labor, occurred in tandem with the growth of California's specialty crops and even greater grower control over laborers.[23] Together, these developments ensured reliable and inexpensive food production and delivery for burgeoning cities.[24]

When the bracero program began, whether the world could feed itself was still an open question. The program was launched prior to Mexico's Green Revolution, the postwar transformation of agriculture through better techniques and the use of chemical fertilizers, pesticides, and hybrid seeds, and public concern about the ability to meet the food needs of a growing global population was still high.[25] U.S. concerns were fueled by recent soil erosion and food shortages, the outmigration of laborers from farms to cities, and the limited increase in agricultural output (33% between 1935–39 and 1944) compared to industrial growth (135%).[26] These preoccupations were even more acute in Mexico, which was then unable to produce enough food for all its citizens; and in 1945 Mexico joined forces with the Rockefeller Foundation to address this need. This research, along with the agricultural knowledge brought back by braceros, was expected to increase food production.

The postwar increase in bracero laborers and California's solidification of specialty crops were not coincidental but part of a larger story that ties Mexican migration to a consolidation of the U.S. agricultural industry.[27] In this consolidation, all U.S. farmworkers, immigrant and domestic, would lose: U.S. farmhands would lose work to braceros, who themselves labored without adequate protections. In the end, the Mexican government—braceros' de jure representative—could never wrest control of the program away from the U.S. government, the de facto agent for growers.[28]

Although Mexico would sign on to the program, the initial offer by George Messersmith, U.S. ambassador to Mexico from 1942 to 1946, was rebuffed on three grounds: the continued discrimination against Mexicans immigrants and U.S. citizens of Mexican descent;[29] the memory of thousands of migrants returning after World War I with little to show for their work; and the forced repatriation of U.S. residents of Mexican descent during the Depression. Acknowledging Mexico's high unemployment, Undersecretary of Foreign Relations Jaime Torres Bodet voiced concerns that workers' exposure to higher U.S. wages would make them unwilling to return to Mexico and its comparatively lower ones;[30] he instead favored the creation of jobs in Mexico via modernization projects already under way.[31] These projects were part of the revolutionary state's movement toward more orthodox economic policies.

President Manuel Ávila Camacho pushed forward plans to modernize industry and agriculture; he undertook road and dam building and electrification projects throughout the north; and, in the mid-1940s, he began a national literacy campaign that focused on rural areas.[32] These policies, like others I have previously mentioned, increased the state's presence (albeit unevenly) throughout the country.

Such policies failed to staunch the stream of migration, and union leaders and northern hacendados, two key government constituencies, pressured to stop the flow.[33] The response to Messersmith's proposal from Torres Bodet's superior, Ezequiel Padilla, Mexico's foreign relations minister, reflects an attempt to balance this pressure. Although the Mexican administration considered it essential to maintain the country's workforce, wrote Padilla, the president also recognized U.S. wartime labor needs; he declared that "no obstacles be placed on the departure of these nationals desiring to emigrate temporarily" but that all "legal ordinances in effect in both countries" be respected and followed. Officials were apparently unaware that U.S. labor laws did not cover agricultural workers.[34]

Still, Mexico's participation garnered diplomatic gains. To begin with, Ávila Camacho cast participation as a sign of hope for stronger collaboration between Mexico and the United States, of an "indissoluble friendship" rooted in "common interests of freedom," and of Mexico's investment in "Pan Americanism."[35] The Mexican American scholar and activist Ernesto Galarza, writing to Ávila Camacho, claimed that "Mexicans are not in the United States just to pick lemons"; their presence would "establish strong and lasting ties between the people of both countries."[36] In addition, Mexico's willingness to share the war burden reflected its stature in the world community of democracies. "Our fight will not be waged in the trenches," said Ávila Camacho, "but in the factories and in the furrows"; nodding to the two countries' disparity in industrial strength, he still highlighted the importance of each contribution.[37] The new ground Mexico gained could help it become the voice of Latin America vis-à-vis the United States and on the global stage. That is, these two strands—one diplomatic, the other a cultural and economic transformation of citizens—reveal the possibilities that the program was seen to offer.

When Mexico announced support for the Allied powers in early 1942, the press coverage of U.S.-Mexico relations began to change. Instead of reporting disparaging treatment and exploitation of immigrants, as had been the norm, newspapers ran stories about rotting crops, abandoned as former farmhands flocked to better paying factory jobs. For several days in May, just as bilateral talks were starting, editorials brought attention to the essential role that Mexican workers could play in fighting the enemies of democracy. Headlines such as "Mexican Workers Urgently Needed in the U.S." and "Only Mexicans Can Save California Harvests" laid the foundation for what would soon be touted as an advantageous official policy.[38] While newspapers were not the first to portray rapprochement with the United States in such a positive light, they were among the earliest to compare the contribution of stoop laborers to that of shiny-faced U.S. soldiers.

Such editorials were just the beginning of a public push for the program. Torres Bodet, alluding to the fascist threat, predicted that "a victory by the democracies would . . . bring progress, harmony, and a just peace to the world."[39] He put Mexico squarely in the democratic camp and declared that a bracero agreement with strong worker protections would symbolize the regard that the United States held for the accomplishments of the revolution. The first agreement appeared to confirm this respect, for it addressed many Mexican concerns.

Throughout August and September 1942, national newspapers trumpeted these benefits. U.S. authorities, well attuned to Mexican sentiment against the program, vowed that braceros would be home for planting season (to placate large northern landowners dependent on this labor) and would do agricultural, not industrial, jobs. Nor would Mexico's national industrialization plan be threatened, for bracero work was temporary work. In addressing the lingering concern that factory workers might want to leave, the provisions defused most resistance in Mexico.[40] Returning home for planting and harvesting, braceros would contribute to U.S. labor needs and promote binational understanding without undermining their country's economic progress.[41] Even Carey McWilliams, long a labor activist, weighed in on the program's behalf; he cited the slogan "From democracies will come victory" scrawled in chalk on trains transporting the first braceros as evidence of a U.S.-Mexico spirit of cooperation.[42] Lending brazos (arms) during the war, many agreed, signaled a significant step toward a more equal binational relationship.[43]

When U.S. growers first expressed a desire for imported labor, they envisioned a program like the informal arrangements of World War I. At that time, growers contracted workers directly and set wages and work conditions without state intervention; workers suspected of union activity were quickly repatriated.[44] Since then, two important changes had occurred. First,

Franklin D. Roosevelt's Good Neighbor policy (announced in 1933) required a different formal posture and rhetoric vis-à-vis the governments of Latin America. This meant that the U.S. government could no longer blatantly ignore the sovereignty of its southern neighbors, act with overt paternalism, or simply demand that its southern counterparts acquiesce to its wishes. Second, in 1938 President Lázaro Cárdenas (1934–40) had nationalized foreign-owned oil fields, such as those of U.S. Standard Oil, long accused of undervaluing capital assets and failing to pay taxes. Although he immediately offered compensation (per the declared tax-roll value), the foreign companies rebuffed the offer as too little. The U.S. government and foreign oil companies boycotted Mexican oil (a boycott Japan, Germany, and Italy would ignore), yet Cárdenas stood his ground, changing the calculus of the U.S.-Mexican relationship. This dispute would only be resolved when the United States entered the war. In the end, U.S. negotiators got most of what they sought: a World War II ally, increased exports of Mexican primary products (in a separate treaty), and the rationalized recruitment and importation of agricultural workers.[45] Still, they capitulated to their partner's major stipulations, including a ban on sending braceros to Texas, where persons of Mexican descent faced discrimination.[46] This capitulation reflected a new fraternal relationship, not a paternalistic one, a relationship that Ávila Camacho could present to a skeptical domestic audience. Yet as the program unfolded, it became clear that the real winners were large growers, especially in California and Texas.

State Expectations and the Arrangement of Agriculture

The ability of growers to benefit from the bracero program relied on shifts that had already occurred: the use of fertilizer and irrigation systems to increase yields, as well as refrigerated rail cars to transport crops across great distances. These, in turn, accelerated large-scale farming's requirement of an increased workforce. Since the early twentieth century, especially in California and Texas (the two states receiving the majority of braceros), farms moved toward labor-intensive specialty crops organized around a proletarianized labor force.[47] Wealthy California agriculturalists resisted the incentive to mechanize, taking three critical actions. First, they forged strong ties between growers large and small, which were then formalized as associations. Under the guise of these associations, the agriculturalists set wages and work conditions for the region and pooled resources to fight unionizing drives by Mexican, Chicano, Filipino, Puerto Rican, and white workers during the first half of the century. Second, growers established connections with local, state, and national officials and the police. And third, they waged public-relations campaigns to spotlight the critical role of agriculture in California's economy and cultivate public sympathy and support during labor actions, repeatedly hyping the "radical" nature of farmworkers' demands. This long-standing sympathetic portrayal positioned growers as vulnerable to economic hardship.

Starting in the early 1910s, farmworkers launched waves of strikes. They received little support from the American Federation of Labor (AFL), which did not officially commit resources to these struggles until 1959.[48] Although Mexican immigrant and Mexican American farmworkers repeatedly pressed for better wages, the required movement of migrant workers—a feature built into the very structure of agricultural labor—limited the possible effects of these efforts, because the workforce changed every season. This constant turnover undercut worker solidarity and minimized the duration or impact of any worker action and grower concession.[49] Moreover, the diverse composition of this labor force made it easier for growers to pit one ethnic, racial, or language group against another. Growers' reaction to worker militancy—along with dust bowl conditions, government-supported crop reductions, and changes in farm technologies—made the availability of work itself considerably less likely.[50]

At the same time that increased collaboration among U.S. growers was working against laborers' organizing strength, the official trade union movement south of the border was expanding. This state-directed movement was fostered by President Cárdenas's incorporation of workers into the state structure and by the cross-border flow of labor organizers, intellectuals, workers, publications, and ideas in the aftermath of the Mexican Revolution. The Confederación Regional Obrera Mexicana (Regional Mexican Workers Federation, which was not part of the state-run federation) encouraged Mexican migrants to join U.S. unions. It also recognized the advantages that ties to U.S. counterparts (in particular, the progressive Congress of Industrial Organizations) would have for Mexicans working north of the border and for establishing a reciprocal willingness to support longshoremen's strikes.[51] U.S. unions, by contrast, saw the value of this closeness only during periods in which immigration policies were loosened.[52]

Paralleling the bracero program's regulated labor stream was a growth in undocumented workers, many of them former braceros who knew how to maneuver in the United States. Employers who viewed bracero paperwork as a burden and wanted to retain the men they identified as good workers often encouraged such former braceros to return unofficially. In 1952 the U.S. Congress, pressed to tackle rising unauthorized migration, passed the McCarren-Walter Immigration Act, making it a felony to import and harbor undocumented workers, although the bill did not institute penalties for employing them; it also prohibited suspected communists and other subversives from immigrating.[53] Thus, the bill simultaneously eased growers' ability to deport "troublesome" braceros without sanction *and* hardened restrictions on union organizers. McCarren-Walter also forbade U.S. citizens from arresting undocumented workers—a strategy that some union activists had used to counterbalance the effects of their presence on organizing drives. The historian James Cockcroft argues that Taft-Hartley, McCarthyism, the Alien Registration Act (1940), McCarren-Walter, and the bracero program were "interrelated parts of a frontal assault on labor activism and the free exercise of Americans' basic civil rights," which delayed a "militant offensive against racism and economic oppression" until the 1960s.[54]

During its twenty-two years the program was plagued by interrelated challenges: a dramatic rise in undocumented labor; a concomitant drop in Mexico's ability to negotiate strong, enforceable contracts; and the high-profile focus (especially in California) on the abuse of bracero and unauthorized workers. On the Mexican side, the economy, though expanding, could never create sufficient jobs to satisfy the demand for work, leading more men to migrate without authorization. The Mexican government thus pushed for beefed-up border patrols and penalties for growers who hired undocumented workers, dragging its heels on agreement negotiations until the United States met these demands. These stalling tactics, however, only intensified the lengths to which men would go to cross the border, and growers were happy to hire men covered by even fewer protections. This cycle further undermined the Mexican government's negotiating position and exacerbated the precariousness of the situation of undocumented migrants, bracero workers, and U.S.-citizen farmworkers alike, as more men journeyed northward for the promise of jobs. By the late 1940s and early 1950s, more than half a million undocumented workers crossed the border annually, with over a million coming in 1954 alone and leading to a coordinated roundup that between 1944 and 1954 repatriated nearly 2 million men and pushed President Adolfo Ruíz Cortines (1952–58) to explore the feasibility of opening coastal land to permanently settle these workers.[55]

After overcoming its initial reluctance, the Mexican government recognized the benefits to be had from sending men north. Foremost among these was a transformation in domestic agriculture sparked by returning migrants. By applying the new skills and knowledge learned abroad, former braceros would improve agricultural output.[56] Their example would also promote the purchase and use of machinery, made possible through a wartime provision that required 10 percent of braceros' wages to be withheld and remitted on men's return so they could purchase tractors and other farm equipment. Taken together, ex-braceros' agricultural innovation would enable the country to feed itself.[57]

Mexican negotiators fought hard for this savings provision. As a case in point, Mexican diplomats held up the negotiation process during the war when U.S. counterparts refused to include it, citing industrial incapacity. Mexico hoped this provision would spur markets for consumer and other goods where none then existed. In a 1944 memorandum to President Ávila Camacho, Manuel Gamio (an anthropologist turned state bureaucrat) recounted his recent meeting with Fowler McCormick, chairman of International Harvester. He wrote of his portrayal of the expected benefits of helping braceros return with U.S.-made agricultural equipment purchased at a moderate price and in installments. A January 19, 1944, editorial in the Mexican daily Excélsior described a future Mexico that did not merely export raw materials for U.S. products but served as a market for these and other commodities. Closer diplomatic and economic ties between the two countries would bring rewards to all concerned: braceros, Mexico, manufacturers, and the United States.[58]

The program, besides conferring more equal diplomatic and economic standing, would be Mexico's contribution to the preservation of democracy. One group of braceros sent a letter to U.S. President Harry Truman, praising the efforts of the Allied nations toward a victory and citing the contribution of braceros toward these efforts: "We [the undersigned] braceros, . . . a small group of the 150,000 [who] find themselves [in the United States], [are] lending our humble cooperation to the world effort to defend the liberty of individuals and communities."[59] Thus, the men's labor formed the basis of Mexico's war contribution and inscribed these migrants as actors for their nation.

Yet this labor was also expected to spur both national and household economies: they worked in the name of the nation, while their consumption—of radios, sewing machines, cowboy hats, tools, and clothes—was promoted as bettering their families.[60] The state advocated such consumption by exempting these products from tariffs (though not from the unofficial demands of individual Mexican border guards). The government encouraged the men to consume U.S. products in the United States even as it fostered industrialization and a domestic market for Mexican-made versions of those products by heavily taxing U.S. goods purchased in Mexico. While production and consumption were critical in the state's sponsorship of the program, production was more valuable. This valuing is not surprising, given the twofold development strategy of import-substitution and public works projects (dams and roads) then under way, a valorization condensed in the figure of the well-built, faceless, Soviet-style male worker shown in public service announcements and campaigns in national newspapers.[61] In unsubtle ways, these images suggested that properly gendered men were to produce for the nation and provide for family consumption. We thus see the gendered logic that provided the program's scaffolding, on which aspiring braceros would draw to position themselves as most deserving of the program's opportunity.

The transformation of Mexicans into desiring modern subjects was occurring not only on the ground in the United States but also in the wider global context. The potential of its global reach was laid out in Truman's Point Four program, which he articulated in his 1949 inaugural address. The world was changing, said Truman. No longer was "exploitation for foreign profit"—what he labeled "old Imperialism"—productive. Now the best option—and new U.S. approach—was modernization, development programs grounded in "democratic fair-dealing."[62] Modernization could rouse the world's people to rebel against their "human oppressors" and their traditional foes of "hunger, misery, and despair."[63] With this language, Truman both recognized the people of undeveloped countries, such as Mexico, as victims of poverty and disease and moved modernization's focus from "national economies to individuated subjectivities." The focus, then, was not on collective national bodies but on "the less developed [individual] subjects of the 'human family.'"[64] The transformation of the backward into the modern individual subject was not a mere by-product of modernization but its fundamental purpose.

Truman's guiding narrative of progress, movement, and arrival was made evident in modernization theory and its successors: development theory, dependency theory, and world systems theory. Modernization theory and the global economic architecture to make it happen came into being during and after World War II as a by-product of the rise of the United States as economic and military superpower, the Soviet (and later Chinese) challenge to its preeminent position, and the connected processes of the disintegration of European empires and anticolonial independence movements in Africa and Asia. Grounded in the logic of evolution and functionalism, modernization theory posited a process of social change, marked by set stages followed first by the United States but common to all societies (evolutionary). This process was homogenizing (societies tended toward convergence), irreversible, transformative, progressive (i.e., suffering for a big payoff), and slow moving (i.e., explicitly not revolutionary). Even Africa, Asia, and Latin America were seen as able to reap the economic, social, and political rewards of a modern industrialized economy—high wages, an educated workforce, a narrowed gap between rich and poor, and a vibrant democracy—for race was not officially a barrier to modernization. This development formula held a radical promise for all, one not envisioned in earlier eugenicist, race-specific renditions.

Still, modernization theory divided the world into modern and traditional societies, a division that brought along with it a gendered component. Interactions based on personal, emotional, and face-to-face contact were understood to constrain the development of proper market relations in traditional societies. Feminine emotionality was deemed to impede the growth of market relationships and its associated (masculine) impersonalism, lack of favoritism, detachment, and indirectness.[65] Traditional societies were viewed as prone to corruption: the distribution of rewards not based on a meritocracy or the neutral, invisible hand of the market.

While modernization theory is first and foremost an economic theory, the payoff was much more than economic; it was cultural and political as well. Economic modernity (advanced capitalist relations) was seen as part of a tripartite economic, political, and cultural package, with democracy as its political component, and particular (U.S. and Western European) values and relationships in regard to and mediated by consumption as its cultural ones. Thus, modernization theory charts the production of modern subjectivities: individualistic, not collectivist; produced through capitalist modes of production and consumption; and mapped onto relations with the state and other individuals and communities. Prioritizing the individual produced through these relations would dilute more collectivist claims (especially those of class, gender, and race), since no longer would constituencies have shared material interests but only more manageable and shifting issues.[66]

Two aspects are critical here: the cultural and the collectivist. The Mexican government implicitly understood the cultural demands of modernization and championed, albeit less publicly, the program's ability to chip away at ingrained negative behaviors, such as alcoholism and poor hygiene, still seen in many migrants.[67] Although delegates to Mexico's 1917 constitutional convention contended that fewer than "two or three of us here . . . have never been drunk," this conduct was nevertheless seen as undercutting the country's progress and prosperity; moreover, it risked the goals of the program, since men who drank spent their money on liquor and "bad women."[68] Protection against such risks—even the elimination of these habits—were important enough that Mexican negotiators insisted on writing into the agreement the requirement that employers "take all reasonable steps to keep professional gamblers, vendors of intoxicating liquors and other persons engaged in immoral and illegal activities away from the Mexican Workers' place of employment."[69] Negotiators also worked to include provisions that gave men access to a primary-school education, skills in English, and instruction in basic hygiene. The willingness of U.S. authorities to incorporate such provisions into early agreements pleased their Mexican counterparts, leading Foreign Relations Minister Ezequiel Padilla to praise the program as an economic opportunity and "a noble adventure for our youth."[70] These dual economic and cultural goals suggest that Mexican authorities' underlying aim for the program was to transform braceros into a certain kind of modern citizen.

These officials also drew on the collectivist strain in the country's revolutionary ideology to allocate the benefits from the program. Individuals would migrate, yet the rewards would spread throughout the country via the agricultural modernization that returning braceros would spark. This allocation and collectivist ethos are constrained in the Mexican state's definition of modern citizen, a stark contrast with the individualist priorities so widely disseminated in the United States. This ethos prioritized the whole over the individual and made the collective the proper recipient of the rewards of modern state projects. This coalesced in la familia mexicana (the Mexican family), a revolutionary understanding of the nation that captured under a single rubric a set of relationships in which the interests of individuals and factions were subordinated to those of a cross-class, unified family or pueblo (people).[71] That is, although a single individual, sector, or family might disproportionally gain or lose from a particular policy, the goal was collective betterment.[72]

The family required a benevolent patriarch, and so did the nation.[73] The state took on this role, positioning itself as protector of collective interests, the true and legitimate inheritor of revolutionary ideals. It took responsibility, said President Ávila Camacho, for the "intellectual, spiritual, and moral preparation" of a nation "anxious" to achieve progress and "conserve the heritage [patrimonio] of liberties"; collective justice and liberty would thus beget progress, just as knowledge would bring victory over misery.[74] In negotiations over the program and its promotion at the national level, officials used a language of collectivity, diplomatic equality with the United States, and respect for a distinctly Mexican vision of the modern nation. At home, however, they were without the financial resources to assuage competing obligations and the internal contradictions (regional, ethnic, language, class, sector, and racial) that those obligations engendered. The program offered a way out of this predicament: individual citizens, with new knowledge, skills, and cash, would help modernize the country, and the Mexican state, through a respectful diplomatic exchange, would establish itself as a U.S. partner. Though the state was unable to resolve its predicament in either the international or the domestic arena, the potential of doing so hints at why Ernesto Galarza—himself prounion, pro-farmworker, and the college-educated son of Mexican migrants—could initially support the program. Ultimately, he would see its flaws and seek its end, but at the outset he believed it would bring about a new U.S. respect for Mexico and Mexicans.[75] In sum, the program, with its modernist frame, presented the Mexican state with the possibility of economic progress, better international positioning, and respect from its northern neighbor. The men who migrated as part of this cooperative gesture were no longer considered a source of social or state embarrassment but rather as national ambassadors and future model citizens.

Migration, Modernization, and the Promise of a Better Life

Whereas previous mass exoduses had signaled the failures of Mexico's development and of the Mexican state, now emigration was perceived as beneficial. This reconceptualization came, in part, from ideas promulgated by Manuel Gamio, a U.S.-educated anthropologist who later became a Mexican government minister. A graduate student at Columbia University in the 1920s and considered Mexico's first professional anthropologist, Gamio came to the conclusion in his study of Mexican immigrant communities that those who had spent time in the United States had changed in ways beneficial for Mexico's future. He found, first, that these migrants were more "advanced" and had "better" work habits than nonmigrating compatriots. Second, they developed new needs during their stay in the United States; their desire for products to meet those needs would create a market where none previously existed. Third, migrants exposed to the supposedly more efficient labor practices, technologies, and cultural attitudes of the United States absorbed the discipline required of "laborers of the modern type," which, Gamio assumed, they would transplant home, fostering economic change and making Mexico "a great industrial and agricultural country." His fourth finding was that the discrimination many migrants experienced in the United States led them to develop a new sense of attachment to Mexico and identity as Mexicans. Gamio's ideas gained currency among Mexican policymakers, and, as director of the Instituto Indigenista Interamericano (Inter-American Indigenous Institute), he advised negotiators and influenced the shaping of the bracero program.[76]

Gamio's ideas are best understood within a longer trajectory. Industrialization, which had taken root by 1900, still constituted less than 15 percent of Mexico's economy (a percentage less than half that of the United States).[77] The fault for this lag, concluded Mexican elites and political leaders, resided with the country's large rural mestizo and indigenous population, seen as biologically and culturally backward. President Porfirio Díaz (1876–1910), whose administration was toppled in the Mexican Revolution (1910–17), sought to mitigate the negative impact of rural nonwhites by encouraging southern Europeans to immigrate in exchange for land. Though few came, it was hoped that these immigrants, deemed white and with the beneficial biological characteristics that entailed, would dilute the deleterious effects of biology through intermarriage.[78] Such ideas persisted after the revolution and found their way into the state's development projects, specifically in the rationale for agricultural projects in the Laguna region in the northern states of Coahuila and Durango.[79]

Northern Mexico in general and the Laguna region in particular became a focus for development initiatives, in part because many of Mexico's revolutionary leaders were themselves northerners, landowners who held large, well-capitalized haciendas and contributed significantly to the country's agricultural output, while their agricultural workers had staffed the revolutionary armies. Politicians anticipated that unless former soldiers were incorporated into the new national project, their mobility and willingness to wage war could undermine the state. On the positive side, many men in the region were presumed to possess the very skills, innate characteristics, and cultural values that the nation needed, since many had spent time in the United States or had been exposed to its values, advantages that would spread to nonmigrants by proximity. Engineers on a state-run project, for example, deemed the region's inhabitants "of Hispanic ancestry, white, bearded, with Caucasian features, tall and robust"; they were "intelligent" and "hard-working," wore "shoes, pants, and jacket," and ate "eggs daily"— attributes that the state sought to instill in the rest of the population.[80] To quash the lingering threat posed by this revolutionary contingent, national leaders sought to anchor former soldiers to the land, converting them into responsible citizens and smallholders rather than collectivized agricultural workers (*ejido* members).[81] The concept of the small farmer as responsible citizen undergirded notions of racial progress framing the program.

In northern regions, however, the small-farmer model competed with other exigencies, especially in the Laguna, where cotton production (a crop ideal for the area's arid climate) was structured around haciendas or large, concentrated landholdings. During the Porfiriato (the presidency of Porfirio Díaz), global demand for cotton encouraged hacienda growth, organized around capitalist production systems dependent on a sizeable labor force. Hacienda labor demands were met by a largely male wage-labor workforce of locals and migrants from other parts of Mexico. Yet this labor demand was seasonal, and most laborers only found work during the picking season.[82] Making matters more precarious, an entire harvest could be wiped out by an unexpected freeze, flood, or hailstorm. The seasonal, sporadic nature of work, then, required a workforce that could shift between temporary factory jobs, agricultural wage labor, and subsistence farming as tenants or smallholders. Still, industrial cotton-production jobs were the highest paid and lured workers from all over Mexico, aided by rail lines laid during the Porfiriato. By 1910 textile factories tied to cotton production had sprung up throughout the Laguna, as it became another stop on international labor circuits that also included Texas and California. The labor system gave "rise to a new, socially unstable," and proletarianized "migrant worker class" not unlike that of its sister U.S. states.[83] This socially unstable, tough, resourceful, and well-traveled working class would form the base of Pancho Villa's revolutionary army.[84] Despite the revolutionary proclivities of northern laborers, the region's large landholding system survived early episodes of land reform precisely because the new revolutionary government recognized that the value of the haciendas came not merely from the land but from the various forms of concentrated capital, such as irrigation systems, that were needed to maintain economies of scale and survive persistent insect infestations, droughts, and flooding. To support the production of industrial cotton, the federal government built Palmito Dam in the Laguna to guarantee water to haciendas in times of drought; it did not irrigate small farms, which continued to depend on the Nazas and Aguanaval rivers.[85]

After the revolution, hacienda workers did not demand the system's overhaul; instead, in the 1920s and 1930s they agitated for better wages and labor conditions.[86] Answering their pleas for support were U.S. and Mexican union organizers, Communist Party operatives, and intellectuals, who flooded the region. Building on the already-established political consciousness of this workforce, organizers denounced their maltreatment, sparking strikes on one hacienda after another.[87] On August 19, 1936, twenty thousand hacienda workers walked off the fields in the middle of the cotton harvest, joined by urban and peasant unions, a few of which had previously called for independent strikes.[88] Although most strikers were permanent employees rather than temporary workers, many of those who listened and watched from the sidelines (and at times even participated) were precisely those men who were sporadically driven to wage work by hunger and underproducing land. The strike ended in September, when President Lázaro Cárdenas (1934–40) addressed workers' complaints by dividing some large tracts of land into small individual plots and communally held property administered by workers' committees. This was not a first step in a march to collectivism, however; instead, the revolutionary state recognized that subsistence agriculture and hacienda-based production needed to end. Cárdenas's move was designed to modernize all production systems.[89]

In the strike's immediate aftermath, owners of new smallholdings were deemed the productive base for export crops such as cotton and were crowned the champions of progress and political stability.[90] The state, in other words, bestowed a place in the pantheon of model citizens to these future capitalized farmers. Yet as often happens, the expected economic stability and boost did not occur; the Depression devastated the global cotton market and put many out of work, just as large numbers of longtime U.S. residents were repatriated to Mexico. In a move reminiscent of that by Porfirio Díaz, many returnees were offered plots of land, remote enough so their newly acquired U.S. work ethic and habits would not be tainted by supposedly uncultured compatriots but close enough that their habits could spread to neighbors. Gamio predicted that exposing nonmigrants to new migrant sensibilities would "elevate the material level of the *campesino* (rural inhabitant) as much as the cultural level."[91] Mexican diplomats folded this understanding of a migrant sensibility—anchored in acceptance of the role of agriculture, especially northern agriculture, in Mexico's modernization—into the goals of the bracero program.

Mexican elites' vision of rural inhabitants and the countryside paralleled the perception that most U.S. urban residents had of their own rural counterparts. The farms and rural areas that were home to almost half the U.S. population in 1930 often lacked electricity, indoor plumbing, and other necessities taken for granted in cities.[92] Depression-era newspapers ran stories of destitute Oklahoma and Arkansas families heading west; Dorothea Lange photographed penniless migrants huddled in shacks; and the Farm Service Administration built camps to house impecunious arrivals to California. While specific New Deal policies targeted such problems, protective labor legislation and the bargaining requirements of the National Labor Relations Act exempted farmworkers. Growers, with legislative help, had maneuvered to exclude stoop laborers from initiatives safeguarding factory workers; farmhands, they contended, were not workers but independent contractors in a patron-client relationship with growers. Thus, amid dreams of becoming yeoman farmers (or regaining that position), most U.S. migrant workers had, like their northern Mexican counterparts, become part of an agricultural proletariat.[93] For Mexican immigrants and Mexican American farmworkers, proletarianization borne of this migration was "the central element" in their racial formation.[94]

At the same time that Congress excluded farmhands from protective legislation, it funded research for capital-intensive solutions to agricultural underproduction. In one 1946 example, the government partnered with International Harvester and John Deere to fund the Cotton Mechanization Project, putting the most extensive agricultural research at the disposal of moneyed cotton interests in the hopes of making mechanized production commercially viable.[95] Although Congress had long dedicated money and personnel (in the form of state agricultural extension services) to developing better farming methods, this capital, as opposed to farmworker, solution ultimately spurred a mechanization revolution and new agricultural practices that further weakened the bargaining position of all farm laborers.

Yet the transition to mechanized farming, says the economist Wayne Grove, was neither simple nor rapid; nor could it be easily adapted to different crops. Grove notes that Congress supported mechanization, even though it offered no straightforward solution to increasing yields.[96] This support came in two forms: first, allowing growers to employ and control low-wage labor, from which they accumulated capital for equipment and additional land (some of the best lands became available when interned Japanese and Japanese Americans defaulted on mortgages); and second, funding research on seed and soil requirements for sustained mechanized farming.[97] These changes simultaneously lowered food prices and enabled huge gains in productivity akin to those in other industries. Only after these technologies were readily available at reasonable cost (in the 1960s) would the bracero program be terminated. The need to blunt the precariousness of the transition to mechanized agriculture, says Grove, was the U.S. rationale for the bracero program. He argues that it was a federal attempt to "guarantee" that growers had access to a "reserve" pool of seasonal—not permanent—employees, part of a "a two-pronged strategy of government-managed economic transition" and a "road to rural development."[98] Not surprisingly, no similar support was available for domestic farmworkers, especially those displaced by the bracero program.[99] Rather, said Representative John Tower (R-Tex.), "the industrial economy and the agricultural economy" are "strikingly different" and "must be treated differently."[100] Braceros would further agricultural changes already under way.[101]

The heart of these changes was in California, where almost half of all braceros would head, and even more so in its Imperial Valley. The valley, encompassing six thousand square miles in the southeastern corner of California, was the epicenter of the agricultural boom and the birthplace of new seeds, techniques, and equipment. It was also at the heart of the farm union movement that had begun early in the century. Bordering the Mexican state of Baja California to the south, Riverside County to the north, San Diego County to the west, and Arizona to the east, this "palm-shaped basin" ranges in altitude from 253 feet below sea level at its low point to Blue Angel Peak at 4,854 feet above sea level on the west side. It is an "ecological transition zone," where temperatures commonly reach 125 degrees.[102] Growers enjoy one of the country's longest growing seasons (more than three hundred days), which enables a two-crop cycle for produce such as iceberg and romaine lettuce, carrots, tomatoes, cabbage, broccoli, squash, cucumbers, asparagus, corn, alfalfa, melons, grapes, dates, citrus fruits, and strawberries.

The Imperial Valley had not appeared destined to become the nation's wintertime produce capital. With an arid climate similar to that of the Laguna (averaging only three inches of rain a year), the Imperial Valley was labeled a "deadly place" in 1776.[103] Its prospects improved when the Imperial Canal was built in 1901, supplying water diverted from the Colorado River. The canal allowed the valley's growers to devote land to agriculture earlier than was possible in the nearby Coachella and San Joaquin valleys.[104] Though this new source of water would change the type of crops farmers grew, they initially planted cotton, a staple of dry-climate agriculture. By the second year of production (1910), the land was successfully seeded with a Durango cotton variety grown in the Laguna.[105] While its strong fiber drew attention from those in the cotton trade, by 1925 Durango cotton lost out to its better-promoted Mexican varietal cousin, Acala, which was heavily planted in the San Joaquin Valley. Imperial Valley growers would cede cotton to this neighboring valley and switch to specialty fruit and vegetable crops whose production also depended on vast numbers of laborers.[106] In fact, the consolidation of California into a preeminent agricultural state required plentiful but poorly compensated farmworkers, whom U.S. Department of Agriculture officials touted as an asset.[107] The availability of this asset accelerated the shift from family- to migrant-based labor. By the end of the bracero program, the percentage of farms relying on family labor (that is, work done by farmers and their families) had dropped to 35 percent statewide and less than half of that in the Imperial Valley.[108] This vast agricultural boom land produced crops valued at more than $100 million per year by 1960 on land concentrated in the hands of fewer than five hundred owners.[109]

While elite growers consolidated their land, fortunes, and control over smaller farmers, migrant farmworkers faced extreme poverty. Men, women, and children labored long hours and lived crowded in what were termed ditch-bank camps, shantytowns of tin or cardboard-roofed shacks situated along drainage or irrigation channels. The Farm Security Administration (FSA), established in 1935 to alleviate pervasive rural poverty, built labor camps in California to address the migrants' unsanitary living conditions and brought rural poverty to the attention of the nation when the agency's hired photographers, such as Dorothea Lange, Russell Lee, and Jack Delano, captured these hardships in graphic images. FSA personnel taught hygiene, first aid, and food safety to camp residents and trained them to run camps collectively. This drew the wrath of growers, who labeled FSA employees socialists and feared their farm laborers would be susceptible to this supposedly un-American ideology.

Indeed, since the beginning of the century, the Imperial Valley had been the hub of farmworker union organizing and militant strikes, which had grown in tandem with commercialized agriculture.[110] During the 1928 Imperial Valley cantaloupe strike, many workers pushing for union recognition were Mexican citizens. They sought help from the Mexican consul in

Calexico, but their efforts were quashed when the local sheriff and district attorney shut down the pool halls and restaurants the men patronized, shuttered the door of the union's headquarters, La Unión de Trabajadores del Valle Imperial (the Imperial Valley Workers Union), and jailed most strikers for "disturbing the peace" or "vagrancy."[111] Union activity was in hibernation when the braceros arrived, dampened by temporary organizer setbacks, World War II's economic expansion, and President Franklin Roosevelt's antistrike measures. Indeed, many braceros were housed in former FSA work camps, not far from established Mexican and Mexican American settlements left empty when their previous tenants departed for factories and the war.[112] After wartime controls were lifted, farmworkers, like their industrial counterparts, sought compensation for wartime wage freezes and no-strike pledges; when this compensation was not forthcoming, organizing began anew.[113] While braceros were prohibited from striking or honoring the strikes of fellow domestic farmworkers, politicians, growers, and regular citizens nevertheless blamed this renewed union activity on communists posing as poor Mexican peasants, who they argued had infiltrated the program and were sowing the seeds of subversive ideology in the nation's fields.[114] This concern (among others) led to Operation Wetback, a governmental campaign that forcibly repatriated 1 to 2 million Mexicans in 1954—some having crossed without documents, others holding bracero contracts, still others U.S. citizens or longtime residents. The U.S. government also reinforced the Border Patrol with new funding and personnel, while increasing the bracero contracts available to Mexican workers. The valley was a California hotspot to which braceros from Durango would come.

Changing Conceptions of Citizenship

Even as the program altered the structure of agriculture on both sides of the border, it furthered a shift in concepts of citizenship and cultural belonging in both countries. In Mexico, privileges and formal ties to the nation had been reshaped in the political contestations and state consolidation that followed the revolution.[115] Instead of a direct citizen-state relationship, as in the United States, Mexico adopted a corporatist model whereby citizens interacted with the state through state-based organizations of peasants, the military, organized labor, and the popular sector. As I explained above, the logic behind this corporatist arrangement (where all opposition is internal to or incorporated in the state itself) was collectivism, under which both state and citizen had responsibilities that, when properly performed, would further the national good.

Citizenship, too, carried responsibilities. For individual (male) citizens, revolutionary citizenship was to be fulfilled through three traditionally masculine activities: military service, civic engagement, and labor.[116] Citizenship was put into practice in daily duties deemed to promote the collective good and instill in men "the consciousness of 'sincere' and 'authentic' revolutionaries." In this way, revolutionary citizens would demonstrate their commitment to county and class by performing civic duties.[117] Yet not all performances of class and national loyalty were equally important in constituting a citizen's place. The primary performances of citizenship and revolutionary consciousness were those that constituted the (male) citizen as modern subject.

Given that most Mexicans lived in poverty and under conditions that the state labeled primitive, measures were put in place to transform these backward people into modern subjects. Because the elites and state officials envisioned citizenship as a male right, the modernization of citizens deemed primitive required the cultural modernization of masculinity—that is, the eradication of male activities and privileges such as wife beating, cockfighting, and imbibing pulque (a homemade liquor from the maguey plant) and excessive alcohol, activities widely attributed to peasants, the working class, and indigenous people.[118] Limiting formal franchise to those "having the quality of being Mexican" and "an honest way of life," the 1917 Constitution officially targeted these "barbaric" holdovers. Substituted for these uncouth endeavors were baseball and basketball, which would confirm peasants' transformation into modern cultured men.[119]

While this configuration of formal citizenship had been in place since the late 1910s, the corporatist model that structured the relationship between citizen and state was only established in 1938. Still, officials, intent on its regularization, looked everywhere for evidence of its acceptance. On the home front, they took as evidence citizens' involvement in political organizations and parties, which, they imagined, visibly signaled a growing "political consciousness," belief in a corporatist vision, and acceptance of the duties of citizenship.[120] As we will see in subsequent chapters, this state version of citizenship had not yet fully or evenly permeated the country's social fabric. Not only did aspiring migrants rely on strands of prior versions to promote their case for a bracero contract; Mexican diplomats negotiating bracero agreements recognized that most men still engaged in the very practices that cultural modernization was meant to eradicate. Officials would push for agreement measures to eliminate them or at least guard against their upsurge in U.S. labor camps.

Race, too, was implicitly woven into Mexican citizenship, both formally and culturally. In contradistinction to the black/white axis in the United States, race in Mexico was organized around a Spanish (white)/Indian (dark) dichotomy, with mestizos—the historical product of a Spanish/Indian mixture—understood in relation to these poles. People of African and Asian descent did not figure prominently in this racial organization. Still, the system was complex. *Indian* was a mutable category of social personage reflecting multiple markers and dependent on social affiliation, language use, geography, clothing, hairstyle, and even the wearing of shoes. In reality this mutability meant that the physically visible boundary between Indian and mestizo was neither clear nor obvious. Mutability became problematic as mestizos began to outnumber Indians and Spaniards. This was a source of concern for elites, who sought to fix the distinctions, and with them the formal privileges (legal citizenship) and bonds of belonging and inclusion (cultural citizenship) allotted by group.[121] By the time of the revolution, however, most Mexican citizens were mestizos who still lived as peasants or rural wage laborers but had long shed the cultural markers of Indianness. A centerpiece of the revolutionary state was the incorporation of such mestizos into the nation, congealed as the nation's protagonists, while *Indian* remained a label of social exclusion. *Mestizo*, thus, became synonymous with *Mexican*.

There is a spatial dimension to this racial categorization, however, insofar as the fuzziness of Indian as outsider was largely mapped onto the countryside, with its communal land and campesino subsistence farming. Rural people were aficionados of cockfighting, pulque drinking, and wife beating, who, in the words of the local bureaucrat Juan Uzeta, had "no custom of work";[122] they desperately needed cultural modernization. If we map these notions of race onto gendered ideas of citizenship, the state's new burden became, first, the sorting of rural Mexicans from Indians; and, second, the transformation of these rural mestizos, identified as Mexicans, into civilized laborers, soldiers, and farmers able to take their place as the nation's new protagonists. Part of the cultural modernization was inculcating these national subjects-to-be with the commitment to work. During bracero negotiations, officials sought to include measures to instill the habits of mind and body required for this national role into the men chosen.

The Mexican racial system allowed those who shed the cultural manifestations of Indianness to become mestizos, hold a recognized place in the nation (cultural citizenship), and exercise official privileges (legal citizenship). In contrast, U.S. legal citizenship had, from the country's founding, been delimited by race and was still circumscribed by it—legally and in practice—when the program ended. Until the Civil War, slavery shut blacks off from the possibility of exercising formal privileges. During the mid–nineteenth century, argues the historian Matthew Frye Jacobson, the larger black/white racial schema shifted such that nationality (e.g., Irish, Italian, German) took on racial connotations, due principally to the massive immigration from countries outside northern Europe.[123] While the 1790 Immigration Act had officially limited immigration to those eligible for citizenship (only free white people), Jacobson claims that nationality then possessed the weight of a racial category, and that Irish or Italian or Jewish was set off from Anglo-American as racial difference. This white racial multiplicity, according to the historian Mae M. Ngai, was reconfigured by the Johnson-Reed Act of 1924, which limited the number of immigrants allowed from each country to 2 percent of their percentage in the 1890 census. This limit, argues Ngai, effectively drew a line around Europe (instead of through it, as earlier), turning all European immigrants into white people and their national, formerly racial, ties into ethnicities, thus uncoupling race from nationality for all Europeans. This uncoupling meant that immigrants from Europe could become American, where "American" was synonymous with "white."[124]

For Mexicans—U.S. citizens, residents, and immigrants—nationality was more tightly fused to race under Johnson-Reed, foreclosing national belonging by marking them as perennial foreigners; regardless of actual citizenship, the label *Mexican* bore the weight of race.[125] Middle-class Mexican Americans, for example, recognized all too well that U.S. citizenship was aligned with whiteness. According to the historian Neil Foley, they fought for their rights during the middle of the century by claiming rights not as citizens but as the (middle-class) whites that they legally were, as a result of the 1848 agreement that ended the U.S.-Mexico War.[126] Braceros entering this racial reconfiguration would find self-understandings reworked as they encountered obstacles to being seen as modern and to the respect that being modern brought, obstacles arising precisely from their racial marking as Mexican. Resident Mexican and Mexican American farmworkers faced a similar terrain. Because growers largely controlled both their own self-depiction and that of their racialized farmworker employees, farmworkers' subjectivities were reshaped as they pressed to extricate themselves from a racial arrangement that a priori denied them recognition and respect as modern subjects. As we will see, being modern was a constituent component of U.S. cultural belonging, regardless of formal citizenship.[127]

The collectivist and individualist conceptions undergirding formal citizen responsibilities and privileges were woven into social practice, and these conceptions are essential to understanding the structures and practices of U.S. and Mexican citizenship. These citizen concepts were the lenses through which braceros would understand their place—or lack thereof—in the Mexican nation, the purpose of their migration, and the broader goals of the program for the Mexican state. These structures and practices of belonging and respect also shaped their relationship to the United States. Try as braceros might to achieve the respect and other benefits the program was held out as offering, they were denied such benefits by a priori exclusion. These structures and practices became the border they could never fully cross.

Conclusion

I opened this chapter by asking why so many men would do almost anything for the chance to work as U.S. farm laborers and what they expected to gain from migrating. This chapter has begun to answer this question by identifying the expectations of the various stakeholders and the historical context into which the braceros came. I also have explored here the key terms framing debate over the program: how it came to be cast as an opportunity for braceros themselves and for the Mexican nation, and how its framing simultaneously opened and closed avenues as braceros attempted to achieve their goals.

The place of agriculture in each nation's development and self-conception is critical if we wish to understand how the program was cast as an opportunity for various actors. Agriculture occupied a central role, both figurative and literal, in configuring the formal and social citizenship of the nation's proper protagonists and in deciding who was excluded from that status. These understandings, together with the promise of the modern, shaped the bracero journey as a space of opportunity that brought about new subjectivities as it tore at the state-citizen alliance in Mexico and furthered the braceros' claims for recognition vis-à-vis the Mexican state and the U.S. nation. In the next chapter I continue charting connections between agriculture and the making of national subjects, examining how elite California growers controlled the boundaries of inclusion and the ways they exerted this control: through the construction of narratives about themselves and about farmworkers.

2

Narrating Class and Nation

Agribusiness and the Construction of Grower Narratives

In testimony before a House of Representatives subcommittee on the bracero program in 1955, William H. Tolbert, a representative of two California growers associations, described the hopes of the American farmer, who never wanted his son to "get up and milk cows at four o'clock in the morning and work until dark and after [that] take care of the chores." Instead, the son should "go to town and become a doctor or business executive or lawyer." For him, announced Tolbert, "we paved the road from the farm to town."[1]

Few, if any, of the farmers in whose name Tolbert spoke milked cows or tended fields at any hour, nor did their sons: farmhands did those jobs. Most instead owned large, profitable operations in the state's booming agriculture industry, yet they understood the benefits of portraying themselves as hardworking, Jeffersonian-style yeoman farmers and self-made individualists.[2] This rhetoric had brought them significant material and political benefits. It fostered what the agricultural economist Charles Hardin would describe in 1958 as a two-pronged "broad political expectation": first, of a government duty-bound "to help people in economic difficulties"; and, second, "that society is made of politically significant groups whose incomes should all be made comparable, if necessary, by public support."[3]

Growers relied on this two-pronged logic of government obligation and parity as the basis for claims to state assistance. Growers' depiction of themselves as yeoman farmers camouflaged the harsh "socioeconomic realities" of workers and racialized them "as docile, innocent, and child-like laborers" in need of "benevolent tutelage" to rid them of their unionizing tendencies.[4] Yet *yeoman farmer* was not the only rhetorical framing on which growers relied. During the mid- to late 1950s, growers would also cast themselves as *modern business owners*. Modern businessmen used machines and relied on science, technology, and the latest research to devise new farming practices.

Their self-portrayal as modern businessmen made these actors legible to an increasingly urban, modern populace and entitled them to the cachet that being modern conferred in the postwar world. They would use this narrative to argue not for parity but for access to the same government support provided to other modern businesses.

Growers' vision of their right to state assistance, whether as small farmers or modern businessmen, also framed their narratives of laborers. As we will see in this chapter, elite growers described workers not as the proletarianized laborers that they actually were but as either peons or unsuccessful farmers. As peons, laborers were remnants of a premodern system out of sync with the core traits on which U.S. democracy was founded. As unsuccessful farmers, they had not invested the hard work and stamina synonymous with independence and individualism and necessary to achieve the success of more accomplished competitors. In either case, workers did not deserve rewards; rather, they were seen as vulnerable to collectivism or leftist agitation, defined as un-American.

In this chapter I examine the narratives that growers constructed about their laborers and themselves, as well as the material benefits that control over these narratives yielded. I take these narratives seriously. Indeed many elite agriculturalists not only started as immigrants but continued to believe in and assert their personal story of "American" opportunity. During the United Farm Workers strike in the late 1960s, growers facing labor actions still described themselves as small farmers to millions of television viewers—that is, as honest, hard-working people, just like the audience. While the broad outlines of the rise of California agribusiness and these grower narratives have been documented, less attention has been paid to how these narratives shifted during the postwar period and the material benefits that they brought.[5] I argue that these grower narratives formed an element critical to the demarcation of the boundaries of U.S. national inclusion, which domestic farmhands were forced to resist, largely on growers' terms. Agricultural elites manipulated the two discursive strains—of small farmers and modern entrepreneurs—to portray themselves as properly American actors, while using race and biology to bar their employees from this same national category.[6] That is, both discourses cast growers as esteemed national actors and dictated the terms of the debate for farmworkers; growers bought their own logic and narratives, justifying their strategic use of a changing set of immigrant workers. Braceros entered a contested narrative terrain that grounded their metamorphosis into transnational subjects. They were figured as good (potentially modern) workers, even as their foreignness denied them a place from which to make claims on the U.S. nation-state.

Growers' Narratives of Self and Other

In Iowa in 1930 Grant Wood posed a stoic local dentist, pitchfork in hand, and the dentist's sister before a cottage whose upper window resembled a medieval arch and painted *American Gothic*. The portrait was widely criticized for attacking the mythic place of the farmer in the U.S. imagination and was understood against Dorothea Lange's photos of farm families leaving the dust bowl for life in California and of the woeful migrant workers they became. These images implicitly contrasted the resourceful fiercely independent farmer to the precariousness of farmers' lives.[7] The public reaction to both visions hints at the emotional resonance that the family farm and farmer held as embodiments of the virtues of democracy and hard work.

While *American Gothic* remains an icon of rural life, the ethos it captured and displayed when exhibited during the 1943 bicentennial celebrations of Thomas Jefferson's birth had been pushed out by structural changes in process well before it was painted.[8] According to the writer and activist Truman Moore, most food grown in the United States was produced on large commercial farms by 1940, with half grown on fewer than 10 percent of the nation's farms. More than one-third of all farmworkers worked for just 3 percent of farm operations.[9] While nearly 20 percent of the U.S. workforce still worked on farms in 1942, land consolidation was accelerating, slashing the percentage of people living on farms from 23 percent in 1940 to 11 percent in 1958; by 1964, the farm activist Edward Higbee lamented that 92 percent of the nation's population resided in places other than on farms. Despite this precipitous decline, six years earlier Charles Hardin, the agricultural economist, had predicted that the farm economy might still flourish because twelve chairmen of the nineteen standing committees in the House of Representatives were from rural districts. "The farm sector *is* a political collectivity," he asserted, and one to be reckoned with.[10]

In California, even more than in other states, large-scale agricultural production continued to expand during the period. The number of large agricultural enterprises, defined as more than a thousand acres in size, jumped 11 percent (from 5,265 to 5,939) during World War II, the greatest five-year increase on record to that date.[11] Still, in 1962 many agribusiness owners downplayed their size. Bill Langenegger, the president of a large growers' association, told Congress, "[Although] the larger grower can afford the high-priced machines, the smaller grower cannot afford to make the investment to purchase an $18,000 machine to pick cotton. So *he must pick by hand.* If handpickers are not available, he has lost his entire year's work because he cannot harvest."[12] Implicit in Langenegger's testimony was the claim that his organization was fighting for the needs of small farmers, rather than for its large grower members. Langenegger could play on public and legislative sentiments that still viewed the family farm as a pillar of democracy. Elite growers promoted their image as small farmers who sweated side by side with their family and field hands as a way to explain both their economic success and the lack of success of those alongside whom they supposedly labored. The narrative, then, was a relational one that divided undeserving farmworker from hardworking deserving farm owner. It was securely grounded in the "myth" of a nation "set apart" by "its freedom" to challenge itself against nature, and California was the shining example of that myth.[13] The critical work of this narrative was "to assuage Jeffersonian objections" to the emergence of a permanent wage-labor class, even as it camouflaged the "radical disaffection and industrial turmoil" beneath the "California-as-yeoman-Eden" image.[14] In California, these objections developed in tandem with industrialized agriculture or "factories in the fields" and in conjunction with the extreme vertical integration of canning, processing, refrigeration, and shipping—all dependent on huge numbers of laborers.[15]

For many growers, immigration was how California would find the large numbers required to fulfill its destiny as a major site of industrialized agriculture.[16] First Chinese and then Japanese, Filipinos, Mexicans, and transplanted poor whites cycled through the state and its farmwork. The narrative of labor uplift contrasted with what Truman Moore labeled the actual "migrant drama" of these "dust bowl refugees" that "caught the nation's attention in the thirties," when "long lines of [white] tenant families—Gasoline Gypsics—crossed . . . into California looking for work."[17] By labeling this a drama and these people refugees, Moore, together with John Steinbeck and Dorothea Lange, implied that these white California newcomers did not belong to the station and space they then occupied—they were out of place; when Filipinos, Chinese, Mexicans, and Japanese—visibly nonwhite and deemed foreign—did this labor, however, they were not. As we will see in chapter 6, the notion of place was critical. Following the logic of eugenics and a century of anecdotes, nonwhites were doing what came naturally. In the process, even those who, like Moore, Steinbeck, and others, defended farm laborers implicitly supported grower narratives and participated in shaping a racial ideology that relegated workers to grueling labor. The exact elements of this agriculturally based racial ideology were flexible, however, for those traits that one grower would apply to Chinese laborers in 1908 — "short-legged, short-backed" workers who could "stand any temperature" — would later describe Japanese, Filipino, and Mexican workers.[18]

The logic that linked racial minorities to agricultural labor was comprised of three essential elements: first, that farmwork required specific skills and demeanor; second, that these skills and demeanor were biologically based; and, third, that specific national (ethnic and racial) groups possessed these skills naturally, in contrast to white Americans who had moved beyond this station. Guiding this logic was a progressivist narrative based on social Darwinism and eugenics, the racial science that advocated certain forms of intervention to improve humans' inherited characteristics, both physical and mental.[19] This logic implied that the work ethic and skills gained through such labor would prepare those currently biologically proficient at it with characteristics required for further uplift.

An example of these linkages comes from Charles Collins Teague, a grower, president of Sunkist Cooperative, and legal counsel for two powerful growers' associations, first the California Walnut Growers Association and then the California Fruit Growers Exchange. In 1944 Teague wrote a book-length defense of his own operations and those of the other large growers against what he felt were unfair public attacks. Perhaps more than any other text, *Fifty Years a Rancher* captures the particular worldview of elite growers and the ways they artfully reframed images and beliefs that broadly echoed popular sentiments. His text shows both how elites maneuvered to secure their status and the sophistication of the argument on which their position was based.

Teague begins by suggesting that proficient stoop labor required innate, not acquired, skills—what he labels as "a natural aptitude." While most who engaged in this labor could become "more skilled" at it, contended Teague, workers without the necessary biological material would never become "really efficient" at these tasks; they instead should do other kinds of work for which they were "better adapted."[20] In his testimony before the U.S. Chamber of Commerce in the early 1920s, he observed that "Americans" were being educated "away from hard work and menial tasks" precisely because very few could do agricultural work "without serious physical consequences." Still, growers needed laborers, ones "fitted to work" in a punishing climate, said Teague, "until Thomas Edison or Henry Ford develops machinery" to take "the drudgery" from the farmworker's labor or "the calluses" from "his hands." This work, Teague implied, should be done by people endowed with the psychological and physical characteristics it demanded: Chinese, Japanese, Filipinos, and Mexicans. Implicit in this vision of a biological suitability was that this labor force was primitive, or at least more backward than the forward-looking white laborers. Such backwardness made these workers biologically suitable; it at times shielded their minds, at others made them vulnerable to the contagion of socialist rhetoric and unionism that spread through the fields.[21] This circular logic, which anchored and upheld the state's "racialized division of agricultural labor," would contribute to making braceros growers' ideal labor source: not only had the Mexican government already deemed them in need of—and ready for—modernization, their current backward condition made them less susceptible to radical labor discourses that had previously permeated the state's fields. This grower narrative about laborers formed the basis for remaking race in the fields of California.[22]

Casting workers as biologically fit for the job required that growers be figured as their opposite: as hard-working small farmers who merited government help but rejected it; they were contrasted with workers, who since the early twentieth century had resorted to union organizing—that is, collectivism. In testimony before Congress and to the media, growers and their advocates shifted seamlessly between depictions of the grind of farm life, their own self-sufficiency, and the value of land (lost as the country urbanized) and proximity to nature. The testimony of Danny Danenberg, a representative of the huge Western Growers Association, is an example. In 1962, he avowed to Congress that California farmers had a long history of "never receiving and proudly opposing Government subsidies," despite being squeezed by rising production costs and decreasing profit margins.[23] As Danenberg saw it, "one of the pressing problems before the American public is the need for a fair return to agricultural labor and investment here in America."[24] Addressing the issue of parity programs that equalized incomes through government support, he presented growers as having rejected state support not because they did not need the help but because they were rugged, self-reliant individualists. In other words, elite growers still held true to the values and character that were disappearing as a result of urbanization, and which farmworkers did not possess.

Yet Teague also likened growers to successful entrepreneurs. His main argument was that large growers, like all business owners, contributed amply "to the advancement of our country, to the security of its people, and to their social development" through the generation of "wealth and employment created by private enterprise." A rancher such as himself, "who runs a business with an invested capital of one hundred thousand dollars and thereby gives employment to one hundred men," was seen as "an enemy to society"; yet, should he "quit his business and give each of his employees a thousand dollars, he would be called a philanthropist." Teague challenged this perspective, positing that the operator of a successful business was in fact of greater societal benefit than the philanthropist. Although "the profit motive was a strong incentive," ranchers and business owners had a higher aim: "to give employment to a large number of people, to raise their standard of living and to improve their social condition."[25] Thus, he intertwined the rhetorics of small farmer and large grower to illuminate the broad benefits of an entrenched agricultural system grounded in a proper racial labor hierarchy and in which the hard work, self-reliance, and economic success that made philanthropy possible were respected.

Despite this portrayal of elite growers as rugged (masculine) individualists, however, in practice, their political and economic clout—the ability to control the value of agricultural products and farmworkers—came through growers' associations: that is, the collective. Yet the right to act collectively was one they continually denied to laborers, who were depicted as falling prey to outside influences. Teague contrasted the current lot with the many second-generation farmworkers who had earlier followed the proper path and availed themselves of an education, "improved their standard of living and [now] occupy a useful place in society." This peaceful progress had been broken in 1941, he contended, when six thousand Mexican citrus workers had been duped into pushing for higher wages. Teague labeled this influence as more intimidation than persuasion, claiming that the majority were "not in favor of the walkout." This walkout, he argued, hurt both growers and workers, employers and employees, because the economic climate had made it impossible to meet workers' demands. Although he opposed organized labor as such, sometimes, he claimed, "it has been necessary for labor to organize . . . to gain fair treatment." The 1941 strike, said Teague, was instead instigated "by professional organizers who had nothing but a selfish, narrow objective" not motivated by "the problems of employee or employer." For workers, "association with a labor union would be a distinct handicap . . . [since] farmworkers are in a much better economic position than workers in large cities."[26]

I call attention to this passage for several reasons. For starters, Teague labeled these laborers workers, not peons, peasants, or proto-farmers, as growers often did, especially in conversations with government officials. However, even as he affirmed farmhands' position as workers, he denied the benefits that might have accompanied unionization, saying "housing conditions are better, their living costs are lower and their opportunity to enjoy life is manifoldly greater" than presumably unionized city workers. Farmworkers, he suggested, had been lulled into believing organizers' lies and collaborating against their own interests.[27] His use of the adjective *farm* to modify *workers* tapped into a popular vision of rural life as more harmonious, salubrious, and community oriented than the alienation and anonymity of cities, even as their rural connection, in turn, negated any claim to being modern. Teague's argument hinted at discursive shifts to follow. These shifts became more pronounced after World War II, when elite growers relied on not just a single thread to garner public and governmental support but an arsenal of seemingly contradictory rhetorical weapons, which they did not attempt to reconcile but rather drew on as needed.

Large growers' claims to self-sufficiency masked the ways they had gained from government programs. In the early 1900s, the U.S. Department of Agriculture created the state agricultural extension service system. These services, originally designed to benefit midwestern and northeastern farmers by conducting research and providing support for local growers, also undergirded an arrangement to improve crop quality and instill best practices to address the effects of packing, shipping, and marketing on spoilage and fruit appearance, a program from which California growers benefited handsomely.[28] The revolution in agricultural knowledge grounded in extension services improved output: from 1950 to 1960, California's agricultural production grew by one-third; its value increased from $650 million in 1940 to over $3.2 billion in 1960. As I mentioned previously, it also fueled land consolidation. The percentage of landowning farmers in the population declined nationwide, from 18 percent in 1900 to just over 8 percent in 1940, alongside an almost 50 percent decrease in the number of farms, even as the amount of irrigated agricultural acreage nearly doubled. In California, this trend meant that between 1940 and 1960, the number of farms decreased by 23 percent, while the number of people involved in this industry (most now as farmworkers) jumped, thus securing the state's position as an agricultural powerhouse.[29]

While the size of California landholdings had been growing long before the bracero program, the trend was hastened after the start of World War II due to another land grab, this time targeting Japanese and Japanese American landholdings. Elite growers had intermittently tried to purchase this land or acquire it by other means. Not only did these farms operate on some of the most productive and fertile acreage in the state, but they were also well capitalized. Valued at $72 million plus $6 million in equipment, this land was worth far more per acre ($279.96) than that of the average California farm ($37.94). Moreover, these Japanese and Japanese American farm owners, known for their exceptional farming skills, controlled part of the produce market and even dominated crops such as strawberries. They produced 40 percent of California's fruits and vegetables, despite farming a much smaller percentage of the state's land.[30] When these highly productive farm owners were sent to internment camps beginning in early 1942 and were no longer able to pay their mortgages, white landowners snapped up this land for mere cents on the dollar.

In the wake of this land grab and the internment of these former farm owners, growers predicted a shortage of suitable workers. To the rescue came women, older students, and soldiers awaiting deployment; some local districts even closed schools so that children could be put to work. Several thousand interned Japanese Americans also pitched in. The Farm Security Administration, too, responded to the call, seeking to relocate a surplus of unemployed farmworkers from other areas of the country to California. Growers were not enthusiastic about these solutions, however, considering them unviable in the long term. Most of these workers were inexperienced, and farm labor was a skill that required a biologically fit worker to avoid ruining crops and losing owners' money. Instead, growers envisioned a solution similar to that undertaken during World War I, when workers were recruited from Mexico. That is, growers wanted a particular kind of worker, one physically suitable and with farm experience who could easily be controlled and would not become a competitor as Japanese immigrants and Japanese Americans had.

During the bracero program, temporary Mexican migrants were the embodiment of this kind of worker. Not long after the program's start, Clyde Rubidoux, secretary-manager of the Glendora Lemon Growers Association, praised them. In an interview with Carey McWilliams, a progressive journalist and lawyer, Rubidoux said Mexican braceros had "saved the day" for California's growers. The men were "averaging three and one-half boxes per hour, or about twenty-eight boxes a day," with some "picking as high as five boxes an hour, or forty-five per day," even though none had worked in lemon groves previously.[31] Rubidoux's assessment, reinforcing Teague's earlier arguments, suggests that the braceros possessed innate abilities. Jack Bias, manager of the San Joaquin Valley's principal growers' association, likewise felt that "those of Mexican nationality" were better "at this type of work" because "of their short stature."[32]

So widely accepted was this view that even a Northern California Farm Placement Service (FPS) representative supported it. "When I first went on the job, I thought the line put out by growers was [exaggerated], but I had to change some of my ideas. I've seen the [braceros] work stooping over for hours at a stretch, without straightening up. An Anglo simply couldn't take it. But it didn't seem to bother these boys a bit." The reason? "Mexicans are generally a good deal shorter than the Anglos—they're built closer to the ground."[33] Another FPS field officer advocated the use of Mexican laborers, claiming that Anglos "wouldn't last a day out there." The organic content of "peat dirt would drive [Anglos] crazy. There are only certain groups who aren't affected by it. Filipinos can work out there, and it never affects them. Mexican[s], the same. But with light skins, it's murder." He would add, "Negroes can't take it either."[34] Even Sen. George Murphy (R-Calif.) would reiterate these ideas in 1960. For him, Mexicans not only actually "prefer[red] farm work," their proficiency at this labor was due to their "manual ability" and "skill in the handling of tools" and the similarity between the climes of Mexico and California.[35] A U.S. Department of Labor field representative explained the suitability of Mexican laborers to the Imperial Valley's 120 degree heat. "When you're out in the fields, they're usually irrigated, and very humid. The combination of the heat and the humidity is just about more than a human being can take. . . . I'm not going to ask an American . . . to do it. I don't know of anybody except the [braceros] who can take it."[36] The repeated references to worker's hands, bodies, work ethic, and biological adjustment to climate and job transformed learned skills into the outcome of biological selection, all with a paternalist twist that depicted them as children—simple, innocent, even primitive. These judgments produced a coherent narrative about Mexicans and their place as the ideal stoop laborers that growers circulated.

Growers, who consented to getting braceros, still complained dearly. We only get "labor only at certain times of the year—at the peak of our harvest."[37] "All the advantages," grumbled a grower advocate, "went to workers and none to the employer." When union organizers protested that domestic workers were being shunned in favor of braceros, William Tolbert, then manager of the Ventura County Citrus Growers, applauded the concessions that growers had made. "We have upgraded the jobs" on behalf of U.S. domestic farmworkers, while "downgrad[ing]" the "menial tasks that the braceros do."[38] By 1951 the U.S. legislation covering the bracero program—Public Law 78—precluded the use of braceros in positions that "operate[d] or maintain[ed] power-driven, self-propelled harvesting, planting or cultivating machinery"; these skilled positions, with some exceptions, were reserved for U.S. domestic laborers. Keeping skilled jobs for "our own people," said Rep. E. C. Gathings (D-Ark.), would "give them the privilege of obtaining good wages." No one, he assured Congress, sought to "bring in foreign workers to do that skilled work." However, manual laborers for the "leaning over type of work" were still in short supply, and growers could use braceros to fill that gap. In other words, while a bracero could "drive a truck" or "take [a] truck to town to get a load of supplies," he could not, contended Gathings, "operate a combine or a cottonpicker."[39]

Gathings's comments are revealing for two reasons. First, by "our own people," he was likely referring to white transplants from Arkansas and Oklahoma, many of whom had recently lost their farms and had come west in search of new land.[40] These new arrivals viewed themselves as farmers, and not farmworkers, which they saw as a temporary condition. They imagined themselves as having nothing in common with farmworker peers for whom the stoop labor was considered natural. Second, Gathings's remarks suggest that the boundaries between supposed skilled and unskilled labor were clear cut. In practice, however, the distinctions were hard to maintain; soon braceros were working as irrigators, mechanics, tractor drivers, and even foremen.[41] Moreover, it made sense that braceros would be given the chance to learn to drive a tractor. Not only was skilled training such as this part of the program's mission, but there was also a provision built into the wartime agreement that encouraged former braceros to purchase tractors on their return, using the 10 percent withheld from checks.[42] While California legislators and other officials heralded these modernizing aspects of the program, growers nonetheless reassured Congress and the public that braceros engaged only in menial jobs appropriate for their class and race, adding further scaffolding to the hegemonic agricultural narrative.[43] In short, the logic of the program—as a means of modernizing braceros—was contested by the racial organization and exigencies of fieldwork.

Thus, growers' narratives cast doubt on the dependability of domestic workers, describing them as "unreliable, winos, incompetent, unstable, or cantankerous," even "damn tramps"—in other words, made redundant (in the Marxist sense) not by machines but by a better set of workers.[44] As Tolbert, the growers' advocate, expounded to Congress, white migrant laborers refused to work. When a "real old honest-to-gosh [white] farm labor migrant" asked how long the harvest lasted and a grower said "'it lasts . . . twelve months a year,'" the worker responded, "'I do not want your job'"—he "want[ed] to move."[45] Tolbert's case in point: although area growers had lodging for more than thirty thousand families, and five hundred of them worked during the winter due to "nice weather" and work "pick[ing] lemons," right "as we reach the peak of the harvest . . . other work begins to come on in other states and . . . they are gone. By summer we have six or seven hundred vacant family houses."[46] The notion that domestic farmhands were loath to the obligatory rhythm of work found its way into Edward R. Murrow's 1960 documentary, *Harvest of Shame*. When he asked if migrants were "happy," a foreman responded, "They got a little gypsy in their blood." Migrants can leave when they want; "they wouldn't do anything else."[47]

We see complexities of this grower narrative. Any racial benefit that made white domestic workers fit for skilled farm labor was undone by their racially incongruent behavior as winos, gypsies, or class troublemakers. In contrast to such unacceptable domestic specimens, braceros were exactly the workers growers wanted. "Near to us" is a population "of a lower standard of living," argued Tolbert. "[They] are very willing to come in and do that job and we, in turn, are helping th[eir] nation . . . to assist [it]self economically by actually working for their money, and in actually producing for us, in obtaining that money."[48] In the end, the narrative portrayed bracero workers as better adapted, biologically and culturally, to agricultural labor than domestic farmworkers, while it foregrounded the particularity of degenerate domestic workers. This theme of white workers' degeneracy and Mexicans' fitness ultimately blurred the racial, ethnic, and national divisions within this workforce, configuring all agricultural workers as nonwhite, regardless of race or ethnicity. Domestic workers would fight against this blurring, as we will see in chapter 6. Moves against it and to restore their position as white were largely unsuccessful and undercut the possibilities of a farmworker class alliance, which braceros would try to support.

Growers' self-narratives and those of their workers came together in descriptions of agriculture's vulnerabilities, especially the shortage of laborers at harvest and planting time. Crops "have sharp peaks of labor requirements," wrote Teague in *Fifty Years a Rancher*. "[They] must be completely harvested in thirty to sixty days or they spoil in the field. This means that many more workers are required at harvest time than reside in the communities where those crops are grown. Hence, there is an absolute necessity for a very large number of migratory workers to follow the peak harvests."[49] The recognition of these vulnerabilities structured the government's farm policies and intervention, and furthered the public's acceptance that growers would at times need support.[50] In fact, the guarantee and regularization of this very large workforce was what the bracero program was designed to provide. It was a state attempt to remove access to labor from the list of uncertainties until growers could eliminate the need for such labor through mechanization—a transition, like the program's provision of laborers, encouraged with state monies and research.[51]

This story, then, is not merely one of how elite agriculturalists secured access to reasonably priced labor until technology could decrease the number of workers required, although it is that. More critically, it shows how growers produced a narrative that both justified the conditions under which workers toiled and constructed a so-called biological truth that reinforced dominant ideas about workers' fitness for stoop labor. This dual accomplishment would ultimately bar domestic farmworkers from the privileges of the modern.

Growers as Modern Businessmen

Thus far, I have mapped out the outlines of California's narrative agricultural terrain: large growers' portrayal of themselves as small farmers and as the embodiment of democratic tradition, and of domestic farmworkers as unproductive loafers. Growers' alignment as upholders of national traditions enabled them to claim that they were due governmental assistance (parity) but had eschewed it, and that farmworkers did not deserve it. At midcentury the growers supplemented their self-depiction as small farmers with a portrait of themselves as modern agroindustrialists.

A four-part *Los Angeles Times* series about the agricultural enterprise, published in tandem with a 1961 lettuce pickers' strike, demonstrates this new image in operation, the advantages it bestowed on growers, and the repercussions it had for farmworkers. Growers used media access and a firmly established self-narrative to position themselves in the public eye as enterprising businessmen able to capitalize on the technological revolution; more critically, farmworkers were excluded from this revolution. What comes through in this coverage is not only farmworkers' lowly stature but the degree to which a grower narrative had permeated the public's vision of agriculture. The ability to control the terms of the debate enabled growers to hide their dependence on a transnational market encompassing both their labor force and their products, and the state's hand in guiding that market. That is, growers could paint themselves as legitimate national actors and their workers as illegitimate and outside the nation. Growers portrayed braceros, who came into this realm, as good foreigners—those who came, contributed, and left— against a set of un-Americans who did not. Their control over these narratives created and fanned a rift between diverse groups of farmworkers for whom class might otherwise have constituted an axis of solidarity.

"Gradually," observed the author of the first article, "and with little public awareness . . . agriculture has become big business." Growers, formerly "at the mercy of . . . weather and uncertain markets," were now portrayed as able to transcend those contingencies. They likely conducted "business on the phone," incorporated "methods of . . . [their] industrial counterparts," relied on "technology and management" and "college-trained specialists," and could now harness "the technical knowledge and economic acumen that [their] fathers probably lacked."[52] By tracing the transformation from farming to agroindustry, the series solidified the differences between elite growers and lowly farmworkers.[53] Farms were no longer a "pastoral" setting of "haystacks and horse-drawn plows," the article explained to its largely urban readership; the "farmer who isn't prepared to invest thousands of dollars in heavy equipment or to contract for services he can't perform himself" will most likely do little "more than feed his family." As one observer argued, "farming here 'is usually an intensive, specialized, commercial undertaking for the purpose of obtaining income from the employment of labor, managerial ability and capital." The series went on to define agribusiness owner: "If he is not a multimillionaire entrepreneur with offices in Los Angeles or San Francisco, the farmer must at least be a competent businessman capable of making large capital outlays and directing his operations in the fashion of a corporate executive." An article pictured the "farmer" as dressed in white button-down shirt and tie, at his desk and on the phone.[54]

Those left out of this transformation of farm to agribusiness, according to one article, were men like Malaqueo Garcia, who owned a farm in San Ysidro, a town just north of the Mexican border. Garcia, said the article, "could never hire braceros" because the "wooden building" that housed his domestic laborers was "filthy," "right out of *Grapes of Wrath*." Unlike his richer agribusiness competitors highlighted in earlier articles in the series, Garcia was "too poor" to make the investment necessary to receive the "much-wanted bracero," and his farm "would never meet the standards set by Public Law 78."[55] The technologically advanced, implicitly Anglo agribusinessman is contrasted with the poor Mexican American farmer (whose name is an obvious cue) unable to support what Bruce Jessup of Stanford University School of Medicine envisioned could someday be "a workforce with a truly adequate annual family income."[56] This unsuccessful (read backward) farmer did not deserve the benefits extended to successful (modern) competitors.

There was an implicit third party in this contrast between poor farmer and wealthy modern businessman: the bracero. If millions of braceros, the article intimated, were ready for the modernizing transformation that the program promised, poor domestic farmers like Garcia were not. Nor was he, by implication, even an adequate worker for modern agricultural ventures; modern braceros were a better choice. The article portrays Garcia as a sympathetic character who cannot escape his own limitations. His was not an isolated case, but simply one example standing in for all Mexican Americans as unfit for the challenges and rewards of the modern agribusiness owner.

Braceros, however, did not arrive similarly laden with the racial baggage burdening Mexican American or white farmworkers. As Robert Lederer of the American Association of Nurserymen said, "Braceros do work which American [white] migrant workers are unwilling to perform and *do badly* and *inefficiently*"; Matt Triggs, of the nongovernmental American Farm Bureau Federation, contended, "Domestics 'are interested in permanent jobs . . . rather than temporary and intermittent employment of the type performed by braceros.'"[57] "In the short time" that braceros had been here, said Rubidoux, a growers association official, they had "learned more than many U.S. workers." He continued, "Their behavior is excellent. Their attitude is inspiring. Their cleanliness, their housekeeping, their self-discipline are amazing. We are most impressed by their production records."[58] This commonsense, long-standing appeal of growers' logic, then, would continue to hold sway. U.S. farmworkers, described as snubbing the temporary jobs that Mexicans took, were no longer the right laborers for modern agribusiness; they were now both too inefficient (i.e., backward) and too advanced (i.e., modern). Braceros, it seems, were just the right combination: modern enough to be efficient, yet not too modern to be productive with a hoe and pick.[59] These gradations of modern, then, speak to the linear narrative of modernization that situated braceros, domestic migrants, and growers at different points on this path.

Thus, we see the divergent casting of farmworkers and growers. Domestic migrants were consigned to the periphery of society, unable to capitalize on its benefits. By comparison, growers, able to "merg[e] . . . traditional farming, mechanized packing and managerial skill," could profit from the riches of the United States. "Machines, in partnership with advanced agriculture technology and an unusual breed of farmers" were "subdu[ing]" the "once . . . trackless desert waste[land]" and turning it into a "valley blossom[ing] under irrigation" and mechanization.[60] As these big-time growers achieved "vertical integration"—"a mechanism whereby *complete control* is exerted over an agricultural product from planting through marketing" that requires "*ownership* of all phases of the operation"—the article's accompanying photo makes explicit just who had built this modern business: the agribusiness owner. His operation was integrated from the foreman reporting to headquarters on the "progress of carrot pickers" via two-way radios, down to the migrants, captured kneeling and at work in the field. Although stoop laborers outnumber the foreman, the picture's placement of the foreman in the foreground alongside an automobile, while distancing the farmworkers, suggests the "social . . . segregat[ion]" the latter experienced. Still, the laborer is positioned close to the foreman, hinting that the supposedly backward and excluded were in fact among us and even closing the gap, unsettling growers' claims to perfect progress in the fields.[61] That is, the photo speaks both to the modernizing possibilities embedded in the bracero program and the lengths to which growers would go to forestall them for some workers.

The unsubtle "farmers-as-competent-businessmen" subtext likewise holds for the second article. It unequivocally linked notions of acceptable risk with growers' refusal to negotiate with union leaders. "We're not anti-union," declared Mike Schultz, president of the Imperial Valley Lettuce Growers and Shippers Association. But neither could growers "depend on . . . small numbers" of domestic workers "to do the harvesting"; growers had "no choice but to use braceros." As Schultz put it, "We don't mind taking a gamble on the *market*. . . . But we can't gamble on having enough labor available for the harvest." Growers knew how to work within the logic of capitalism, but farmworkers, as we have seen, were unpredictable. Refusing to accept a farmworkers' union was, by implication, a sound business practice.

These "rugged individualists" would not knuckle under to "union bossism," a phrase reinforcing unions' supposed antidemocratic and antimeritocratic structures. "Everyone [stood] to lose" from a harvest strike, said Schultz, "the farmer, the worker and the consumer who [would] have to pay more for whatever produce he can get at the neighborhood market."[62] And just in case readers did not understand the "quiet revolution" modernizing agriculture, the series spelled it out: "The machine is the principal ingredient in the evolution of farming from a family-oriented status to its emerging agri-business form."[63] Farmworkers pushing for a union, the Los Angeles Times seemed to say, were preventing this revolution.

Just as growers were described as modern in their use of technology and advanced practices, so too did the articles establish, beyond a doubt, that domestic farmworkers were backward and outside the nation. While elite growers "exert[ed] . . . complete control . . . over an agricultural product from planting through marketing," relying on an $82,000 machine to "scoot . . . among rows of freshly-baled alfalfa," farmworkers could not control the conditions of their lives. In one article, Hobert Rush, a domestic farm laborer, was said to "shar[e] two dingy metal huts that rent for $18.60 a month . . . with his wife and six children." Having only worked a few days, the Rushes were "down to their last $2," to be spent "on some lard and flour." The living space of these domestic laborers was contrasted to those of braceros residing in a model labor camp that was "sanitary and rather pleasant." Thus, one article in the series described "over a thousand braceros . . . eat[ing] well" and "earn[ing] considerably more than [they] would in Mexico."[64] The point of this comparison between bracero and domestic laborer was revealed in the Los Angeles Times article's next sentence: "Rush, an American citizen, is left pretty much to his own devices. The bracero, a citizen of Mexico, has the U.S. and Mexico governments looking out for his welfare."[65] U.S. citizen farmworkers deserved no state protection, while braceros received it from two national governments.

By casting domestic farmworkers' lot in this way, the article implicitly obscured other possible reasons behind their condition. It diverted readers' attention away from questioning the structures of commercial agriculture, the reigning depiction of farmworkers, and the root cause of their condition. In concentrating on character flaws and individuals' failure to avail themselves of possibilities, the series left no room to inspect forces at work beyond farmworkers' control or to question the seemingly commonsensical nature of this elite vision. So deeply rooted was this narrative that, despite extensive reporting on farmworker strikes, the *Los Angeles Times* did not inspect, much less challenge, it.

In the end, growers were depicted as properly dominating agricultural production, braceros as safeguarded by the United States and Mexico, and domestic farmworkers as lacking self-reliance and initiative and therefore undeserving of protection. This grower discourse framed domestic migrants and braceros as dependent—that is, unable to act as modern individual subjects—and thus with tenuous claims on the nation and its benefits. Though domestic migrants repeatedly fought for better wages and material conditions, as we will see in chapter 6, even their advocates, such as Catholic priests, largely accepted the commonsensical framing that constructed farmworkers as needing protection. The legacy of this narrative, then, was the denial of farmworkers' agency and their continued depiction as backward and thus outside the nation.

Conclusion

Growers' narratives of farming and farm culture impacted how the material rewards of agriculture would be allocated. Landowners alternated between describing themselves as small farmers and as modern business owners, while portraying domestic farmworkers as lazy, collectivist-minded, un-American, and at times too modern. Growers' small-farmer narratives marshaled an abundance of long-standing images about farming as meritocratic and the seat of democracy. Workers unable to benefit from this meritocracy, then, were either peons (seen as the antithesis of democracy) or lazy—that is, not meriting farming's recompense or state aid. Small farmers, however, deserved governmental support for their self-reliance, despite supposedly refusing such help. By midcentury, this picture would add another narrative thread: of growers as modern business owners. That thread drew on a national fascination with technology and science, and everything anchored in them, as the height of the modern.

Growers used these images and narratives to earn handsome profits. Urgent pleas of labor shortages pushed government officials at the local, state, and national levels to prop up elite interests by securing through the bracero program a type of laborer modern enough but not too modern. That is, growers drew for their economic success on state aid, diplomatic influence, and manipulation of labor markets—all reliant on power relations beyond the nation. As the United States emerged from World War II, farming's earlier depiction as nonmodern became more problematic. Changing to fit the postwar world position of the United States, farming was reconfigured as a modern business, and growers updated their image to conform to the shift. They maintained that they still acted on behalf of the nation and rhetorically marginalized farmworkers as poor and uneducated, downplaying the transnational relations on which their success depended. These transnational relations, in turn, fostered the formation of an elite grower class and anchored its power. Just as gender and race are relational constructs, so too are elite and popular classes made in relation to each other.

Grower narratives cast farmworkers' economic position as the result of innate laziness and the gypsy in them, thus connecting poverty to a rejection of farming's opportunities. At times, domestic migrants contested this portrayal, for they recognized that it denied them the privileges of citizenship. In the end, they could not overcome the stigma of this image, which undercut their claims to whiteness and ultimately confined them to the realm of the foreign. While, as we will see in chapter 6, they would challenge their foreignness by claiming difference from braceros, this strategy ultimately worked against their material interests, as it cut farmworker solidarity along national lines. In the end, the narratives that furthered the formation of a grower class of and for itself simultaneously undermined the constitution of a farmworker class.

The next chapter turns to the braceros. It explores where these men came from, what they sought from the bracero journey, and how they claimed they should be chosen for such an opportunity. This is critical for understanding how experiences in the United States would shape men's self-perceptions.

3

Manhood, the Lure of Migration, and Contestations of the Modern

"The euphoria about the bracero program was incredible," a former bracero told his questioner. "Everyone wanted to go. . . . I realized that it was very good opportunity to avail myself of resources."[1]

In Santa Angélica, a similar collective sentiment was repeated by the men of the barbershop. Ramón Avitia, one of the town elders, said, "We all thought we were going to get rich."

"Yes, that's what we thought," agreed Álvaro García, the barbershop's owner. "If we worked hard, did what our bosses wanted, we'd make a lot of money."

"I thought that things were fair in the United States," interjected don Ramón, "that it was not about whom you knew, like it is here, but about how hard you worked. . . . I'm not sure anymore."

"I worked hard; it was hard work picking fruit," concluded don Álvaro. "I didn't come back rich, but I did set up this barbershop."[2]

Despite braceros' initial euphoria, not everyone sought to participate or did so for the same reasons or goals. The desire to migrate, I suggest, was instead a product of specific local and national conditions that intertwined with social systems and place.[3] In part, these conditions were shaped by the expectations promulgated by the Mexican state. As we saw in chapter 1, Mexican officials envisioned the program as a component of the nation's modernization; selected men would head north, acquire agricultural knowledge and techniques, and transplant these to communities in Mexico, stimulating a transformation. The braceros, however, had their own reasons for wishing to migrate, ones based on conditions affecting individuals, families, and communities. Critical at the local level was men's tenuous grasp on manhood, an adult status grounded in the ability to sustain a family. Drought, disease, and economic factors often sent men teetering on the edge of losing this social position. These factors, as I show in this chapter, are constitutive of aspiring migrants' desire to go north, a desire framed in specifically gendered terms—as specifically *men's* reasons.[4] This gendered desire to migrate anchored the central transformation that occurred on men's journey: from braceros into transnational subjects, a new sociopolitical subjectivity or sense of themselves.

Physical Terrain and Social Relations in Durango

I first arrived in Victoria de Durango (the official name for Durango City), or simply Durango as locals call the capital of Durango State, in July 1994. I saw a bustling city of nearly half a million people, more than a mile high, surrounded by half-barren mountains that took on a purple cast in the late afternoon. Situated in the central southern part of the state, the city had plentiful sun, few clouds, and the temperate climate for which I had always wished in my hometown of Chicago. Cars clogged the streets, fighting for space with bicycles, exhaust-spewing buses, and farm animals pulling carts laden with produce, equipment parts, and furniture. Located more than seven hundred miles south of the U.S.-Mexico border, Durango City was also covered by a layer of dust that soon coated my clothes, my breakfast table, and found its way into my eyes. That year, like many years during the bracero program, the state was stricken by drought. Rain or the lack thereof would be a prominent theme in my conversations with former migrants, especially town elder don Ramón.

Durango state is bordered to the north by the state of Chihuahua, to the northeast by Coahuila, to the southeast by Zacatecas, to the south by Nayarit and Jalisco, and to the west by Sinaloa. Physically the fourth-largest state in the country, it has the second-lowest population density, in part because lack of rain has made agriculture difficult. Rich in natural resources, Durango has four distinct climates and geographic terrains: desert, semidesert (the majority of the state), valleys, and a forested region. The desert area, located at the foot of the state's western mountain ranges, was home to mining in gold, mercury, silver, and especially iron.[5] The discovery of these metals fueled the region's initial settlement in 1563. Centuries later, the state's business and political leaders acknowledged that the mining growth had been hampered by the lack of roads and railways. At the time, the only area linked to Mexico City was the Laguna, the economically vibrant cotton-producing region in the northeastern corner of Durango that stretches into the neighboring state of Coahuila (a state boundary so located, in part, because the topography was flatter and more easily conquered than the steep rocky terrain of the mining region to the west). With intrastate rail connections woefully inadequate, in 1933 the state government imposed a one-year tax to fund a Laguna–Durango City connection.[6] Today cotton is still a major state industry. Other notable activities are ranching and farming. There was a Coca-Cola bottling plant in Durango City, and in the lushly forested northwestern section logging is the primary activity. In this part of the state, reminiscent of Northern California with trees and lush vegetation, heavily laden logging trucks slowly wind down the mountains on narrow gravel roads. My research, however, focused on the semidesert area of central Durango that cyclically thirsted for rain.[7]

During the drought-stricken time of my fieldwork, smaller communities in this semidesert region were even dustier than Durango City. Roads leading to the *pueblos* were not paved. My light blue 1985 Honda Civic, nicknamed Sarge, had to negotiate gravel roads once we traveled past the highways heading out of Durango City. Luckily for Sarge, these roads contained only small craters, around which I could maneuver so as not to scrape his underbelly. The first time I visited the area, I was struck by its panorama, vast and open, which seemed more so against the cloudless bright sky. There were no power lines or billboards to mar the view, just an occasional small store where I would stop for a soda. Leaving Durango City, the road began to wind, hills verged on mountains, sparse vegetation dotted the area, and scrawny cows meandered about in search of a few blades of grass. Telephone and electric lines appeared out of nowhere at a *pueblo*'s entrance. The telephone signals were sent over distance by wireless technology and then funneled into wires to reach the few individual homes that contracted service. Electricity was not reliable, and lights would flicker periodically, often disappearing for several hours at a time. Still, with breathtaking scenery, no wonder the state has been the setting for so many westerns.[8]

I surveyed a number of communities in Durango and selected two in this central swath for in-depth analysis and oral historical and ethnographic research. Santa Angélica and San Andrés were typical of Durango *pueblos*. They had a couple of general stores, packed to the ceiling with produce, canned goods, batteries, clothes, videos, tools, and other odds and ends. Small adobe houses with metal or tile roofs kept their inhabitants cool in the summer and warm in the winter. They were painted various shades of yellow, peach, and blue. None had heating, a testament to a generally mild climate with only brief cold snaps, as well as to the wonders of adobe. The homes of current migrants were, as in Durango City, noticeably larger than those of nonmigrants. They had more elaborate designs and facades, often reminiscent of ones found in the United States, and second or even third floors. San Andrés did not have a formal central plaza; instead, a corner acted as the meeting place for the *pueblo*'s elderly men. Santa Angélica, outwardly the more prosperous of the two, was home to a tiny Catholic church that former (and now current) migrants had been called on to support, despite the lack of a priest. Located in the municipal district of San Juan del Río and formerly part of Hacienda El Casco (land awarded to settlers in the early 1700s), at midcentury Santa Angélica had more than fifteen hundred residents, down somewhat from 1900.⁹ When I was there in the mid-1990s, both *pueblos* had only about three hundred inhabitants, as many former residents or their sons, daughters, and grandchildren had moved to the United States. One prosperous man commented that he saw more people from his town on the streets of Chicago than in their supposed homes.

In both communities, many residents worked land located far from their homes. Don Álvaro's farm, for example, was twenty minutes by car from his house; other people traveled greater distances. These were not idyllic small farms adjoining small, neatly appointed houses. The terrain in both areas was relatively flat. Santa Angélica was situated about seventeen hundred meters above sea level, which gave the area a climate favorable to both humans and crops. Because of this climate and the *pueblo*'s proximity to the intensively worked Avino mine, the area was among the first settled by the Spanish, despite the presence of Tepehuan and Zacatec Indians, pushed further inland in the nineteenth century.¹⁰ In San Andrés, located closer to the economically vibrant Laguna region, former peons received land when the surrounding three haciendas were broken up in 1926; one of these haciendas, Santa Catalina del Álamo, the largest in the state, had comprised more than 1 million acres before it was subdivided after the revolution.¹¹ Today, children play hide and seek and animals roam through the huge rooms of the crumbling, once luxurious main house.

Neither *pueblo* used irrigation. Instead, farmers depended on rain, and they cyclically faced severe droughts, often lasting four or five years. During the program, circumstances that would spark a national competition for bracero contracts were exacerbated by these droughts, along with occasional freezes. "The daily salary that [peasants] earn," contended Durango state representative Juan Pescador Polanco in 1953, "isn't even sufficient to acquire [items] most indispensable for survival." The problems resulting from the previous freeze, which destroyed almost 50 percent of harvests, Pescador noted, were "truly disturbing." Entire villages showed up at the state capital hoping to join the program and go north to find work.[12] Drought, however, was not a new phenomenon. Whenever it struck, the *pueblos'* men had gone to seek work elsewhere, frequently finding employment in Laguna textile factories or picking cotton on haciendas. In 1995 I met several elderly Durango residents who, in the 1920s, had walked for two months to the United States to find work.

Drought was only one cause of migration, however; another factor was shifting demographics. Even though the state was underpopulated, by the 1940s economic and health policies had created major population and land pressure due to the need to feed larger families on the same size plot.[13] The number of calories consumed by families, wrote Daniel Casarrubias Ocampo in his 1956 study, was "deficient." It was a diet of "tea, tortillas, chiles, and beans" for breakfast, "tortillas, chiles, and beans" at lunch, and for dinner, "the same as in the morning."[14] A 1945 study faulted postrevolution land reform. Deemed "a lamentable waste," the policy did not grant access to water, credit, seeds, or other services to make the land viable.[15] Although in 1935 President Lázaro Cárdenas made agricultural credit a permanent 3 to 4 percent of the budget, his successor decreased the amount while the number of small farmers eligible for credits increased.[16] Nor did these farmers have access to "technology." "In 90 percent of the cases," declared Casarrubias Ocampo, peasants used "colonial-era" methods when they desperately needed to be "educat[ed]" in modern ones.[17] Whether for lack of knowledge or access to water, credit, or seed, many from Durango's central semidesert region were unable to survive off the land and were lured instead into the bracero program. At times, drought and the lack of other services so hampered farm yields that government officials recognized the likelihood of undocumented migration and allotted the state a large number of bracero contracts, although the number allocated could never meet the need. Thus, the push off the land, begun early in the century, continued during the program, making Durango a state of entrenched outmigration.

The offroad locations of the communities I studied made them seem totally isolated, an isolation marked by dirt roads, lack of telephones, and miles to the neighboring town. Yet during the revolution and in subsequent decades, the entire region was alive with the movement of people and communication. Even as early as the U.S.-Mexico War (1846–48), Mexicans of the region were beckoned across the border to lay railroad track in formerly Mexican lands. Later, they travelled north by foot or by rail, where they also participated in the great 1917 strike at the Phelps-Dodge mine in Bisbee, Arizona; worked as cowboys on Texas ranches; and labored in California agriculture from the beginning of the century. This movement brought them into contact with an array of ideas, social practices, economic systems, and products not available in their *pueblos* but common in the United States and even other parts of Mexico.

Durango's men were also exposed to a host of ideas within Mexico via news spread by contact with peasant soldiers in Pancho Villa's army and from what they saw and heard as soldiers themselves. They carried news between *pueblos* on foot or on horseback. They walked to jobs as seasonal wage laborers on plantations and in textile factories, mines, and commercial ventures in the Laguna area; and small producers transported crops to market. Some men met U.S. organizers from the Industrial Workers of the World, who had been drawn to Laguna factories after the revolution, and heard their message of working-class solidarity and consciousness.[18] By the late 1930s, Mexican movies and radio were more common outside Mexico City, exposing all who watched or listened to a multiplicity of ideas. Mexico's presidents, seizing on radio's ability to speak to the entire nation simultaneously, used the medium to promote their goals and deeds. Although broadcasts were special events in small *pueblos*, most people would have still known of them. Thus, by the start of the program, Durango residents already found themselves enmeshed in the ideas, movements, and social upheavals transfixing the area. Made "tough" and "resourceful" by hardship, men of this region were also "well traveled."[19]

In sum, the region that I experienced as remote and isolated was, during and after the revolution, awash in change. By the program's start, word of the government's premium on modernization had filtered down to men living beyond the Laguna, alongside stories of workers' rights and peasants' and workers' strikes. In this area formed by local, regional, national, and transnational forces lived men who even before trips north of the border had been exposed to wage labor and development schemes similar to those they would find in the United States.

Manhood, Migrant Expectations, and Production of the Modern Subject

Men not selected as braceros sent letters to Mexican presidents arguing that they would better represent the Mexican nation in the United States and should have been chosen for this role. These letters implicitly challenge collectivism—the discourse that undergirded the revolutionary state's consolidation and formed the axis of revolutionary nationalism. The reasons mobilized in the letters reveal not only the unevenness and partiality of the penetration and acceptance of collectivist discourse but the struggle over the kind of relationship that would prevail between state and citizen. The state, still cohering after the revolution, was pushing two interrelated ideas: first, a corporatist relationship (organized around the collective connections structured indirectly through state associations); and, second, the "modernization of patriarchy": that is, the destruction of "regional patriarchal networks of power and provisioning, in favor of national, horizontal [that is, fraternal] networks."[20] In both aims, the federal government, rather than localized patronage webs, would be the bearer and distributor of resources. While it would allocate these resources based on need and immediacy of threat, the destined recipients would be individual patriarchs and through them, families. That is, state officials envisioned the emergence of national lateral bonds and the containment of hierarchical ties within the domestic sphere.

As we will see, the letter-writers did not always accept the state's vision. Using an eclectic set of rationales to push their case, they refused to surrender the rewards of patriarchy from which they gained authority. At times in men's letters we see their reliance on collectivism, the benefits they saw in the state's patriarchal responsibilities, and the ways they advocated for themselves as individuals. As such, the letters illuminate a key moment in the production of Mexico's state-citizen relationship and the axis around which this relationship would revolve. This relationship, as we shall see, was under much stress throughout the bracero program.

Men from Durango greeted news of the program with optimism and responded in numbers exceeding available spots, standing in line sometimes for days.[21] Interviewed by reporters, those program hopefuls indicated they "desired a better life" and were "full of faith" that work in the United States would bring "the prized necessities that the homeland denied them."[22] They picked up on the government's official rendition of the program as part of the country's path to modernization. Thousands were turned away, though, and many opted to migrate outside official channels. Others who could not get a contract directly sought help from elites or pleaded their cases in letters to Mexican presidents or officials. In the letters, of which there are hundreds at the Mexican National Archives, signatories argued that they and their families were destitute, desperate for work, and needed the chance the program offered. Destitution alone, however, did not qualify them over those actually chosen, since most picked were equally needy. Thus, letter writers intertwined program goals (or the writers' versions of the goals) with reasons why they were the best men to achieve them.

Writers made strategic and inventive use of the state's framing of the program, offering evidence of the hard work, respectability, and sacrifice for family that it implicitly required, manifest in character recommendations mandated for program eligibility (requirements also included a birth certificate, evidence of military service, and proof that the applicant was not a member of an *ejido*). Letter writers sought to impress presidents with impeccable personal qualities, as well as the culturally legitimate reasons for, and severity of, their economic misfortune. Not all men could be entrusted with fulfilling the program mission, men wrote, for very few would put the needs of country before their own. Only those whose manhood was untarnished brought together all the characteristics government officials believed were required to make the program a success. Petitioners argued that they, in contrast to many chosen through prescribed channels, possessed the stipulated characteristics.

In brief, proper manhood required being a head of a household that included a wife, children, extended family, and often unrelated members. This kind of man worked hard, provided for his family, and monitored and controlled the labor and sexuality of his wife and children without abusing the privilege of control. Only heads of household had the weighty responsibility of covering family members' needs, anchoring notions of work as central to manhood.[23] As the anthropologist Ana Alonso found in her work in Chihuahua, a man able to fulfill his role as head of household gained a reputation as a "good community member" and "man of respect," where respect was "the social esteem" extended to men deemed "honorable." Honor, in turn, formed "the basis for the legitimacy of men's status and authority" in both "the domestic domain" and "the public sphere of community life." From work, concludes Alonso, a man gains "not only economic but . . . social value"; a "good reputation" was a "prerequisite for almost all social activity," and a "bad reputation" was "tantamount to social death."[24] Thus, honor, good reputation, and the ability to shoulder financial and social responsibilities were the essence of manhood, which in turn afforded full personhood. Marriage was a double-edged sword. The principal vehicle through which a man secured manhood and participation as a full community member, it also frequently undercut his status, since poor, working-class, and peasant men were at regular intervals unable to provide for their families.[25]

This vision of manhood—as head of household, good community member, honorable patriarch, and man of respect—was buttressed by movies making their way to villages and countryside, through the character of the *charro* or cowboy. "The *charro* was a symbol of Hispanic masculinity: light-skinned, handsome, and respectful of the 'inherent' divisions" within a society undergoing rapid revolutionary change. For Durango men, often believed to be fairer-skinned and taller than those not from northern Mexico, the *charro* "personified" and "glorified" "a specific kind of Mexican machismo" and masculinity familiar to them.[26]

This figure of the *charro* was deemed "protector of the peons against the powerful [plantation owners]" and a symbol of virility, even as he "maintain[ed] the patriarchal system that kept classes, races, and genders in their places." The film *Allá en el Rancho Grande* (1936) venerated a nation where "everyone resume[d] his or her social and gendered place, and everything return[ed] to normal." This resolution was made possible when the *charro* and the plantation owner ultimately "resolve[d a] quarrel," enabling the consolidation of the revolutionary state. The film's mixed reception suggests that the future direction of the country was still very much in flux. While critics saw it as confirming a stereotypical foreign vision of a backward Mexico of "cowboy dandies" and "peasant girls wearing colorful shawls," scholars understand this and other films as moments where Mexican audiences "came to recognize themselves as subjects of the nation."[27] As we will see, men saw the recuperation of manhood so critical in their relationship to the state and place in the nation at stake in their ability to migrate.

One letter asking for presidential intervention described a husband whose family was "so sad" and who had no way to feed his children. He continued, "I will be grateful [to] you, the powerful [leader] of our nation, [for] whatever help that you give me. . . . I want to work."[28] This excerpt highlights four ideas found in a majority of the letters I read: first, a distinction between the president (good ruler) and local government representatives (bad officials), harkening back to the colonial disjuncture between good king or president and bad officials or representatives;[29] second, the notion of *social indebtedness*—my term for the complex web of hierarchical relationships rooted in and emergent from the asking and granting of favors; third, an assertion of the writer's need to work; and, fourth, an explanation of the writer's need to work as due to circumstances beyond his control and not of his making.

The act of appealing to the king and president is a venerable tradition in Latin America. The king signified the beneficent and legitimate ruler, in contrast to corrupt and illegitimate local administrators. When faced with a problem, residents of New Spain appealed to the king to intervene. He was positioned above politics, and petitioners saw themselves as having direct access to him. This disjuncture was reconfigured after the revolution in the divide between president and caudillos—the local political machine bosses whose maneuverings were built on entrenched patronage, family bonds, and corruption. In writing to the president, aspiring braceros mobilized this tradition; they drew on a president's reputation as good and his position as all-powerful and not bound by the program's selection rules or local political favoritism that had thwarted the writers' pursuit of contracts. The good president possessed capabilities and wisdom to see beyond local constraints and act as Mexico's symbolic father and mediator of all interests. If made aware of problematic or corrupt procedures, he would take measures to resolve the selection of men so that those deemed most desirable by the program's own rhetoric would be chosen.

The writer also acknowledges that he would be grateful for the president's help. This plea signaled that this help would be a favor, a grant of assistance based on kindness and generosity, and not aid the state was required to give. In recognizing this aid as a favor, the writer signaled his willingness to repay it, thus burdening himself with an open-ended social debt. This debt would, until settled, link him to the president, embedding him in a social hierarchy. The act of taking on this debt and inscribing oneself into a social hierarchy and the relations it entailed reveals much about local constraints and the cost of resolving them. Financial instability repeatedly forced poor people to seek aid and economic relief and support from more established members of society, by asking for and receiving jobs, loans, or credit at a store. The process of asking for, granting, and receiving favors enmeshed both receivers and grantors in a community of ties, as favors requested and favors granted became a form of currency—what I term *social debt*—acknowledged by both parties, connecting the poor to their benefactors and structuring social relations. Because the poor found it difficult to extricate themselves from their social debts, these social hierarchies were largely immutable. Returning braceros would use both the money and the social capital they gained through the program to loosen the binds of their social indebtedness.

When the petitioner asserted that he sought work, he challenged the prevalent image of peasants as neither working nor wanting to work. Despite the clamor for bracero spots and long lines at contracting sites, Mexican officials were so convinced that the campesinos targeted for modernization were indolent and lazy by nature that negotiators made exposure to and adoption of a U.S. work ethic a program goal. That is, they built into bilateral agreements steps to replace campesinos' presumed propensity for drink, fighting, and fiestas with a dedication to hard work. Indeed, braceros were initially offered classes in English and hygiene.[30] While the presumed indolence of rural people was not a new idea, the program created another avenue to eradicate such traits deemed backward.[31]

This letter writer, in avowing that he wanted to work, challenged the state's assessment of peasants and rural life. He instead implied what other letters spelled out: that men without true need, defined as those burdens associated with families, would easily succumb to the lures of women, alcohol, and modern U.S. life. They might squander their earnings instead of investing in the future of their families and, by extension, that of Mexico. Some might not even return. Only men such as this author, who accepted the heavy burden of family, who kept his woman in check, and who wanted to raise his children well would resist temptation.[32] While officials assigned to select braceros could not differentiate between those desiring adventure and those without a "place to work," other writers contended, the president *was* able to see.[33] For example, the signatories of another letter, "worried about the economic interests of [their] homeland," did "not agree that peasants with land [should be able] abandon it to . . . work outside the[ir] country." By failing to prevent the exodus of men already able to support families, the state was inflicting "serious harm" on the national economy and threatening a social order predicated on established gender roles and authority.[34] Dovetailing with the first letter's assertion of need, this letter casts the migration aspirations of those who were not heads of households as synonymous with a desire to escape *pueblo* life, as well as family and national responsibilities; these men only wanted adventure.

Notions of real need, in contrast to the desire for adventure, worked to regulate specific configurations of manhood and womanhood and inscribed— if not into law, then in official discourse—these behavioral boundaries. During the 1940s and 1950s, many individuals—mostly women—petitioned the courts to obligate their spouses to "fulfill their responsibilities." Often wives wanted a divorce when their husbands could not or had not lived up to their legal responsibilities to support them and their children. At other times, rather than divorce, women sought to bring the power of the state to bear on economically or socially wayward spouses, in an attempt to force them to meet their responsibilities. While it is nearly impossible to ascertain how often this legal action was the remedy of choice for women, or whether women filing petitions were pleading for government intervention for stated reasons, these petitions do convey ideas about accepted gender responsibilities and roles. Over and over again, petitions used a specific language to describe the role of wife. They labeled her "a woman of the house," charged with "the duties [quehaceres] of her sex." These petitions brought these relationships and tasks under judicial jurisdiction. Wives, then, "became" legally responsible for taking care of the house, while husbands were entrusted with making sure that wife and children were fed, clothed, and had a place to live.[35]

Marriage protected each spouse's reputation and enabled men to claim that they and their families were truly needy. This we see in their description of the duties and responsibilities that marriage assigned each spouse. Women, former migrants instructed me, got married because they needed someone to provide for them, a husband who would keep them fed, clothed, and with a roof over their heads. For husbands, marriage brought the security of knowing that they would return to an orderly, child-filled house, a warm meal, and clean clothes. In fact, as one pueblo resident told me, since most women who live in pueblos "don't work," there was no way that they could provide for themselves. The need for economic support, he claimed, was why most women got married. For women, marriage offered the present labor of their husbands and the future labor of their offspring.[36]

Yet men's position as heads of household offered them considerable latitude in actual behavior; as long as men tried to fulfill responsibilities as husbands and fathers, they maintained the honor associated with manhood and could claim real need. For example, one migrant told me that every Sunday, when he went to Arkansas, braceros would get together and "get drunk." He, of course, did not. While he admitted imbibing a beer or two and sometimes even hard liquor, he made sure I understood that he had "drunk but [he] didn't get drunk."[37] Whether or not his claim is accurate, clearly in his eyes and, we may assume, the eyes of others, excessive drinking impaired a man's ability to work, jeopardizing his manhood and, thus, his legitimate reason to migrate. That is, this behavior—in this case, that a man drank—was not automatically delegitimizing. Men whose behavior undercut their work, however, had succumbed to the desire for adventure. They displayed, for all to see, a comportment that threatened not only their manhood and claim of real need but also their commitment to the Mexican collective.[38] In the end, then, most letter writers took the position that the only legitimate rationale for bracero migration was to support families.[39] To allow otherwise, they predicted, would threaten the cohesion and security of the Mexican nation.

The first letter engaged the notion of real need and wanting to work and extended it to a critical aspect of manhood. The writer testified that his family "found itself [*se encuentra*]" with a need for, but inability to find, work. By using the reflective construction, he acknowledged the family's financial straits while eschewing responsibility for creating them. Like other letters that used the materiality of ruined corn, parched plots, or dead animals to refute blame, this claimant, too, contended that his economic plight was due to neither lack of motivation nor character flaws.[40] Rather, his material circumstances were outside his control. In this case, asking for assistance did not jeopardize his manhood, just the opposite: he asked for help precisely because he would recuperate his manhood if he could fulfill this responsibility, for which he needed the president's intervention.

Many petitioners, eschewing responsibility for creating ruinous circumstances, instead attributed hardships to state inaction, inefficiency, or to officials' outright greed. These state missteps, they claimed, were outward signs of the failure of the revolution. In chapter 1, I suggested that a paternalist state was created out of the revolution's rubble. Designed to protect citizens from harm, this state fostered a rhetoric that said all citizens would vie equally for state support and resources, which would be allotted according to need. It put the needs of the nation above those of any individual or particular faction. Most critical, the state cast itself as the arbiter among competing sectors, structuring all dissension and opposition into the state itself through a corporatist model. This model had only been instituted four years before the start of the program, during the Cárdenas administration, so it and the collectivist vision undergirding it were unevenly accepted. We see that lack of acceptance in the letters men wrote. In highlighting officials' indecision or avarice, and faulting these—and not themselves—for their inability to secure a bracero contract, letters tied men's own situations to a failing of the revolutionary promise. That is, men again relied on the split between the president as good leader and state officials as illegitimate representatives; this, at its heart, speaks to the tenuous grasp of collectivism—the state's discourse about its responsibilities to citizens and those of citizens to the state and one another.

"The Revolution," alleged a letter, had "favor[ed] all its accomplices, without remembering Mexico's needs." Government officials and new elites destroyed the haciendas "with the pretext of liberating the peon," seizing "the best for themselves." Since corn and beans did not "produce sufficient dollars, they converted the production of these grains into export[s] such as sesame [and] cotton." Although "everything [was] in abundance, according to propaganda," people were experiencing shortages of basic foodstuffs. To solve this problem of hunger, the president had to restrain the "voraciousness" of these "exploiters without conscience."[41] Here the writer subverted what the state had extolled as successes, using them instead as signs of broken promises and the bastardization of national unity. The revolution's leaders, he contended, were rife with avarice, putting the economic desires of the wealthy above the needs of the most vulnerable. A privileged group of state insiders, the letter contended, threatened not only national unity and social solidarity but, more fundamentally, the state's portrayal of the relationship between governing and governed, on which rested national stability and the state's very legitimacy.

"It would be much appreciated," began another letter, if the president would authorize the writer to travel north "as a visible act before Mexico and its history." Doing so would "evidence" the president's "great dignity" in service to "the homeland, as the guide of the Mexican people."[42] Thus, signatories linked dignity to legitimacy. The president's dignified service to the homeland would assuage allegations of elite privilege, corruption, and dishonesty, insulating him from charges facing others preying on hopeful migrants. His grant of bracero contracts would instead demonstrate true stewardship of the nation and secure the state's legitimacy and his place in history.

The following passage, while not directly condemning the revolution, still ascribed community problems to lack of state attention to the needs of men, women, and children of the popular classes. Such men were experiencing difficult times "together with" their families. The writer protested, "[It is] not fair that, because of a lack of individual guarantees on the part of our government, we suffer through a lamentable situation."[43] This letter, like earlier ones, spotlighted the unresolved tension between the trope of community or collective and that of the individual. Yet here the writer saw individual guarantees as a way to accrue benefits not for a single individual or family, but for the community. The community was again foregrounded as the proper unit in a relationship between governing and governed, with the difficulties experienced by the entire community attributed to a lack of individual guarantees. Through this juxtaposition between individual and collective, letters pointed to the disjuncture between the state's rhetoric, which put the health of the collective above the individual, and its policies, which prioritized undeserving individuals—elites and high-level bureaucrats.

While the state draped all its projects in a collectivist discourse born of the revolution, one 1950 letter, like many of the period, suggests a widespread questioning of—if not resistance to—such rhetoric. It touted the ideal of Benito Juárez, the esteemed president of Mexico from 1861 to 1872, who repelled the French invasion, restored the Republic, and instituted liberal reforms. "How difficult it is to find . . . men [like] Benito Juárez!" the writer lamented. If today's government officials "were as don Juárez was, Mexico would be great." The writer continued, "We beg you to extend valiant help to workers actually without occupation due to the close of the cotton harvest." This writer used Juárez, a leader of impeccable honesty, to depict the economic circumstances in which the writer and fellow petitioners lived as truly bleak and outside their control and themselves as above reproach. "Our economic region will benefit greatly," contended this author, since contracts would bring it "great progress."[44] Thus, he solicited help by insisting that aid for the few truly needy would mean progress for the many.

Exactly who was covered by the term "our"—whether the petitioners' region or the entire country—remains open to question. Still, the writer's use of both Benito Juárez (individual) and Mexico (collective) suggests a parallel: in the first instance, "our" probably refers to the particular region, while in the second it hints at both. Thus, this letter justified the rewards due particular men from this particular community by implying that benefits reaped locally would transcend the specific and benefit the whole; thus he reproduced the logic in play about both the program and other public undertakings of the period. The collective good came from individual betterment; and the state, as benevolent patriarch, was best situated to apportion individual sectors' access to resources so as to bring about this collective good.

In many ways, the act of writing (and by extension reading) became complicit in the irreconcilability of the tension between individual and collective. In pencil, pen, and professionally typed, men young and old solicited help in obtaining the elusive contract. In Durango villages, scribes set up stalls in town plazas and markets, offering their pens or pencils (and later typewriters), along with often rudimentary literacy and letter-writing skills, to those who lacked them.[45] Indeed, the state, affixing knowledge to independence— individual and collective—then to overcoming misery, called illiteracy such a hindrance to national progress that in 1944 it instituted a nationwide literacy campaign.[46] The act of becoming literate, it contended, would secure the goals and promise of the revolution and the nation's success as modern.[47] Thus, we must see letter writing as a symbolic act though which men shaped themselves (and were shaped) as the promise of the revolution and the very people whom Mexico should be sending north: exceptional individuals and the exception to their class. In so doing, petitioners again challenged the state's collectivist rhetoric that structured the program.

Given this state framing, we might expect that it would permeate not just men's letters but also the responses they received from officials. Such responses, we might expect, would foreground the president as the nation's infinitely wise patriarch and the state as the actor best placed to adjudicate members' competing claims. However, this patriarchal relationship was not fostered; instead, responses depict a formalized bureaucratic ideal that disregarded personal connections and favors. When in 1952 Representative Enrique Rodríguez Cano responded to a letter from Margarito Morales and Juan Morales de Jesús asking for help finding work as braceros, he merely instructed them to wait.[48] Another response, this time from the government bureaucrat José Rocha, would bespeak a similar formula. Thanking the petitioner, Rocha indicated that the ministry would "take into consideration [his] suggestion to install a Contracting Center in that state."[49] The state, suggested Rocha, would "compile lists of the hopeful, with the expectation that" the petitioners would find themselves "duly prepared."[50] Again, no immediate help was forthcoming—merely a clarification of program procedures so that the petitioner could be duly prepared for the next call, for only the duly prepared would be selected. Each request was redirected to formal channels and away from a patriarch-client relationship. Juxtaposing bureaucratic responses to the paternalistic way the state framed the program itself, these petitions again illuminate the gap between the state's collectivist language and its willingness—or ability—to follow through on that rhetoric.

Yet letter writers did not easily surrender the paternalist relationship. Actualized in social indebtedness, this relationship was one to which writers were accustomed and from which they saw themselves as benefiting. "I would like you to help me obtain permission," wrote Rafael Elizalde, "so that I can go and work on the other side. As I told you, I make very little here." If the president complied, he continued, "I would owe you much." "With no remaining hope," he said, "I say goodbye to you, your friend and humble servant."[51] In contrast to the formalized style and language of government responses, this aspiring migrant mobilized gratitude and a promise of lasting service indicative of paternalistic bonds between governing and governed. Thus, although state officials' formalized responses implied a relationship stripped of these bonds, letter writers did not easily concede a benefit that they drew from them. In this case, Elizalde refused to relinquish the patron-client relationship that held each partner to established rules and responsibilities and from which he directly gained.

Men writing letters, we should remember, had been rejected after going through the prescribed process, or else their village had not been eligible for contacts; they were not among the individuals destined to bring home the program's collective benefits. Most writers did not challenge the overarching logic that the collective benefited through individual success; their letters, instead, questioned *which* individuals were best able to bring home the benefits. Urging reconsideration of their claims, men thus intervened in a discussion not just of how the rewards of *this* program should be allocated, but how a state with limited resources should resolve *all* competing claims on benefits.

A group of writers touched on this logic when they cautioned the government to "take special care" to ensure that those with "an occupation from which [they can] make a living" did not leave. Too many of the men selected, these writers alleged, did not meet the "truly needy" criterion; they were poor but not without other options. Administrators should review "special statistics" on unemployment, so that only those without a stable means of support *and* whose absence would not affect the country's economy should be allowed to participate.[52] Another letter contended that its signers were "worried about the economic interests of our fatherland." The petitioners predicted "serious harm" to the national economy if landholders were to "abandon" their farms to work abroad; they asked for the president's "valiant intervention" in getting credit from the National Bank of Communal Credit and forestalling the "well-known economic consequences" of the "exodus."[53] Other letters requested help on behalf of landless campesinos, heads of household in "an extremely agonizing situation," or asked to be put on the bracero list for the sake of their families and "the good of themselves."[54]

Here we see a concern that the nation as a whole would suffer if those without real need were allowed to migrate. By selecting those who were capable of supporting their families, the state abdicated responsibility to judge between competing claims, putting the entire economy and national collective at risk. Equally important, in permitting such migration, the state threatened the social order and boundaries founded on gendered spaces and roles. Here community leaders paint a picture of economic devastation with future consequences. Because of the community's financial situation, they say, "thousands and thousands of women, the majority of whom ha[d] children," were on the verge of becoming prostitutes, creating "a serious social problem." These leaders requested the president's permission for these women to "work honorably in the United States, be it as maids." This would allow them to resolve their financial difficulties and still "return to their homes and children."[55] These local leaders emphasized the seriousness of the community's plight by pointing to the coming gender breakdown. Not only would women sell their bodies; worse still, they would take to the streets—the space of men and disreputable women—to do it. Leaders implored that economic opportunities be created for women as well as men. By choosing the best men for bracero jobs, the president would protect individual women and families, and thus the nation.

But who were these best men that the president should choose? This was the question to which all letters spoke. The best men were, as described in one letter, "healthy," in "good condition to work," and "heads of household."[56] This last condition—head of household—established legitimate need beyond a doubt, in stark contrast to those men—young and old—without family responsibilities. In aggregate, these heads of household, letters contended, deserved preference over those selected men because their acceptance of family responsibilities demonstrated a willingness to put collective (family and national) needs above individual ones. In the end, these letters leave unresolved the form the relationship between state and citizen should take. Braceros, however, did attempt to resolve this uncertainty by holding the state to its promises for migration. As we will see in subsequent chapters, in their repeated acts of pressure, they not only reconfigured their relationship with Mexico but asserted claims on the United States.

Conclusion

Many components—the physical terrain as well as social, economic, and political organization—shaped expectations that Durango braceros brought to journeys north. At stake was the meaning of Mexican manhood and whether poor folk could claim the rights and privileges that manhood entailed and achieve a manhood that brought full citizenship, a status heretofore undercut by class. Letters to Mexican presidents written by men denied a bracero spot speak to a particular set of masculine values then in play and situate their authors as those best embodying the qualities the state deemed crucial for a successful program. They give clues as to how the conditions of possibility critical for being a man, as a privileged gender position, had eroded or maybe never existed for rural people, and how the program raised expectations for the claiming or recuperation of manhood.

The letters, then, reveal the multiple, often conflicting, ways that men couched their claims to being more suitable agents for the nation than those actually selected as braceros. In joining this conversation, letter writers did not refute the state's vision for this program, but they did challenge a changing discourse on relations between state and citizen more generally. They refused to let the state relinquish responsibilities it had taken on as a patriarchal state, from which it ultimately drew legitimacy and men their particular rewards. In this process, then, the men were produced as men—that is, as specifically gendered sociopolitical subjects—and their claims against the state and the nation were framed as men's claims. Men also expected that as braceros they would play a central role in the country's modernization. Their letters draw on the state's celebratory rhetoric and allude to the progress, both individual and collective, to be gained through the program; and men not selected portrayed themselves as those who best exemplified the characteristics of integrity and hard work that officials deemed necessary to bring such progress. Rejecting the state's conception of them as country folk responsible for their own and the nation's backwardness, they instead threw the onus for their precarious economic position, and thus their shaky claims to manhood, back on the state. Relying on a state conception of the Mexican family that depicted the state as benevolent patriarch, writers refused to let the state abdicate the patron-client relationship from which the men drew privileges and security, and around which the revolutionary state was consolidating its power and legitimacy. As we shall see, this refusal to let the state off the hook, so to speak, would have significant consequences as the state's inability to fulfill revolutionary promises and those for the bracero program became increasingly clear. In the end, its hegemonic project was mutually constructed along with men's production as gendered political subjects.

Thus, the vision of the relationship between citizen and subject was not merely imposed by the state from the top down, it was also constructed from the bottom up, in a dialectical process. Men, in their letters, both reacted to state discourse and preemptively acted to shape it, drawing on what they felt were shared cultural values. The dialectical process, here directed toward the state, would continue throughout the journeys of braceros and prove critical in their interpellation as transnational subjects.

Men hoping to migrate were put through elaborate selection procedures, which I outline in the next chapter. The selection ceremonies, as sites of direct state contact with men, became the arena in which the state put forth ideas about the modern, bracero responsibilities to state and nation, and the ideal relationships between citizen and state and citizen and nation. While the notion of Mexico as a modernizing nation was promoted in these arenas, it was also challenged by the constraints examined in this chapter: life structures common among the poor, who maneuvered within sets of patron-client relationships. These stages for action, as we shall see, sent mixed messages about the modern and the gulf between the ideal and the possible, conflicting messages that men attempted to resolve.

Part II Bracero Agency and Emergent Subjectivities

4

Rites of Movement, Technologies of Power

Making Migrants Modern from Home to the Border

One warm afternoon, Álvaro García told the crew in the barbershop how proud he was to have been selected. "I was proud, too," said Ramón Avitia. State officials "told us we would teach the Americans about Mexico," that "we'd bring progress to Mexico, to Durango."[1] Erasmo Bolívar echoed this sentiment in a 1950 letter to President Miguel Alemán Valdés (1946–52). When he headed north, he wrote, he wanted to take along his "undying pride" in Mexico, "along with [his] sombrero."[2] "What I wanted was an adventure," explained Mariano Chores Alarcón, "[but] we were soldiers of agriculture." If not for Mexican farmworkers, he continued, winning the war would have cost the United States a lot of work.[3] "The idea," said another, "[was] to progress."[4]

Some braceros sought money for families, others adventure, still others to "enrich the nation 'that gave them life' and subsistence."[5] Their sentiments of patriotism, progress, and products echoed the Mexican government's stated reasons for supporting the program. Yet braceros also came to the program for their own reasons and did not automatically endorse state goals, once they learned of them. State goals were most intensively articulated during the lengthy screening and selection process. Each step in the process was a portal that men navigated to earn the right to migrate, and in each of these they were exposed to the state's (mixed) message. Men incorporated those pieces of the message they deemed advantageous and rejected others seen as undercutting their own goals.

The process, however, communicated not only Mexican state goals for the program but also the value that Mexican and U.S. state actors placed on aspiring migrants. For Mexicans, this migrant was a national actor, while for U.S. officials he was a stoop laborer. Screening men's bodies, then, was part and parcel of the differentiating, ranking, and attendant valuing of particular kinds of bodies, cut along racial, gender, and class lines with a national valiance. The selection process entailed *practices of border*: evaluative rituals that symbolically recreate the border in quotidian ways as incommensurable difference. In that way, the work of the border would be reproduced in future exchanges with U.S. growers, foremen, and community locals, reshaping how braceros understood themselves and their nation. That is, while screenings officially assessed whether men possessed the skills and physical traits necessary for agricultural work, the messages communicated by the screenings effectively recast current definitions of what it meant to be Mexican, campesino, worker, and citizen. This recasting and the ways men struggled against it would engender their transformation into transnational subjects.

The Selection

"I remember hearing about the program from my *pueblo*'s mayor," don Álvaro told me during my first visit to his barbershop, "so I talked to some of my friends and we decided to go. . . . We decided to go north for the dollars."[6] Just minutes before, he had unlocked the doors of the *peluquería* and welcomed me and several town elders. Sitting on the barbershop's long benches, men talked about the announcement of good-paying jobs, enticements from friends, and reports of easy money and adventure north of the border.[7] All had heard about how braceros had returned sporting new clothes, their pockets stuffed with cash and trinkets for their families. These stories and images, alongside economic "desperation," had piqued curiosity.[8]

Some men, don Álvaro informed me, expected that they would go for the length of a contract or two, get out of debt or save a little money to finish a house, or buy a plot of land, seeds, or a cow. Others sought to purchase shoes for their children, a marker of civilization.[9] Jesús Saucedo, with "no education," had his family on his mind: "I wanted something for my children."[10] Carlos Labastia, who was walking around the municipal seat, saw "a gringo" in front of the recruiting office and was invited to go but was not drawn by financial need. "What piqued my attention was the idea of getting to know America and having an adventure."[11] Still, most got caught up in the quest for dollars and headed north with great hopes for the benefits outlined by the state.[12]

After the program was announced and the *pueblos* and municipalities that would benefit were listed, the labyrinthine selection process began. Its initial phase obligated aspiring migrants to compile information about their past and reputations, such as a birth certificate and proof of completion of military service. Men also had to certify they were not members of *ejidos* (communities where land was held jointly).[13] The government's agricultural plan allotted an important, if only ideological, role to these communities, predicting complete agricultural disruption if members migrated. One former bracero acknowledged the government's right to prevent such migration. "Peasant[s] will sell the parcel or rent it out," said Isauro Reyes, leading hacienda owners to ask: "For what purpose did [peasants] want land? To abandon it?" Reyes referred to the state's land reform program, which was still contentious. "Is that why the government took our land from us?" This, he suggested, was too often what happened. "That's how we discredit our government."[14] While some accepted the state's role as redistributive, an unbiased patriarch who mediated conflicts for the good of the nation, many *ejidatarios* (members of these landholding communities) hoping to migrate worked around the ban, and often officials would issue a letter certifying their nonmembership in exchange for a small bribe.

Men also needed recommendations of good character. Officials were looking for "good men, family men mostly," ones who were "hard-working," said Paco Zermeño, a friend of don Álvaro.[15] Many good family men asked the local mayor to affirm their high moral standing; others approached prominent citizens, such as successful storekeepers or landowners. Still others sought out the resident political boss or local priest to confirm their willingness to work.[16] Even if no money was exchanged for these recommendations, as I indicated in the previous chapter, they still came at a cost as men were indebted to the grantor of the favor.

At first most men obtained official documents without charge, yet officials began to spot the possibility for gain. As more men sought contracts, a growing number of officials, as well as those with official-sounding positions or connections, began to charge for documents, both official and fake, especially *micas* or identification cards. So it was that when Magdaleno Escalante enrolled in 1957, he had to pay a fifty-peso enlisting fee; others paid two hundred pesos each, proceeds "distributed among the associates in the 'enterprise.'"[17] These practices would come to permeate all levels of the program. "The government wouldn't *give* us a card," said an ex-bracero, but instead would charge for free forms and required documents and "pocket the money"; interested applicants had to "buy a contract."[18] Local officials often added their own requirements to the list of official ones. In areas, such as the north, where labor was scarce and elites still owned large tracts of land

and had entrenched connections to politicians, men not only were forced to work the harvest or planting before leaving but also had to show pay stubs or letters from landowners for whom they worked, possibly waived for a bribe.[19] Charges of corruption did, at times, force officials to investigate allegations and root out networks. Government radio and newspaper notices stressed that all necessary documents were free. This widespread corruption chipped away at the initial optimism with which men entered the selection process and undercut the credibility of state's collectivist rhetoric. The inability of eradicating a host of program problems or living up to its rhetoric would weaken state legitimacy.

After allowing hopeful migrants time to gather documentation, the town mayor brought the aspirants to a central meeting place, usually within a couple of weeks. There, one by one, he, together with local elites, reviewed men's documents and weeded out those without the required credentials. The names of those passing this initial inspection were then compiled into an official list, which traveled with the men to the migratory station, the regional-level stage in the process. Migratory stations were located in state capitals and other major cities, with processing generally occurring within a few weeks of the initial review. There aspiring migrants faced a second round of scrutiny. They would congregate outside the site, usually a stadium or large public place, and wait for officials to call their name. Some sat on the ground, some squatted, and some milled around, while others stood or leaned against the stadium wall; some slept, while others gathered with friends and sang, accompanied by an old guitar.[20] Women and children, too, were present and vocal, hawking food and drinks.[21] Children often performed songs or wandered about, shining shoes in hopes of earning a few cents.

This scene contrasted dramatically with the formal procedures happening inside the stadium. Within these walls, barricaded from onlookers, would gather the program's regional director, local military units, members of the press, other government officials, and influential citizens. In Durango City, the selection process took place at the Francisco Zarco Stadium, at the city's west end. There young soldiers faced each other, forming two straight lines that ran half the length of the stadium. In lines stretching toward the center from both sides of the entrance, armed soldiers standing at attention lined the path leading to where the director and other important individuals were seated.[22] For men entering this space, the use of the army, standing silently in formation, signaled the significance of the event, the prestige to be accorded those men bestowed a bracero contract, and the power of the state itself. This power was twofold: to those not chosen, the display projected the state's ability to curb unforeseen unrest; to those selected, it offered a reward, which officials extended as men passing inspection were welcomed into the nation.

This national incorporation was done, in part, through explicit instructions given to the men as they waited. "You are going to be representatives of Mexico in the U.S.," they were told. "Be an example of honesty and show what good workmen you are." In this case, the instructions were code for being obedient and docile. "Don't go on strikes or make trouble for your bosses. Remember, if you make good, you will be wanted again and again in the future."[23] Thus, these migrants were told of the possibilities of future contracts and instructed in their role as Mexico's ground-level "ambassadors" in the promotion of binational understanding.[24]

To begin the selection process, lists containing the names of those in contention for a contract were thrown into a receptacle. One by one, the director pulled out each list and read the names, until the allotment of bracero contracts was exhausted. As the names of aspiring braceros boomed over the loudspeaker to the thousands waiting outside, the specified man would enter the stadium and walk down the narrow pathway created by the soldiers to the table of waiting examiners.[25] In linear procession, each man moved through the double lines of soldiers, the grand approach to the table where documents and hands were scrutinized. "It [was] enough," said one witness, "to see their hands, how they [were] dressed, their general appearance," and ask them about agriculture to know if the men were peasants.[26] At this second inspection and in the presence of this auspicious company, the director questioned each man about his general health and strength, his agricultural knowledge and work experience. Then he, or one of the other officials present, examined the worker's hands. As I was repeatedly told, officials were looking for the "hands of a worker"—rough, weathered, "used."[27] "Calluses," don Álvaro interjected into the barbershop conversation six men and I were having. "They wanted hands with calluses."[28]

Those selected would head to the Department of Photography, where three pictures would be taken: one for the *mica*, another to be filed in the Central Contracting Office, and a third to be archived at the local contracting office.[29] Those with the requisite weathered hands and documents in order exchanged the latter for an official identification card complete with name, age, marital status, town, state of origin, photograph, fingerprint, and name of beneficiary in the event of death or accident. This *mica* indicated that the government had chosen its bearer for the program. The selectees would then continue on to the next site for final approval. These men, sometimes carrying a small bundle of belongings but often nothing more than the clothes on their back, were hustled onto waiting buses or trains for the lengthy ride to the border.[30]

This regional-level scrutiny functioned as an act of confirmation, a way of conferring on these previously invisible residents the rights and responsibilities of revolutionary citizenship. Extended in this moment was *social visibility*, that is, as I define it, the recognition—by an individual, others, and the state bureaucracy—that an individual is a member of the nation, with the ability to impact its social and cultural boundaries and reap the rewards of state protection. Social visibility exceeds juridical citizenship and is inseparable from the process of nation formation.[31] It—and not, I contend, the widely used notion of legal citizenship—marks the degree and kind of inclusion and benefits that national subjects reap. The social visibility awarded through the selection ceremony contrasted starkly with the men's perpetual social indebtedness. Incorporation into the nation, like the beginning of a direct state-citizen relation that the selection process established, contrasted with the kinds of hierarchical relations in which they were usually bound. Thus, the process occurring inside the stadium became a highly ritualized moment in which men formerly outside the Mexican nation became visible—if only momentarily—as new members and symbolically included and given the privileges of such status. It became the first step in the modernization of both the men and the nation.

We can better understand the connection of the selection process to national ritual and modernization processes through a reading of the stadium setting. Twentieth-century stadiums, says the literary scholar Rubén Gallo, were "the most unusual technological medium in postrevolutionary Mexico." In 1924 José Vasconcelos, Mexico's first minister of education, oversaw the building of Mexico City's prestigious National Stadium, which he anticipated would be the first structure in the new civilization of the "cosmic race." This term emerged from his ideology, which glorified the progeny of the historical melding of Indian mother and Spanish father, a national progeny who bore the best qualities of each parent and whose civilization would inevitably clash with that of the Anglo-Saxon. According to Gallo, these twentieth-century edifices, built of concrete and steel (in contrast to their nineteenth-century stone cousins) and made for "purely domestic . . . consumption," hosted important political rallies and inaugurations, along with state-sponsored artistic, gymnastic, and choral events broadcast over radio. Emblems of progress and a "new postrevolutionary modernity," stadiums comprised part of a "carefully crafted image" that Mexico belonged to a "select group of developed nations."[32]

Staging the event in this circular, open-air venue, then, was no neutral act. No matter how pedestrian the actual stadium, in using these unenclosed settings as program sites state officials trumpeted a particular array of ideals and a revolutionary reconfiguration of the relationship between state and citizen. The circularity of the arena represents democracy, nonhierarchical divisions, and unity between people, in contrast to earlier aristocratic architectural models, with their many small dark rooms, thick walls, enclosure, and isolation from the masses outside.[33] Roofless stadiums, in contrast, do not close off the people gathered there but instead connect the spectators to the light and open air—symbolizing a transparency of action and clarity of motive, freedom, and liberty. Stadiums host competitions between adversarial equals.[34] Holding the ceremony in a stadium made the program inseparable from the revolutionary ideals of stability, order, and harmony, the instantiation of the state's "affirm[ation of] principles of justice and liberty."[35] Transformed from mere procedure into national ceremony, the selection process became part of the state's arsenal of revolutionary rituals celebrating democracy and the arrival at the modern.[36]

Names of men selected formed the official list from which U.S. officials at the reception center, the final selection site, would award contracts. Since mix-ups did occur and as a measure against the likelihood that those with fraudulent documents would obtain contracts, only those whose names appeared on this list could be awarded a contract.[37] Indeed, complications developed immediately. As early as 1944, two years after the program began, the Mexico City daily *Excelsior* estimated that military officers had *already* swindled braceros of at least forty thousand pesos through the sale of counterfeit certificates. In one incident, police went to Mexico City's Alameda Central, the central park where thousands had gathered to await final inspection. Some lucky men possessed *micas* or identification cards of earlier screenings, while others without them were hoping their plight would persuade a sympathetic official to let them go regardless. According to the article, on this particular morning several uniformed police convinced numerous men with *micas* that they were collecting the documents to facilitate the departure north. Men handed the coveted *micas* to the police, who then trotted to another area of the park and resold them to others able to purchase a supposedly sure bracero ticket. Another article described how police—or those dressed in uniform—stood in the entranceway to the National Stadium "extorting from peasants the identification cards they had been given." The swindlers purported that the documents were fake, "but not ten minutes later, they were [re]selling them for at least fifty pesos." This abuse of humble citizens by state officials could not pass without the reporter's comment: "Even the police take advantage of and discriminate again these poor men," most of whom were "without shoes."[38] Program corruption became so widely known that the April 12, 1954, edition of *El sol de Durango* could state that "Mexican workers . . . are [regularly] asked for 'guarantees' in order to go to the United States." So pervasive was the demand for guarantees that a late-1950s investigation documented that almost 80 percent of program participants had paid for a contract.[39] Ultimately, the men who "lost" documents, as well as those who purchased phony ones, were sent home—neither possessed the right paperwork. In such exchanges, only officials profited.

As buses filled to capacity with the chosen and headed for the U.S. reception center, one newspaper article described the tears that men wiped from eyes as they left families. These tears, it claimed, were a sign of the distinctive "silent suffering . . . of savage [*bravía*] people": that is, those desperately in need of modernization.[40] Yet as more men sought a contract, great numbers of them were not peasants, but rather skilled workers from the cities. When Diego Hernández tried to migrate, he was told to wait to be called. "I waited about a month and no call. All I kept hearing was, 'let the specials through.' . . . I asked myself, what the hell is so special [about] these 'specials?' I soon found out that these 'specials' were mechanics, waiters, bakers, carpenters, and construction workers. These guys were not campesinos, they were fake ones."[41] A small bribe, it seems, could turn anyone into a campesino, even though many of those the state hoped would learn modern agricultural skills had already left the land.

Men whose *pueblos* were not allotted spots frequently headed to a contracting locale anyway, hoping to snag a contract. "I waited for two months in Mexico City before I was put on [his state's] list and permitted to go to Empalme," then a regional migratory station, a former bracero explained. "When I got to Empalme, I waited another fifteen days before they sent me to El Centro," a reception center in California.[42] Too often located in cities without adequate housing, sanitation facilities, or food, these sites "were like pictures of hell," ventured Jesús Saucedo. "Three to four thousand people would wait to be called." There the migrants might wait three or four weeks.

"It was a crazy situation. If you did not have money, the chances [of getting a contract] were very slim. One either had to give bribes or just pray that you would get picked."[43] For another bracero, it was easy. He gave the contractor "two turkeys and a pot of mole" and was put on the list.[44]

After men selected had boarded the departing bus, one man was entrusted with transporting the official list. As the barbershop owner don Álvaro announced one afternoon, the carrier of the list was someone whose "exceptional character" was well documented and known to the program director. This exceptional individual was given a carrying pouch, kept hidden from others at all times. The pouch "was like a fanny pack. . . . Every time I went to the other side after the first time, I was chosen," said don Álvaro. "The director knew me. He trusted me. I always carried the list. . . . It made me important."[45] Another list carrier recalled, "Although it was supposed to be secret, most of the men knew who carried the list."[46] The list guardian would board last and ride the last bus to depart; the remaining part of the selection procedure could not proceed until he arrived.

Although the ride to the reception center could take twenty hours, some men portrayed it as "not so bad," noting that they traveled on "nice buses."[47] "I had never traveled first class before. The seats were comfortable and there was [enough] room. It was okay."[48] "Buses were clean," a man told me, "[with] no animals. Although I hadn't traveled much, besides . . . visit[ing] relatives, I had only traveled on buses with animals, with chickens and pigs." Don Álvaro remembered the "comfortable seats."[49] Some men were not so lucky. Instead of traveling on first-class buses, they rode north aboard crowded boxcars on the Mexican National Railroad. As one Mexicali official said, "When the men come in freight cars . . . many times there is no drinking water. There is no heat. . . . There are no toilets. . . . Men who have gone before take tin cans with them. . . . But many . . . lean . . . out of the big sliding doors. . . . Several times [trains arrived] . . . with two or three men missing because they had fallen out [during the trip]."[50] Former braceros I interviewed believed that first-class accommodations reflected their status in the eyes of Mexican officials. Others not so well accommodated cited this leg as the part of the program they liked the least.[51] Such sentiment says a lot, given the long hours and strenuous labor men did once they arrived, the isolation in which they lived, and the discrimination they often faced.

Even those transported on coaches, rather than boxcars, frequently had an unpleasant trip. One bracero was disgusted by overcrowded trains with no drinking water and broken or clogged toilets. The "U.S. government," he lamented, "pays the Mexican government for this transportation, and it is supposed to be good transportation. But something happens along the way. . . . It [is not] good transportation." An anonymous Department of Labor (DOL) official remarked, "[I wish] there were something we [U.S. monitors] could do about the way they haul [braceros] up to the border. Something needs to be done. It is the weak link in the chain. But the matter is taken out of our hands. . . . We don't dare say anything. If we do, it's considered a breach of the good relations between the governments. Mexico is very touchy about this whole program . . . and if we don't handle her with kid gloves, she's just liable to pull out of the whole thing."[52] The statement is interesting, for it provides a window onto the status of Mexican sovereignty as viewed by a U.S. federal employee. Initially this man appears generous—as wishing to improve braceros' transportation but unable to do so as any move would breach good international relations. This generosity it undone by his assessment of Mexico as touchy, needing to be handled with extreme care, like a delicate, finicky female prone to capriciousness and inappropriate reactions. By extension, the Mexico described by this program bureaucrat brought little independent authority to the table; rather, U.S. officials were forced to appease her in the name of diplomacy.

At reception centers, buses and trains from migratory stations across Mexico converged for the final step in the process. Before the men, tired and hungry from the long journey, were allowed to eat, they received a smallpox vaccination, and their bodies were again scrutinized. Their hands were examined, this time by Mexican *and* U.S. officials from the corresponding health departments. "[The examiners] touched our hands," said one bracero. "They were the knowledgeable ones, they chose people, they decided who would go and work, and who wouldn't."[53] Men who came from the cities, suggested another, "spen[t] several days rubbing their hands with rocks." When the recruiter saw the calluses, the man continued, he would pass the candidate through. "I fooled the doctors and all." Another man took chalk and rubbed it on his own soft hands, "until they turned hard," to convince them he was a peasant.[54]

Those passing muster had their information typed up by young Mexican women sitting behind long tables.[55] After this inspection, men would disrobe, said a former bracero, and a doctor would give each one a physical exam, searching for lice, disease, and physical injuries, along with an x-ray to check for tuberculosis. A doctor, he said, "would make sure that we didn't suffer from hemorrhoids or any disease."[56] Some scholars suggested that men were screened for "epilepsy, idiocy, craziness, chronic alcoholism, psychotic personality, and other problems difficult to diagnose."[57] "The doctor would examine your eyes, your ears," don Álvaro informed me. "He'd look into your mouth and examine your teeth. . . . I remember that he'd especially search for scars—new scars. They didn't want new scars."[58] Man after man informed me that officials scrutinized bodies for evidence not of poor work habits but of recent injuries and pain. For U.S. officials, new scars called into question a man's ability to withstand the backbreaking labor. For bracero candidates, in contrast, they put at risk the claim that his body was a strong, virile instrument, thus undercutting his claim to manhood.

Men were then deloused with DDT and their clothes washed and disinfected while they showered. "Thousands came every day," said one bracero. "Once we got there, they'd send us in groups of two hundred, as naked as we came into the world, into a big room about sixty feet square. Then men would come in masks, with tanks on their backs, and they'd fumigate us from top to bottom. Supposedly we were flea-bitten and germ-ridden," he recounted.[59] "Clearly many had lice," said another man, but others didn't.[60] "No one," he was told, "had lice but because of how we were dressed and what we looked like after traveling so long, they assumed that we had them."[61] "We were hot and covered with dirt when we arrived," a man remembered. "Often we didn't have real shoes. We looked like we would have bugs."[62] "The United States," don Álvaro stated frankly, "did not want any lice, any bugs from Mexico coming into their country."[63] Migrants conveyed strong sentiment about this point in the journey. The idea of having bugs, of being covered with dirt, of not being dressed properly, offers a window onto the men's experience at the border. They crossed at a time when parasites signified dirt, disease, and a life without access to running water. In this forced inspection, they were flagged as potential carriers of disease and, in the process, linked to racialized poverty.[64]

Arriving braceros were not screened just for parasites and physical ailments; they were also examined for the character traits that would make them ideal workers: youth, servility, humility, and docility. Growers and labor contractors contended that, after years of working with farmhands, they could spot the good ones. As a former bracero related, after processing, candidates were sent to "a huge bunk house" to be looked over by contractors from California growers' associations. "The heads of the associations would line us up. When they saw someone they didn't like, they'd say, 'You, no.'

Others, they'd say, 'You, stay.' They didn't want old people—just young, strong ones. And I was young, so I never had problems getting chosen."[65] "You see this fellow here?" one grower explained to health researcher Henry Anderson during the late 1950s. "He's the ideal worker." How did this man know? "This one," said the grower, pointing to the man, "[is] the right size. He's built right. He's a farmworker, you can tell that." More important in signaling this man as a farmworker was his demeanor: "He hasn't any big ideas. He's got the right attitude. He's humble, not fresh or cocky. He's an Indian type." Singling out another described as "tough," the grower remarked, "We'll have trouble with him. . . . We'll have to haul him up on the carpet at least once, and maybe after that he'll behave himself." Labeling a third a "smart alec," the grower assured Anderson that this worker was "lazy and irresponsible." He described still another as a "ladykiller," who would not "pay attention to his business." If intelligence was thought to be an asset, the grower nixed that: "This one is a type I don't care for," he contended. "He's no peon. He's too well dressed. Looks too intelligent. Almost white. He could pass for a Frenchman or anybody. The trouble with those kind [sic] is that they're too ambitious. This is no place for them. They end up telling off the foreman and there's trouble." When Anderson queried as to what should be done with this type of worker, the grower responded nonchalantly: "Let them stay in Mexico."[66] In the mid-1950s, Immigration and Naturalization Service (INS) officials moved to do just that. To keep grower-identified troublemakers in Mexico, they interviewed men as they passed through reception centers, comparing individual names to those on the list of undesirables: that is, communists or labor organizers in braceros' clothing.

While growers screened for docile workers, U.S. officials frequently treated men as animals.[67] They were slapped, berated, and cursed, often for asking a question. "I saw one bracero go up to the Immigration man," reported an observer, "and ask him, 'Where do I go now?' The Immigration man, instead of telling him where the next [inspection] was, said 'Bete [sic] a la chingada.' This means 'go screw yourself,' only worse. "You hear this all the time . . . from young guys, even when they are talking to older braceros [who] don't do anything about it. They just stand there and stare." The witness described the shameful way that DOL employees treated the braceros. "Nobody has any patience. Immigration, Public Health, Labor Department— it's all the same. Everybody curses at the braceros and shoves them around." Men were grabbed by their hair and shaken. The eyewitness even observed a photographer "bang one old man's head against the wall three times, so hard [he] thought it would break open." The old man "had something wrong with his neck, and couldn't hold his head straight." The observer recalled, "Migrants usually just stood there and took the abuse—what else could they do—they felt pretty bad about it. I have seen a lot of braceros cry after they were talked to in this way."[68] He concluded, "It takes a lot to make a Mexican man cry."[69]

Hopeful braceros, especially those who had come more than once, understood what growers were looking for and tried to act the part. "I had a lot of trouble getting contracted," a man told Anderson. "They found out that I had six years of school. They only want dumb people." "I always wear shabby clothes and sandals [instead of shoes] to get contracted," said another. "After I am selected, I take a shower and change. The growers seem to prefer the dirty, poorly-dressed men. They think that all the clean, well-dressed men are *coyotes*"—which Anderson defined as "sharpsters" or "cityslickers."[70] Whether by growers or U.S. officials, peasants and city slickers alike were tested, their "muscle and health" subject to scrutiny "much as Negroes sold at auction in the pre–Civil War years were 'sized' up by plantation owners."[71]

These moments of selection reflected more than mere physical intrusion; they were games of strategy. For migrant aspirants, they were casting calls, scenes in which men—bakers, mechanics, waiters, carpenters, construction workers, and agricultural wage laborers—were required to perform backwardness for U.S. officials and growers down to the last detail: no belt, cowboy hat, or shoes; only *huaraches* (sandals), the quintessential sign of indigeneity. No city slickers, with schooling beyond their life's station, need apply. Men were reduced to their hands, calluses, and muscles. Those chosen performed this backwardness well, acting like the docile humble Indians that growers sought. Moments of scrutiny and the performances that they demanded from braceros came to stand for the border between Mexico and the United States, a physical line which symbolically mapped the signs of nationality and national difference for which officials screened onto a specifically U.S. gendered class and racial hierarchy. As we will see, these differences screened for at the border, and the hierarchy they supported, would be reproduced as social practice—practices of border—in braceros' subsequent interactions with growers, foremen, other migrant farmworkers, and U.S. government authorities. Through the mandated performances such men, many of whom left home considering themselves men from their village or Durango or northerners, began to understand themselves as Mexican, where Mexican stood for a racialized national category. Onto these men, who came for money and whose physical appearance after the long journey branded them as probable carriers of lice or other vermin, were etched notions of disease, danger, and foreign contagion, all of which was conflated with Mexicanness. The racialized notions were then instantiated and given continued life by practices of border within the Unites States.

At the reception center, men moved from station to station, room to room in groups, without much privacy.[72] After showering and redressing, the famished men, close to being awarded contracts, were served a meal in a large military-style mess hall furnished with wall-to-wall benches and tables. They devoured the food, for many had not eaten much, if anything, en route. The man in charge of food service at El Centro's reception center noted, "When the men arrive here . . . they are practically starving. They dig into the food we give them like a bunch of hungry wolves."[73] After eating, they were subdivided into groups, each man given a number; they had their photographs taken and connected up with representatives—or, rarely, the owners themselves—of the farms or orchards where they were going. At this time braceros were instructed in the provisions of work and given official contracts detailing pay scales, rights, and farm owners' responsibilities. Then they were given another *mica*, this time from the U.S. government, containing their name, home address in Mexico, and a photograph; this authorized them to work legally for the contract's duration.[74] Braceros were handed a sack lunch and shuttled onto rented school buses, old and often dilapidated, which would transport them to farms. "I took a look at the lunches they were handing out to the men as they were getting on the busses" for their ride to the individual farms, a U.S. government employee confided to Henry Anderson. "They consisted of two sandwiches, and nothing else. The bread was so hard and old nobody could have eaten it."[75] Not surprisingly, he noted, the streets around the centers were littered with the uneaten repasts.

While braceros were scheduled to leave reception centers for farms within hours, at times delays were unavoidable—or imposed. At those moments, they frequently faced hostile U.S. authorities, who scrimped on food and other amenities. In an incident reported by the *New York Times*, a contractor was charged with serving dog food to unwitting braceros at the Eagle Pass reception center.[76] When Henry Anderson visited El Centro, he found "no provision for heating the barracks." An official responded, "There'd be no sense in . . . installing stoves in these places. They'd never be turned on. Or if they were, the men would . . . open all the windows. . . . When you get a barracks with twenty or thirty [Mexican] men in it around here, the heat from their bodies is enough to keep it warm all night, even on the coldest nights of the year," even though each man was provided only a single blanket.[77] There were other similar incidents. In one case, the home of a California INS employee needed a sewer line. According to Anderson, this employee, in cahoots with an official at the reception center in El Centro, detained for a week "a couple of lucky braceros" said to have caused trouble during their crossing, requiring them to complete the sewer line. Afterward, the men received their contracts and were hurried on their way. "Pay?" asked Anderson. "Nothing so crass . . . sullied this relationship."[78]

Extracting labor without compensation, however, was not the only way officials benefited from the program; they often used administrative positions at reception centers to direct lucrative rewards their own way. The case of the Fuller Commissary Company is telling. Not only was the business entrusted with running daily camp operations for one growers' association, but the company's president used his day job as office manager for the El Centro reception center to win a contract for the Fuller Commissary Company to deliver the mandated bracero insurance. While such connections were not illegal, the program generated deep webs of corruption from which U.S. officials capitalized. This setup, remarked one inspector, resulted in "cozy relationships."[79] These relationships between local business people, growers, and officials overseeing aspects of the program inherently challenged the image of the United States as modern—that is, as operating under pristine bureaucratic rules where everyone received equal treatment.

Those who failed this final inspection, usually due to signs of tuberculosis, other contagious diseases, or radical politics, were returned to Mexico. Although authorities were to deposit men at their homes, this was not always done; sometimes they were left just south of the border. "Why do they bring us all the way [here] to tell us we can't have contracts?" bemoaned a discharged man. "I spent the last of my money. I do not have five cents in my pocket. How do they expect me to get back home?"[80] One man, rejected along with five of friends, complained to all who would listen: "All of us are ruined, since all of us went deeply into debt to come to try for a contract. I sold my farm . . . to raise money for the trip. My wife and six children are waiting at home, waiting for me to send them money from the United States. Now there will be no money and there is nothing for me to go back to. I guess my children will have to beg." He shook his head, "I wish I were dead."[81] Men in this situation frequently scurried back across the border to jobs alongside braceros, albeit for less pay and under harsher conditions.

Throughout the selection process, the Mexican government intimated the motives and stature of the program in a multitude of ways, both to the men selected and to the nation as a whole. The decision to participate was initially framed as the country's contribution to the war effort, where stoop labor was deemed as essential as shooting a gun. This message reached men living in *pueblos* far from the capital's usual reach. "I was going to work hard. Yes, I wanted the money, but I also wanted to demonstrate what Mexicans could do. . . . We aren't lazy; we work hard; we could contribute."[82] Even the Mexico City daily *Tiempo* concluded that migrants understood the importance of their work. Men's worries "regarding food and 'the lack of chiles and salt,'" it said, "were compensated by the idea that they were serving the cause of democracies."[83] Indeed, braceros even told activist and lawyer Carey McWilliams that they saw the merits of "exchanging skills and talents" between the two countries "on a planned basis."[84] Migrants saw themselves both contributing to the war as heroes and representing a Mexico inhabited by proud, hardworking men. Yet from the competition for contracts and stadium displays of the military to the presence of prominent officials, citizens, and the press and doctors' examinations of external body parts, we see the reach and mix of state visions and men's strategic use of them. The celebratory state rhetoric about the men and the program would be called into question by long hours, low pay, isolation, racial discrimination, and by Mexican officials' inability to resolve realities that challenged the spirit and letter of the bracero contract.

In many ways, then, the selection process paralleled the path to modernization. Both were imbued with celebration and stature, and each individual man's movement—from room to room at the reception center, like that through the stadium—mapped Mexico's path toward progress. We might see the selection process, then, as part of the linear transition from rural resident outside the nation to socially visible modern citizen-subject. Yet while men moved singly through the process, at multiple points they would coalesce in large mess halls or subsequently on U.S. farms, in labor camps, and in outings as a collective force. That is, they were being schooled nationally and transnationally in a Mexican vision of the modern, one that championed an individuated relationship to the state mediated through the national collective. Still, the messages men confronted were mixed. As we have seen, aspiring migrants were berated, scrutinized, forced to offer bribes, and made to don the persona and dress of unworldly peasants. For them and the entire nation, the trip north was no simple journey or labor outflow. Those crowned braceros became the exemplars of their presumed peasant class, ready for modernizing, even as they were again reduced to sweat and muscle.

Selection as Celebration, Journey as Status Confirmation

When ex-braceros told me about their inspections, I listened in disbelief at how they seemed to feel about them. I had read accounts of earlier immigrants, angry and humiliated at customs officials' interrogations, doctors' examinations, and forced showers that washed off the dirt and disease of their class and race.[85] When I talked with former braceros, however, I sensed a distinct lack of anger or frustration at the experience. Throughout the journey, their character had been questioned, their bodies probed and penetrated, their hands evaluated. Yet instead of acting as if they had been abused, most recounted their journeys with a degree of pride that they passed the rigorous selection procedure. The repeated proving grounds had confirmed their bodies strong and healthy. And their role as rural laborers had made their hands "men's hands—callused and hard, . . . hands that . . . were used."[86] "Not women's hands," don Álvaro told me, "all soft and tender."[87] "Yes, men's hands," another man in the barbershop added.[88] Nodding in feigned agreement, I refrained from pointing out that I had never seen a rural woman's hands that were not callused, hard, or used—the same adjectives these men had used to describe their own *men's* hands, the body part made synonymous with the ability to support families and reclaim manhood.

Former braceros with whom I spoke smiled, even chuckled, as they remembered the doctor's inspection. Sitting around don Álvaro's barbershop, they talked openly about their first x-ray and how they passed it. They spoke of drinking "a lot of milk" right before the examination, to fool or trick the machine, as they put it, if they feared that it would find a trace of contagion that would disqualify them from a contract.[89] Others, including those in the doorway of the barbershop, concurred verbally or nodded their heads. Henry Anderson also found a man who, initially rejected for tuberculosis, had ultimately bested the x-ray machine. "I cured myself by drinking Pulmotol," he said, a tonic of questionable value.[90] It was not "manly," concluded Anderson, to be "sick or to admit that one ha[d] been sick."[91]

Men's understanding of milk as a foil for the machine is interesting. First, they conferred on a fluid synonymous with the female body the power to override the seemingly omnipotent power of the (male) modern. Second, *milk (leche)* is a slang term for semen.[92] While some might see men's use of the milk/semen reference as self-emasculating, reflecting a weakened patriarchal position within households and communities, I suggest, instead, that their ingenuity, which enabled them to harness women's bodily force for their own benefit and dilute the strength of the machine, was key to their salvation. Overcoming the critical obstacle—the x-ray machine—became a step toward regaining their manhood.

When former migrants told me about a doctor's physical examinations, they appeared pleased that a doctor, with his white smock, medical knowledge, trained eye, and advanced medical tools for measuring bodily functions, had bestowed on them the official stamp of good health and approval. As don Álvaro explained, up until then no modern machine had "peered into [his] body."[93] Instead, when most men were sick, they visited a local *curandero* or *curandera*, healers who lacked formal medical training and recommended various home remedies to rid bodies of the injuring poison, disease, or spirit.[94] The visit to a *curandero* was a visual contrast to the sterilized setting of a doctor's office, even in the improvised, sparsely appointed setting of the reception center.[95] Relating their experiences, former braceros spoke one minute with playfulness and amusement at having cleverly challenged the sanctity of the doctor's realm, and in the next they reaffirmed their faith in the doctor's tools, expertise, and diagnosis. Health as determined by a doctor, it seems, symbolized strength for these men, marking manhood and the potential to become modern workers, although not necessarily in ways that the U.S. and Mexican states anticipated.

Also notable is what is absent from migrants' narratives: a language of class. Many, if not most, Durango men who became braceros had already worked for a wage and were privy to languages of workers' rights, had participated in agriculture and factory strikes, or had witnessed work stoppages in which they did not take part. These men, therefore, came to the bracero program and its promise of modernization with prior experiences and analytical frames grounded in class rhetoric and workers' consciousness. Why, then, did braceros not read the process through this frame?[96] Doing so, I suggest, would have betrayed as fiction their performance as peasants and undercut the ways men understood why they earned a contract. Mexican and U.S. officials and growers' agents were expecting backward bumpkins—anything to the contrary would have eliminated the chance of migration; and men hoped for employment to regain their manhood. The frame of class, then, had not disappeared; it would reemerge to contextualize men's treatment at the hands of growers. Migrants, as we will see in the next chapter, would call on it as they pressured U.S. and Mexican officials to force growers to honor the bracero contract.

Even after men had been admitted to the program, they went through another appraisal, this time from growers or their agents. "One question that each [of us] was asked," explained a former bracero, was "what have you worked in? One [would] say, in cotton." The grower would follow up by asking, "Okay, how many pounds have you picked?" As it was the first time this man migrated, he responded, "No sir, I don't know anything about pounds; I know about kilos."[97] Growers would then inquire about where a man had done his picking and compare the answers to his appearance. "[Growers] looked at your shirt, they looked at your clothes, they looked at you. . . . Perhaps you were lying. . . . If you [were] saying that you ha[d]n't gone and they saw something different in your clothes, you went back."[98] "We learned that we shouldn't wear anything made in the U.S.," volunteered another man, "especially belts."[99] "You'd be surprised how growers would treat [us]," said Benny Carranza. "They even opened [our] mouths and looked at [our] teeth—like a horse. We felt degraded."[100] Although some men felt pride at passing the doctor's examination, they reacted with humiliation to growers' scrutiny of their bodies. Whereas the doctor's stamp of approval brought men the confirmation that their bodies were strong and capable by an instantiation of modern knowledge, in this appraisal their bodies were studied as if they were livestock by a person whose occupation did not carry the same status or reflection of the modern. This evaluation was merely a disgrace.

Grower's questioning and visual dissection helped weed out men who had previously migrated, for few wanted workers who knew too much about the labor process and might cause trouble; nor did they want laborers who might demand that the contract be enforced. "We learned how to stand [to get chosen], you couldn't stand up too much, stand too erect. [That person] was considered too independent, too rebellious."[101] As one bracero concluded, "They want us to be dumb and dirty. Next time. . . . I will wear my old clothes and I will pretend to be just as dumb as the next man."[102] Indeed, the very criteria growers used to select the braceros—not standing too erect, being dumb and dirty—together with men's need to comply—oppugned braceros' claim to manhood. Instead, migrants' clothes and demeanor bespoke subservience and a willingness to accept whatever was demanded of them. While men could refuse work from a particular grower, there were consequences in doing so, since it meant that they understood their rights and were not afraid to exercise them, a combination that all but guaranteed a quick return to Mexico. California growers, in particular, adhered to invasive screening measures because the state was the premier site of U.S. farm union organizing. Screening procedures would become more important during the late 1940s and throughout the 1950s, when the threat of communist infiltration was said to peer from behind every corner, and every potential bracero was a weak link in the armor of U.S. security.

In sum, growers' insistence on a malleable workforce, along with men's need for work, helped shaped a seemingly perfect set of laborers: temporary foreign migrants blessed with a compliant temperament and whose racialized bodies were thought to withstand heat and hard labor. This supposedly docile workforce, however, did not turn out to be particularly compliant. As I show in chapter 5, in letters, labor actions, and exchanges with officials, they pressured growers and officials for the modernizing rewards that the program promised. These men expressed great creativity in realizing their goals and used and circumvented established lines of authority, setting the terrain through which they would become transnational subjects.

What my analysis of the selection ritual shows, then, is the slow, constant chipping away of the optimism with which men entered. In the beginning aspiring migrants were willing to buy into the Mexican state's framing of the program and the benefits that would accrue to those chosen. However, as men were repeatedly examined and reduced to their bodies, they could no longer keep their disgust and humiliation in abeyance. They admitted fooling U.S. and Mexican officials and the machines in whose trust authorities put total faith. They learned the expectations that Mexican and U.S. officials and growers held for them and how to best maneuver this set of expectations so as to appear as lowly peasants, suggesting the great lengths to which men went for a contract. These steps, then, were portals to migration.

Conclusion

The experience of traversing these migration portals marked the men in a specific way. The selection ritual first imbued them with a celebrated status and prestige, heralded as part of Mexico's road to modernization. The competition for bracero contracts elevated dirty agricultural jobs to hot commodities with significance for individual and nation; the required recommendations attested to braceros' good character as deserving men; the march through the stadium extended them social visibility and gave them an individual relationship to the state; their rough hands affirmed them as good workers; the solemn presence of the military accorded them an official and public status; and a doctor's trained eye confirmed their health and bodily strength. Yet the importance of being a bracero was undercut at every turn by the need to perform a backwardness that conflated Mexicanness with the rural, the uneducated, the peasant, the Indian.

The very selection ritual that imbued the men with status and prestige later demanded that they perform the backwardness of their class. And each retelling of this ritual brought its contradictions to the fore. In exchange for this new esteemed status, men withstood bodily inspections, read not as forms of wage-labor discipline but as signs that they were potentially modern. For these men, class was not the primary lens through which they understood the need to look "dumb and dirty" or dress in "shabby clothes and sandals." While many had come to the program with exposure to a class language and logic, here they did not use it. These class-shaped experiences were not erased, however, but merely relegated to subtext. Although some migrants would later draw on a class lens, not doing so during the selection process hints at the enticement that the modern initially held, as even those familiar with harsh labor discipline did not openly question the program's promise. Instead, they held tight to the hope of the program's future rewards.

Yet the selection ritual's allusions to the traditional and hierarchical were also palpable: not only were men's contributions those of manual labor, the required recommendations and demand for bribes also forced men to seek out those whose word counted with proverbial and actual sombrero in hand. This requirement reindebted the powerless to the powerful; it reembedded men within local hierarchies and made migration the only way out. Isauro Reyes, for example, bemoaned the indebtedness of his land collective to officers of the Banco Rural, their "patron" and "boss." "We c[ould]n't make it as farmers," he lamented; they instead had to migrate. Social indebtedness, augmented by yet another favor in the form of the recommendation, meant that men, whether selected or not, then, owed additional social debt to those who aided their pursuit of a contract. In other words, those already "hopelessly indebted" to local elites, bureaucrats, or political institutions became further enmeshed in this complex social web, from which it was nearly impossible for poor families to extricate themselves.[103]

Thus, though we might want to see the selection ritual as a push by the Mexican state to establish a direct relationship between state and citizen, the required recommendations also hint that the state was reluctant to destabilize entrenched power relations. Rather, we might read the process as an attempt to reinstantiate—even expand—webs of power, for if recommendations marked men as exceptional and exemplary of their class, they also showed aspirants to be exploitable. The display of docility and honor—crystallized in the state's injunction for men to "be an example of honesty," "good workmen," and to avoid "mak[ing] trouble"—became a prerequisite for the promised full incorporation into a yeoman farmer class, even as their class exceptionality—their selection as potentially modern men deserving of this unique opportunity—brought them social visibility, introduced them into the realm of the nation, and made them worthy of inclusion in the state's consolidated national-popular political project. That is, the same process that identified men as exceptional for their peasant class and would transform them into modern yeoman farmers simultaneously reinscribed them in hierarchal social relations *and* brought them into an individuated relationship to the state. Revealed, then, is the complimentary relationship between visibility and indebtedness, a complementarity akin to that between the modern and the backward. The state's promised inclusion as the nation's agents of the modern would become fundamental to the ways braceros exerted pressure on the Mexican state to fulfill these promises.

Braceros' need to negotiate between the lure and reward of the modern, on the one hand, and the demand for backwardness, on the other, was the contradiction underwriting the program and the actions of the major players involved. Initially, aspiring migrants were willing to take the Mexican state at its word: that it was an impartial redistributive patriarchal state offering a prestigious opportunity that would transform its humble participants into national actors. This we saw when hopeful migrants were brought into the stadium, celebrated and anointed as new actors for the nation, and sent out to do its work. Yet this optimism slowly dissipated. Repeated instances of corruption and humiliation chipped away at men's willingness to invest in the state's self-portrayal and sign on to its vision of what the program would bring them, their families, and the nation. Men began to understand what lay ahead in the journey and got a glimpse of the cost of migrating and what was at stake. In this process they started to recognize that their interests and those of the state were incommensurate.

Thus, my examination of the selection processes reveals the terrain of dialogue within which men would seek the rewards the program promised. This analysis thus exposes three issues. First, it shows the rhetorical place of the modern in the ongoing Mexican projects of nation and state building, of which the program was one example, and how the latent tension between the modern, as social visibility, and the traditional, as social indebtedness, was endemic to this modernization process. Second, it exposes the multiple levels and spaces where the work of the border—understood as incommensurable difference—was done and the ways this work was instantiated in everyday social practices (practices of border). Third, it suggests that the real impact of this negotiation between state and migrant, lived alongside practices of border, would be the transformation of braceros into transnational subjects. These were lived as the program's key paradox.

Communicated to men throughout the selection process, then, was this troubling paradox, and they arrived at final selection sites changed by it. It would be their window onto the rest of the process and the program as a whole, the understanding with which they would confront hostile treatment and admonishment anew, this time from U.S. officials. While eyes, teeth, muscles, hands, and attitudes were scrutinized by officials north and south of the territorial border, the border did not anoint men as modern national subjects of a sovereign nation-state but instead reduced them to their racialized bodies. In the United States, these so-called temporary workhorses were strictly precluded from the modern by race and nationality, for, as other scholars have suggested, Mexican was an altogether racialized label.[104] It did not carry the weight accorded other labels of nationality, such as English or French, which at the time of the program were recognized as markers of fully sovereign nation-states. Without Mexico's designation as such, the clash between modern and backward at the border would become racialized and replicated in subsequent interactions men had with growers, foremen, domestic farmworkers, U.S. officials, and community residents throughout the United States, in particular in California's Imperial Valley. That is, while braceros were promised that the program would make them modern, in reality work in U.S. agriculture fields offered no such thing. The pervasive practices of border (quotidian interactions that reproduced men's screening at the border) made becoming modern the border that braceros could never fully cross. Practices of border, as we will see, would become the lens through which migrants understood their journeys northward and the terrain on which they would fight for inclusion in the modern. This terrain, in turn, would shape how they would became transnational subjects. Tied to nation and state projects—to Mexico as citizen, to the United States as farmworker, but not completely synonymous with either one—this subjectivity was the terrain from which men would push for the rewards held out by both nation-states.

In the end, Mexico's lack of standing as a sovereign nation-state would not only affect migrants but also take a toll on the Mexican state. While many welcomed, and the Mexican state publicized, the program agreement as evidence of the country's newly acquired status as an (almost) equal U.S. hemispheric partner, my analysis suggests that this equivalence was largely fictive. Instead of two sovereign states sharing equally in this process, we have seen here the making of a transnational space in Mexico that aspiring migrants were forced to navigate to even arrive at the official border. The fictive nature of Mexico's sovereignty in the eyes of U.S. officials and growers will become even more evident in the chapters to follow, as Mexican state options grew increasingly limited. State options were constrained not only by the pervasive economic need of braceros and undocumented migrants, but also by growers' ability to exploit that economic need (with the implicit support of the U.S. government). As a subaltern state built on paternalism, redistribution, and the collectivized growing pains of modernization, Mexico could not fulfill its promises to braceros.

In the next chapter I follow men's journeys from the border reception centers to the places they would reside for the length of contracts, exploring the conditions of work and the relationships they formed. These contrasts created spaces and contexts in which practices of manhood, race, and nation were thrown open, contested, and renegotiated by braceros themselves.

5

With Hunched Back and on Bended Knee

Race, Work, and the Modern North of the Border

"It's a picture of San Andrés before the revolution," replied Mauricio Herrera to my question about the black-and-white photograph hanging next to one of Pancho Villa, revolutionary hero and Durango's legendary son. "We didn't own any land; we worked the landowner's." While reform policies subsequently apportioned land to many Durango residents, that land still did not yield enough to support don Mauricio's growing family. "[There was] not enough rain, no credit, no government support—so I had to go to north." As Guillermo, my escort and assistant in this community, and I sat in the main room of don Mauricio's small home, he began telling us about his time as a bracero. "I picked lots of different crops," he recounted, "but beets—that was very hard work. And I didn't earn much money—I thought I would but I didn't."[1] He abruptly pushed himself away from the table and slowly stood up. Bent at the waist, with arms outstretched toward the floor and crossing one leg over the other in a sort of scissors step, his body reflexively assumed the familiar pose of nearly fifty years ago. I watched him, frail and nearly blind, and struggled to imagine a much younger man with hopes for a better future.

I did not come to know don Mauricio as well as some ex-braceros I met, yet his words and bodily portrayal of grueling labor were critical to understanding his bracero world: in particular, its overwhelmingly homosocial living spaces, bars, and fields.[2] The presumably backward peasants who inhabited this world battled its organization so as to transform themselves into modern men and reap rewards tied to this transformation as promised during the selection process. The realities of this world counterbalance the implicit hopefulness of the selection ritual, which bestowed social visibility on formerly invisible, though legal, citizens and imbued the men and their labor (deemed to instill a "revolutionary consciousness") with an importance not formerly conferred on these bodies.[3] The symbolic capital—social visibility— that the selection process accrued to braceros: how far did it reach, and how long did it last?

My analysis reveals a radical assault on the configuration of men's worlds and, specifically, on the patriarchal rationale used—implicitly by the Mexican state and explicitly by the men themselves—to legitimize migration. Men attempted to overcome these obstacles and recuperate their manhood. Though nearly three-fourths of bracero applicants were single and younger than twenty-one—that is, future patriarchs—recuperation was still made necessary by men's homosocial living and working spaces, and the attendant lack of legitimate access to women's bodies, which further undercut claims to manhood already suspect due to their inability to support families in Mexico.[4] Braceros would position themselves as workers (not future yeoman farmers) as a way to gain respect for their labor and themselves, and to push for growers' compliance with contract stipulations believed to accompany this modern social position. Migrants' struggles for compliance and respect highlight long-standing practices of border. The very enactments of race, class, gender, sexuality, and nationality that had marked men as foreign at the border were reproduced in California's arrival celebrations, barracks, bars, and fields. Men struggled for confirmation as modern subjects within the set organization of the program, against U.S. practices of border that reproduced their exclusion from the modern and limited the economic and social benefits that migration was expected to bring. That is, the configuration of U.S. membership along a modern/nonmodern axis structured the program benefits available to braceros and the lines along which they fought for these benefits. This configuration, then, *became* the U.S.-Mexico border.

Welcome to El Norte

When braceros finished the selection process, they were assigned to growers associations and began the last leg of the journey.[5] The same scrutiny their bodies and character had received did not extend to the transportation that ferried them northward. While contracts mandated minimum safety standards, in practice growers chose the mode of transportation, just as they would choose the form that would haul men between labor camps and work sites.[6] Be it in old school buses, large stock trailers, or open-bed trucks, most men arrived without injury. However, the bus that barbershop owner don Álvaro rode in "broke down several times during the trip to the farm." The train that another rode in took thirteen days because it detoured before arriving at its destination.[7] For men "in a hurry to start work," such delays were torture and hindered men's primary goal: getting to fields to earn money.[8]

Men found many aspects of the trip alienating, challenging their recent coronation as Mexico's modernizers. On one trip don Mauricio "rode in an old school bus," while on another he traveled by stock trailer, pressed up against other men for many hours. "It was hot and uncomfortable."[9] Another had sat three to a seat on torn seats, while Samuel Carrillo and several men rode on a single wooden bench.[10] Another man, for whom things had not been so bad, had gone in the early days of the programs. "The boss got us a nice bus," he noted, "old but comfortable."[11] Men found the box lunch, with its prescribed two sandwiches, piece of fruit, and soft drink, strange at best.[12] For Diego Hernández, the trip was "quiet and lonely." Hernández, who went without relatives or friends, chatted with the other braceros, but "no one seemed to say much."[13] For many, the long bus ride was their first time away from home. "In our Mexican tradition," said Jesús Saucedo, "a family is never divided. We move from town to town, but we never separate."[14] In one incident, seventy-five braceros were stranded when their driver was arrested and jailed for defective brakes, running a red light, and driving on a suspended license. The *Houston Post* reported that police fed a "stew supper" to the braceros who had spent the day milling around the police station lawn, "hungry for food and smokes and scurrying for shelter during the thunderous afternoon downpour."[15] The majority of migrants overlooked these difficulties in return for cash and with it, the possibility of reclaiming their manhood.

When men initially arrived at U.S. residences, they often dressed in serapes (cloaks) and sombreros, toting guitars, baskets, and small bundles of personal effects. During World War II, crowds of men, women, and children supportive of Mexico's efforts would meet arriving trains and cheer as braceros disembarked. At times, new arrivals found themselves besieged by people wanting to purchase their seemingly ordinary items.[16] According to the *San José Mercury News*, newcomers "represented every conceivable type found south of the border." Some "could have stepped straight from the pages of *National Geographic* magazine, with their closed Indian faces, their shoulders enshrouded in blankets and their hats made of straw which never saw the inside of a factory and looked as if they might have been handed down from father to son for several generations."[17]

Early on, the activist, journalist, and lawyer Carey McWilliams acknowledged the program's possibilities for building mutual goodwill. The generosity expressed as local communities staged fiestas for new arrivals, appointed welcoming committees, and established education and recreational facilities—more than sixty bracero night schools were founded in rural California—would ultimately "serve a useful international purpose." It would afford braceros, he said, the "opportunity to learn something about North American agriculture, to learn to speak another language, and to become familiar with the manners and customs of a neighboring nation." U.S. rural communities would gain a chance "to know, understand, and appreciate these visitors from the south."[18] Although he would ultimately withdraw his support, for McWilliams, the program initially offered bidirectional benefits.

Like cheering crowds and welcome committees, local government officials also greeted braceros during World War II. Men tired and anxious to get to fields were first delivered to stadiums, sports fields, or large parks, where they were venerated in speeches whose celebratory tone replicated that of the Mexican state. "Citizens of Mexico," one governor welcomed, "you have come to help us in our most difficult . . . [and] important wartime task": "harvesting our crops . . . [and] starting them on their way to provide food and clothing and necessary equipment for our fighting men." Braceros' service symbolized Mexico's commitment to the "full share of the burdens of this war," to defending the right of "all men of good will . . . to live as free men in a free world" that "knows no boundaries of nationality, race, or creed." They and their nation were acting on behalf of the "common cause," bringing "the day of victory a little nearer by [their] own personal efforts."[19]

Yet braceros were told they were not just coming for economic or even patriotic reasons but to "absorb" U.S. culture and values. The "desire to see a country so different from your own," continued this governor, "[to] travel to new surroundings, to earn money," all helped them decide to come.[20] Not only did these pronouncements dovetail nicely with those of Mexican program officials, who had favored nationalistic and consumeristic ones (agricultural knowledge, cash, and consumer goods), they also repositioned braceros as enlightened, self-interested subjects: their basic needs already met, men could pursue individual interests, aspirations, and desires. Desire, here, was linked not to physical demands of hunger, thirst, and pain, but to passions—both sexual and for different knowledge and experience—and signaled needs to be quenched after those of survival. That is, braceros were imagined as motivated by not social indebtedness and hierarchical relationships but individual desire.

Taken together, these many descriptions suggest the impact of this range of hopes and expectations for the men and the program. On the one hand, U.S. newspapers portrayed braceros as frozen in a historical past. Their homemade hats and serapes made them foreign and strange, as they delighted waiting crowds in their exoticism. On the other hand, welcoming ceremonies offered, albeit momentarily, the possibility that migrants could be positioned as (proto)modern for their contributions to freedom and democracy. These priorities both detached men from their nation and local communities and confirmed connections to a global democratic community. The governor hoped that the men would enjoy their stay and that they would take away "pleasant memories of a visit among friends."[21] That is, he framed in a specific way the experience awaiting braceros, linked the two countries and their citizenry in solidarity, and granted the two partners equal standing. Patriotism, self-interest, and individual desire—not hunger or poverty—became men's motive for migrating. In transforming their needs into desires, these welcoming ceremonies moved Mexico rhetorically forward along the modern-backward continuum.

This public glorification of bracero labor is also seen in Mexican government rhetoric toward migrants in the United States. In a 1945 presidential speech read aloud by Secretary of Foreign Relations Francisco Castillo Nájera before a large crowd of soldiers and workers—that is, braceros and other people of Mexican descent—at a Los Angeles celebration of Mexican independence, President Manuel Ávila Camacho proclaimed that Mexico "admire[d]" these people's "efforts." "On this day of national rejoicing," he told them, "[the nation maintains] a place for you under our sky."[22] Many in the audience had left during the revolution, yet they, like braceros, were not "absent from [the country's] thoughts."[23]

Undergirding the speech was a particular definition of *patria* (homeland). It was not, wrote Ávila Camacho, "a geographical limitation defined by geographical accidents or by artificial conventions," but rather a "treasure accumulated over centuries, in which spiritual perfection commands a high price." *Patria* signified the nation's "entire past with its sadness and glories." But, the president continued, it was also "the present, with its struggle and the hope of a future of betterment and happiness." In "homage to those [heroes] who gave us the Patria," he asked listeners to make a firm commitment to work so that their "sainted homeland" could complete "the historic mission that marks [its] eternal destiny."[24] Here, *patria* decoupled place of residence from place of belonging, as all Mexicans shared a past of (male) heroism and (female) abnegation and a present fight for democracy.[25] No longer were Mexicans residing in the United States an embarrassment or a sign of backwardness.[26] Their achievements could now be recognized precisely because of Mexico's own progress—and they could be brought into the nation through the granting of social visibility. The state was now able to protect all its members, regardless of residence, for it had the clout vis-à-vis its northern neighbor, to do so. Braceros would pull from the multiple strains of logic offered about the program, as articulated by Mexican and U.S. officials, and shape the ways they claimed place, rights, and privileges in both countries.

A Man's World: Disruptions and Migration Experiences

The Barracks: A New Domestic Space

When braceros arrived at their places of residence, they were drawn into a migrant world comprised largely of men. By day they faced long hours of backbreaking labor in the fields. By night some men called military-style barracks home, while others shared small shacks with as few as five to seven migrants. Some dwellings had individual toilets and shower stalls; most men, however, used large collective bathroom facilities, many with only cold water.[27] "I lived in a barracks," a former migrant recalled. "Each man had a bed and a small place for his clothes and things. . . . Some nights you'd see clothes hanging up to dry."[28] California had four kinds of labor camps: those owned by large growers, which were older and had often housed both immigrant and domestic workers; growers' association camps, which were relatively new or remodeled barracks housing more than one thousand workers each; fringe camps, which had previously been chicken sheds or storage; and family camps for growers with fewer than five workers.[29] While some called accommodations "filthy" and basic, Diego Hernández commented on his good fortune. On the first day, he and his comrades awoke to find that they "had everything: toothbrush, soap, shavers, toilet paper, you name it and we had it."[30]

Braceros' hygiene was the subject of much talk by camp managers and Department of Labor (DOL) representatives. When the men first arrived, claimed one manager, "we [were] lucky if we [could] get them to take a shower . . . once a week. . . . After a man has been here [for a while], he insists on having his shower every day."[31] This same theme was repeated by DOL employees. At one labor camp, an employee declared, "they have people stationed at the doors of the mess hall, and they inspect their hands. Won't let 'em eat unless they wash their hands. . . . After they've been in this country for awhile, they begin to use the facilities." At another, he continued, the foreman and his family ate alongside the braceros. If a man sat down to eat with his hat on, or ate with his fingers, the foreman, this official noted, would instruct them in "civilized" behavior and ask that they conform so they could "eat like decent, civilized human beings." "You can do a lot [with braceros] if you really want to," he concluded. "There's nothing basically wrong with the[m]. . . . they haven't had the same . . . education we have."[32] U.S. officials and camp managers similarly scrutinized men's bodies. Men who arrived, as "skin and bones," claimed a Southern California camp foreman, headed home "weighing ten to fifteen pounds more."[33] This concern for men's bodies and manners, like the repeated assessments of muscles, hands, and physical health during the selection process—and men's evaluation on these bases—meant that this sort of "sizing up" was integrated into the program's daily working.[34] These everyday interactions and attendant evaluative reactions came to symbolize differences between the two countries and shaped how braceros would come to see themselves as men, Mexicans, braceros, and ultimately, transnational subjects. It was an instantiation of the border that became part of producing braceros as this particular gendered, classed, and racialized social category.[35]

Braceros' living arrangements helped draw distinctions between self and other. Men commented on the "lack of facilities for washing, poor ventilation in summer, drafts and leaks in winter, overcrowding, dirty bed covers, no sheets, lack of recreation facilities, isolation from others, frozen pipes in winter, lack of good drinking water and nearness of passing trains."[36] Lacking blankets, at one camp men tore out the flooring of their barracks for bonfires, "huddle[ing]" around the fire "as it was too cold to sleep inside."[37] At another camp that had previously held Italian prisoners of war, with signs still in Italian, men resorted to writing instructions in Spanish, in chalk. One man, joking about the irony, suggested, "Surely someone had more appreciation for an Italian prisoner than for a Mexican democratic ally," since the latter did not merit that signs be written in his own language. "They charge us for this [accommodation]," remarked another.[38]

Work schedules, like living arrangements, were also not of the men's making. A camp manager saw the rigid schedule—up early, days doing physically taxing work, and to bed early—as an asset. "You don't have to worry about [braceros'] off-duty hours. They get up at 4:00 or 5:00 in the morning. After they dress and eat, they go out to the fields." After work, the men ate and got cleaned up. "They're mostly in bed by 8:00pm."[39] According to another, the constant work and a lack of structured leisure activity, which would have bored most Americans, was not a problem for braceros. "A Mexican boy doesn't require much in the way of recreation or entertainment," he argued. "[They] don't go in . . . for sports and games the way we do. . . . In the evenings they just like to sit around."[40] These two aspects marked men's experiences. First, braceros' work was routinized, highly structured, and organized by a clock.[41] For some this contrasted markedly to life in Durango, where men planned their days around work on individually or collectively owned plots. For others who had merged this labor with farm or factory wage work, the discipline was not new. Still, in Durango men could choose to leave, here an option far more difficult to exercise. Second, though braceros, as poor people, had been evaluated by Mexicans in authority, in the United States officials judged migrants vis-à-vis a standardizing American masculinity. Braceros were not men but rather boys who needed training—to wash their hands, to take their hats off at the table, to use silverware—to civilize them.

When braceros spoke of their world, many used benign terms to depict the same-sex environments in which they lived, worked, and relaxed. Ramón Avitia, in a barbershop moment of reflection, summed up his experiences this way: "We worked together all day; we cooked together; we drank together; we slept together. We spent all our time together."[42] Other ex-braceros within earshot nodded in agreement. Don Álvaro picked up the conversation. "I lived with many other men, in a barracks. I remember lying in bed at night, right before the lights went out, and listening. Men would be talking to one another; you could hear every word that someone said. After we had been there awhile, . . . [and] had gotten paid and bought radios, you'd hear lots of music, all different kinds, from different radio stations, some Mexican, some American . . . a circus of music."[43] In my many conversations in men's homes and the barbershop, most talked not of abuse but of distinctive lives that were formative in shaping men's senses of themselves, others, and their place in a transnational world.

Radios had unusual resonance. While not new to Mexico—there were ninety commercial and twelve government stations by 1940—their cost was still prohibitive for members of the lower classes. Approximately three hundred thousand units, concentrated in cities, were in circulation then for a population of 19.6 million (about one radio for every sixty-seven people). This contrasted sharply with the United States, with some 30 million radios, or one for every four people.[44] Thus, radios in Mexico were most often a community resource. In California, however, braceros were not only able—and encouraged—to buy them, they could also choose from a wider range of programming. As men learned a smattering of English, radios functioned as a source of information, transmitted across great distances, and a symbol of modern life. Although Ávila Camacho's government had pushed hard to reconfigure the state's relationship to culture, and he had used radio, art, plays, movies, and opera to incorporate places far from the capital like northern Mexico into the nation, that incorporation was inconsistent and uneven.[45] Thus, while radios were not absent in Durango *pueblos*, national programming—both cultural (traditional music, plays, skits, historical content) and political (presidential speeches and announcements)—formed part of a nation-building effort. It "reassert[ed] the nation as the dominant social framework in the face of . . . alternative sources of social identity and allegiance."[46]

Against radio's national valence in Mexico, in the United States the acquisition of a unit signaled a bracero's individual choice, work success, and adherence to the program's mission; a radio was a consumer product. The Mexican state, however, was initially more focused on capital equipment. During World War II, remember, the agreements dictated that 10 percent of salaries be held in escrow and returned to migrants to buy tractors and other equipment, a policy designed to transfer U.S. knowledge and increase farming efficiency. Mexican negotiators fought hard for this provision, although braceros, earning thirty to seventy cents an hour, would have found the machinery (too costly even for many U.S. farmers) beyond their means; U.S. officials at times claimed they could not comply with this stipulation because most U.S. factories had retooled for war materiel. If braceros could not likely afford such equipment, something else was to be gained by Mexican negotiators' demands for this provision. To begin with, growers initially used braceros not in conjunction with but in lieu of farm machinery. In fact, growers argued they needed braceros precisely because the growers themselves could not afford to buy farm equipment or because mechanization did not yet exist for certain processes.[47] Ironically, then, a program that offered growers the luxury of not investing in—or even demanding—new technologies was anchored in the premise that men would learn how to use this equipment. Second, when machinery was used on farms, the binational agreement specified that braceros not operate it, reserving such tasks for U.S. domestic laborers with supposedly higher skills.[48] While braceros would incrementally take over this mechanized work (allotted to "specials," braceros deemed to possess these skills), when debates over this provision raged most intensely, the majority of braceros had little or no contact with the very machines that Mexican negotiators envisioned they would later use on Mexican plots. Thus, more important than how many—if any—men actually bought machinery, the desire for objects labeled advanced reveals the modern's cachet. Machines signified a U.S. present and a Mexican future, as well as the symbolic capital that the program was to accrue to Mexico.

Although ex-braceros described their living quarters in innocuous terms, these descriptions still show marked differences from Durango homes. At any given time, some men would be drinking, some sleeping, and some doing various activities. Many would take to bed ill or exhausted after their first or second day, for the "climate, good water, and other factors" would at times elicit "serious physical maladjustments."[49] *Falsos*, or fake campesinos, those who had not formerly engaged in agricultural activities or lived in rural areas, found the transition particularly difficult. For others there was too much commotion. One camp manager spoke of a man who had requested to move from the barracks to a tent for "more privacy." When asked why, the bracero responded that "he had bought a phonograph and a set of records, and was trying to teach himself English. He sometimes listened to the records late . . . after the men were in bed, and he didn't want to disturb them."[50]

Amid the mélange of music and men, women, too, might be part of the mix. While camp managers were legally bound to keep "persons engaged in immoral and illegal activities" out of the barracks, most did not rigorously enforce this rule.[51] "Women go out to the camps. . . . Why kid ourselves?" said a manager. "I'd like you to tell me how the hell we are supposed to keep [the women] away from the men. . . . It's like flies and honey."[52] "I have heard eyewitness reports," said Reverend James L. Vizzard of the National Catholic Rural Life Conference, "[of] signs tacked on the barracks doors indicating the schedules and prices of the prostitutes." Another priest commented, "More than once, I have had the experience of saying Mass at a camp at night [when] a car drives up outside the barracks. One of the men goes out . . . [and says], 'You can't come in yet. The *padre* is still here.' . . . Early in the morning—3:00 or 4:00am—I would find the prostitutes in the barracks."[53] Camp managers who refused women entrance found their efforts thwarted. "What do you suppose [braceros] do? They go to whore houses and booze it up."[54] Another complained, "[Prostitutes] simply drive around to the back—

or maybe park in the middle of the orchard—and go about their trade. . . . Big old Packards . . . are really whore houses on wheels."[55]

Much of this activity speaks to braceros' isolation and lack of free movement, and to the meaning behind this lack. In California, camps were located some distance from town and beyond public transport routes and camp managers frequently locked the gates at night; in Mexico, however, men came and went as they pleased. Men's ability and right to move freely, in contrast with that of women, who required a husband's permission, was at the heart of Mexican manhood; also key was the recognition and servicing of a man's sexual needs. Having prostitutes come to their camps mediated their lack of movement. Bars directly profiting from the Mexicans' presence also catered to these needs. To lure the men to their establishments, owners often provided transportation to and from the camps. One bar owner even furnished prostitutes. He considered this a service—for the men, who would find women anyway (providing a safe place to satisfy their needs prevented them from being assaulted and robbed by locals resentful of their presence), and for the community, because the practice kept the Mexicans away from nice local girls.[56]

Bracero advocates, however, saw prostitution as a sign of men's corruption and, as we will see in chapter 6, that they needed protection. In a 1958 congressional hearing, Reverend Vizzard testified to the breakdown of men's "moral practice." Though the "basic morality of the Mexican people [was] as good or even better than might commonly be found in this country," Vizzard had reports from "many parts of the country of excessive drinking, high-stakes gambling, drug addiction, and prostitution," as women of ill repute "prey[ed] on the weaknesses of men separated from their homes and families."[57] A researcher also concerned about morality interviewed a local judge, who estimated that between eight and twelve braceros and locals "appeared in his court every Monday morning" from 1944 to 1946, charged with knifings or shootings resulting from conflicts over women or jobs.[58] Friction erupted, concluded this researcher, because area growers increasingly sought the labor of this "unpopular group." But local women also often dated braceros, lured by the men's newly earned money.[59] "They come in and take jobs away from our own people," said a local resident, "because they work for almost nothing; the braceros get the jobs and our people have to go on relief." Braceros were "a real menace to society," concluded another, because they carried diseases from Mexico. "The braceros aren't like the rest of us who came to California to make homes," ventured still another. "They don't care about the community—they get drunk and get into fights and give the Mexican people a bad name." That is, instead of faulting the program, residents blamed braceros' backwardness: "[They] usually come from the country; they are campesinos, indios [a pejorative term for Indians], and fools who are pretty ignorant. They don't know much and can't get along well in the United States."[60]

At some camps, braceros took steps to avoid such problems and maintain their own respectability and that of their living environments. Sixty-five men at one camp elected one of their number to serve as camp manager. They then drew up and signed a set of rules forbidding women and liquor on camp grounds, set fixed meal times, prohibited fires in the camp, created a volunteer firefighting service, and "set a regular schedule for camp clean-up."[61] Whether by using prostitutes or through maintaining camp discipline, men maneuvered within program strictures to regain freedoms and rights central to manhood.

Like living arrangements, food and rituals around eating also marked differences between Mexico and the United States and sparked reactions. Most men disliked the "lack of tortillas," strange foods, and unaccustomed cooking techniques. "Down in Mexico," explained an ex-bracero, now a U.S. permanent resident, "they are very poor. . . . [Some] only have one meal a day. That is very common. . . . And that one meal will be very simple. No meat. No fruit or vegetables. No milk. Just beans and chiles . . . [and] tortillas." This stood in contrast to the eggs, bacon, bread, and milk he had eaten for breakfast as a bracero.[62] Meals were also the moment when many locals expressed anger at braceros for their presence, and braceros took offense at the lack of respect they were shown. One morning, a man who migrated in the early 1960s stood in line for breakfast and witnessed a mechanic spit into the oatmeal being served. "It was sickening!" he exclaimed. Attributing this behavior to the mechanic's "evilness," the bracero left without eating: "I felt as if I was going to die. It was so gross."[63] The anthropologist Manuel Gamio evaluated the effect of changes in diet and kind of work for President Manuel Ávila Camacho. "In Mexico, the diet is poorer, . . . [but] the labor is easier and more spread out." As such, concluded Gamio, "In the beginning, the bracero doesn't have sufficient physical energy to take on the American workday, which is hard and continuous." Meals were "more nutritious and abundant" but the new tastes were not readily accepted. Braceros, unaccustomed to such foods, ate little and worked hard, a combination that brought about "serious crises that often require[d] that the bracero be sent back."[64]

Still, poverty, concluded other researchers, was not necessarily the reason that people ate poorly. "We ate with many people who had herds of cattle or fields of palm trees, who ate like paupers. . . . Sometimes they just do not know any better."[65]

The men with whom I spoke did not like (at least initially) yellow American cheese served with lunchmeat on white bread, a staple in the bracero diet.[66] Many longed for Mexican food: beans, chiles, and tortillas.[67] "No Mexican, in those days, ate [a meal] without chiles and [corn] tortillas."[68] "It's who we are," don Álvaro elaborated.[69] Andrés Morales considered American food to be bland. "You Americans don't like spicy food," he said. "We [Mexicans] need chiles but [as braceros] we ate tortas, you know, a sanveech, with meat and yellow cheese."[70] Many camps, especially the small camps, lacked tortillas, while others had mass-produced flour ones. When asked which they preferred, white bread, flour tortillas, or corn tortillas, almost 69 percent of braceros chose corn tortillas, 22 percent flour tortillas, and only 6 percent liked bread best.[71] To the average villager, "the noonday meal, consisting of meat and vegetables prepared in oil or lard, is the hearty repast of the day. . . . The evening meal is of little consequence with a stomach well fortified at noon. In the United States, however, a short lunch of ham or bologna 'sandweech' is more or less the accepted noonday meal. The Mexican is unprepared for this. He often throws out his sandwiches in disgust and so, hungry and dissatisfied, works all day without lunch. By night, when according to American ideas, he is expected to eat his 'big meal,' he is too exhausted to digest it. From his point of view the subsequent distress is due to the outlandish food."[72]

Unfamiliar situations with unexpected repercussions arose not only over what men ate—or did not eat—but who purchased and cooked food.[73] Cooking was considered the domain of wives and mothers, yet men sometimes found themselves preparing their own meals. "We had to cook our own meals," said Federico Garciniego. They had to do their own shopping as well. "So every . . . Sunday, that being our day off and when the truck went into town . . . [some of us] went grocery shopping. . . . This one time it was my turn to go," said Federico. "[We] didn't have much money. And no one could speak English very well. . . . No one could read. . . . We bought the usual stuff—beans, rice, tortillas. . . . Then we saw these cans of what looked like meat. . . . So we figured, okay we'll buy them." He continued: "The meat wasn't great, but . . . on tortillas, with beans, it was okay. So the following week, we bought them again. We ate that meat . . . until one man—he had been there for a while and he could read some English—he asked us if we knew what we had bought. We said, 'no, not exactly,' but that it was some sort of meat. So he told us." Federico paused. "We had been eating dog food. . . . It wasn't bad, but we didn't buy it anymore."[74]

Radios blaring at night, English-language records playing, buying unknown food, eating bland meals, cooking together—these experiences highlight the gulf between Mexican homes and same-sex U.S. living spaces. In Mexico, domestic arrangements were organized around nuclear and extended heterosexual family units in which all members—men, women, and children—held economic and social responsibilities and privileges.[75] The family was seen as the "basic nucleus of society" and an essential building block of "the capitalist order" as envisioned in Mexico.[76] Men's inability to support their families, a fate to which most poor and working-class Mexican men often fell victim, threatened manhood; bracero migration, with its job prospects and the promise of greater economic security, was set up to recoup it. Little did it matter that at times nearly three-quarters of aspiring braceros were bachelors under the age of twenty-one.[77] The point critical for the Mexican state was to induct all men—current heads of household and future ones—into a particular gender logic grounded in a (future) maintenance of family and authority over self and family, even though U.S. conditions would deny braceros this self-authority and challenge wider claims to manhood.

Another difference: most braceros lived in camps where someone else made the food. Braceros, said a government official, "are technically given a choice between eating in the camp facilities and cooking for themselves. We do everything we can to discourage their cooking for themselves." One estimate found that less than 2 percent of all braceros in California cooked for themselves, in part because the camps made money by providing board, but also because employers and government bureaucrats alike were convinced that men ate better and were safer when they were supplied meals. Few men knew how to cook; some would not eat if food were not in front of them; others required to cook relied on inexpensive prepared foods, such as canned sardines, cinnamon rolls, canned beans, and soda pop. Men seeking to save money, confirmed a California Department of Public Health investigator, often starved themselves to death.[78] Ernesto Galarza, estimating that only one out of every thousand braceros prepared his own meals, concluded that braceros faced the choice between eating prepared food "or else." "Men don't want the 'or else,' so there is very little trouble."[79] The "or else" was most likely a threat to send men home. "Free societies," suggested Henry

Anderson, "operate on the premise that men shall have the right . . . to make mistakes, to be foolish, to do things which are not in their best interest." This he contrasted with "a system in which an employer or a bureaucrat . . . says, 'You will do it this way because I know what is good for you.'"[80] Yet these freedoms, required for the status of fully adult male, were exactly what employers and government officials refused to extend to migrants; they considered braceros children, in accordance with grower narratives (chapter 2), or at least not fully adults.[81] As children, their daily existence was organized by others, and they were instructed in so-called civilized behavior. While braceros were legally afforded "a certain freedom of choice," many involved in the program concluded that braceros deserved no more freedom or respect "than any other commodity shipped in international trade."[82]

Thus, the acts of shopping for, preparing, and eating food took on new significance in the United States. Men began to recognize themselves as different—foreign and out of place—in ways made more palpable by racially segregated farming communities. The senses of self and of collective being created north of the border contrasted markedly with the (often weak) feelings of Mexicanness that men had at the start of their journeys. These senses instead became representative of new racialized gender subjectivities and threats to old ones, set within an explicitly transnational logic and context. While initially migrants claimed that the lack of chiles and tortillas were inconveniences offset by "serving the cause of . . . democrac[y]," differences from and attacks on the particular (Mexican) form of life from which they as (proto)patriarchs drew their agentive position began to symbolize a more general assault on their status as authoritative (male) subjects, one they would attempt to reclaim in other ways and sites.[83]

How should we understand this identitarian process under way, given that braceros from Durango and outside of Mexico City more generally (the majority) were still in the process of becoming Mexican? How did the contrast between men's living conditions in the United States and those in Mexico figure into this process? After the revolution, the state had engaged in nation formation as it attempted to cohere the population behind a particular sense of the nation as Mexican. At the same time, many people—in particular, rural folk, the poor, and those not living in Mexico City—remained partial to their local and regional identities. In this respect, men left as only tenuously Mexican; for them, the program functioned as an accidental exercise in nation building. Thus, although bracero quarters, like homes in Durango and the rest of Mexico, often lacked indoor plumbing and electricity, these took on significance explicitly because this new social organization undermined the heteronormative logic from which men derived rights as (proto)patri-archs—and it did so *outside* Mexico.

Men read everything through these differences in social organization. For example, on some farms, they did their own laundry, while on others, owners arranged for local women to offer this service. At the farm on which Andrés Morales picked Mississippi cotton, "local women—they were all black women—used to come once a week . . . to wash our clothes. We had to pay. . . . It was much better than doing it ourselves. . . . I wanted to save money, [so] in the beginning I washed my own clothes. . . . But it was hard work, and after working all day, I didn't want to do it. So I had a woman wash my clothes. . . . It was worth it."[84]

In this man's remarks the gendered framework that legitimated migration becomes evident along with the implicit contrast between Durango homes and U.S. labor camps. *Not* paying for laundry service demonstrated his pri-oritization of family needs over his own, for in saving money he could send more to his family and thus reclaim his manhood and title as household patriarch. Yet even as his claim was undone by the "hard work" that wash-ing clothes entailed, all was not lost to him. The washer of his clothes—a woman—was someone to whose labor he, as proper patriarch, should have had access, maintaining the accepted gendered boundaries of domestic re-sponsibilities. Thus, the ongoing struggle between spending money, making bracero life easier, and supporting the proper division of labor, on the one hand, and saving money, making life harder, and undermining this labor division, on the other, was framed as a struggle over rights to the title of proper patriarch. This conflict did more than refashion gender subjectivity: produced vis-à-vis Mexican social categories in a non-national context, this subjectivity thus became both Mexican and transnational.

Regardless of how this particular man's laundry decisions were resolved, for braceros more generally the same-sex environment of their living spaces provoked anxiety about themselves as properly gendered beings, and its loca-tion outside Mexico saddled seemingly mundane decisions with new weight, rousing questions over ties of belonging. For surrounding communities and the states involved, the barracks' homosociality aggravated suspicions about the men and their sexuality, further marking them as foreign and distinct from the local community. As we shall see, migrants sought to reclaim their status as properly gendered men through wartime participation in parades and music festivals, and social rituals of drinking and socializing, often with women other than wives or girlfriends.

Public Performances, Private Spaces, and Subjectivity

During World War II, braceros were invited to participate in local celebrations for the Fourth of July, Thanksgiving, or local holidays. "Many men know their own country dances. Many play guitars or other musical instruments, and almost all of them sing," averred one report. Here they had the chance to participate in an "American affair" and show something about their nation to their U.S. hosts, which they did with "greatest enthusiasm." Dancing, performing music, participating in parades, or playing Mexican songs on a radio program while wearing the national colors of their homeland gave these foreigners "a thrilling opportunity."[85] At these moments braceros were called on to be Mexican: to display the Mexican flag, play Mexican music, sing Mexican songs, and dance traditional Mexican dances. Initially, braceros may not have considered the things they did Mexican, per se; rather, they played or sang whatever they knew, from local or regional *corridos* (a narrative form of song and poetry) to popular songs.[86] In short, men who had previously called themselves *norteños* or of a certain *pueblo* marched as Mexicans to the applause of U.S. citizens.

I first learned the role of parades and music in braceros' lives when I visited the Durango home of Antonio Ramírez. Hesitant to talk at first, he relented when my local chaperon, Guillermo, reassured him that I was not from the CIA or any Mexican government office. Hanging on the turquoise walls of his dimly lit house were several instruments, including guitars. I looked around at length, engaging him about the instruments, before he— blind, frail, and seventy-seven years old—described how as a strong young man he had picked California plums, peaches, and pears.

Don Antonio first migrated in 1945, at the tail end of the war, and was one of his *pueblo*'s first program participants. He traveled north at a time when migrants were welcomed in the United States, likened to soldiers in the fields, and portrayed in Mexico as national emissaries in a cooperative mission.[87] In interviews, many men invoked their identity as Mexican to describe aspects of migrant journeys, and don Antonio was one of those men. "I am a musician, I play the saxophone," he said. After some people found out about this, he was invited to play at a prison. "I didn't want to go—it was a prison," he emphasized, "but some friends convinced me to go, so I went. They went, too. . . . I played Mexican music because that was all I knew. And when I was finished playing, they wouldn't let me leave. No, they wanted me to continue. . . . So I did, for a long time, song after song, some more than once. . . . They clapped; they wanted me to play and play. . . . I guess they didn't have many visitors."[88]

Don Antonio brought up this experience in the course of talking about his journeys. It stood out among the numerous times he migrated. Although he situated the incident in the context of talking about his ability to play and the reception of his music, the story reads as a moment in the continuous (re)making of Mexicanness. Don Antonio was constructing it through his interaction with the men who heard the music, an audience he never described and about whom I did not ask. Yet his use of the adjective *Mexican* to name the music that he played suggests that for him (and maybe his friends in attendance), this staged semipublic performance was critical in situating the music and its purveyors as Mexican, easily distinguished from listeners across lines of nationality, race, and language, among other things.

Like don Antonio, José Moreno also recalled music as an important aspect of his journey. An energetic man, slightly hard of hearing and in his mid- to late seventies, don José told us how he learned the saxophone. He and his friends didn't have much money. "Like them, I sent a lot home for my family—so we couldn't do much . . . on weekends. I had time to learn. . . . A man taught me how to play, he taught me what he knew. It wasn't much, but after awhile, I could play a bit. But I practiced and practiced. When other men went out drinking, I practiced." He used the instrument that his foreman had lent to the man who was teaching him.[89]

Don José's recollection foregrounds his dedication to music as a way of locating himself vis-à-vis other migrants. After he learned to play, he and his friends would stay in the barracks and sing. "We didn't need to go out, to spend money in bars. We could enjoy ourselves without trouble." He told me that he had been asked to play publicly, during his second bracero trip in the late 1940s and early 1950s. "I got pretty good," he said. "I even played in a parade for the Fourth of July. . . . There were bands of Americans playing music I didn't know. . . . They asked me to play Mexican music, so I walked in the parade and I played, with a friend . . . who played the guitar. . . . The Americans applauded for us when we went by. . . . I still play, even now that I'm an old man, and on the same sax I brought back with me."[90]

This description lends itself to a critical reading. As don José and others stayed in the barracks, singing or listening to him play, a distinctly bracero community was fostered. Don José understood the barracks as a place to have fun "without trouble," safer than spaces where brawls precipitated by alcohol broke out with locals.[91] But fights also frequently erupted in the barracks. Thus, his understanding of their safety seems to refer not to literal safety but rather to a particular kind of safe space: a bracero space. Likewise he mobilized the adjective *Mexican* to label the music. While at the outset migrants most likely considered *Mexican* a national label, in the United States, they confronted its racial weight.[92] Taken together we begin to understand how Mexicanness was being recast in the United States: initially framed in home-grown terms and then communicated through selection ceremonies, it was now denigrated by bracero conditions structured through racial, gendered, and class markers. This recasting would weigh heavily in the constellation of men's new subjectivities.

The Bar: Space of Seduction for Cash

As we have seen, the braceros' living conditions—isolated sex-segregated barracks and the requirement that men engage in domestic tasks—highlighted their lack of legitimate access to women's bodies and called into question their already precarious claims to status as proper patriarchs. Braceros looked to recoup this status, often through social rituals of drinking. Whether married or single, the act of drinking, in barracks and at bars, became a common way to escape the drudgery, monotony, and isolation of their physical labors and surroundings. The bar became a space where men could socialize and even meet women, for it was organized around the promotion and fulfillment of men's desires and needs, whose gratification was considered a fundamental part of male privilege. Social jousting for position among men was critical to fulfilling those needs. Braceros used the act of drinking with friends, spending money as saw they fit, and meeting and talking with women to mark those who enjoyed to excess as womanizers, spendthrifts, and irresponsible men and themselves, who respected limits, as proper patriarchs.[93] This fundamental division between proper patriarchs and womanizers would be structured into these rituals and the space of the bar.

Yet there was another dimension that made this division more complicated for meeting gender expectations—in this case, supporting their families—gave men the right to adventure and social rituals like drinking. My discussions with former migrants suggest that they found a resolution to this seeming contradiction: the rights of a proper patriarch had limits. The general consensus was that while they "didn't drink very much," "everyone, almost everyone did." According to Samuel Carrillo, "every Saturday night, some Fridays, too, when we weren't working on Saturday morning, men went to the bar. . . . I went sometimes—I drank a little. But I was never drunk."[94] Others, it seems, spent nearly all their leisure time there. "Mostly, I didn't," Alejandro Medina told me. "It wasn't that I didn't want to—I did. But I had a family to support. I couldn't spend my week's wages in just one night. I had young children. . . . I couldn't drink very much. . . . I behaved myself."[95]

Don Alejandro hints at both the right to socialize with friends after a week of hard work and the limits of that right, as well as the elaborate mechanisms by which men justified their choice of behavior. In the case of don Alejandro, a husband and father of young children, he had a family to support; he did not deny his right as patriarch to participate in these social rituals, but he saw that right as limited. Other migrants, too, confirmed this limit. As Paco Zermeño told me, "Some men—married men, too—met women in the North. They had girlfriends, they went out with them on weekends, they bought them things, they spent lots of money. I didn't do that much; I had a family, and they needed me to help with the bills. I drank with my friends, but not very often; instead, I saved my money. . . . We have this house because of the money I made in California."[96] "Yes," Félix Ávalos acknowledged, "I went drinking at the bar. . . . I lived with my parents and still sent some money home, although not as much as I could have, like other men did. But I wasn't married, I didn't have a family—I had a girlfriend, but I didn't have a family. . . . I went for the money, but for adventure, too . . . to see things. . . . I had a [local] girlfriend . . . but I didn't marry her. . . . [Some men] left wives and families. . . . They found other women and stayed. . . . I came home for my girlfriend."[97] Aníbal Bañales recalled, "I met a woman when I was working in the United States, and she became my girlfriend. I had a wife and my daughter was young then, but I found a girlfriend. After all, a man needs a woman. My wife, she had her friends, her parents, my daughter; a man needs a woman. I had a girlfriend, but . . . I came back here, to my wife, family."[98]

The above descriptions suggest two ways of resolving the threat that domestic arrangements of the barracks posed: either men went to the bars and exercised male privilege in an attempt to (re)secure their tenuous claim to manhood, or they recouped their manhood by attributing their refusal to participate in social rituals to the need to send money home and fulfill patriarchal responsibilities. Many men with whom I spoke confirmed that they drank and went to bars. "But, I wasn't married, I still sent money back to my parents, so it was okay," said don Álvaro. Thus, being single (partially) negated the need for limits. "I met lots of women that way," don Álvaro told the barbershop audience. "Lots. They knew we'd come on Saturday nights and they'd be there. They liked Mexicans. . . . They liked that we were hard workers; they liked that we dressed well and had money. They used to come around the bars that we went to. . . . They really liked the Mexicans."[99]

Still, using sexual involvement with local women as a way to counter the threat to manhood signaled by the homosocial bracero space came at a cost. Migrants were frequently accused of loose morals for impregnating local women and refusing to marry them or support the children.[100] Others laid the blame for such behavior elsewhere. One man repeated the frequent observation that the program was "like the Army" in its "traditions and agencies" intended to keep men in line. "[Yet] there is no discipline in bracero camps, and so . . . anything goes. Homosexuality, anything. This is not because braceros have loose morals to start with [but rather] employers . . . could provide discipline . . . if they wanted" but failed to do so. "I have never met an employer . . . who gave a damn about the morals of his men," he continued, "so long as the work got done."[101] Thus, the critical caveat: as long as braceros lived up to their responsibilities as men, they could justify their activities and still claim their position as proper patriarchs. They could refuse the specter of the patriarch's destabilizing opposite who might reside in a sexually unregulated space: the drunk, carouser, womanizer, and spendthrift. That is, the broader circumstances that framed men's drinking—not *if* they drank—functioned as a marker for a claim to manhood and being a proper patriarch.

The complexities of the bar are hinted at in don Álvaro's claim that local women "liked Mexicans." This gives clues to the kind of women braceros frequently met and the relationships they had. Although men were rumored to have met, married, and stayed with U.S. women, no man with whom I spoke admitted to knowing anyone who had done so; in fact many noted the limited interactions between braceros and locals.[102] In short, the relationships that don Álvaro raved about were most likely ones in which men exchanged cash, directly or indirectly, for socializing and sex, even though he portrayed these relationships as based on love and heterosexual attraction, ones in which gifts and favors were given for romantic possibilities.[103] That is, the men saw and justified their actions vis-à-vis Mexican gender conventions. Regardless of how a migrant spent his money, he could reclaim his manhood and the label of proper patriarch if he supported his family in Mexico.

In short, drinking, spending money, having sexual encounters and relationships were both potentially at odds with being a good worker, husband, and man *and* the very entitlement for being so. Yet migrants' claim on the title of proper patriarch was always only partial. In Mexico, it was partial because they could not live up to the foundation of patriarchy and support their families—the very reason they sought to migrate. In the United States, their domestic arrangements made their heterosexuality suspect, and the men's absence from Mexico undercut their control over the sexuality of children and wife, who was made even more vulnerable and available to other men. Thus, braceros' romantic and sexual interactions with local women, which simultaneously "strained relations" with local men, put pressure on men's vision of patriarchy and the rights associated with it. While braceros had come to "make money," in the end, all their social relationships, including ones deemed the right of patriarchs, were commodified.[104] This commodification encapsulated the very process of proletarianization that these migrants were undergoing.

The process through which braceros maneuvered to reclaim their manhood ultimately generated other subjectivities integrating different forms of connection—local, national, racial, and class based—that emerged through men's particular experiences in the United States. These emergent subjectivities drew on a specifically Mexican version of citizenship, with its lateral as well as hierarchical affective ties, which the Mexican state propagated domestically and in the program's selection rituals, and of Mexicanness, which it pushed in national holidays and schooling. To further explore the impact of shifts in subjectivities on braceros' reading of journeys, I now turn to the fields—the space of work—and the creation of a workers' solidarity.

Generating Solidarity: The Fields, the Barracks, the Bar

Like braceros' regimes of living and leisure, work, too, was a highly structured and predominantly male world. Most men arose before sunrise, ate breakfast, and picked till noon. After lunch, workers had the afternoon off to avoid the midday sun. Others began work at ten o'clock and labored till dark, with a short break for lunch. Still others worked from six in the morning to seven at night. Their migrant world was formed around mentoring and friendships. "We helped each other," said don Mauricio, who had shown me how to pick cotton.[105] "Everyone had their good days and bad days. I really felt sorry for the *falsos*, [who] suffered the most. Many of them fainted or got sick. Some . . . were sent home because they couldn't handle the work-load."[106] Men who aided compatriots were compensated in many ways. For example, one bracero who had been a barber in Mexico "gave everyone a haircut," recalled Reynaldo López. "The men wouldn't pay him, but the next day they would dump a couple of sacks of pears in his bin, which was pretty much the same thing, plus it helped the friendship. Another man was a good musician. . . . Men would ask him to sing a particular song for them, and then the next day they would buy" him "beer."[107] But men also competed with each other. One man recalled how he had been part of a work gang, the Golden Shears. "Not another gang could beat us."[108] "You bet," concurred an-other former bracero. "We were the fastest at filling those crates. . . . There's a knack to everything."[109] Ignacio Ochoa Perdomo remembered himself "as a champion" who had "beat[en] out thirty people" in picking competitions.[110]

Seasoned braceros brought new arrivals into this setting of competition and rivalry, orienting them to the structures of work. "The first time [I went], I didn't know how to pick beets," recalled don Andrés. "I remember the first day . . . I took . . . my sack and started to pick. It was hard work, so I watched the others and tried to imitate them. That helped, but not that much. Finally, one man . . . who had done this for a long time—he was Mexican—he took me aside and showed me how. 'Like this,' he said. 'It's much easier.' And it was. . . . We got to be friends. And then later . . . I showed other men. . . . That's how it worked."[111] Don Mauricio remembered a sack he received the first day: "I carried it around, trying to fill it as quickly as I could. . . . But I was slow. . . . The experienced workers, it seemed, worked much faster than I. They were filling their sacks faster, much faster." He told me how he had worked several days like that "before I got to be friendly with someone. He—he was a northerner like I was—he showed me how the experienced workers did it. He had cut the bottom of his sack and restitched it, making it easy to empty. He said all the experienced pickers did it this way. I tried it and it took less time . . . I could empty . . . much faster. . . . I earned more money."[112]

These structures of work created both new relationships and conditions productive of new subjectivities. Often newcomers "couldn't [read] the contract" and "used to throw [it] away," said Ignacio Ochoa Perdomo, but established workers knew what it said and would orient others about its provisions. "We talked about the clauses among ourselves in the camp."[113] Veteran migrants also shared with younger braceros how to organize for bet-ter food or pressure for compliance with mandated pay scale. "One time," said Ramón Avitia, "a group of us, we didn't like the food—it was horrible, the taste, plus, no tortillas or chiles. . . . Those with some experience got together and threatened the boss. We told him that we weren't going to work if the food didn't improve. It didn't, so we left, about ten of us. . . . We found other jobs, without contracts, but the food was better. That's important. . . . The work was okay, the boss, too—but not the food."[114] Don Álvaro also had worked at a camp with poor food. "We only ate sandwiches, ham and cheese, eggs, lots of eggs," he said. "So we got a group of men together and . . . talked to the foreman. He told the boss. . . . The boss talked to the cook. . . . The food got better. . . . I imagine that [the boss] had heard of other men leaving, of walking out. I wouldn't have left, but some would have."[115]

Established migrants not only shared information about work but also taught newcomers about other aspects of braceros' lives, often about more "recreational" activities. During one long conversation, don Álvaro recounted that, after receiving his first paycheck, some friends and he met a more experienced migrant. "He said he knew exactly what we needed. Now I figured . . . that he'd be taking us into town. We all needed clothes, you know, things. . . . But do you know where he took us?" Don Álvaro paused and glanced around the barbershop. "Sure, he took us into town, but instead of taking us to buy clothes, we went to a bar . . . where everyone knew him. He had credit; he could drink as much as he wanted even if he didn't have the money. . . . We all drank; we drank a lot. I spent almost my whole paycheck that night. . . . He did it every weekend. . . . So did some others." He continued: "It was fun, but I didn't do it too much—once in awhile."[116]

Male relationships flourished out of living, working, eating, and drinking side by side, and longtime migrants passed knowledge gained through experience on to new arrivals. This transfer of information—that is, of knowledge acquired through bracero work—helped attenuate (if only slightly) the power of strong growers' associations, for growers and foremen traded names of workers who "caused trouble"—code words for attempting to improve working or living conditions or stop the rampant discounting of wages. In sharing this knowledge, in showing newcomers shortcuts, and, in turn, helping them earn more money, in organizing for better food or wages, returning migrants often exercised a worker solidarity and shared their take on the practices of border—that is, the axes of difference, exclusion, and hierarchy—that organized their lives in the United States.

Markers of difference through which men came to understand their migrant world were built into the organization of work. "Work in the United States was different from Mexico," Jesús Saucedo said. "In Mexico we did not have machinery, we did not have irrigation, we did not have land. The work was hard . . . [but] compared to America, U.S.A., working in Mexico . . . was a piece of pie. In Mexico we 'campesinos' are used to working strenuous labor and not getting paid for it. [But] all of our work was for our own survival." Self-survival contrasted with cash and wealth for growers: "A big difference!"[117] For other men, language grounded this world. On separate occasions, men commented to me on how some foremen "looked Mexican" but "didn't speak Spanish."[118] "When I first . . . looked at [my boss]," said Juan Luis Martínez, "I thought he was Mexican. He looked Mexican, but he wasn't; he didn't speak Spanish. . . . One day, I started talking to [him] in Spanish, but he just looked at me and then walked away. He didn't understand what I said. Or maybe he did but he didn't want to show it—I don't know. But he paid attention when a few friends and I got together and talked."[119] "Usually," said Mr. Yamato, a grower interviewed in the early 1960s, "Spanish-speaking Americans [were] hired as foremen to handle the immediate problems with braceros and to perform the role of an intermediary between the employer and the Mexican workers."[120] These passages suggest that language became a salient dividing line for braceros: those who spoke Spanish "were" Mexican; and those who did not "were not"; men became Mexican negotiating this line and the racism to which it spoke.

Analyzing migrants' living and working conditions reveals the ways that bracero experiences generated new subjectivities, ones in tension both with their place as nonnational (foreign), nonwhite (Mexican), nonmodern (farmwork) migrant laborers in the United States, and with the agentive position they had been led to believe they would occupy for Mexico. In the United States, braceros were "separated . . . from family and friends," "isolated from American communities," "confronted with new foods not to their taste," and forced to capitulate to demanding bosses "known to exploit them."[121] In Mexico they were husbands, sons, and brothers; lived in families, units of men, women, children, and often, older relatives; socialized with friends, had sex with wives, courted girlfriends, and came and went as they saw fit. Each family member derived responsibilities and freedoms as a function of age and gender, and as a part of that unit and in relation to its other members and community norms. Ideally, men worked outside the house and left domestic chores to women folk, a line that was not crossed.

However, work in the United States was all about crossing lines, physical and imaginary. Here, braceros could not maintain even the appearance of the entrenched demarcation between "women's" and "men's" work, between "men's" and "women's" spaces. Food needed to be prepared, dirty pants washed, and ripped shirts sewn. Yet women, for the most part, were not available for such work and definitely not without being paid. So braceros were forced to engage in what was seen as women's work. And they had strong feelings about these gendered transgressions. "We had to wash our clothes," don Félix told me. "We had to cook, we had to shop for our food, we even had to repair torn clothes. I didn't like it much; I didn't want to, but I had to do it. I wanted to eat."[122] Another man agreed: "We arrived from a day's work," he said, "[only] to work again . . . patting and flipping tortillas, preparing supper, preparing fried beans for the next day, cooking the meat— in a word, we did everything. . . . We cooked, washed, ironed, and did all the housework."[123] Don Ramón said that before he migrated, he "didn't know how to cook." "Some of the other workers taught me. . . . I still remember how, so once in a while, I'll prepare something for my family. . . . It's not so hard. . . . Nowadays women complain, but it's not so hard."[124] Don Álvaro eloquently declared: "All day we worked in the fields; all day we picked. From lemons to tomatoes, we dragged our sacks and we picked. Then we went to our barracks and we cooked dinner; we washed our clothes, we cleaned, we went to bed. . . . After doing 'men's work' all day, every evening we did 'women's work.' . . . We did men's work, [and] we did women's work, too."[125] His words bring into relief the previously unbridgeable divide between "women's" and "men's" work. Men's work, in their eyes, was physically taxing and demanded physical strength: men lugged around heavy sacks of fruits or vegetables; they got dirty, their bodies ached, and they earned money. Men's work gave them men's worn and callused hands.[126]

Yet herein resides the conflict: while braceros engaged in a men's work not unlike what they had done in Mexico, they had still crossed an official border. Not merely the work itself but the space in which it was done demanded that these same callused, used men's hands—required by growers and Mexican and U.S. government officials for men to become sanctioned migrants—also do the work of women. The words of the men bespeak both a pride and shame at having done this women's work. "It isn't so hard," men repeatedly told me when talking about cooking and washing clothes. These words hint at a pride of self-sufficiency and of being able to do something new. Still, they also communicated shame, as the men discounted the difficulty of women's responsibilities, the same ones that, when they did them, threatened their claim on manhood. Ultimately, braceros' inability to provide for their families required them to cross a physical border, one that relegated them to the homosocial arena of the barracks and the fields and whose segregated arenas, in turn, denied them legitimate access to female bodies. In so doing, their hold on manhood and patriarchal privilege was again made tenuous, this time in the United States.

Recuperating Manhood

Faced with a denial of the rights and privileges of patriarchy, braceros sought to overcome this threat. Those whose claim to manhood had been precarious in Mexico had seen migration to the United States and the attendant prospects of a job as a way of meeting these expectations. But how could men recuperate that manhood? They could not. In Mexico, their claim to manhood was attenuated by an inability to maintain families, while in the United States living arrangements built not around familial ties but around same-sex work relationships further called it into question, even as this distorted domestic space buttressed the formation of a particular Mexican identity produced in the fields. How, then, could these men (re)secure manhood rights and privileges, despite the need to take on tasks labeled "women's work?" That is, what might have enabled braceros to transcend their predicament? And how were approaches to and attempts at transcendence connected to the workers' solidarity emerging and relied on in the fields? Stymied in the recuperation of manhood by this predicament, men used what they had at their disposal: the subjectivity as workers, grounded in the homosocial space of the barracks and created in the fields, vis-à-vis white and Mexican American bosses and foremen, competing migrants, and earlier experiences and knowledge from Durango (and Mexico).

The many accounts of clashes between bracero farmworkers and foremen and bosses suggest how braceros mobilized a workers' subjectivity to their own ends. When thirty-five-year-old Francisco Hernández Cano was approached by a newspaper reporter in 1956, he was on his way to Washington to "get . . . fair pay and treatment" for himself and other braceros with whom he worked in California's Salinas Valley. His coworkers, he told the reporter, "had passed the hat to get [his] bus fare," and he was off to talk to the Mexican ambassador, whom he hoped would resolve "complaints—of pay deductions for tools, blankets and insurance; of bad food and housing; of days wasted waiting for work." While acknowledging his and most men's "ambition . . . to come every year to work in California," he lambasted growers. "'Under the contract I can make $18, even $35, in one week sometimes," said Hernández Cano. But, he lamented, growers "do not obey the contract. They take out so much money sometimes a man gets only $5 or $10 for his week's work. Some men get only a few cents for the whole week." As the newspaper article suggested, Hernández Cano—and the "million other Mexicans . . . [who] came north to work—wanted their contracts enforced." In Mexico, they "had no land and no job."[127]

These men, then, the ones who made this long trek northward, were not peasants—as the newspaper said, they held no land. Nor did they see themselves as such. Rather, they described their economic situation in terms of wages—the amount of money that a man could make in a week—and appealed to rights due them as workers. Like workers elsewhere, they wanted the contract—the bilateral agreement—enforced. While specific agreement provisions allowed braceros to elect one of their own to represent them in attempts to settle disputes, growers generally refused to meet with worker representatives or negotiate with braceros. These migrants thus faced an irresolvable dilemma. Although they did engage in work stoppages, sit-down strikes, and other forms of solidarity, the contract explicitly forbade them from striking or from honoring local strikes of other workers by refusing to cross picket lines.[128] Moreover, their representative was not allowed to renegotiate substantive issues, such as salary, delineated in the official agreement. In turn, growers—and their agents, the foremen—denied braceros the best avenue for resolving disagreements. Given this institutionalized obstacle, the most powerful weapon that most braceros had was their feet—they left. According to Immigration and Naturalization Service statistics, "within one month" of the arrival of the first round of braceros in 1942, 15 percent had deserted.[129] Hernández Cano and the other striking braceros, by contrast, refused to "skip," a term that became a category of worker used by growers and officials alike. They, instead, attempted a class-based strategy, asserting their rights as workers. One such group of striking workers argued, in an October 1961 telegram to the Mexican ambassador, "We ten Mexican agricultural workers were brought to the United States with guarantees of fair treatment . . . [but] have received very bad treatment. . . . When we complained . . . we were told to be quiet or else be sent back to Mexico . . . [The growers' association] is now threatening to repatriate us against our will. We have refused to go back to the filthy conditions, cursing, and bad treatment at these camps, and we have refused to go back to Mexico before our contracts expire. We have some rights." As if the point needed clarification, the telegram continued: "Please help us get justice. Do not let them send us back to Mexico, and do not let them treat us like animals."[130] They appealed to the power of the Mexican ambassador—and thus, to a particular version of national identity and state authority—to get this justice.

Though this petition was ignored by then-ambassador Antonio Carrillo Flores, braceros' worker-based claim to rights was, over the course of the program, increasingly supported by U.S. union officials and labor activists. The need to unionize braceros was made clear in an extremely bitter 1947 California strike at DiGiorgio farms. While striking DiGiorgio domestic workers held out for over two years with unionists' support from around the country, their efforts failed precisely because braceros (and their undocumented brethren) were available, and because U.S. and Mexican officials were willing to ignore agreement regulations that stipulated that braceros' presence not influence the outcome of any strike. In the aftermath of the strike, steps were taken to insure that unionized farmworkers would never again be undercut by nonunion associates.[131] First, although U.S. officials refused, American Federation of Labor representatives advocated for a place on the bracero program negotiation team, asserting that it was essentially a labor agreement, and not an immigration one. Second, in 1950, the farmworker activist and scholar Ernesto Galarza organized local California braceros into a specifically bracero union. And third, Galarza established connections with local union organizers in Mexico. Together, seekers of a solidarity that transcended national boundaries took steps to inform workers of contract rights before they left and urge migrants to join Galarza's bracero union prior to departure. While such attempts were short-lived and largely unsuccessful, unions and braceros themselves still claimed that this arriving labor force was a force of workers and due workers' rights (see chapter 6). Growers rebutted this portrayal by painting farmwork, and thus those who did it, as part of an established paternalistic relationship, even as growers gained exorbitantly from the flexibility that a formal, wage-based relationship permitted: braceros then constituted around 95 percent of all tomato pickers, 90 percent of lettuce pickers, and 80 percent of citrus harvest workers.[132]

Braceros, however, gained little in this strategy that cast them as workers, due to entrenched relationships between the Mexican state and U.S. growers and to the program agreement itself. While some Mexican consular officials (such as those in Arkansas) relied on program mechanisms to resolve contract disputes, many others—specifically, in California and Texas, states with a history of abuse and discrimination of Mexican workers and the highest numbers of braceros—often had more to gain from maintaining a good relationship with growers than from supporting their countrymen. Usually they chose the more lucrative option.[133] "The Mexican bracero does not have an advocate or counsel [to resolve] the differences that arise between him and his employer," wrote Galarza. Mexican consulate and embassy staff, whom program agreements officially assigned such responsibility, were "even in worse condition than the Department of Labor in respect to adequacy of staff."[134] Braceros lived these effects. "No, Father, the Mexican consul is not my friend," said a bracero to a priest. "He is the friend of the boss."[135] Moreover, the remedies available to consular staff were constrained by the agreement's procedures. Not only was grievance-filing discouraged, it was often impossible, since men generally did not know how or where to file and were usually located a great distance from consular offices. On rare occasions when men did submit complaints against growers, a principal, though not the only, remedy available to bureaucrats was sending the offending braceros back to Mexico. Instead of pressuring growers to honor the letter and spirit of the agreement, administrators too often applied pressure on workers to either back down or return home.[136] "When you are sent back, you are sent back in a hurry," recalled one former bracero. "They give you the notice in the morning, or maybe at noon, or when you get back from work. You tie up your bundle and [you're gone]."[137] In the face of such explicit threats, men not ready to return to Mexico exercised the options of workers: they either gave in or "skipped" in search of a better job.

In the end, changes were occurring in barracks, bars, and fields. Braceros, finding little help from those charged with mediating disputes, banded together to resolve problems, be they bad food or poor living and working conditions. In the process, men came to see themselves as workers vis-à-vis foremen and bosses. Yet this class transformation was occurring outside of Mexico, and it was grounded in the strange diet and lack of female bodies of a distorted domestic sphere, the competition of the fields, and the pleasures of the bar. It was also constructed vis-à-vis a Mexico that was invented, negotiated, and incorporated in the United States. Created, in the process, was a particular workers' subjectivity, one not only used by braceros later to reclaim positions as patriarchs but made in relation to non-Mexican employers and fellow braceros *as Mexicans*. Thus, while the Mexican state had predicted and expected a class transformation that would turn peasants into yeoman farmers, the result of the bracero program was a gendered and racialized transnational proletarianization.

Conclusion

What, then, does this contrast of the spaces in which men lived, worked, and spent their leisure time reveal about the aims of the program, the expectations that braceros and the Mexican and U.S. governments had, and the resulting transformations? One implicit goal for the Mexican state, we should recall, was the metamorphosis of peasants into yeoman farmers who would be entrusted to produce sufficient food for the Mexican nation. Yet no former bracero I met or interviewed had small-scale agricultural production as his primary source of income. Rather, some men opened small stores or, like don Álvaro, barbershops. Others followed the internal migration stream to large cities within Mexico. Still others (maybe the majority) refused to give up the benefits that bracero migration brought, moving from stoop labor to jobs in factories or small businesses, before handing the migratory baton to children, nephews, cousins, and grandchildren—male and female. This transformation into small shop owners or national and transnational workers came in tandem with the reconsolidation of land in the hands of large Mexican agribusinesses, changes not unlike those that occurred earlier in the United States. The conversion of peasants into yeoman farmers promoted by the Mexican state was made highly unlikely, if not impossible, by the changing configuration of agriculture in Mexico, along with the nonagricultural background of many braceros selected. Exploring braceros' renderings of the barracks, bars, and fields shows the power of a subjectivity from which they drew reward, as well as the (proto)patriarchal privileges that they refused to relinquish. It also highlights the flexibility and resiliency of subjectivities under sustained attack, and the complexity and depth of the class transformation that the program accelerated.

Yet the class and other transformations occurring during the program, seen here, were not part of a strictly Mexican or U.S. context or logic. Rather, they were arose from broad, interrelated changes transpiring in both places. As we saw in the last chapter, south of the border, braceros had been celebrated and stoop labor jobs became prized opportunities (farm salaries in the United States were nine to sixteen times higher than prevailing wages in Mexico).[138] Yet the men had also confronted officials' greed and humiliating scrutiny.

This celebration collided with the conflicting messages workers received from and in the United States. In reception centers they showered off unwelcomed bugs and dirt, then rode in cattle trailers, not first-class buses, to lives of seclusion and grinding routine in all-male barracks, not family units. They spent days in the fields and nights doing women's work, while cut off from legitimate access to women's labor and bodies. They were repeatedly instructed to imbibe modern information and advanced agricultural techniques, even though the work and work sites were not unlike those in Durango. They bought radios and clothes, which, at home, had been out of their economic reach. And, in local festivals, they were called on to be Mexican.

The result was the creation of a transnational proletariat whose subjectivity as workers was grounded in processes and relationships within *and* outside national boundaries, and vis-à-vis gender and race. Acknowledging that this class transformation was multisited affords a unique window onto the production of subjectivity that was simultaneously Mexican and transnational. The celebratory and degrading messages made the border that the men traversed not a single line in the dirt but a continually reenacted point of crossing. And this border was always based on a racialized, classed, and gendered reading of Mexicanness that mapped these distinctions onto the dichotomy between modern and nonmodern. In both countries, then, braceros had been seen to live a nonmodern life. The supposedly fixed national border, between a so-called advanced country and one deemed synonymous with the past in the program's rhetoric and goals, functioned as a fictive and moving boundary that braceros experienced, probed, and repeatedly challenged. That is, while the border was to be ceremoniously crossed, in reality, practices of border, repeated throughout their time in the United States, made that crossing impossible.

Thus there were limits to braceros' claim to being modern workers. These limits resulted from an entrenched growers' narrative about the agricultural process, its actors, and its needs (which I examined in chapter 2). In the next chapter I explore domestic workers' refusal to relinquish claims to shaping this process. Analyzing the DiGiorgio strike and another by domestic migrants and their media coverage reveals the ways growers pitted braceros against U.S. workers. Domestic farmworkers were sundered from their bracero counterparts by growers' control of the narrative and its broad acceptance beyond the fields, which halted any movement toward a transnational farmworker class.

6

Strikes against Solidarity

Containing Domestic Farmworkers' Agency

"Sure, the work was hard . . . and the food, sometimes it was hard, too," said Ramón Avitia, in a moment of levity. He glanced around the barbershop at me and the four men on the bench, who nodded in agreement. "Growers," he continued in a somber tone, "didn't always respect the contract or pay us what it said. But it was hard to advocate for ourselves and our rights. We were far from home, didn't speak the language, and often had no one to go to for help. Mostly we braceros struggled alone."[1] Don Ramón's recollections coincided with an earlier vision: "In camp[s] . . . we had no names," said a man. "We were called only by numbers." These indignities had "to be tolerated in silence," added another man. "There is no one to defend our guarantees. In a strange country you feel timid—like a chicken in another rooster's yard."[2]

These comments convey alienation—from surroundings; from the labor process; from presumed class allies, domestic farmworkers—stemming from the near complete control growers exercised over the organization and quotidian details of the agricultural labor process. This control, maintained through a set of interrelated narratives, was enforced through the racial and national hierarchies of farm tasks (see chapter 2). And it took its toll. Braceros' emergent subjectivities as workers (not as the yeoman farmers the Mexican state wanted to create nor as the cheap, disposable foreigners sought by growers and U.S. state agents) readied them for a class struggle alongside fellow domestic farmworkers. Yet, as I show here, a farmworker class struggle that transcended race and nation was not to be for growers' discursive and material control over the labor configuration of industrial agriculture weakened domestic farmworkers' lateral class attachment to braceros.

I explore this weakening by examining two strikes—the 1947 strike against DiGiorgio Fruit Corporation, one of the largest growers in the state, and the 1961 lettuce workers strike—and the response of one set of important supporters, Catholic Church activists and religious leaders. While by 1961, there was more public and U.S. government support of farmworkers, the outcome in both cases was the same—the strikes failed. Analyzing these cases reveals that farmworkers and activists alike largely operated within the terms of debate that growers set.[3] Although they used different tactics and discursive strategies to fight for a more equitable distribution of agriculture's rewards, without directly attacking the logic of the fields, they could not accomplish their aim. Domestic farmworkers, still not seen as workers, would instead fight for privileges as Americans. Thus, we see the limitations of worker as a key node for farm laborer agency.

Strikes and Intra-Farmworker Conflict

After World War II, the U.S. economy expanded in response to unbridled consumer demand, and workers, whose push for better wages had been forestalled by government regulation, began to lobby for their fair share. Rank-and-file laborers filled the streets in shows of strength and discontent—in 1946 alone, 4.5 million workers engaged in labor actions, rattling industries from steel to coal and oil to trucking.[4] From business interests, there was much criticism of these actions. Charging workers with "irresponsibility," they pushed for passage of the Taft-Hartley Act (1947).[5] Although this legislation did not formally overturn the Wagner Act (1935) that guaranteed industrial workers' right to organize (farmworkers and domestic help were exempt), it severely constrained this right. By 1960 workers' high expectations were over, and the labor movement was in partial chaos.

Labor agitation in California contributed to this disarray. After the war, farmworkers, like their urban counterparts, pressured for wage increases. Leaders of the National Farm Labor Union tried to explain to urban workers the need to make common cause with agricultural laborers, excluded under the Wagner Act.[6] Farmworkers' frustration came to a head in 1947 in the nearly two-year-long strike at DiGiorgio Fruit Corporation.[7] The ranch's owner, Giuseppe DiGiorgio, was a major landowner in Kern County (northwest of the Imperial Valley). His fortune in real estate and other interests, according to the *Los Angeles Times*, "def[ied] the imagination."[8] The strike, ultimately galvanizing workers across the nation, had humble beginnings. Months of knocking on doors and conversations in fields brought 858 of DiGiorgio's more than 1,300 employees into National Farm Labor Union (NFLU) Local 218, making the area again California's heart of farmworker organizing.[9] These workers—overwhelmingly Anglos from Arkansas, Oklahoma, and the Midwest, along with Filipino Americans and Mexican Americans—sought better working conditions and ultimately coverage under Wagner. They sent DiGiorgio a letter asking for a meeting to discuss a ten-cent hourly wage increase, a seniority system, a grievance procedure, and recognition of the union as their collective bargaining agent.[10] The latter, said Fred West, then president of the Kern County Central Labor Council, was the most important demand: "If we get union recognition . . . we'll get money later. . . . We don't want a closed shop, or even a union shop. Just grievance machinery."[11] "Somebody ought to tell Joe DiGiorgio . . . to sit down with his fruit pickers," wrote "Inside Labor" columnist Victor Riesel, since the workers' primary demand was "a living wage."[12]

Mr. Joseph, as DiGiorgio was known, refused. Born in Corsica in 1874 and fond of recalling how he worked for $8 a month, this man of modest beginnings heralded his immigrant status; he had risen from New York fruit jobber to owner of the "largest individual farm in the United States." In a 1946 *Fortune Magazine* interview, DiGiorgio credited his success to an "early perception that the *small* grower and the city jobber who supplies the small retailer both require a free, open, and honest market." Ignoring the intervention of prosperous relatives, DiGiorgio attributed his good fortune to his "honor."[13] Intimated in this interview was his claim to being a small farmer, like the other so-called small farmers "from places like San Francisco, New York City, and Havana, Cuba," who sat on his company's board of directors.[14] This he insisted on, even though when the strike began his operation's yearly water usage was nearly 15 billion gallons—equal to five months of water for all of San Francisco—and revenue from his holdings (labeled one of the world's most profitable vertically integrated agricultural corporations) topped $18 million. Although he portrayed himself as a father figure to his workers, he refused to meet with them. There would be no strike on his twenty-two-thousand acre property, he insisted.[15]

DiGiorgio held that the labor action threatened his "right to cheap labor." While he contended that "fruit is nothing but water, labor, more labor and freight" delivered on a "meticulous timetable," the activist, scholar, and DiGiorgio strike organizer Ernesto Galarza claimed that the "favorable state of affairs" that emerged to meet that timetable, which elite growers had so long enjoyed, "was being threatened." The union, which crossed racial lines of segregated mess halls and housing, was training grassroots leadership and "provid[ing] the community with the machinery of democratic experience."[16] This budding democratic practice was a frightening development for Mr. Joseph and all California growers.

On October 1, 1947, DiGiorgio's shed and field workers, irrigators, and tractor drivers formed a picket line at the gates. In solidarity, 130 braceros laid down their tools, only to be forced back to work two days later, threatened with contract termination and immediate deportation by a local sheriff, a U.S. Department of Agriculture (DOA) employee, and the Mexican consul (telephoned by DiGiorgio himself).[17] Also siding with DiGiorgio was Edward Hayes, head of California's Farm Placement Service and a DiGiorgio stockholder.[18] Although the agreement expressly forbade braceros' participation in either side of a dispute, government officials "openly escorted" them across picket lines. The DOA official Norman Lepper saw this agreement irregularity as "living up to its contract with DiGiorgio." "It was our job," contended another government official, "to see that [braceros] got work."[19] To do otherwise, claimed an Associated Farmers representative, would allow any farmer with braceros to "have a picket line thrown around his farm" and his Mexican workers deported. "Who will do the stoop labor?" he added. "American workers won't."[20] Seven days after the strike's kickoff and a few days after braceros were returned to work, a DOA ruling ordered them out of the fields. This union victory was short-lived. Siding with DiGiorgio, a Mexican Embassy spokesperson told the *Bakersfield Californian* that there was "no dispute between [braceros] and the ranch. Conditions are favorable; they are satisfied with the pay and housing and meals and working conditions. They do not want to be moved away or to go on strike." Heralding this move, an area grower argued, "We need food production. . . . This is a poor time to pull a strike. . . . Every effort should be made to produce food and get it to market, [especially] where perishables are concerned."[21]

During the six subsequent weeks, while strikers faced mass arrests, aggressive company tactics, a drive-by shooting, and an influx of strikebreakers from around the country, braceros remained at work.[22] Their presence mitigated the effectiveness of the walkout and allowed DiGiorgio to bring crops to harvest, even as he recruited—and was lent by other worried local growers—additional braceros.[23] On November 17, 1947, only after multiple union protests and legal actions and over DiGiorgio's strident objections, Mexican migrants were removed from his fields to the thunderous applause of picketers. The specifics of the bracero agreement were ultimately honored, yet braceros, coerced into working, were removed only when their labor was no longer required; the crops had been harvested and shipped to market unimpeded.

Growers crippled the strike by charging domestic workers with being Communist supporters. Even before it began, DiGiorgio urged California State Senator Hugh M. Burns to investigate the NFLU for communist ties. While the State Senate Committee on Un-American Activities, of which Burns was a member, found no ties, the moment the strike erupted the committee questioned Frank Spector. When this local painter and admitted party member was asked whether the Communist Party supported the DiGiorgio strike, he replied, "The Communist Party supports all strikes of workers everywhere, and especially farm workers." Not surprisingly, the *Los Angeles Examiner*'s afternoon headline read: "Communists Support DiGiorgio Strike."[24] Though DiGiorgio's congressional friends supposedly unearthed documents that confirmed that more than eleven hundred workers had resisted the union's Communist ideology, an "independent check" by Richard E. Combs, the committee's chief counsel, "found no [such] influence."[25]

Denying such an assessment, members of NFLU 218 charged DiGiorgio with making false allegations. As evidence, they cited an interview he had given where he had blamed the union for "using 'communist maneuvers' in organizing his workers," a stance the union rejected. Clearly, he had told the paper, "this agitation is Communist-inspired by subversive elements."[26] Despite union attempts to dislodge the charge, it was made credible by growers' narrative portrayal of workers as lazy, unable to capitalize on farming's opportunities, and incapable of advocating for themselves. Since only outside influences and agitators could inspire normally indolent men to action, the very call for collective action was evidence of such intervention.

The union's legal maneuvers, which finally removed braceros from the fields, triggered a powerful backlash. In December 1947, shortly after the strike started, local growers toured DiGiorgio's property. They subsequently published findings in *A Community Aroused*, a forty-two page pamphlet containing an introduction by a successful grower and professional photos of modern workers' housing, a swimming pool, a spotless recreation center, and children happily playing games. Complete with black-and-white pictures and using large type for easy reading, the pamphlet indirectly refuted Local 218's principal contention: that workers were maltreated, underpaid, and lived in substandard housing. It likewise used payroll data and statistics on operating losses incurred for housing to buttress DiGiorgio's claim that no strike had ever occurred; rather, it was a simple "labor disturbance." It cast growers as "the pioneers who built Kern Country" and "made America great," a vivid contrast to the strikers as "agitators, crack-pots and left-wingers and associates of known Communists" and the NFLU as "power-greedy farm labor union organizers."[27] Robert DiGiorgio, Mr. Joseph's nephew and administrator for the corporation, labeled picketers as "pawns of 'outsiders.'" These were not merely poor workers, he said; strikers instead wanted to "make themselves the *bosses* of Kern County and eventually all California agriculture."[28] In using the term *boss* he insinuated that the union was neither democratic nor meritocratic, but akin to the Mob. As bosses of agriculture, these field hand bullies would be out of place. He suggested that, instead of respecting the accomplishments of hardworking growers, undeserving "agitators" and "crack-pots" were bullying those who deserved wealth, prominence, and their place in the agricultural hierarchy. The local press picked up the story of the pamphlet, which was distributed for free to win over the reading public.

With newspapers aligned with growers, the union could not rely on them to depict workers' plight sympathetically.[29] Instead, it wrote a strike song to generate solidarity from other workers and increase internal cohesion, and to publicize workers' troubles. Songs were first used in organizing activities in 1908, when the organizer J. H. Walsh orated to bindlemen who "tramped from farm to farm to harvest grain" toting their worldly possessions "in a blanket on [their] back" but found his voice drowned out by a Salvation Army band. He responded by putting together his own band, contending that singing roused the crowd and had positive "psychological effect upon the poor wage slave." Thus began the tradition of using songs to draw a crowd to "the interest of the working class." A year later, the Industrial Workers of the World would compile *The Little Red Songbook*, printing fifty thousand copies to be distributed at rallies and meetings.[30] Songs thus became part of labor movement culture.

During their heyday, strike songs and union ballads were sung before meetings and as strikers walked the picket line. They told the world why workers were fighting, despite often unfavorable odds. Singing enlivened dull moments of picketing, maintained discipline and morale, and generated solidarity. It also animated enthusiastic onlookers, who often shouted or clapped to the rhythm. Strikers and supporters would bring guitars and tambourines to the picket lines to raise spirits, a form of musical support vital especially when workers could not afford record players or did not have

Bracero Agency and Emergent Subjectivities

a steady source of electricity. Strike songs were works of art and tapped resonant images. Ernesto Galarza, whom NFLU President H. L. Mitchell named as the composer of the popular DiGiorgio anthem, drew images from John Steinbeck's 1939 novel *The Grapes of Wrath* and its 1940 film adaptation.[31] While their use might initially be thought to reflect Galarza's elite education and be too literary to resonate with workers, this novel was, in the words of the Steinbeck scholar Peter Lisca, a "phenomenon on the scale of a national event. It was publicly banned and burned by citizens, it was debated on national radio hook-ups; but above all, it was read."[32] Galarza then, utilized imagery popular with working folk that provided resonance beyond the fields as a means to publicize the strikers' plight. The anthem, moreover, reminds us that the labor movement was also a cultural movement, with its own songs, stories, and art.[33]

> Pickets standing on the line
> Looking down the country road,
> Saw a lonesome stranger coming
> And he said his name was Joad.
>
> Now the stranger stood besides us
> And his face was pale and thin,
> Said he'd like to join the Union
> So we said we'd let him in.
>
> Thursday night he came to meeting
> And he raised his snowy head,
> With a voice like Resurrection
> Spoke, and this is what he said.
>
> "There's a fence around Creation,
> There's a mortgage on the sun,
> They have put electric meters
> Where the rivers used to run."
>
> "God Almighty made the valley
> For a land of milk and honey,
> But a corporation's got it
> For to turn it into money."
>
> —"Ballad of the DiGiorgio Strikers," by Ernesto Galarza

Of import here are several images and themes. The first is Tom Joad, the highly recognizable main character of *The Grapes of Wrath*: the "lonesome stranger," "pale and thin," weary from his cross-country journey. Like the strikers themselves, this white man, "with a voice like Resurrection," did not deserve such treatment; his was not mobility—a choice—but forced movement. He, as they, was being alienated (in the Marxist sense) from nature, the song's second set of images. God-given lands and open spaces, which farmers had worked and people enjoyed, were being harnessed by corporations. The ballad's use of imagery of God and nature was a deliberate antidote to the charge that strikers were communists; it was intended to purge any hint of atheism, reestablish the strikers as religious, and make their cause righteous and legible to the wider public. It also served to highlight the claim that the strikers were former farmers, who had lost their lands, not longtime farmworkers. This legibility, built on their belief in God and appreciation and knowledge of nature, whitened these workers, while distancing themselves from and racializing as foreign those whose movements God would not justify.[34]

The third critical image is that of the corporation. Its position vis-à-vis God and creation furthered the claim that those working the land were more closely connected to humanity and reality; they were "civilization's caretakers."[35] The strikers, and not the corporations extracting a profit from what God created, respected nature and all living things. They sought a return to a vision that "idealized rural life untouched by the ravages of capitalist enterprise."[36] That is, these former farmers turned farmworkers valued hard work and individualism, and exhibited these qualities. Unlike corporations, whose predatory use of land and water was backed by the government, they relied on their own sweat and stamina to eke out a living and succeed.

Notably missing from the ballad is a theme central to Steinbeck's novel and the film adaptation: the family. Here the union—a fraternal, rather than paternal, organization whose bonds transcended kinship ties—substituted for (and reconfigured) the family. In Steinbeck's novel, the explicitly biological paternalist organization that anchored the Joads became a larger, more inclusive community whose bonds were based on the commitment of each member to the whole. In the song strikers appealed to the union, a specifically fraternal entity whose members were united by that fraternal bond which provided fortification and strength as they waged their struggle.[37] The ballad condensed a key theme in the novel: humans' inhumanity to their own, seen in the devastation faced by the Joads and other migrants that was not inflicted by God or nature, but by poverty, greed, and class inequality. This poverty resulted from humans' refusal to recognize the humanity of others and treat all with respect. This plight could, however, be solved by humans as well, workers argued.

While *The Grapes of Wrath* was indeed a popular reference, workers' use of its imagery was not unintentional. When it was first published, elite growers throughout California were indignant. Agriculturalists in DiGiorgio's own Kern County not only held a book-burning party and brought about its two-year ban from local libraries; they also used their clout to bar the movie version from area theaters. Growers were even alleged to have offered almost a third of a million dollars to the person who could lock "the book and the book rights in a heavy safe and row [them] out on the Pacific Ocean and dump the whole thing overboard."[38] In using a medium over which growers lacked control to tell a story in images known to rile them, strikers implicitly challenged the agricultural status quo, despite limited media access to do so.

Strikers would continue various attempts to disseminate their messages. Not only did the union leader H. L. Mitchell publicize the strike in an opportune ABC radio broadcast to the American Federation of Labor (AFL), the Hollywood Film Council, an AFL member union, filmed *Poverty in the Valley of Plenty*, a documentary about the strike that implicitly challenged *A Community Aroused*.[39] It featured close-ups of campsites whose "landscape is done with junk" and of workers with ragged clothes and hollowed eyes. The narrator spoke of the multimillion-dollar industry's denial to its employees of "rights and opportunities . . . granted to all other industrial workers," which farmworkers had long argued they endured.[40] The background track was a rendition of the strike song.[41] Although the documentary did not mention DiGiorgio, his corporation, or the strike by name, the allusions were unmistakable, for all three were then national news. Unfortunately, ventured Galarza, *Poverty in the Valley of Plenty* "did not draw a sufficiently sharp line between the generalizations about the industry and the specific statements on the strike," a lack of distinction for which Galarza and the NFLU would pay dearly.[42] Though the union had legal precedent on its side, DiGiorgio filed a libel suit at the very moment his friends on the U.S. House Committee on Education and Labor were holding hearings in Bakersfield, California.[43] The committee uncovered no evidence of libel, but the notoriety still weakened union support. Not satisfied, DiGiorgio demanded an official reprimand. This he received in an appendix to the *Congressional Record* signed by, among others, Richard M. Nixon.[44] This still did not appease DiGiorgio. He sued and countersued Galarza and the NFLU for more than fifteen years, depleting the union's small treasury.[45] In the end, a filmic portrayal of bucolic farm life substituted for one of workers' abuse, closing off one avenue to contesting growers' narratives.[46]

The strike, then one of the longest in California history, lasted for thirty months, during which DiGiorgio used financial and political muscle to starve strikers into submission. Though agricultural workers were not covered by the 1935 Wagner Act's industrial labor protections—an exemption for which growers like DiGiorgio had pushed—his lawyers still argued that strikers were subject to provisions of Taft-Hartley (1947) that had modified Wagner's reach. Ironically, then, workers unable to benefit from Wagner were bound to act in accordance with Taft-Hartley's limitations.[47] Though the court initially found for DiGiorgio, the case was reversed on appeal, a reversal that came long after the harvest was over.

The strike officially collapsed because DiGiorgio had access to another source of labor—braceros—and because of pressure on the union from Congress and the California state Senate Committee on Un-American Activities. More fundamentally, it was undone by the organizational structure, temporary nature, and narratives of agricultural employment, and by the willingness of U.S. local, state, and federal employees to accept those narratives and prioritize elite agriculturalists' needs over those of workers. Resisting this joint government-grower onslaught, the NFLU leader H. L. Mitchell reminded farmworkers that they were "fighting a long-term war, not just one battle."[48] Yet the union's dearth of resources and inability to force DiGiorgio to the bargaining table would make an ongoing labor war hard to wage.

While workers struck for better wages and working conditions, at the core they were fighting for dignity, respect, and recognition: dignity for themselves as workers, respect for their work, and recognition for their contributions to U.S. society. Growers, in labeling farmhands "agitators, crackpots and left-wingers and associates of known Communists," delegitimized these claims.[49] Using the rhetoric of democracy and patriotism, farmworkers fought growers' allegations head on. They were poor but not unpatriotic, outside the nation, or a threat to it with alien—that is, communist—discourses.[50] Rather, organizing and expressing solidarity were workers' unique forms of "doing" democracy, and dignity, manifested in better wages and working conditions, was linked to a broader vision of freedom. In so doing, they challenged the increasingly entrenched consumption-based version of democracy.[51] The union, contended a striker, was their "democratic way."[52]

Backing for the strike came from across the country. Unions caravanned supplies of food, clothes, and cash to strikers; the AFL urged members to donate canned goods or money, while some unions unlawfully boycotted "hot" DiGiorgio fruit and wine.[53] A strike support committee of distinguished citizens and religious leaders even formed in New York.[54] Despite this outpouring of aid, Local 218 members wised up to what farm laborers before them had learned: that they would never win while battling the soaring number vying for work, on the one hand, and an extremely powerful opponent with clout and deep pockets, on the other.[55] Had braceros been able to align themselves with U.S. domestic workers by walking—and staying—off the job, the strike trajectory might have changed. Had Mexican officials immediately demanded that braceros be pulled from the fields, as the agreement stipulated, the balance of power might have swung toward workers and DiGiorgio might have been forced to negotiate. Moreover, the program's enforcement mechanisms, together with a lack of government funds, made investigations of any complaint sporadic at best, and theoretical at worst. Neither the Mexican Embassy nor local consuls insisted that U.S. federal and local officials honor the agreement, most likely because consuls had entrenched relations to growers whose support brought lucrative rewards. Moreover, despite the Mexican negotiators' struggle to enact strong agreement provisions, migrant remittances, then the country's third-largest source of hard currency, provided Mexican communities with an infusion of cash, assuaging local hunger, poverty, and the likelihood of protest, and the Mexican state with a reason to continue the program.[56]

At the heart of allegations leveled by DiGiorgio and fellow growers against strikers was that they were acting collectively—the exact behavior in which these agriculturalists, through powerful associations, were engaged. Growers had collaborated to publish *A Community Aroused*, to lobby influential friends in state government and in Washington, to investigate the union, to push local law enforcement to arrest striking workers, and to pressure the courts to rule against the strikers. They, acting in concert, claimed the position of self-made community pioneers, while dismissing workers' collective action as a telltale sign of susceptibility to alien—i.e., communist—ideology. Growers, as individuals, were honorable men and valuable members of the nation, while workers, acting as a unit and succumbing to a foreign rhetoric of class conflict, did not possess the fortitude of character for national inclusion. Twenty years earlier, growers had lobbied to deny farmworkers the protections, social security, and minimum-wage guarantees extended industrial laborers—*not* because farmworkers acted collectively, but because their relationship with growers was not a modern employer-employee relationship but rather an unmodern patron-peasant one.[57] Strike leaders countered this twin depiction by describing agriculture as a modern enterprise and themselves as modern workers who, like their industrial counterparts, should be recognized as members of the nation.

Ultimately, DiGiorgio won the media war by adhering to the established narrative line: that he respected the logic of individualism with its refusal of government help, that as a small farmer he embodied U.S. values and traditions, and that as an immigrant he had followed the quintessentially American story of hard work and progress. He concomitantly downplayed the influence of friends who had delayed the removal of braceros from fields and had even lent him more. Also minimized was the judicial finding that held workers governed by legislation from which they could not benefit, and the congressional and state investigations into the union itself. That is, DiGiorgio reiterated his adherence, like that of other growers, to the U.S. "foundational fiction" of hard work and self-reliance, while proclaiming as out of place the strikers who invested in alien values.[58]

Compared to DiGiorgio, the January 1961 Imperial Valley lettuce pickers' strike affected many more braceros and occurred when federal officials were no longer resolutely on the side of growers. Yet, as with the DiGiorgio strike, officials did not mitigate the effects of braceros' presence, even though growers provoked the strike in the first place. Told by the California Department of Employment that all farmworkers, domestic and foreign, had to be paid the same, the Imperial Valley Farmers Association (IVFA) reduced the hourly wage. Domestic laborers, formerly making between two and three dollars an hour, found their wage decreased to ninety cents. Some union officials, reluctant to call a strike, recognized that farmworkers were "in a fighting mood" and that no small growers would be hit by the strike. Rather, those who would feel the pressure—the valley's large ranches—were highly dependent on braceros, a dependence the union sought to contain.[59] Besides, capitulating to this wage reduction would indicate union weakness. The IVFA manager Edward F. Hayes, formerly the director of the state Farm Placement Service, predicted the union's reaction, telling the audience at a Kiwanis lunch that they should "watch out for 'flying union goons' in the winter."[60]

The Agricultural Workers Organizing Committee (AWOC), the NFLU's successor, chose the peak of harvest as the moment to stage resistance to this wage reduction and publicize the plight of the nearly ten thousand lettuce workers, eight thousand of whom were braceros.[61] Like DiGiorgio, affected growers refused to negotiate, instead lobbying local, state, and national officials for rescue; they even contended that local farmhands had benefited from the braceros' presence. Describing the short ninety-day window to harvest winter lettuce, strikers, they claimed, had put them in a vise. This window, said one grower, "makes the stock market seem tame by comparison." A single work stoppage, concluded a *Time* magazine reporter, could "ruin a season."[62] Although growers' contentions were featured in extensive radio, television, and newspaper coverage of both sides, their grip was weakening. Even California Governor Edmund Brown spoke of balancing the needs of growers and farmworkers. While "agriculture . . . [was] the greatest wealth producer [the state] ha[d]," he said, and government officials sought to ensure its continued prosperity, they were "interested in human beings, too."[63]

From the strike's inception, braceros were the focal point. Union leaders, knowing that getting braceros out of fields where domestic workers were striking hinged on official recognition of the strike, pushed California's Department of Employment for certification.[64] Growers, in contrast, argued that foreign workers could not be removed.[65] Appealing to the *Los Angeles Times*, growers claimed that "the Imperial Valley was 'peaceful' and there was no threat to the safety of Mexican nationals."[66] Losing the six hundred bracero workers at this point in the harvest, said the article, would push growers to either "recogniz[e] the union and [pay] higher wages to domestic workers or [see] their crops rot in the fields."[67] As in the DiGiorgio strike, unaffected growers collectively rallied to the aid of those hit by the strike by loaning hundreds of their own braceros to affected ranches. Harvesting continued.[68]

Three hundred union loyalists reacted to this donation of braceros. According to *Time* magazine, while growers staked "No Trespassing" signs in fields and domestic farmworkers targeted the Farm Placement office for failing to hire them, a motorcade toured the area and promoted the strike.[69] Carrying signs that read "Bracero, Pide Tu Libertad" (Demand your freedom), union members staged a sit-down demonstration outside a bracero camp to block workers from going to the fields; thirty-eight strikers "beat up the camp cook and two braceros with broom handles" at another camp, threatening to set it on fire. "The melee," concluded the reporter on the scene, "was broken up by a flying squad from the sheriff's office, which later stormed into a meeting at union headquarters and arrested six union leaders." Although growers armed themselves with firearms, "searched for strikers[,] and communicated by radio," they avoided stirring up further trouble "lest the Mexican government withdraw all [local] braceros."[70]

The AWOC demanded that the Department of Labor and the state Board of Agriculture remove all seventeen hundred braceros from the fields and return them to Mexico, in compliance with the agreement. As the AWOC's Norman Smith had argued in an earlier strike, "They have to give [domestic migrants] the jobs. The law says so." During a work stoppage, he argued, "federal law prevents Mexican [braceros] from working on that farm."[71] Union representatives charged that braceros, then used as strikebreakers, were being put in harms' way in grower's attempts to obstruct picketing.[72] The state Agricultural Board, in a 3–2 decision, supported farmworkers' right to organize and declined to rule against strikes during the harvest.[73] Governor Brown urged a "peaceful settlement," encouraging growers to offer better wages that would draw U.S. workers, inherently undercutting growers' contention that domestic laborers had benefited from braceros' presence.[74] Acquiescing to the Mexican government's request, Brown ordered that braceros be removed for their safety and to honor the agreement.[75]

Despite the union's momentary victory, growers ultimately squeezed out another win, this time with the help of President John Kennedy's labor secretary, Arthur Goldberg. Goldberg, himself a veteran of the labor movement, refused to promptly remove braceros from fields as the agreement demanded.[76] While he eventually ruled to withdraw them, his narrow ruling, charged the AWOC organizer Smith, allowed growers to harvest their crop with a reduced workforce, blunting the strike's effectiveness.[77] Even Goldberg admitted that he deliberately delayed their removal. "I stalled on the [Mexican government's] request in the interest of the local economy and all the people involved."[78] After losing the strike, the AWOC immediately focused unionization attempts further south in the state, but these also failed. Like organizers before them, the committee concluded that unionization would only succeed by eliminating the bracero program and terminating the ready supply of replacement labor. The agreement's prohibition against braceros' use as strikebreakers, wrote Henry Anderson to Ernesto Galarza, "was never meant to be taken seriously"; using them as such was, in fact, the agreement's very goal.[79] Although AWOC and federal officials both claimed to protect braceros' welfare, neither sufficiently advocated for them.[80] The agreement's only option was men's deportation, which no one wanted—neither Mexican migrants, nor growers, nor state officials. They therefore became pawns in California's ongoing labor contest. The least powerful actors in the struggle, braceros were forced to remain in the fields, even if they supported the strikers. They could not exercise rights as workers.

Growers and their minions often echoed the logic that braceros aided both growers and labor. Domestic workers, alleged A. R. Duarte, manager of the San Joaquin Farm Production Association, a growers' organization, were "protected from wage depression" because the Farm Placement Service was required to conduct a survey of each area's and crop's prevailing rates before braceros could come.[81] Wage rates for braceros were then set accordingly, acting as a bulwark against downward wage pressure. Refuting this as absurd, Galarza argued that state officials, long in the pockets of growers, had not even conducted such surveys. His letter to the editors of the *Stockton Record* insisted that growers' association members had merely met and collectively set the wage scale for the crop. This wage was then sent to Edward Hayes, chief of the Farm Placement Service, who certified the association the very next day for 750 braceros to pick carrots at the same wage the growers had agreed to. In closing his letter, Galarza implored the newspaper to bring to light "all the ways in which the prevailing wage," a presumed indicator of an open process and barrier to wage fixing, could "be manipulated."[82]

Despite attempts by Galarza and others to publicize government collusion with growers, agricultural narratives, which cast growers as held hostage to farmworkers' capricious demands, still carried sufficient weight, especially during strikes, when such imagery counted even more. Growers couched themselves as "far more vulnerable" to labor actions than industrial employers precisely because of the fixed crop schedule. This supposed vulnerability meant that farmworker unions would result not in shared power between workers and growers, but rather the "submission of *farmers* to labor union *leaders*." In this inverted hierarchy, these agricultural pioneers would be out of place.[83] Growers claimed they were not against unionization per se, just farmworker unionization.[84] Still, in labeling farmworkers' collective action unnatural and an inversion of farming's natural order, growers not only reinforced the notion that they were successful because they were better and more deserving farmers but also denied laborers the same right to act collectively on which they themselves relied.

At the core of these strikes was an entrenched grower narrative that mapped job and economic status onto a supposedly natural ethnic and racial hierarchy that seemingly permitted the most perseverant and independent to succeed while justifying a system in which the least unsuccessful were forced to move in search of work. This narrative, then, confirmed agriculture as a fluid class system that allowed for upward mobility and faulted farmworkers for languishing in the lower class. Unions, in countering this depiction, configured all forms of solidarity as expressions of workers' rights and their fight a workers' form of democracy. Yet worker for them remained a nationally bound term. Program stipulations, which denied braceros the chance to act as workers in concert with domestic farmhands, had a priori severed this class tie. Without attacking this nation-based framework head-on, domestic workers succumbed to and reproduced the growers' narrative and undermined the possibility of building a farmworker class movement. Braceros, refused the right to participate in unions, were denied the claim to being workers, in which the possibility of being modern was anchored. This denial fundamentally affected both groups: braceros were made superfluous in the struggle *and* instantiated as foreign competition and backward (or at least not fully modern), while domestic farmhands of the same class were similarly deprived of this title and its benefits. In the end, what prevailed in a setting that might have generated a *transnational* narrative by farmworkers of *inter*-class conflict was a naturalized grower account of *intra*-workforce competition grounded in *national* ethnic and racial divisions, which marginalized both groups as alien and unmodern.

The Limitation of Farmworker Agency

Strikes brought a surge in interest in domestic and foreign farmworkers. They also changed the nature of church, largely Catholic, involvement. Early on, the Department of Agriculture asked priests and lay ministers to address the effects of migration on braceros' spiritual health.[85] Initially this meant organizing programs for the Día de Guadalupe, a Mexican holiday celebrating the nation's patron saint, including processions with songs and guitars, and conducting special masses in Spanish.[86] However, with more contact, activists began to see the bracero program not as an isolated problem but as part of "the bulwark of an immoral system of agriculture."[87] Recognizing the interconnections between Mexican American poverty, the exploitation of braceros, and traffic in undocumented migrants, Archbishop Robert E. Lucey rallied more than two thousand priests, nuns, and lay ministers from around the Southwest into the Catholic Council for the Spanish Speaking to find "Christian solutions" to these systemic and interconnected concerns.[88] When asked by a reporter to explain the committee's focus on nonspiritual concerns, Father James L. Vizzard, director of the Washington office of the National Catholic Rural Life Conference, argued that "a minimum of material security and well-being is required before the spiritual can flourish." The "spiritual welfare of souls," he insisted, demanded social justice.[89]

This orientation toward justice would continue. During the debate on a Department of Labor agricultural minimum-wage proposal for domestic farmworkers akin to the measure covering braceros, Reverend Julian Kieser of Kern County's Council of Churches backed the increase. Citing a survey that indicated that the average California farmworker earned a mere $1,450 in 1950, Kieser argued that farmhands were "living in squalor on inadequate diets . . . because of low income." While religious leaders conceded that a "rise" in farm wages might result in a small increase in the cost of food, "no injustice is done to consumers if they are asked to pay a price which allows [farmworkers] a decent wage and [growers] a fair profit."[90] In response, spokespeople contended that growers only had the best interests of farmhands in mind; a minimum wage, they said, would hurt farmworkers in the long run because it would push growers out of the state and shrink the number of jobs. The Catholic press rejected these contentions. Behind a language of burden, fairness, and concern for farmworkers, suggested *The Catholic Worker*, was the reality that domestics could not accept the low wages that growers offered braceros; these "family breadwinners"—men of color and poor whites—would not compete against "the underpaid 'men only' imported from Mexico." According to the article, some domestic field hands were forced onto "relief rolls, despite the animus this arouse[d] on the part of local taxpayers and taxpayers' associations, who brand[ed] them as lazy and shiftless."[91]

Catholic advocates thus linked the bracero program to U.S. farmworkers' fewer economic possibilities and their lack of moral compass, yet they also saw it as bad for braceros, for men, whose wives remained in Mexico, were "deni[edl] . . . normal family life" and turned to prostitutes. This "denial," contended the Catholic *Monitor*, forced them to live "abnormal lives," furthering their "social segregation" and "corruption."[92] Not questioning men's need for sex, priests asserted that braceros drowned "the drudgery of work and the monotony of camp life in drunkenness, prostitution, and gambling." The program, they said, brought about "a terrible *moral* situation," both for braceros and for families in Mexico. Many became "demoralized" and forever "incapable of fulfilling the responsibilities of family life"—code for threats to heterosexuality;[93] often they abandoned families. One priest who had followed the program for eight years "noticed a change in the men." When they first arrived, they were "unspoiled." They sent "money home faithfully." But gradually, he said, "they begin to break down."[94] For church officials and activists, this vice-infested isolation could not be "ameliorate[d by] . . . pastoral care alone"; it required a material solution.[95] The entire situation, they contended, constituted a U.S. "national badge of infamy."[96]

The sacrifice of "normal family relations," which precipitated men's moral breakdown, was not a concern of church activists alone, but part of a more general anxiety about the pervasiveness of homosexuality. With the Cold War, homosexuals, like their constant communist pairing, were imagined as everywhere, even infiltrating the United States by crossing the border disguised as Mexican peasants. In largely isolated, unregulated camps, where only men resided and where few but priests and the unsavory would tread, communist agents would exploit men's need for sex to lure the unsophisticated into an unnatural and un-American—communist or gay—life. If the United States allowed this incursion and the barbaric farmworker conditions that encouraged it, what did this say about the morality of the country, especially as the Cold War pitted U.S. social and economic systems against Soviet ones?[97]

Attacking the program as bad for domestic and foreign farmhands, Catholic activists condemned the farmworker conditions and labor structure that pitted U.S. citizen against foreigner. What began as an approach to end the program based on both issues soon became, says the historian Gina Marie Pitti, a campaign against the general immorality of industrial farming and the dangers that it precipitated.[98] It was dangerous to foreign workers because it risked their physical and spiritual health and perverted their nature; it was dangerous to domestics because the presence of foreigners undercut the economic livelihoods of U.S. citizens; it was dangerous to the U.S. nation because some men were "Communists, saboteurs, and troublemakers"—ideological radicals and homosexuals;[99] and it was immoral because the conditions in which men lived bordered on slavery. This specter of slave labor racialized the workforce and tainted it as nonmodern. It left only victims in its wake.

Despite the good intentions of church activists, in the end, the frame they used to attack the organization of agriculture—immorality—contained the scope of their influence, for only religious voices, the arbiters of conscience, were able to speak in this moral register. Moreover, domestics and braceros were never put forth as capable of bettering their own lives, nor were they taught to speak for themselves—instead, they were victims who needed outside help.[100] As such, they could never be modern workers or part of a modern nation. In the end, then, for farmworkers little changed. By challenging the agricultural system on moral grounds, church activists left grower narratives intact. They too fell victim to this discursive control.

International Competitiveness versus Intraclass Coordination

While religious activists critized the program's immorality, NFLU organizers railed against the use of "temporary" foreign labor when U.S. workers were available.[101] After losing the DiGiorgio strike, the union regrouped, and by 1949 meetings drew hundreds of unemployed workers, who denounced wages, which had fallen significantly due to increasing labor supply, along with growers' continued preference for braceros. With nearly three-quarters of local residents unemployed, domestic farmhands were "extremely bitter" about this preference, concluded Ernesto Galarza.[102] Union organizers were "not opposed to anyone," a NFLU radio program assured listeners. "Our union is made up of racial and religious groups of many different colors and creeds. . . . [Our goal is] to win our jobs back and to care for our fellow farm workers of American background, before we allow temporary imported labor into our area."[103] A 1952 strike song even cautioned against "tak[ing the striker] for the rival of the contracted bracero."[104] While commendable, this supposed openness did little to combat deep resentment against braceros, and foreign workers more generally. Few rank-and-file domestic farmworkers fully appreciated braceros' inability to honor strikes, and many blamed them for lower wages. Plus, locals were still fuming, one observer said, because when they had gone off to war braceros had "moved in on their girl friends and sisters."[105] Indeed, the existence of a song entitled "El bracero y la pachuca" hinted at the prevalence of these relationships.[106] "Fifteen years ago," said a worker, "you could work in the vineyards for $1.00 an hour. . . .

You could live on that. Now [braceros] are doing that work for 85 cents an hour. . . . I think it is best . . . if the [braceros] go their way, and we go our[s]."[107] For these locals, the struggle was an economic one partitioned by nation; braceros were national interlopers, not brothers in a working-class fight.

Galarza, however, imagined an alliance built around class solidarity. Braceros, he noted, had initially honored the DiGiorgio and other strikes, despite threats of repatriation. Moreover, Mexico had a strong union tradition, and earlier cross-border flows of labor and ideas had sparked labor activism in the Southwest and California specifically and helped ignite a Mexican American civil-rights push during the New Deal.[108] Galarza saw braceros as inheritors of these traditions, a force to be brought into the union. The question was how to build a binational organization and foster the lateral attachments that grower narratives had precluded. Braceros saw the need for such an organization: not only did more than five hundred members of the independent National Alliance of Braceros from Mexico (Alianza Nacional de Braceros de México), an organization formed in the late 1940s, seek to join NFLU Local 218, but twelve other braceros had enrolled in the union, only to be told by a contractor when they sought to attend a meeting "that if they persisted," they would be "deported."[109] During the intense 1951–52 organizing drive, union broadcasts "inform[ed] braceros . . . of their rights." Even though messages helped convinced them to join the union, the Associated Farmers' response—trucking in undocumented workers from Mexico—ultimately made it more difficult for all union workers to find work.[110]

Not to be outmaneuvered, Galarza escalated his binational strategy. He sent staff to organize the Imperial Valley, then home to more than six thousand domestic farmworkers, as well as five thousand braceros and an estimated ten thousand undocumented workers. As the NFLU leader H. L. Mitchell remembered it, the "organizers got the cooperation of the Mexican unions across the border"; this allowed them to "successfully organize practically all . . . domestic workers." After 1954 the United States–Mexico Trade Union Committee, consisting of Mexican labor organization representatives and the AFL-CIO, was created to combat worker exploitation. "Workers of both nations," it contended, "w[ould] always stand solidly together."[111] Mexican unions now readied braceros prior to their journeys, telling them to get in contact with the NFLU when they arrived.[112] Galarza and Mitchell also demanded that labor representatives participate in negotiating the bracero agreement. "Vital interests of the workers of both countries," concluded a

United States–Mexico Trade Union Committee member, "ought not be excluded from the negotiations. . . . We . . . urge [the U.S. government] to grant organized labor full participation."[113] Despite insistence, no labor representative was ever permitted to join.

Not surprisingly, U.S. growers resisted unions of domestic and bracero farmworkers as well as an official union presence at the agreement-negotiating table. While Mexican negotiators "accepted the principle," opposition came from the Mexican Ministry of the Interior. A union press release maintained that this ministry was "preparing legal action to make it a crime for Mexican workers to cooperate with the American Federation of Labor in the struggle to . . . raise living standards in this hemisphere." Bureaucrats of both governments, said Galarza, "harass[ed]" and "intimidate[d] the friends of United States labor," specifically the National Alliance of Braceros. Affiliated with the AFL through an "inter-American regional confederation of free trade unions," the Alliance had attempted to engage in collective bargaining on behalf of braceros. While negotiators from both countries were engaged in closed program meetings, he contended, the Alliance, the Railroad Brotherhoods, and the AFL were working "to break through th[is] curtain of censorship" and counter the "intergovernmental drive to lower working standards in every trade and craft."[114]

Galarza valued the Alliance's partnership, for he saw the same forces at work in the loss of U.S. farmworkers' jobs, braceros' exploitation, and the influx of undocumented migrants. Yet he also understood that one small union, even one affiliated with the AFL, was not strong enough to counter these forces. He began talking to other Mexican unions, and on March 2, 1951, the NFLU signed an agreement with the Unión de Trabajadores Agrícolas del Valle de Mexicali, a member of the official Mexican labor confederation, the Confederación de Trabajadores Mexicanos.[115] Reprisals, however, came quickly. Not long after the NFLU-Unión pact, the wife of the Unión's president was detained by the Mexican police and "questioned about her husband's connections with the AFL Farm Labor Union"; he was later taken into custody, "charged with . . . conspiracy to organize Mexican farmworkers in cooperation with the NFLU." As H. L. Mitchell explained in a letter to George Rundquist of American Civil Liberties Union, the NFLU was afraid he would be "railroaded to prison or murdered." "Years ago when the rights of individual workers in our own country, and even other countries, were threatened, organizations, such as yours, often were able to do something to prevent trouble. Can you do something about this case?" Mitchell asked.[116]

This was the contested ground into which braceros came. Despite the NFLU's methodical work and a small crew of domestic and foreign farmhands ready to support better wages for all, little would come of this coordination. Braceros could not band together with local farmworkers to form a union. They could not join strikes or support them by refusing to cross picket lines. Gestures of solidarity brought state threats of deportation braceros did not want. And having been denied these labor rights, they were seen by their domestic counterparts only as foreign competitors and the cause of lower wages, rather than as workers and part of the same farmworker class. Ultimately, this denial made the Mexican state's investment in the program ironic. On the one hand, Mexican authorities officially publicized it as a way to modernize first braceros and then the nation; on the other, by restricting migrants' ability to act and see themselves as workers in conjunction with other workers—the very purpose of unions—officials not only perpetuated an intraclass and nation- (and race-) based conflict, they also limited braceros' chance to act as agents for themselves. Unable to act collectively or on their own behalf, braceros could never fully achieve the status of modern agents that their migration had promised to bring.

The Possibility of Change

Change on a few fronts was coming. The consolidation of the United States's international position in the aftermath of World War II exposed the disjuncture between its democratic rhetoric and the domestic experiences of non-whites, making urgent the need to portray citizenship as racially blind.[117] This disjuncture, which helped frame political rhetoric from the administration of Harry S. Truman through those of John F. Kennedy and Lyndon Johnson, provided a focal point around which to mobilize toward ending discrimination and opening citizenship.[118] The result was an explosion of civil-rights organizations and worker activism over wages that had stagnated during the war. Though California farmworkers' wages still approached those of southern sharecroppers, news reports on the DiGiorgio strike and subsequent farmworker actions, along with later policy shifts and an expanding economy, brought the extreme conditions under which farmhands of all races and nationalities labored to the nation's attention.[119]

Lingering below the surface in farmworker actions and other labor struggles, more generally, was the question of what and who "America" was. Was it, as had been portrayed during World War II, a modern democracy in which all citizens had pulled together to defeat fascism? If so, would everyone reap the benefits of this global win? Were farmworkers, still denied the labor protection offered their industrial counterparts and, thus, outside the bounds of the modern, to be included in the rewards? Or were they, despite legal citizenship, to remain excluded? In short, how did a country that imagined itself as democratic and modern reconcile this poverty and exploitation? After the DiGiorgio strike, the nation began to question farmworkers' place in this vision. While not framed in these terms, a scathing report issued in 1951 by President Truman's Commission on Migratory Labor came to two overarching conclusions: first, that domestic laborers could not compete economically with braceros, as the presence of the latter depressed agricultural wages, even for so-called skilled jobs reserved for domestics; and second, that despite complaining that the program was unworkable, growers found braceros preferable to U.S. workers. The temporariness of braceros' contracts made them easier to discipline, since so-called agitators—anyone pushing for better working conditions—could be readily deported. "[Men] who complain," one priest put it, "are always threatened, called Communist agitators, and sent home."[120] Although the commission exposed the range, degree, and ways in which all farmworkers were exploited, it did not propose an immediate end to the program or a legislative solution with wage guarantees and the bureaucratic mechanisms to enforce them. Rather, it lamely mentioned that "future efforts" should abolish the "dependence on foreign labor" and instead prioritize farm jobs for domestic workers.[121]

A deep discussion of these workers' place in a modern democracy would not emerge until the early 1960s, although it was foreshadowed by the agricultural economist Harry Schwartz nearly twenty years earlier. "Our farm labor program has been formulated and administered," he wrote in 1943, "with an almost complete absence of farm worker participation." Such a situation, he contended, was wholly "undemocratic."[122] Still, the report by the president's commission intimated the conundrum surrounding migrant workers. Migrants, said the report, "move restlessly over the face of the land [yet] neither belong to the land nor does the land belong to them. . . . they pass through community after community, but they neither claim the community as home nor does the community claim them." Theirs was movement forced by economic survival. Migrants, then, neither belonged nor were entitled to the privileges of belonging. "Domestic migrants are citizens of the United States," it continued, "but they are scarcely more a part of the land of their birth than the alien migrants working beside them."[123] Forced to roam by the structure of agriculture, they were alienated from the land, the very entity understood as the seat and giver of democracy, and robbed of ties of national belonging. Not seen as part of the national body by the commission or the public, domestic farmworkers were denied U.S. social visibility and the benefits it brought.

The bracero program was renewed throughout the 1950s, as California agribusiness had staunch allies within the federal government. President Dwight D. Eisenhower and his modern Republicanism, aided by economic expansion, would weaken these bonds when Secretary of Labor James P. Mitchell, a political moderate, took steps to enforce the program agreement (returned to DOL jurisdiction). Labeled the "social conscience" of the administration, Mitchell enacted policies to better monitor reception centers and the treatment of braceros, and his department investigated complaints against wage fixing. Yet braceros still contended that "Mexican work inspectors and consuls only rarely show up and they don't always take notes about our complaints"; and they explained to the journalist Ted LeBerthon that their "right to complain to the Mexican consulate [wa]s theoretical," as complaints usually "ended with the camp foreman," the very individual with whom braceros often found fault. The DOL official Robert G. Goodwin dismissed such allegations. Unlike "indentured servants" or "prisoners of war," he insisted, migrants "were free to return to Mexico any time for any reason." Armed guards lined prison camps, but bracero labor camps had none.[124]

Still, support for the program was waning. Not only did the 1960 Democratic Party platform condemn it, but Mitchell and Arthur Goldberg, whom John F. Kennedy selected as labor secretary in 1961, pressed for substantive changes to it. Pressure to end the program or at least strengthen its worker protections came in part from Mexican American groups, who in California had voted en masse for Kennedy. He renewed the agreement but promised stronger enforcement and oversight, arguing that the decision acquiesced to the needs of the Mexican government, which could not immediately absorb the return of thousands of soon-to-be ex-braceros. Growers consented to stronger regulation, for they finally saw that the program was in serious jeopardy, their coalition fractured by the mechanization of cotton farming. Texas and California cotton farmers, previously a major (if not the largest) user of bracero labor, no longer needed this source, for by the early 1960s 95 percent of cotton production was mechanized. California tomatoes were next. Mechanization, developed with federal funds, divided the invincible bloc of large agriculturalists and rolled out precisely as reports of farmworker poverty and rhetoric criticizing such poverty proliferated. Thus, California's growers of specialty crops, now the only significant users of braceros, faced an increasingly uphill battle.[125]

Broadcast in the midst of this changing context was *Harvest of Shame*, part of Edward R. Murrow's famous CBS Reports. Aired the day after Thanksgiving in 1960, the documentary graphically depicted the squalor in which migrants lived and the labor regime under which they worked. Muddy children as young as two, seen playing with rats, were left in the charge of six-year-old siblings while their parents picked the fruits and vegetables served on viewers' dinner tables. The faces of Murrow's migrant workers were both black and white, yet *Harvest of Shame* more than hinted at farm labor's resemblance to slavery. "We used to own our slaves," announced a grower on camera. "Now we just rent them."[126] Murrow, known for explicit coverage, brought the clash between the modern and this most premodern of labor systems directly into U.S. homes. Footage challenged the ideal of a modern United States as it exposed the poverty of farmworkers and the greed of growers and fused two then-unconnected issues—poverty and labor—in the public's mind.[127] Ultimately, the rural-to-urban demographic shift, alongside its political and cultural realignments, reduced the congressional presence and clout of members tied to a powerful agricultural constituency and (temporarily) gave increased relative weight to the priorities of organized labor and progressive groups.[128]

Conclusion

Strikes and the actions of religious activists and union leaders present a useful way to begin thinking critically about growers' physical and discursive monopoly over agriculture. A class-based approach uniting domestic farmworkers and braceros was a possibility, as braceros recognized their class connections. These connections were forestalled by the power of growers, like DiGiorgio, and the local sheriffs and police allied with them. They were also blocked by U.S. officials unwilling to follow the binational agreement's directives and pull braceros immediately from fields affected by strikes. When Mexican consular personnel also failed to demand adherence to the agreement and braceros' removal from work, these men found themselves forced to remain on the job under threat of deportation.

The connections were also thwarted by these laborers' supporters, in particular, Catholic Church activists. Although church supporters were logical allies in these struggles and argued forcefully against industrial agriculture on the basis of its immorality, their use of such grounds implicitly portrayed farmworkers as helpless and in need of rescue; it did not encourage farmworkers to help themselves. They were seen not as active subjects, but as passive objects. As objects, they had no place in a U.S. national narrative that prized independence and initiative—growers alone held that prize.

Connections were ultimately undercut by the domestic farmworkers themselves. Their refusal to recognize braceros as welcome class comrades doomed their struggle as they framed agriculture's rewards in national terms and reproduced the intra-class divisions and narrative that growers had fostered. Theirs, then, was a class consciousness already severed along national lines. Thus, we see the material impact of growers' discursive control.

These class divisions would be bridged temporarily by César Chávez's United Farm Workers. His 1965 strike against table grape growers, and the movement it sparked, riveted the nation for five years with its creative use of pan-Mexican cultural symbols, dislodging or at least tempering growers' long-standing narratives. As this movement framed it, striking farmworkers had "only one problem"—"growers."[129] Yet even the United Farm Workers movement could not withstand the accelerated global restructuring and free-trade policies that political and economic shifts would bring, ones that hastened the actual and discursive demise of domestic farm labor in favor of an almost entirely immigrant workforce in the new millennium. This was most likely not the "social revolution" in "California agriculture" that the director of the California Department of Employment, Irving Perluss, predicted at the height of the 1960s strikes.[130]

Still, braceros would have appreciated a transnational class approach, for many had come north already versed in the lateral connections that bound them to domestic farmhands. This was particularly the case for those from Durango, previously exposed to militant labor actions. While they joined domestic workers in the strikes examined here and many others, they were repeatedly forced to back down; their removal from disputed fields was the only program option available, even to supportive officials. Thus, braceros were rendered helpless in labor actions, denied the possibility to advocate for themselves and their class brothers. Refused this possibility, they could never be seen as modern—the very reward that work in the United States was to offer. Instead, they were made to feel foreign and out of place, like the chicken in the unfamiliar pen of a more powerful rooster.[131] These men, who had left Mexico as national citizen-subjects, thus became foreign, backward laborers. Their individual and collective efforts to overcome the abuse they faced were never sufficient to eradicate the structural and discursive mechanisms through which growers (and state agents) perpetuated farmworker abuse. Theirs was neither perfect agency nor perfect victimhood.

We thus see connections between the material impact of growers' narratives and the limitations of class as a prism through which farmworkers could understand their experiences. With waning but still significant power toward the end of the program, growers still fanned intrafarmworker tensions, delaying the possibility of a farmworker subjectivity that would bridge divides of nation and race. Few union leaders, save Galarza and Mitchell, were imagining such a labor configuration. Without it, braceros had little chance in the United States of realizing the modernizing benefits that migration was held to bring. We therefore begin to understand why men had to return to Mexico, on which I will focus in the next chapter. It was the only place where they could reinvest in a vision of themselves as (proto)patriarchs and modern agentive citizens. By then, the border was no longer a liminal position but an ongoing predicament.

Border of Belonging, Border of Foreignness

Patriarchy, the Modern, and Making
Transnational Mexicanness

One afternoon in the barbershop, Raúl Molina mentioned crossing the border back to Mexico. "I was coming back," he told the assemblage of men in their sixties and seventies. "I got off the bus and walked up to the border guard. . . . The soldier was young, although I wasn't that old then either, and he wanted some money from me. When I wouldn't give him any, he tried to distract me and take some. I said to him, 'We're *compatriotas* [countrymen]. Why do you want to steal from me?' I couldn't understand."[1] Other men have described similar border exchanges. One was ordered to pay a Mexican guard a fifty dollar bribe in order to cross. "I told [him] that I wouldn't give him anything because my money cost me." In the end, he gave the guard five pesos as a token bribe to cross.[2]

What can we make of border guards' demand for a piece of braceros' bounty and the braceros' refusal to comply? To what connection did don Raúl refer when he labeled the guard a *compatriota*? What did the second bracero mean when he attributed a cost to his money? In examining two particular moments in braceros' return—border encounters with guards and reincorporation attempts in home *pueblos*—we see how the modern as an ideological frame and the daily enactments of social differences screened for, labeled, and ranked at the border—what I have termed practices of border— not only shaped men's experience of going north but also configured their reintegration. Exposed are the tensions embedded in the meanings braceros gave to migration and the real cost of the material benefits extracted from those who left their homes.

One tension concerned the divide between forced movement—which in the United States signals a lack of place, home, and belonging—and mobility as a symbol of liberty, freedom, and (masculine) independence. In the previous chapter I suggested that the organization of agricultural labor, which demanded that migrants follow the harvest, stripped them of a key component of U.S. cultural belonging—an official claim of place. Their required movement, in turn, racialized the work and lives of all farmworkers, including braceros.[3] In Mexico, however, mobility was set against the forced immobility of prerevolutionary debt peonage, in which peasants were tied to the land by generations of debt—at least theoretically. The contradictions between these two versions were instantiated in the border, produced on the U.S. side as racialized difference between the modern and the backward, and supported by a racialized geopolitical relationship between the two countries.

The divide between forced movement and mobility brings into relief a central bracero tension—that the journey brought both opportunity *and* exploitation. And this tension structured men's reintegration. The journey brought opportunity because it offered the possibility of economic freedom—living up to responsibilities as (proto)patriarchs—and social visibility; it brought exploitation because braceros' work racialized and gendered their bodies so as to render them forever backward, and it meant that similarly placed white and nonwhite U.S. farmhands were unable to recognize them as fellow members of a farmworker class. Returnees sought to resolve this class misrecognition by investing in a particular set of values and lifeways in their home *pueblos*. These values and lifeways delivered benefits through claims to being modern and properly masculine subjects, which structured private lives and community social position. That is, modern gender privileges compensated braceros for their exclusion from rewards in the United States on the basis of race and nation. Critically, the context against which men understood these rewards was not just home *pueblos* but larger Mexican *and* U.S. communities—that is, a transnational arena. Revealed in this analysis, then, was what was at stake in migration: its rewards and its costs.

The Border: Commodities, Conflicts, Corruption, and Claims

When braceros' contracts ended, they packed belongings and headed home, often laden with gifts for family and commodities for themselves, just as their government had encouraged. Most had long traded homemade straw sombreros for Stetsons, and they now sported new clothes, and often watches.[4] Border guards greeted them not with a fraternal welcome, but with envy, and former braceros complained that guards had demanded a share of their take.

Luis Camarena, a San Andrés man of slight stature, then in his seventies, had gone north in the 1950s when cyclical drought had ravaged the livelihoods of local peasants. He compared the places he worked and things he saw with his village, which at the time lacked electricity and a doctor, and where house-wives still washed clothes by hand. Recalling all that had changed, don Luis shifted to things he had purchased: in particular, a radio. "Everyone bought radios. Crossing the border . . . a guard stopped me, a Mexican," he said. "He tried to take my radio from me—this made me angry. I asked: 'Why are you trying to take that [radio], *compadre*? I'm Mexican, like you."[5]

Most migrants I spoke with indicated they had experienced some sort of border altercation. One afternoon, amid the barbershop bustle and the snip, snip, snip of don Álvaro's scissors, Francisco Medrano, who had been sitting quietly, announced that he, too, "had a problem once." "After work-ing two contracts and not coming home, I tried to cross the border. A guard stopped me. He wanted money." There was a pause in the conversation, and don Álvaro glanced over. "The guard," said don Francisco, in his late sixties, "looked at me; he wanted money. I looked him in the eye and told him, 'I'm not giving you any of my money. I worked for this money and I'm going home. Take me to your supervisor if you want—I'm not giving you any money. I'm not giving any to him, either.' And with that, I left. . . . And he didn't stop me."

The barbershop erupted. "Border guards," said don Álvaro, "always wanted a payoff." Shaking his head, he summed up his own border interaction cross-ing back into Mexico: "The guard, he was Mexican like me."

"I got stopped once," added Félix Ávalos. "They wanted my cowboy hat."

"Little things," interjected Aníbal Bañales. "They wanted little things, a little money, or something. A token."

"Imagine, Mexican like me," repeated don Álvaro, shaking his head.[6] He, too, it seemed, had encountered a guard seeking unofficial compensation; his "Mexican like me" recalls don Raúl's "*compatriota*." Both men asserted a national connection to the guard.

Nation, especially for men as they returned home, was a fraught frame. Braceros had expected a migration opportunity that would modernize them and enable them to subsequently fulfill their responsibilities as patriarchs. In the United States, many had instead been denied the benefits of an opportu-nity whose rewards were framed in racial and national terms. Nor had they been welcomed by domestic farmhands as temporary coworkers and part of a broader farmworker class. Men from Durango, whose own experiences or those of older relatives had schooled them in their class position and interests before migration, were likewise refused class inclusion. In framing a connection to border guards in terms of a common nationality, men pressed a claim along the very axis on which U.S. domestic farmworkers had rebuffed their class connections in the United States.

Border guards, invested with the power to block men's return and unafraid to exercise it, often demanded money, jewelry, clothes, or electronics. Returnees confronted these officials of the state at the precise moment they could again communicate without struggle or derision. Border exchanges might be seen as evidence of public officials on the take: even as Luis, Raúl, Félix, and Álvaro prepared to return to Mexico, all four collided with a guard who used the authority granted to him by the state not to benefit or protect the nation but to enrich himself. However, I suggest that men's responses point to an attempt to affirm membership in the national collective, possibly as individual citizens or, like the guard, as national representatives, recalling the selection ceremony that had anointed them the state's valued migrant workers.

Yet Luis asserted ownership of the radio, Raúl of his cash, and Félix of his cowboy hat. The items in question were personal property, not for the collective taking. This exchange, then, could signal a struggle over who had claims to migrants' hard-earned consumer goods. Did they belong to the individual, as Luis, Félix, and Raúl contended? Or were they property of the collective, as the guard's demand might imply? Or was the request a transparent financial transaction—a quid pro quo where admittance to Mexico came at the cost of cash, a hat, or a radio? For these storytellers, the compensation sought by the guard was, at the very least, a bribe, a payoff. It was grounded not in an established social relationship with a past, as were their relationships with local elites or officials with whom the request of a favor became a social debt, but in an unreasonable demand from a paternalist state or a single corrupt official. Moreover, Luis's refusal to comply, and the language in which he couched that refusal, like that of Félix and Raúl, conveys a way of thinking and feeling about the accumulation of personal wealth and property, and with them, the emergence of a particular kind of subjectivity. Men claimed the surplus value of their labor as their own; it was not the property of the state. Their refusals, moreover, imply a set of expectations former migrants had with respect to the behavior of representatives of the state and their recognition of braceros as citizens. In other words, no one expected the same exclusion and exploitation from members of the Mexican state as they had experienced in the United States.

Braceros asserted a connection to the guards and were irritated when this connection was questioned; this response might have come from the men's sense of national belonging and embodied Mexicanness. In the aftermath of the revolution, the Mexican state recognized the need to instill a widespread sense of the nation, strategically implemented through public education and celebrations, as well as in the bracero selection ceremony.[7] Yet, as we have seen, part of what these migrants had come to understand as Mexican emerged not in the domestic context or merely vis-à-vis the Mexican state but through an array of bracero interactions—with U.S. and Mexican officials, U.S. growers, foremen, labor organizers, priests, shopkeepers, and tavern owners, and in same-sex labor camps. That is, when braceros were called on to play what others termed "Mexican" music, when they lobbied for chiles, beans, and tortillas that came to be understood as "Mexican" food, or when they were forced to do chores they recognized as unbecoming to a Mexican man, migrants learned to see themselves as Mexican. Mexican also acted as the frame through which they came to see and express bonds to each other and alienation from domestic farmworkers. Thus, Mexican had not always possessed deep resonance before men left Mexico. Returnees brought the term's new shape and significance to border encounters.

At the heart of the struggle over Mexicanness was its imprint on the formation of subjectivities. In challenging the guard, don Luis asserted not only his claim to being Mexican, but the validity of his version. Don Raúl's "*compatriotas*" and don Álvaro's "Mexican like me" suggest a similar investment. Having already been granted social visibility through the selection process, the braceros, in refusing the guards' right to their possessions, may have been insisting on that visibility; they also may have been protesting state exploitation and demanding that the state fulfill its paternalist role. Yet this refusal might also have been men's claim to being part of the state. After all, braceros had been knighted the state's "soldiers of the fields" and agents for international understanding, with their cash and consumer goods deemed the reward for fulfilling such duties.[8] In this reading, then, the border exchange brought together two state representatives—migrant and guard. The demand for a bribe could indicate a guard's refusal to extend to the bracero the same honor that the uniformed officer possessed, or it could point to an aspect of state collectivist ideology used to frame the program that entitled guards, as recognized state representatives, to men's proceeds, preempting a need for subsequent redistributive actions.

A collectivist sensibility comes through in the terms braceros used to frame their relations to guards; this language is suggestive of a state formulation that constituted the nation as a family bound together by a set of deep and historical horizontal ties and, critically, headed by a benevolent state-father. Don Luis's term *compadre* is particularly expressive of this sentiment. The word translates not only as "friend" or "pal"—a lateral connection—but also as "godfather"—an epithet for fictive kin.[9] This nation-as-family idiom was also used in a 1957 report in the Chihuahua daily *El heraldo*. The paper featured a photo of Juan Silos, bloodied from a clash with border police, with a caption quoting Silos: "I don't know why they talk about discrimination against braceros outside Mexico. . . . Here they almost kill us, our very *hermanos de raza* [racial brothers]."[10] The accompanying article attributed these conflicts to state betrayal: "It is shameful that, upon arrival in Mexican territory, these [men] are transported in freight trains, piled high as if they were beasts. And what is worse, so that the [men] enter in an orderly fashion, they are beaten with metal sticks."[11]

Although newspapers had repeatedly publicized state negotiators' dogged attempts to obtain strong agreements, the article inferred that the state had abdicated its protective role. Braceros sent north as heroes were received home as "beasts," and as beasts, they were perennially backward and without a place in the modernizing nation. The border stories of Juan, Álvaro, Félix, and Raúl simultaneously claimed national membership and chastised the state for its behavior. But so did the reporter. "With the unending avalanche of people coming back without any resources," he wrote, "*we* should be offering . . . food . . . medical attention, and housing."[12] This journalist staked out a space for braceros as national citizens owed recognition (social visibility), respect, and material benefits, and he held the state accountable for those benefits. Juan Silos's comments also hint at another reading of the guard-bracero relationship, not as one of coequal citizens or state representatives but as *hermanos de raza*, suggesting a biological connection inflected by race, people, and ancestry. Possibly he intertwined the state's formulation with "the cosmic race," the educator José Vasconcelos's term for Mexico's superior mestizo progeny of Spanish father and Indian mother. The result was a "unique national character and culture" contingent on a "complex ontology" that incorporated "racial, linguistic, and performative differences under the banner of multiracial or multiethnic unity."[13] Broadly conceived, Mexico was an imagined family born of a racial and gendered logic of conquest and reproduction.

Still, the affective ties required for this mestizo national project had only begun to take hold. Despite exposure to this state vision through mandatory primary education, national holidays and celebrations, and literacy and other campaigns, people had other options for making sense of their relationships, including local, regional, and class ties. Aware of these options, the state had tried to sever citizens' long-standing bonds with local and regional elites and power brokers who anchored such alternative ties, but it chose to negotiate, lacking the ability to completely rupture such ties. This negotiation, as scholars have suggested, led to the project's different versions and uneven acceptance—the local specificity of the national—allowing strong local and regional identities to continue in Durango and the country generally.[14] Recognizing this unevenness is critical to analyzing braceros' use of terms such as *hermano de raza*, *compadre*, *compatriota*, and *mexicano*. In reading them alongside a rhetoric of national family, we begin to see the complexities of men's denunciations of guards' actions; their reliance on national terms suggests that the state's framing had taken hold, however partially and maybe even north of the border. Lest we forget, Silos was beaten en route home from the United States, where he had likely seen or faced racial discrimination. Thus, his use of *hermanos de raza*, not merely *hermanos*, might signal the impact of a U.S. reading of Mexican as a particular race. Don Álvaro's "Mexican like me" and don Raúl's "*compatriotas*" suggest myriad influences, for, in the years since their return, they had continually been exposed to visions of the United States from movies, television, and their migrant children and grandchildren who visited for holidays.

Together these multiple incidents point to an aspect of the program that the state likely did not anticipate: that self-identification as a member of the nation was occurring outside state control over form and content of the national imaginary and the impact of that process. While Mexican negotiators insisted on (though rarely achieved) wages that would enable braceros to purchase commodities, and state propaganda encouraged them to do so, such purchases were intended to further modernization, not (re-)Mexicanization. Braceros, however, could not separate the two; both processes were happening simultaneously, instantiated, as we saw above, in dual claims to national inclusion and to the commodities with which they returned.

Still, migration produced a component critical for the state and for returnees: desire. Seen to fuel and be satiated through consumption, desire was, however, unrealizable at home. Promoting the program as a way of fostering (individual) desire and the local (collective) markets to sustain it, negotiators incorporated into the early agreements provisions to escrow 10 percent of braceros' wages beyond the reach of swindlers, greedy bosses, or spendthrift men themselves. Officials waved tariffs on returnees' U.S.-made commodities such as shoes, clothes, radios and encouraged men to invest in U.S.-made tractors and farm equipment with the escrowed funds.[15] Yet few men received, or were even aware of, these funds. Hence, although the state sought to modernize migrants by ensuring they could return with commodities and purchase capital machinery once home, in practice, *pueblos* enjoyed only an influx of commodities because this capital (escrowed wages) was unavailable. This made the purchase of agricultural machinery still beyond braceros' economic reach. Thus, while the desire for commodities, seen as an important component of modernization, was sparked, only further migration, not life in Mexico, could quench it.

For their part, the poorly paid guards, exposed to new products at work, in newspaper ads, and at the movies, did not have the resources to consume.[16] What braceros framed as an unauthorized (state) claim to the results of their labor might be a window onto tensions within Mexico's state structure that (rhetorically) constituted all conflict as internal. It might also reveal the emergence of class as an important axis of subjectivity, indicative of a transformation from peasant to proletarian occurring not only for braceros, but also in other sectors. Increasing commodity circulation among a limited segment of the population fostered the contestatory process through which the desire fundamental to modernization was instilled. Yet this period also revealed the limitations of a third-world state without the financial means to undertake extensive bureaucratic modernization. The guards, like the military, other police forces, and the general state workforce, had yet to be fully professionalized and paid a wage reflecting that professionalization; without professionalization and corresponding remuneration, many—if not most— turned to so-called corruption, using their position to exploit the citizens in whose name they worked. Braceros' refusal to pay bribes at this point in their journey (in contrast to before they left) might have been their new demand for bureaucratic modernization, with its routinized, impersonal state practices.

Exchanges in which returning migrants expected a welcome instead frequently functioned as moments where braceros' national belonging was questioned or denied. By using labels such as *mexicano, compatriota, compadre,* or *hermanos de raza*, braceros demanded membership. In many ways, such as the social visibility extended during selection ceremonies, membership was all the state could offer. As a subaltern state, Mexico lacked the economic resources to deliver on often competing promises made to various national sectors—even, as in this case, the state's own representatives. While it could not offer braceros many concrete rewards, the state grew increasingly dependent on what they produced: remittances. By the mid-1950s, migrant remittances constituted Mexico's third-largest source of hard currency. Thus, in asserting national belonging, returnees were, in a sense, forcing the state to honor its self-designated role as national protector; they demanded that protection be a component of the new modern bureaucratic relationship, not a quid pro quo for favors—what modernization, with its push toward transparency, called personalism or even corruption.[17]

In pushing their connection to border guards, braceros were advocating a complex moral position: they asserted individual rights to the surplus value of their labor (rather than its collective expropriation by the nation) while appealing for guards to fulfill their assigned protective role rather than extend a covetous hand. Yet state negligence began before men left, when eager officials demanded money or gifts for free program prerequisites or to guarantee a spot on the list; and it continued throughout their stay. Migrants' moral position, then, was the insistence that the Mexican state act like a legitimate state. Part of this insistence can be seen in braceros' selective use of discursive strains then in play. Migrants couched their refusal to fill guards' outstretched hands in individualist rhetoric—only they, the migrants, were entitled to the fruits of their labor. This individualistic rhetoric, in tension with a Mexican collectivist logic, hints at how experiences in the United States might have shaped braceros' claims and sense of self as members of the nation. Even if men would have resisted state claims to their possessions before going, they now had additional support for such resistance.

Yet braceros did not totally relinquish a collectivist discourse. Their choice of terms (*compatriota, mexicano,* and *hermanos de raza*) shows that these men, who claimed national inclusion, also pushed for promised state rewards and protection. We might initially be tempted to see such strains as merely the absorption of the dominant, alternately Mexican and U.S., state gaze, yet the simultaneous discursive adoption *and* challenge of these strains might better be explained as their questioning of state legitimacy. The promises of protection and of migration's material rewards and political inclusion, which braceros had to some degree accepted, were still elusive, signaled by unmet contract provisions in the United States and by border challenges. Hence, unmet promises, the structural fallout of Mexico's subaltern position, became the grounds on which migrants challenged the state's contention that it—and only it—could speak for the nation.[18]

Braceros' use of individualist discourse to frame border exchanges reveals the strength and allure of the modern as lived in the United States; yet their refusal to relinquish a collectivist rhetoric forces us to recognize the benefits men saw this rhetoric as offering. The use of both strains suggests the difficulty of acquiring the prizes of the modern: Mexico could not offer the men material rewards, only social visibility—that is, rhetorical inclusion; while for the United States the modern was so tightly bound to class and race that its rewards were limited. Taken together, braceros' desire for the modern's material and discursive dividends shaped claims made on the state and nation, the contents and contours of those claims, and the resulting subjectivities. I again tackle migrant claims on the U.S. nation in the epilogue. Here I turn to how returning braceros used their cache of U.S. commodities and knowledge to reposition themselves within a local hierarchy and advance different kinds of local claims.

The Return

Gifts, Knowledge, and Difference

Braceros' repositioning emerged through their attempts to realize promises of migration not always fulfilled in the United States. Some spent the money they had earned on food, clothing, and land in Mexico, or established small businesses;[19] others brought commodities back for family members; one migrant brought clothes for his wife "something pretty for her," along with shoes for his children.[20] Still others lugged toys for their children and appliances for their wives: "a sewing machine, a toaster."[21] When commodities were displayed on bodies and in migrants' homes, they confirmed a man's commitment to his family and his prowess as provider, dislodging the taint of adventure, the lack of control over a wife's sexuality that had come with his absence, and migration's other potentially destabilizing effects. Although items with which men returned might have been selected for their use value, their distinctiveness from local goods signified the modern and a migrant's knowledge of it. By donning, in Mexico, objects exemplary of the modern, braceros accrued cachet and reinforced the idea of the United States as the space of the so-called advanced and new.

Yet commodities did not merely *mark* a difference between Mexico and the United States; they *became* the difference. When don Álvaro mentioned that Durango lacked electricity and therefore could not power his U.S.-made radio, he remade the spatial boundary between the modern and the backward, between those who knew about the modern and those who did not. In this case, he was among those who knew. This line, however, was not a stable boundary, at least for braceros. One U.S. labor camp manager, who operated a small store, explained, "I pick up khaki shirts and pants in town and sell them out here for just what I pay for them." However, "peddlers" would come around and sell "seconds" right outside the camp at the same price or even lower. "It falls apart after [the man has] worn it once or twice. . . . These [braceros] don't know anything about buying clothes. So they think the peddler's is a good deal."[22] For the manager, then, unmodern braceros were those without the knowledge to judge; they had to be protected to prevent exploitation of their ignorance.[23] Once back in Durango, the same braceros who had been deemed unknowledgeable in California now flaunted their newly acquired knowledge vis-à-vis nonmigrant family and friends. Now it was they who judged who was or was not modern, in the process redeploying much of what U.S. growers, foremen, farmworkers, and state officials had said about them, this time toward those without their experience. This process instantiated the border in a different place and form; Durango became backward, compared to a modern United States, while they, able to cross the border, rose above Durango's stigma.

While nonmigrant family and friends often envied the former braceros' modern commodities, not everything modern was welcomed in the men's home communities. Some ideas were thought to be too socially threatening, even attracting "national levels of interest" and a push for a "rapid solution"; many residents feared that cultural shifts might provoke "violent [local] changes." Of note was the Catholic Church's reaction to "deformed customs, language, and way[s] of living" and the bars and pool halls "flourishing" in locales of outmigration. These male spaces where no decent woman ventured, noted church elders, were socially disruptive, for they allowed men to "spend [money] and brag about what they had obtained in the United States," and to divert dollars from family support to the "acquisition of such businesses."[24] Already concerned about sending the truly faithful to the land of Protestantism, such elders predicted that if these changes were not contained or, better yet, migration curtailed, local social structures would be undermined.

Authorities and nonmigrants were disgusted by both a Spanish "deformed" due to the influence of English and the prostitutes invading small communities.[25] The former bracero Isauro Reyes complained that those who went to the United States "just to get money" returned to Mexico "strut[ting] around every day drinking and showing off, every day, pretentious." "They bring bad habits," he said. "They come back dressing in fancy clothes, first-class; they become self-centered. That's not good. They discredit their country. . . . The ones who bring back money and act with reserve, invest it well, put it in the bank to work, live with their children, with their wives, they're the good ones."[26] This casting, of a modern both beneficial and destabilizing, complicated the space between the modern and the backward, the work of the border, and the position of braceros themselves.

In addition to gifts for family, migrants often returned with *regalitos*— small gifts or tokens of appreciation—for those who had aided their journey. Be these people shopowners, landowners, local priests, recommendation writers, or officials who chose them from among countless contenders, migrants sought to acknowledge help and compensate favors in accordance with community standards and local etiquette. Perennial asking of favors— credit at a store, for example—and reciprocating them tied men to local elites in a social system from which most could never emerge, save with a stroke of luck. Local officials and elites often dismissed the unequal power relations that both enabled them to help migrants and required migrants to call on them. "Often, when the men came back," said Mario Valero Salas, a former Durango program director, "they would bring a little gift for me. . . . I didn't *need* anything from them, but they *wanted* to express their appreciation." Sometimes, don Mario remembered, a favor was compensated with a gift from the United States, at others, with cheese or mescal (bootleg liquor made from agave cactus).[27] For this influential citizen, it was braceros' generosity that motivated gift-giving, not a strict social order. Former braceros' lower social standing obliged repayment, as a family's very survival often depended on the extension of favors—that is, debt, both monetary and social. Migration frequently became the stroke of luck that allow them to repay and free themselves from such debt. As Félix Ávalos told me, "it was important" to give a gift. "[The official] helped me and I wanted to show him that I knew [of his help], that I remembered."[28] "I also brought something back for the local official who helped me get the contract," said don Álvaro. "Not much, a small gift. I wanted to reciprocate the favor."[29] Symbolized in the act of bestowing gifts and in the gifts themselves was men's acknowledgment of their status and social indebtedness; they perpetuated hierarchical ties, even as they used the fruits of migration to climb the social ladder. The gift, indeed, often symbolized the shifting hierarchy.[30] The repeated acts of indebting and repaying, then, functioned as a complex process that integrated a *pueblo* resident (and family) into a larger web involving the requesting, extending, and reciprocating of favors. As such, borrowing and repaying were mechanisms through which hierarchical relations and community membership were enacted.

Social indebtedness as an analytic concept thus offers a way to think about how returning migrants were reincorporated into communities and how they understood this reincorporation. It affords a window onto how the material conditions in which men lived prior to migration and their understanding of these conditions affected the ways they made sense of their place in a transnational migratory system. It suggests that migrants did not enter the United States without knowledge of exploitation or discrimination; their life options were configured according to their place in an often crushing social hierarchy. The impact of this prior experience in shaping migration has largely been ignored, and men's U.S. experiences have frequently been construed as objectively more exploitative than those in Mexico. Lost in this false comparison is the impact of this prior experience on men's reading of migration's potential and how the experiential frame shaped the understanding of the gains of going, both during the journey and after their return.

Notions of social indebtedness can help explain migrants' reactions to border guards, their willingness to compensate local elites, and their eagerness to dispense presents to family and friends. With the first, there was no relationship in place: they did not owe anything to that *particular* individual, who was but one instance in a broader state relationship. In contrast, former braceros had deep prior ties to families, friends, and even local elites, albeit largely unequal ones. By returning with presents for their relations and money in pockets, men were fulfilling their role as proper patriarchs. Positing their prior social relationships as a primary lens through which braceros understood their social webs makes it possible to reinterpret both their motives for migrating and the meanings and value they accorded to going. Only by recognizing the prior indebtedness—economic *and* social— that structured these men's lives, how it had defined their life options, and the ways migration reconfigured aspects of that indebtedness, can we begin to appreciate how braceros made sense of the daily expressions of class and racial inequalities lived in the United States, and how this understanding, in turn, shaped ideas of the modern in Mexico.

Success, Manhood, and the Modern

Migration held out the promise of benefits, yet these were no sure thing. "In the past," confessed a former bracero rejected for another contract, "I returned to my home . . . [my] suitcase full of new clothes, and I always arrived home in a taxi. This time," he lamented, "I will arrive at night. I will have to sneak [back] . . . and hide myself. . . . I will probably be put in jail because of the money I owe." Without another contract, he was "ruined."[31] This man went from prominence and relative wealth to financial and social disgrace, debt, and constraint. Prominence, then, was always a delicate balance, for disaster could send men tumbling down the social and economic ladder and, as I elaborate later, encourage cyclical migration.

From suitcases of clothes and riding in taxis to repaying favors with *regalitos* and establishing small stores and enterprises like don Álvaro's barbershop, these displays acted as physical signs of a man's time on the other side, ones unrealizable without the (even small) infusion of cash from their time and labor as migrants. Performing the economic advantage that migration was imagined to bring was no small feat, however, for returnees were drawn back into local practices of exchange that depleted their meager resources. Social convention called on returnees to invite male friends and family members for drinks at the local cantina, to homes for a meal or small presents, and to *pueblo* and family celebrations. Successful migrants, like local elites, were asked to sponsor local religious feasts and celebrations or to act as the *padrino* (godfather or sponsor) for a young couple's wedding. In poor (and especially peasant) communities, where few families had individual resources sufficient to host celebrations, festivals were largely collectivized. Everyone would sponsor a portion, with the wealthiest and those closest to the celebrants underwriting more expensive items and those least able contributing something small. Families unable to fund a celebration had to borrow from others and accrued a financial and social debt to those able to lend. Sponsorship, then, became a subsequently compensated favor. Collectivization redistributed wealth and capital within peasant and poor communities, insuring that no individual or family overaccumulated. A man's inability to demonstrate the success of his migratory stint through these social conventions called into question his right to a contract, a right grounded in patriarchal claims and the need to fulfill these responsibilities. Pressed to live up to expectations yet unable to do so, many braceros became trapped in cyclical migration.

Although braceros claimed that their migration had been successful, a success they displayed in terms of commodities and claimed in terms of being modern, in many ways their perspective reflects a vision of the modern that was still in process. I see this in the ways that former braceros discussed freedom. "For a Mexican outside his beloved country and customs, far from his way of living," maintained one former bracero, "it's very tragic, very difficult, to find oneself suddenly with something different and distinct. For that reason," he continued, "we were so excited to return quickly to our country and to enjoy this freedom and our way of life, despite so many tempting offers that were made to us [in the United States]."[32] The return home, then, brought the freedom to enjoy one's way of life. For many ex-braceros, this "way of life" referred to knowing how things worked and to having control over one's time. Money was not the essential ingredient—control over the organization and rhythm of life was; it was the basic ingredient for manhood.[33] "No one" in Durango, said don Félix, "tells me what to do or when I have to do it."[34] Men of the barbershop lived this precept. In some sense and within certain (tolerable) limits, Mexican *pueblos* offered returning braceros the ultimate prize: being able to do what they wanted, whenever they wanted.

Patriarchy was at the root of this prize. The patriarchal household was built on the man's rightful authority over the time, movement, and labor of others. While in Mexico poor men could not usually support families—the burden of responsibility that balanced their patriarchal rights—they were nevertheless still free to structure their own time. In the United States, in contrast, lives were organized by growers or foremen, even though braceros could drink, have sex, spend money, and gamble without many of the social sanctions that frequently accompanied such behavior in Durango. While freedom was a fundamental component of male privilege and not contingent on family maintenance, meeting such obligations through migration allowed men to fully reassert this privilege and act without hesitation on its accompanying freedom. Hence, in exercising freedom, men displayed and reclaimed the self-mastery and independence at the core of manhood and patriarchal authority.

The notion of freedom as time of one's own was inadvertently supported by a program structure that sent men home when contracts expired, and it had implicit repercussions for understandings of work. "I always went home between contracts," said don Álvaro. "I worked for forty-five days, two months, or six months, and then I went home. I saw my family, I saw my friends. Then I went back, usually to the same boss."[35] "Sometimes I renewed my contract," said Gerardo Huerta, "but I always came back here from January through March. . . . My family needed me."[36] "When I came home, I didn't work," explained don Álvaro. "I returned to work after a vacation [here] for several months."[37] Here we see the prioritization not only of a certain kind of work—wage labor—but of the space of work—the United States—despite the recognition by most that work in both places was similar.[38]

Before migrating, braceros did not automatically conceive of work as physically or temporally separated from leisure or supposed nonwork. Though many in the two communities that I studied had mixed subsistence agriculture with wage labor a distance from homes, wage labor had nevertheless not been a part of the daily routine. Wage labor took them away from home for several months, after which they returned to their families and plots. Strictly speaking, if illness or misfortune hit, men could return. Thus, work was not automatically severed from nonwork. In California, in contrast, work was divided from leisure in terms of both space and time, and men brought this conceptual framing back to Durango. Inherent in don Álvaro's separation of work from so-called vacation is also a gendered divide: between productive (men's) labor and reproductive (women's) labor, grounded in the gendering of place. Regardless of the tasks migrants undertook during their stays in Durango—most likely planting and harvesting—a refusal to label these tasks as work ultimately feminized Mexico and situated it as the site of family and community reproduction, not modern production. Labor that was presumed nonproductive became women's work, the series of endless tasks for hands without calluses—women's hands, as don Álvaro labeled them. His ability to identify (his) labor with the United States, the modern realm in a transnational spatial divide, made his U.S. activities productive and valuable, a productive labor that, in turn, justified his patriarchal authority in Durango. In the end, this spatial divide made proletarianization—as an uneven, gendered cultural and economic process—possible. Only certain labors would become part of the process of transforming peasants into workers, while other tasks, those defined and gendered as nonproductive, would anchor rural people to their rural place.

Even as men used specific cues to divide work from nonwork, even as they experienced (the routines of) work in California as distinct from labors in Durango, these two places—Mexico and the United States—were linked through space and freedom. The freedom migrants felt in Durango was juxtaposed to and grounded in rigid U.S. schedules. At home, men determined when they would plant, harvest, and seek wage work, an apportionment of time that accommodated local fiestas and family obligations. In the contrast between the two settings and the emerging distinction between work and nonwork, Mexico became the site of freedom. That is, the freedom so crucial to braceros' claim to manhood was only made possible by the money earned and knowledge accrued in the United States; yet it was this control that enabled them to structure their lives as they wanted. While I initially wanted to discard their conception as idealized memories of a moment long past, I found that they provided clues to how braceros understood their isolation and constraints on mobility and how the recuperation of manhood thus came at a cost. Maybe these constraints and isolation were what the bracero meant, in the vignette with which I opened this chapter, when he said that his money earned in the United States had "cost" him.[39]

Freedom, Patriarchy, and Webs of Social Indebtedness

Given that most men with whom I spoke described the rhythm of work in both places as more similar than different, the question becomes what this mapping of freedom and constraint might tell us. I suggest that it reveals what was at stake in the program, the rewards held out in men's return, and the patriarchal underpinnings of a modern negotiated broadly and selectively vis-à-vis a transnational set of social practices and conventions. That is, it shows how the logics and practices associated with each place—and men's ability to meet these expectations—depended on and were fueled by a larger transnational system.

To begin with, what migrants experienced in Durango as freedom and a lack of work was constructed against their rigid daily schedules in the United States, and it was dependent on this transnational framing. Moreover, men could only experience freedom within their *pueblos* and adjust work routines to accommodate this autonomy after months of sweated labor outside home communities. The physical move across the border gave men the possibility of extricating themselves from unmet financial responsibilities and thus the constraints of social indebtedness. The very contrast between the two settings and the emerging distinction between work and nonwork made Mexico, and its attendant flexibility of time and schedule, the site of freedom.

We also see the interdependence of seemingly separate logics and practices in the *regalitos* and the reciprocation of favors, through which migrants repaid debts that would otherwise have required a significant investment to disentangle. Former braceros used *regalitos* to acknowledge and express appreciation for help and the act of gift-giving itself to acquire a better position within the social hierarchy. Thus, men's ability to ease bonds of obligation in Durango required the rewards of work in the United States. Yet the migration so critical to loosening these oppressive bonds and recuperating manhood simultaneously put another tenet of the latter at risk: the known quantity of a man's character. In Durango, men were known; in California, they were anonymous and lacked a past; migrants had come together with others from all over Mexico. They escaped the prying eyes of family and neighbors and lived among men who, while not always approving, largely overlooked behaviors such as sex with prostitutes or heavy drinking, considered privileges of manhood. As we have seen, manhood, in Durango and Mexico more generally, demanded that men be known and mark their presence in a community's physical and metaphorical place. And only a man accorded full selfhood for his patriarchal position and reputation reaped such privileges. One's manhood, then, enabled the occupation of public spaces, even as a lack of visibility (his behavior in the United States) and transparency of motive (whether he sought adventure or family support) undercut this claim. Only a fully adult man was allowed the freedom and possibility of physical movement outside the known space of home *pueblos*, and the privileges that accompanied this freedom, without automatically threatening his reputation. And only in the United States, with its economic possibilities, could migrant men establish, solidify, and protect from *pueblo* intrusion their right to the comportment occurring in these hidden spaces.

My point is not that behaviors were condoned in one place and condemned in another but rather that the behaviors, differently valued in each place, were inherently constructed against their valuing in both places. Men frequently suffered no consequences for dalliances or unacceptable behavior in California. As a current migrant told me, what happens in the United States does not count.[40] That is, there were no consequences as long as such behavior did not undermine men's ability to fulfill the central legitimate reason for migration: family support. Still, the physical separation between Durango and California that often made such behavior easy at times weakened their authority. Men not only lost tight control over the actions and movement of women and children; they were also stripped of their individual reputations, for growers and foremen relied on nation-, race-, and class-based designations. For growers and foremen, then, braceros had no past or future but were part of a nameless, faceless, anonymous group confined by race and class to the margins of U.S. society. This anonymity acted as a counterweight to the social restrictions of home *pueblos*, allowing braceros a freedom of movement and comportment not experienced as such in Durango.

While migration enabled men to introduce myriad new ideas, consumer goods, and practices into local communities, and to gain status from these novelties, they also refused to render—that is, modernize—aspects of their lives, such as patriarchy, from which they garnered privileges. Those with whom I spoke naturalized the privileges that, as men, they had within patriarchal marriage and the corresponding constraints put on women, framing these constraints as a form of "security" based on "interdependence." In a particularly lively barbershop discussion, former migrants discussed the reasons that motivated each gender to pursue marriage. Women needed someone to "provide" for them, the men as a group concluded. Women needed a husband to keep them fed and clothed, with a roof over their head. For husbands, marriage provided the security of returning to a clean, orderly, child-filled house, a warm meal, and clean clothes. And "men need sex," everyone agreed. "We cannot go without it for long periods of time." Wives and single women concurred.[41] Although wives insisted that their husbands would never have sex outside marriage, manhood as constituted in Durango gave men the right to express their "nature" and often demanded that they did, as long as it did not interfere with the primary responsibility of supporting a family. That is, men and women generally accepted as fact prevailing notions of male sexuality, which dictated that (most) men would stray from the marriage bed, and a version of male privilege that permitted them to do so. Given this organization of households and the patriarchal division of responsibility and authority from which men gained so much, they were loath to change such arrangements.[42]

Nor were Mexican officials eager to disturb this family arrangement, for the state and individual officials, too, benefited. Though negotiators had targeted signs of backwardness, including gambling, gunfighting, and excess drinking, for eradication, patriarchy as a whole was not up for revision. Still, its modernization was already under way.[43] While the revolution had weakened certain hierarchical bonds, the emergent state could not do away with them entirely, as it had little concrete to offer in their place. Thus the state, as the people's benevolent protector and patriarch, drew men into its revolutionary project by resecuring—not undermining—conjugal privileges. This relationship between state and citizen was unsettled by the program, however, when Mexican officials proved either unwilling to intervene in U.S. disputes over wages and living conditions or unable to resolve them equitably. By contrast, the shared experience of struggle in California heightened lateral ties, and returnees brought invigorated fraternal bonds, together with their position as knowledge holders, to exchanges with border guards and community elites. This emergent subjectivity did not undermine men's role as household patriarchs, for the state made securing, supporting, and leading the family the road to national inclusion. In this way, it grounded the program in a heteronormative appeal that developmentalist language and ideology could accommodate—that is, modernization did not preclude patriarchy but rather strengthened it. In the end, braceros' ability to gain socially from migration and to be recognized as modern citizen-subjects came not in the United States but from their manipulation in Durango of the meager rewards that migration offered.

Reconfiguring the State-Citizen Relationship

Braceros, then, were located at the nexus of multiple competing versions of the modern. In the United States they could not be considered modern because of their nationality cum race; yet, as we have seen in this chapter, they could—and did—claim to be modern in Durango, where they showed off clothes, electronics, and information that conveyed a modern knowledge. Although they sought the rewards and privileges that the U.S. modern promised, braceros at no time bought into a conception of the modern that replicated this U.S. version whole cloth. While they pushed for its benefits in the realms of citizen-state relations and of production—growers' adherence to contract stipulations, recognition as workers, and backing from Mexican officials—they advocated no such revision in terms of domestic and community privileges from which they gained; like Mexican officials, they did not see the sphere of reproduction and community as needing change. Instead, they wanted to sustain the *pueblo* bonds, values, and lifeways that, without migration, were difficult to reproduce.

We have also seen braceros push for a less personalistic relationship to both the state and the nation. Although some migrants clearly framed their desire to return home in terms of family need, others described it as a challenge to the United States as the singular site of economic opportunity and the modern. "For me the United States was a great place to work," stated Manuel Rodríguez, "but my homeland . . . offer[ed] me the same fruits that the United States did and obviously my interests lie in Mexico. . . . I'm not sorry I didn't stay. . . . My work and my efforts were well compensated in Mexico."[44] Even though the director of the Ensenada Chamber of Commerce called braceros good salesmen for U.S. ideals, Catarino Hernández agreed with compatriot Rodríguez: "The bad thing is that [migrants] enrich [the United States] with their work. It's better to enrich your own."[45] These statements suggest that at least some braceros returned with a sophisticated reading of the modern that linked duty to one's country to the possibility of a different kind of relationship between state and citizen. In refusing to succumb to the lure of the U.S. individualist version of the modern, they cracked opened the potential of multiple versions. More than merely asserting that Mexico, too, could become modern, their understandings reflect a deep engagement with the parameters of the modern that the state asserted were critical to modernization. Some braceros, at least, subscribed to the state's vision and acknowledged that citizens had responsibilities to nations and states, just as states and nations had responsibilities to citizens, and they were willing to sacrifice for this collectivist modernist vision from which all were seen to inevitably benefit.

This willingness was not unlimited, however. "Now," said a rejected ten-year veteran of the program, "[the screeners] tell me I cannot come again, because they say I have tuberculosis. I have never been sick a day in my life. How can I have tuberculosis? If they are going to reject us, why don't they do it [in Mexico]? Why let us come so far? I suffered three months at [the border]. I slept on the ground, I went without food, I was away from my family. All for nothing." He recognized not only the hardship he had endured and the Mexican state's role in it, but also the modern's arbitrariness—even when he had played by its rules, he lost. Worse yet, his time and energy had gone not to the prosperity of his own nation, but to that of one that did not accept him: "I have spent the best years of my life working for your country."[46] We thus see the limit to men's willingness to invest in this collective responsibility; it could go awry or be subverted—explaining braceros' anger over bribes and this man's rage over the state's duplicity.

This bracero's rejection calls attention to the fleeting hold that he and all

Mexico had on the modern and its benefits. This hold was indeed ephemeral: in the aftermath of World War II, the United States invested millions of government dollars to rebuild Europe and Japan, while pushing Mexico and the rest of Latin America to seek private monies for development.[47] During the latter half of the twentieth century and beginning of the twenty-first, these countries would once again be stripped of the possibility to be future homes of industrial production, repositioned as the source of manufacturing inputs—materials and cheap labor. Without the ability to dictate the terms of the modern and its actualization, both this individual bracero and subaltern Mexico as a whole would be subject to the whims of the United States and the industrial global world. Locked out of a U.S. modernist project, braceros turned their attention back to Mexico. They advocated a version of citizenship and Mexicanness that reflected their experience on both sides of the border and that challenged the version of national identity instilled in school curricula, holidays, and other expressions of a so-called Mexican national culture.[48] In many ways, migrants' eclectic use of these different versions shows not only that national identity was being made outside territorial borders but how migrants themselves were critical to the process.

By spending time in the United States, braceros defined, solidified, and dismantled the borders of these two imagined nations. Armed with a vision shaped by the practices of border that structured lives in the United States, men began to broaden the spaces and contexts against which they negotiated their belonging and the ways belonging was performed and displayed. In claiming a place in the Mexican family, migrants maneuvered against not merely nationally constructed hierarchies and social categories but the depiction of "Mexican" as a racial marker in a U.S. hierarchy. That is, experiences outside the national territory acted as the salient backdrop to this reorganized world. Still, beneath the surface, each vision hints at the desire to establish a particular relationship between state and citizen, one confirmed as modern and exemplified in deed and attitude. We thus begin to see the complexity of braceros' version of the modern and its impact on Mexico.

Conclusion

Woven throughout the above analysis is a fundamental question: What is the proper target of the modern? Was it the nation, as in the Mexican notion, where the state claimed to undertake economic development on the nation's behalf while also instilling modern attitudes and actions? Or was it, according to U.S. contention, the individual modern citizen-subject, imbued with individual longings and desires and unfettered by the state in fulfilling them? Was it the U.S. sphere of production, as migrants advocated, a sphere whose knowledge of which should enable men to meet their gender responsibilities and derive their gender privilege? Or was this target the realm of the domestic, as recent work on migrant sexuality contends?[49] The latter, as we have seen, was not open for renegotiation in the mid-twentieth century. The modernization of the sexual subject would come later, brought about by changes from continued migration and global restructuring.

Attention was focused elsewhere. While economists such as John Maynard Keynes were concerned with the nation-level development of less-developed countries, Harry Truman, contends the literary scholar Maria Josefina Saldaña-Portillo, was interested in "a set of *attitudes*," in particular, the "attitude toward freedom from want," where development is aided by "'all who *long* for . . . security and abundance.'" Thus was created "the desire for development-as-freedom," instilled within underdeveloped "subjectivity," manifest "in 'wishes,' 'desires,' [and] ultimately choice." With Truman's talk of individual desires and wishes, no longer can underdeveloped countries pursue or not pursue nation-based development, argues Saldaña-Portillo, for millions of desperate individuals "*desire* development" and, as we saw in Félix's, Luis's, and Raúl's refusals to surrender precious commodities, actively "choose it . . . for their own lives." Critical here is that the modernizing transformation was no longer geared only toward countries—now the focus was on the "less developed subjects of [Truman's] 'human family'"; "*individuals* [were] available for development."[50] This unresolved tension over the proper site for the modernist project was exactly the conflict at the heart of the program—in the U.S. version the individual triumphed, while the Mexican state's rendition intertwined the individual with the nation. Braceros, too, were engaged in resolving this tension, as we can see in the material objects they brought back and displayed, the gendered social benefits they reaped from these objects, and how their gender prerogative was fundamentally bracketed from revision.

Although the Mexican state imagined the program, and migration more generally, as a short-term solution to rural backwardness, for many, maybe most, braceros, meeting their families' needs on an ongoing basis was elusive. As migrant needs (food, clothing, shoes) morphed into desires (radios and cowboy hats in the past, and now video games, iPods, and computers)—an intended program objective—men were propelled into a cycle of migration; the Mexican state has had to manage this objective discursively since it cannot solve the problem materially. In late 1995 I interviewed Miguel Bermúdez Cisneros, then minister of Durango's Ministry of Labor and Social Welfare. When I explained that I was researching migration from Durango, he told me directly, "Men don't really need to migrate." Dismissing state responsibility for the pervasive poverty, he attributed the large outmigration to the search for "adventure." While people *might* have once needed to migrate to the United States for work, Durango now offered a broad range of new industries, in which hardworking men could labor and earn a decent living. Migrating, he said, had instead become "a rite of passage for young men," a sort of quotidian ritual through which boys "became" men. "Have you ever been to Santiago Papasquiaro or Tepehuanes?" he asked me, speaking of two small villages. "They have houses nicer than many here [in the city of Durango]." In juxtaposing urban/modern/wealthier to rural/backward/poor, this official suggested that "[migrants] just go to escape the [restrictions] of their families and villages, to be with their friends, to see the United States, for the adventure." Durango's new job opportunities for "hardworking men," he claimed, removed need as a justification for leaving.[51] In framing migration in this way, Bermúdez Cisneros delegitimized both the supposed reason for migration—need—and what was to be gained from it—modern desires. Desire, apart from need, then, is illegitimate.

Notice, too, the adjective "hardworking." In invoking this boundary between hardworking and lazy, the official suggests that men who migrate do so not only for an adventure but also because they are afraid of or want to avoid hard work, the litmus test of manhood. In this formulation, the government is not shirking its responsibilities, for there actually are economic opportunities. Instead, through the circulation of notions of adventure and fear of work, the government can dismiss claims that Durango lacks jobs and complaints of the government's own negligence. In mobilizing these notions, this official exploits the illegitimacy of these reasons by positioning them as decoupled from—and contradictory to—supporting a family and "real" need. Through this decoupling the government merely confirms what it has always suspected of these men: they give into their individual(istic) desires and forsake collective responsibilities. While migrants questioned the legitimacy of the state because of what they saw as inadequate protection and lack of transparency, here we see the state disposing of any obligation to citizens by labeling them as illegitimate and unworthy of protection.

Written out of the picture are the increasing numbers of women—divorced, widowed, or single mothers—who are joining the northward stream as workers and not just wives. Many of them work as domestics, but many too are found on farms and in factories, constituting the current preferred class of worker in California's tomato industry.[52] As they enter the realm of paid domestic and other work, these women leave their families and domestic duties in the hands of mothers, grandmothers, sisters, aunts, and friends, while they themselves are forced to perform chores for and care for the families of upper-class U.S. women. This family form, which stretches across borders and is termed "transnational motherhood," in many ways perpetuates the earlier linking of the United States with production (gendered male) and of Mexico with reproduction (gendered female).[53]

Too often migration did not fulfill its implicit promises of self-sufficiency, either for individual braceros or for Mexico. For most, a single stint begat another and another. The desire for commodities and a belief in possible self-sufficiency left sons and nephews—and now daughters, nieces, and granddaughters—to continue the migration cycle when their fathers or uncles no longer could. Despite the program's talk of a southward transfer of farm knowledge, Mexican agriculture has never been able to produce enough food to feed its citizens and continues to fall back on imports. Still, the state grew reliant on braceros' remittances. This vital source of hard currency enabled it to expand services (at least initially), even as migrants were better able to address family needs, lessening the pressure on the state to do so.

Although braceros could not fully achieve the modern, this failure was not a personal one; rather, it reflected the constraints on all underdeveloped countries. Without capitalization and with a desire for commodities, at home they found the benefits of the modern ephemeral. For braceros, then relentlessly drawn to the material and social rewards that the modern brought, the only answer was ongoing migration. Regardless of their adherence to a modernist logic assumed to facilitate their arrival as modern, in the end, this arrival, like Mexico's, was continually delayed. Few, however, were willing to quit pursuing it altogether, for its potential payoff was too great. They would continue to migrate, the legacy of which we are still witnessing. Behind the modern's rhetoric of self-sufficiency and masculine independence, then, is a U.S. imperial project grounded in and coeval with Mexico's economic dependency, a coevalness required for modernization and for the uneven distribution of its rewards to the people of Mexico and the United States.

I do not mean to wrap up the changes in braceros' lives too neatly. When I met them in the mid-1990s, many men, including don Álvaro and don

Ramón, still worked the land. Well past middle age, they employed a few younger people, often relatives, to help them with their fields. And many used tractors. For those successful few who owned this machinery and had, like don Álvaro, purchased it long after their return, tractors were capital. They were not only used on the owner's land but also rented or lent for use by others; they thus accrued to the owner both income and social capital. The tractor, in other words, stood as an axis of social indebtedness. Once again we see the legacy of the class transformation at the center of the program.

This chapter, then, brings braceros' journeys to a close, yet the impact of their migration and desire to migrate resonated beyond these men as individuals or their communities: it also constrained the options and influence available to the Mexican state as it ultimately emboldened U.S. growers and state. Within Mexico, braceros teetered uncomfortably on the divide between a proletarianized (worker) world and a world of subsistence agriculture (peasant), but they were not fully of either. As migrants, they were supposed to bring back tractors; instead they brought back radios. They were supposed to bring back capital; instead they returned with consumer goods. They were alienated in the United States, but they also saw the possibilities it offered for a better economic future and a social status dependent not only on time outside Durango, but on their knowledge of the United States. That is, to keep what they had gained, men had to keep migrating. Their social and economic position depended on living lives that straddled the border. In many ways, it was a tension they could never resolve. We might think of the tractor that don Álvaro owned and lent as symbolic of the border these men inhabited. Nowhere were braceros offered a complete and secure modern package, for what they had come to know, want, and depend on required both sides of the border and the ability to move between them. For some, that ability came with U.S. permanent residency, made possible through changes to immigration law in the program's aftermath. For most former braceros, however, this freedom of movement is yet unrealized. The next chapter pans back to consider the repercussions of these men's migration and demand to migrate on the larger struggle between the United States and Mexico and on the formation of a transnational arena, and how this pressure opened up and constrained the options of these state actors. We thus see the impact of braceros' agency in the limited measures available to both sets of state protagonists.

A Mexican official assesses a line of men waiting to apply for farmwork in the United
States, 1956. Note the men's sandals. (Leonard Nadel photograph. Courtesy of Division
of Work and Industry, National Museum of American History, Smithsonian Institution.)

Aspirants for work in the United States wait in line in Mexico City, 1956. Many men wear sandals, not shoes, and carry their belongings in various kinds of sacks. (Leonard Nadel photograph. Courtesy of Division of Work and Industry, National Museum of American History, Smithsonian Institution.)

Women prepare food and drink for braceros as they wait to enter the migratory station in Monterrey, Mexico, 1956. (Leonard Nadel photograph. Courtesy of Division of Work and Industry, National Museum of American History, Smithsonian Institution.)

Outside the migratory station in Monterrey, Mexico, braceros enjoy an impromptu concert, 1956. (Leonard Nadel photograph. Courtesy of Division of Work and Industry, National Museum of American History, Smithsonian Institution.)

Braceros stand in long lines grouped by state of origin at the migratory station in Monterrey, Mexico, 1956. Vendors, including women and children, sell refreshments and food. (Leonard Nadel photograph. Courtesy of Division of Work and Industry, National Museum of American History, Smithsonian Institution.)

An official examines a bracero's hands for calluses during the selection process in Monterrey, Mexico, 1956. (Leonard Nadel photograph. Courtesy of Division of Work and Industry, National Museum of American History, Smithsonian Institution.)

A bracero on a train bound for California, ca. 1942. Note the wartime "Bien-venidos Los Trabajadores Mexicanos" (Welcome Mexican Workers) tag the man is wearing and the words painted beneath the window: "Braceros Mexicanos—Viva Mexico" (Mexican Braceros—Long Live Mexico). (© Doro-thea Lange Collection, Oakland Museum of California, City of Oakland. Gift by Paul S. Taylor.)

Mexican migrant workers travel by train to Los Angeles, 1942. Note the "V for Victory" signs the men are making and the wartime tags they are wearing. (Los Angeles Times Archive, Department of Special Collections, Charles E. Young Research Library, University of California, Los Angeles.)

Braceros headed to Texas or environs east walk over the bridge from Reynosa, Mexico, to Texas for final selection, 1956. (Leonard Nadel photograph. Courtesy of Division of Work and Industry, National Museum of American History, Smithsonian Institution.)

Franklin Gettinger (center) takes the temperatures of braceros headed for the Imperial Valley during the final step in the selection process, January 27, 1954. (Los Angeles Times Archive, Department of Special Collections, Charles E. Young Research Library, University of California, Los Angeles.)

Men are fumigated, probably with DDT, at the reception center in Texas, 1956. (Leonard Nadel photograph. Courtesy of Division of Work and Industry, National Museum of American History, Smithsonian Institution.)

An agent for the Texas growers association examines the musculature of a bracero during the final step of the selection process, 1956. (Leonard Nadel photograph. Courtesy of Division of Work and Industry, National Museum of American History, Smithsonian Institution.)

A man displays his just-awarded permit to work in Texas, August 22, 1964. (© Otto L. Bettmann/Bettmann Collection, CORBIS. Donated by CORBIS-Bettmann.)

The first trainload of braceros arrives in Stockton, California, October 1, 1942. Note
the styles of hats the men wear. (© Otto L. Bettmann/Bettmann Collection, CORBIS.
Donated by CORBIS-Bettmann.)

In California, a bracero picks peppers, 1956. Notice the short-handled hoe
on his belt. (Leonard Nadel photograph. Courtesy of Division of Work and
Industry, National Museum of American History, Smithsonian Institution.)

(opposite) In a California field, a bracero strips a head of lettuce of bruised
leaves, 1956. (Leonard Nadel photograph. Courtesy of Division of Work and
Industry, National Museum of American History, Smithsonian Institution.)

Hard at work, braceros use short-handled hoes in California fields, 1956.
(Leonard Nadel photograph. Courtesy of Division of Work and Industry,
National Museum of American History, Smithsonian Institution.)

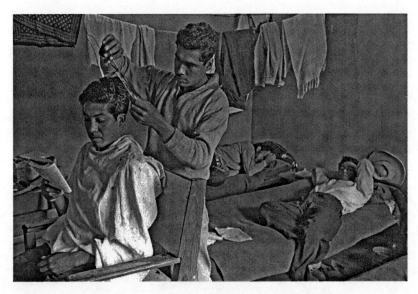

A bracero cuts a man's hair in the living quarters of a California camp, 1956. (Leonard Nadel photograph. Courtesy of Division of Work and Industry, National Museum of American History, Smithsonian Institution.)

A bracero, posed on his California camp bed, reads the grammar book, *Método de inglés sin maestro* (Method for English without Teacher), 1956. (Leonard Nadel photograph. Courtesy of Division of Work and Industry, National Museum of American History, Smithsonian Institution.)

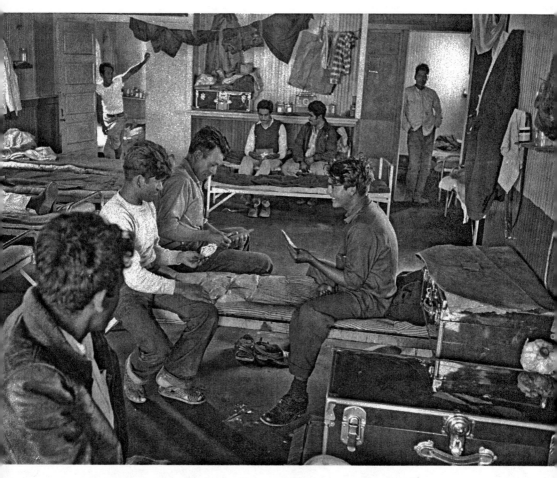

Braceros play cards in their California living quarters, 1956. (Leonard Nadel photograph. Courtesy of Division of Work and Industry, National Museum of American History, Smithsonian Institution.)

At home in the barracks after a hard day's work, braceros relax by watching television, August 15, 1959. Men pooled their earnings to buy television sets. (© Otto L. Bettmann/ Bettmann Collection, CORBIS. Donated by CORBIS-Bettmann.)

Braceros examine their paychecks in Watsonville, California, 1956. (Leonard Nadel photograph. Courtesy of Division of Work and Industry, National Museum of American History, Smithsonian Institution.)

Headed home by train, wartime braceros display silver dollars and paper money for the camera, May 1943. (© Otto L. Bettmann/Bettmann Collection, CORBIS. Donated by CORBIS-Bettmann.)

Aspiring braceros congregate at the border in Mexicali, Mexico, January 17, 1954. One laborer lifted up in the melee is aided by a U.S. border guard as more than 800 men strain forward toward the international line; some men faint in the crush. The 1954 border incident demonstrates the lengths to which men went to migrate, which in turn limited the options open to the Mexican state. Scores were injured in the month-long episode; only a few were admitted. (Los Angeles Times Archive, Department of Special Collections, Charles E. Young Research Library, University of California, Los Angeles.)

Part III The Convergence of Elite Alliances

8

Tipping the Negotiating Hand

State-to-State Struggle and the Impact of Migrant Agency

"I went only once," Ramón Avitia told me, referring to his bracero journey. "I didn't earn much money and it was hard work, but with what I made I built my house and bought a few cows."

"I went several times," don Álvaro said. "When I came home the last time, I opened this barbershop."

During one of our barbershop conversations, many men spoke of coming and going between Durango and California. Whether they went once or several times, most men I spoke with were drawn by the promise the program held out.

"They said it was an opportunity," Felipe Castañeda told us. "For me, it was an opportunity, sort of. My family has a house. My kids got shoes. I went lots of times. Although life got better, the opportunity came at a cost."

Don Felipe raised his left arm to show a scar.[1]

Opportunity or exploitation: this dichotomy underscores a central tension in the program. These men (indeed, their nation) had been promised that the program would bring capital and agricultural knowledge to modernize Mexican farms; men would go, work, learn, and return—the end. The unspoken promise was financial independence for individuals as small capitalized yeoman farmers, and economic sovereignty for Mexico. However, as we have seen, most braceros never achieved this goal, nor did most want it, though all sought the program's promised rewards. When these were not forthcoming, men continued migrating, turning a single trip into many sojourns and a revolving migratory door. When migrants could no longer head north, they handed the baton to their sons, younger brothers, nephews, and eventually grandchildren. For these men and millions of their compatriots, the trip was less a lone experience than a way of life, one braceros began and families continued. In the end, the journey embodied the critical contradictions that the program was expected to resolve: making braceros modern while jump-starting Mexico's capability to sustain their modern desires through a return with capital. Yet although some men did come back with cash and consumer goods, they often could not hold onto new financial resources or a claim to being modern without continuing to migrate. The necessity of constant movement, then, is the dark side of an ever more integrated global capitalist system, where opportunity always comes at a cost.

Because demand continuously outpaced availability, many men wanted to migrate but did not get contracts. Some therefore took matters into their own hands, crossing the border without documents and contributing to the "wetback" problem, a pejorative colloquialism for those who waded the river.[2] Others congregated at the border hoping for an elusive spot. Both strategies called attention to men's unmet needs. Several critical moments illustrate the pressure that aspiring migrants exerted on state actors, for these men went to great lengths to accomplish their goals. These actions and their consequences have much to tell us about the U.S.-Mexico relationship, the possibilities and limitations of modernization, and how these migrants shaped the seemingly impervious terrain of U.S. and Mexican state options.

1948: The El Paso Incident

From the program's outset, migrants returning with dollars in the pockets of their new clothes piqued the interest of many who had never thought of heading north. Talk of higher wages and adventure so enticed men without contracts that they often journeyed to the border, either in hopes of sneaking across or to wait for the next contracting session. The number of contracts was raised after World War II, urged by Mexican negotiators, who aimed to bring undocumented migrants into the documented stream.[3] But it was also done at the behest of U.S. growers. This expansion in contracts, along with the actions of its citizens, undercut Mexican officials' ability to garner strong protections and enabled their U.S. counterparts to win concessions.[4] Yet even this increase did not meet the seemingly insatiable demand. An October 1948 report estimated that at least seventy thousand undocumented migrants were working in the United States; by 1952 this figure had risen to 1.5 million.[5] A state representative called it a "conservative calculation" of the number of braceros who had remained after their contracts expired; it did not include those who had entered without them. However, U.S. and Mexican border patrols, he said, were working together to staunch the unauthorized flow.[6] This cooperation translated into a visibly enhanced two-state presence and power. Aspiring migrants responded by going to reception centers or border cities, like Ciudad Juárez, and waiting, rather than attempting to sneak across.[7] This strategy was inadvertently encouraged when the Mexican government, capitulating to U.S. pressure, started to allow those congregated in border towns to be contracted for work immediately.

Until October 13, 1948, U.S. border officials actively prevented undocumented migrants from entering the country. That day, however, everything changed. Border agents in El Paso (directly across from Ciudad Juárez) blatantly "desisted in their efforts to stop the illegal entry of Mexican agricultural workers into North American territory," wrote the Mexican newspaper *El nacional*.[8] For five days in mid-October, men "waded the shallow river in sight of the Border Patrol [in El Paso], which received them with formality, herded them into temporary enclosures, and immediately paroled them to . . . cotton growers, who trucked [them] . . . at once to the fields."[9] *La opinión*, a Spanish-language Los Angeles paper, denounced this action as a "flagrant contradiction" of the binational arrangement. "The corresponding authorities from both governments," it continued, "will take all measures to avoid the illegal migration of Mexican[s]."[10]

While press coverage portrayed U.S. officials as merely refraining from fulfilling their duty to stop unauthorized crossers, in actuality, U.S. border guards intentionally and unilaterally opened the border. Stating that fall harvests were in jeopardy, local agents pulled back the gates, allowing waiting men to stream across.[11] The seven to eight thousand men crossing during the momentary opening were instantly "dried out" (a play on "wetback"), offered contracts by growers or their representatives, who "happened" to be waiting for them, and then dispatched to fields across the country.[12] Mexican authorities, not surprisingly, condemned this move as a violation of the agreement and an assault on the "spirit of cooperation and the Good Neighbor policy." The U.S. government apologized a few days later.[13] This unilateral action further tilted the power imbalance into U.S. hands and broke Mexican negotiators' grip over what growers had decried as slow and cumbersome procedures for getting workers to the fields. The $3 daily wage pushed by Mexican officials in ongoing negotiations—already down to $2.50 in actuality—dropped as low as $1.50 following the influx of workers.[14]

The public display of human bodies rushing across the border crippled Mexican negotiators' ability to secure fundamental protections for its citizen-workers. Negotiators, like migrants, were caught in the middle, compelled to acknowledge the now patently visible "never-ending poverty" facing hundreds of thousands of migrants.[15] With so many struggling to find jobs, by either "legal or surreptitious means," and with others leaving work on Mexican haciendas not far from the border, prominent citizens at home and in the United States called on the Mexican government to "stop lying" and admit the "uncontestable truth" that the nation's "agriculture continue[d] in crisis."[16] This pressure, however, was multisided: from below, by would-be migrants, and from different elite factions in a sort of lateral force. Together these moves further constrained the Mexican government's already limited ability to broker adequate protections. The result: U.S. authorities accrued an edge in bargaining, and growers an advantage in warding off a labor movement.[17]

This predicament occurred in some measure because Mexican negotiators had not conceded to two specific provisions: making individual growers the agreement's employer of record and locating reception centers close to the border. To the first provision, U.S. officials, capitulating to grower lobbying, had fought to overturn Mexico's original mandate that the U.S. government act as the employer of record and party responsible for enforcing the agreement. From 1948 to 1951, the period in which Mexico conceded this provision, contract abuses skyrocketed as the federal government ceded to growers more authority over the program's day-to-day operation. To the second, the two sides had, from the beginning, haggled over reception center sites, and by summer 1948, Mexican negotiators finally agreed to put one reception center on the border in Mexicali in exchange for keeping others in the interior of the country.[18]

These concessions highlighted Mexico's waning diplomatic clout and foreshadowed negotiators' limited ability to win on issues of transportation costs, domestic agricultural interests, tighter control over the program, and undocumented migration. In terms of transportation, the agreement stipulated that the U.S. government shoulder the cost of transporting braceros from reception centers to U.S. farms and back, with the Mexican government picking up the tab for expenses up to that point. The issue was key because each party sought to pay as little as possible. In terms of agricultural interests, the Mexican government needed to placate powerful northern agriculturalists, whose operations depended on a sizeable but poorly paid labor force. Seeing former workers beckoned across the border by higher salaries, northern plantation owners demanded that reception centers be located in the country's interior.[19] In terms of control over the program, the Mexican government sought to retain decision-making power over which, how many, and when men would migrate. Officials needed to balance the needs of northern agriculturists and of local politicos, who distributed contracts for political favors, while still reserving a labor supply for state modernization projects—all potentially impaired by a mass exodus of workers. They also met insistence from U.S. officials, especially Texas Governor Coke Stevenson, who claimed that Texas had dismantled long-standing discriminatory practices and that this state should be taken off the blacklist and braceros allowed to work there.[20]

When the El Paso incident occurred, Mexican officials immediately walked away from negotiations, although they refused to terminate the program outright. This refusal, like Mexican officials' hesitation to demand that braceros be immediately removed from DiGiorgio's fields, suggests that negotiators were resigned to the necessity of the program, despite mounting criticism from elites and trade unionists, both of whom were important political constituencies. Huge sums of money that migrants remitted to families meant that at least the most urgent of basic needs were satisfied, lessening rural poverty and the demand for state resources at a time when they were being channeled into development projects and other state responsibilities. A decrease in poverty was also expected to decrease the likelihood of another rural uprising; with the revolution barely thirty years old and other rebellions since it, the specter of the militant peasants who had joined in droves in northern areas like Durango weighed heavily on bureaucrats' minds and pushed them to continue the program, even if that meant without stringent protections. Negotiators figured that migrants were better served by an official program with weak protections than by no program and no protections. Despite its weaknesses, the agreement struck after the El Paso incident was portrayed in the Mexican media as one between good neighbors and diplomatic equals. In the end, Mexican authorities were unable to protect their migrant citizens because the interests of the state (strong diplomatic leverage, ability to protect workers) and those of citizens (access to work) were incompatible.

Bringing Braceros into the International Arena

In 1950, two years after the El Paso incident, at the United Nations' Fifth General Assembly meeting in New York, a Polish delegate accused U.S. growers of treating braceros inhumanely and the U.S. and Mexican governments of negligence. This accusation followed an earlier session's discussion at which the United Kingdom had alleged that the Soviet Union was engaging in forced labor, a practice denounced under the Universal Declaration of Human Rights. When the United Kingdom and the United States again charged the Soviets with using forced labor, the Polish delegate asked why only the Soviet Union was subject to reprimand, since Mexican migrants faced a similar fate working in the United States. He alleged that braceros were doing the equivalent of forced labor and read into the record a statistical account of braceros. These workers, he insisted, received neither the pay nor the guarantees stipulated in the agreement but rather "wages of hunger"; they were subjected to "racial and economic discrimination" and "iniquitous exploitation"; and they were not covered by workers' protections, such as Social Security or worker's compensation, offered to U.S. industrial workers.[21] Moreover, he charged, braceros were forced to purchase toiletries and other sundry items at company stores, an implicit reference to the *tiendas de raya* that had tied peasants to landlords through generations of debt incurred through the extension of credit. A rallying cry for the Mexican Revolution, the *tienda de raya* and inheritable debt more generally had been outlawed, but they still constituted a potent charge. The Polish delegate thus implicated the Mexican state in the exploitation of its citizens and challenged its claim as inheritor of the revolution.

Incensed, Senator Pedro de Alba, a Mexican delegate who later wrote about the incident, refuted Poland's charge, which he claimed was based on "adulterated data." In his memoir, he described the "dirty game" (*juego subterráneo*) going on, which used braceros "as projectiles or witnesses against the United States." The real intent of the allegation, he insisted, was to "retaliate against Anglo-Saxon countries" and let the Eastern Bloc "present itself as supporters of human rights and protectors of migrant workers." Mexico's delegation, with a measured but forceful response, acknowledged that there was both a grain of truth in the statistics and "much exaggeration." Mexican workers may have been mistreated in the past, said de Alba, but now U.S. and Mexican officials were partnering to protect them and "guarantee" their "just demands." "We condemn the ensnarers [*enganchadores*] and traffickers [who] operated in earlier epochs," he asserted, telling the U.N. General Assembly that "times have changed." The government of the revolution, he continued, "would never have relinquished the protection of its citizens"; nor would it have consented to being the "provider of migrant labor" had this labor not been afforded "the same treatment" as U.S. workers and protection from discrimination. De Alba maintained that the bilateral agreement shielded Mexican workers in ways advocated by the International Labor Office (ILO) in Geneva, to which "all countries of the world . . . contributed morally and economically."[22] Yet as de Alba touted the partnership between Mexico and the United States, braceros were bringing increasing complaints against growers. President Harry S. Truman was forced to appoint a commission to investigate these complaints and lessen the "political heat" that he faced.[23] Although Mexican negotiators had steadily lost negotiating clout vis-à-vis their U.S. counterparts, at the United Nations—the world's highest democratic body—the country's delegates were obligated to claim that Mexico was an equal and respected U.S. diplomatic partner.

Five years later, Mexican representatives once again faced the charge that braceros were forced laborers, this time at the 1955 ILO conference in Geneva. At that occasion, delegate Emilio Calderón Puig admitted that program conditions were not as favorable as Mexico had "hope[d] that they would be." Still, he argued, there was no forced labor. "If these conditions were actually similar in any way to forced labor, I can solemnly affirm that the Government of Mexico would not allow a single one of its sons to leave the country to undertake such work."[24] Calderón Puig, ILO chair in 1957–58 and again in 1963–64, insisted that the bilateral arrangements were "based on good faith" from "both Governments" and "on the desire to improve conditions of work continually." Akin to the U.N. delegation's earlier contention of a true U.S.-Mexico partnership, Calderón Puig claimed that current negotiations were "carried out in the favorable atmosphere resulting from the excellent and cordial [binational] relations." Not only, he contended, were these relations ones between "neighbors geographically-speaking," but, more important, they signaled a mutual "friends[hip]" grounded in the "common love of liberty."[25]

Calderón Puig's portrayal before this international audience set the United States and Mexico as equal and respected diplomatic partners, yet the previous year this equality had been tested by a second border incident that again raised the ire of Mexican authorities. The vivid spectacle of bodies, guards, and guns spotlighted Mexico's inability to curtail unregulated outmigration or raise the standard of living for the country's vast numbers of poor. Again we see the government's range of options and ability to negotiate constrained by the very citizens on whose behalf it advocated.

The 1954 Incident and Operation Wetback: Pressures from Aspiring Migrants and Elites

Whereas in the 1948 El Paso incident local officials had responded to local growers' needs without high-level intervention, in 1954 the impetus for opening the Southern California border came from uppermost levels.[26] On Friday, January 15, 1954, after months of negotiation had not produced an agreement that satisfied Mexican negotiators, representatives from the U.S. Departments of Labor, State, and Justice took matters into their own hands.[27] They issued a joint press release stating that the government would begin awarding contracts to migrants who crossed the border.[28] Incensed, Mexican officials implored men to not be lured by such offers and halted agreement negotiations. They accused U.S. negotiators of wielding a "stick" to "force" acceptance of unacceptable conditions, thus tipping the scales in the diplomatic stalemate.[29]

Men kept heading north, joining the massive numbers who, after failing to get a contract, had taken up residence at the border. One witness reported "see[ing] so many sick people hobbling around . . . begging in the streets." Those "physically able," he continued, might try and jump the fence; the others would "just rot."[30] In response, the Mexican government threatened to increase the number of troops, pledged that no one would be permitted to cross, and promised swift punishment for those who tried.[31] U.S. Representative Ken Regan (D-Tex.) noted the pool of waiting laborers, the urgent needs of U.S. growers, and the breakdown in negotiations; he lamented the two countries' inability to settle differences and doubted whether closing the border would deter anyone. "Mexicans," he concluded, "need North American dollars and we need their labor. [Migration] is an aid to the Mexican economy and to ours."[32] Not surprisingly, the Mexican officials depicted the situation quite differently, putting the blame on the unilateral decision of the U.S. government to contract workers. Despite a December 21, 1953, avowal to continue talks, they cut off negotiations and chastised U.S. authorities for not agreeing to guaranteed minimum working standards.[33] Rather than hammering out an agreement, the United States was "encouraging men to violate the law" and endanger their lives.[34]

The throngs of men gathered in Mexicali, however, did not care whose fault it was. They saw migration as their ticket to prosperity—or at least less grinding poverty. After waiting, some for more than six months, most men had no money. "Thousands of workers," claimed Baja California's director of migration, were "milling around in Mexicali's streets," in "dire need" of "food and a place to stay" and impatient with the delays and diplomatic finger-pointing.[35] By mid-month, troops were dispatched to Ensenada, Nuevo Laredo, Nogales, and other border points.[36] In Mexicali, five hundred men retaliated for this display of state force by marching on the governor's palace; protests and demands for food and work were greeted by soldiers wielding fire hoses.[37] *La opinión* reported that there were "hordes of braceros" who wanted nothing more than "to be allowed to cross . . . and work."[38] Tired of government words without actions, they were out to achieve their own betterment. President Adolfo Ruíz Cortines (1952–58) quickly took steps to defuse the situation. Announcing a plan to extend credit to small landowners and communities with communally held land, he hoped to deter men's desire to cross. Baja California Governor Braulio Maldonado sweetened the deal.[39] With over twelve thousand men congregated at the border and more arriving daily, Maldonado offered free transport home and possibilities of work.[40]

Some men took Maldonado's offer, but no appeal could persuade the majority to return to their villages or dissuade others from heading north. A reporter from *La opinión* labeled the situation, growing more dangerous by the day, "a house over a barrel of dynamite." In one report he wrote that some men in the crowd, impatient and weary, threw rocks at photographers perched on rooftops; he described another incident later the same day as "a playful occurrence." During this playful event, men lifted a bus into the air, complete with passengers and driver.[41]

When U.S. border guards opened the gate on January 22, pandemonium ensued. Hundreds of hopefuls rushed in. Mexican soldiers grabbed their countrymen and yanked them back, while U.S. guards helped the migrants to cross. Mexican troops pelted compatriots with fists, guns, water, and clubs in a vain attempt to contain the rush of bodies.[42] Meanwhile, officials and growers on the northern side instructed undocumented workers already there to "step over" the invisible line and "legalize" their presence. This momentary step-over would mean that migrants had officially returned to Mexico, and having met the U.S. requirements, could "reenter" with the sanction of the Immigration and Naturalization Service and be given an official contract.[43] These men, too, found themselves "grabbed and beaten" by Mexican police and soldiers.[44] This was in marked contrast to the comportment of Mexican border soldiers in the past, when they "did little to stop this immigration" and instead, "literally rode herd on groups" of undocumented workers to assist growers, letting "the responsibility for preventing migration f[a]ll to the United States Border Patrol."[45]

Seeing the crisis that his government's muscular posture was igniting at home, President Ruíz Cortines tactically reversed course. He declared that no Mexican authority would impede anyone from crossing.[46] In response, U.S. officials stated that border guards would again regulate migration and would unilaterally put in place an interim migration program starting the following Monday. Even these measures did not ease tensions, however. On Wednesday, January 27, five days after the initial incident, more than twenty-five hundred impatient men "rioted" on the Mexican side for about an hour. Amassing at the border at six in the morning, they had inched their way toward the gate and to "the promised land."[47] A photo in *La opinión* captured the agitated crowd pressed up against the steel fence dividing the two nations.[48] With U.S. immigration officials and police forming a human chain to repel the onslaught of these waiting men, this deluge of contenders was finally broken up by a torrent of water from fire hoses and by local Mexican police driving squad cars into the agitated crowd. Miraculously, only one person was seriously injured, with others receiving what *La opinión* termed light bruises.[49]

Mexico's minister of the interior realized he had on his hands an explosive situation and a public relations nightmare. He ordered soldiers not to detain anyone, only to ask a man's name, age, and occupation. Officials also found themselves denying charges that they had increased the military presence at the border or issued orders to obstruct migrants' crossing. Yet such measures still did not defuse the tinderbox. Men had seen their companions shoved, stepped on, and kicked in the previous day's skirmish. With Monday's date fast approaching, authorities on both sides feared renewed mayhem.[50] And they were right. Aspirants started lining up at the border in the wee hours of Monday morning. At first subdued and orderly, the crowd's mood quickly turned when the mere five hundred contracts were allotted in twenty minutes. As *La opinión* described the spectacle, masses of men streaming toward the border ran head on into local Mexican police determined to hinder their crossing. "This morning," claimed the reporter on the scene, "between eight and ten thousand farmworkers threw themselves over the gate posts in Caléxico, while on the U.S. side authorities, aided by police and fire fighters, stood [ready] to repel the avalanche of braceros whom they found on top of them the moment that the gates were opened. . . . Officials used tear gas and hoses to turn the crowd around."[51]

A close-up on the front page of *La opinión* showed "a humble worker" caught in the melee, "exhausted from lack of air."[52] At one point, the men leading the crowd could neither advance nor retreat; to their front, they faced a "human chain" of Mexican immigration officials, while from behind they were blocked by thousands of other disillusioned men pressing toward the forbidden territory.[53] With every prod, push, shove, and inch forward, a few men collapsed and were trampled by others attempting to squeeze into the vacated space. Even soldiers trying to control the crowd at times lost their balance on account of the pressure, ceding the momentary breach to the advancing human force. Border agents on the northern side also got into the fray. A photo captured one man being fought over by a U.S. border guard and a Mexican policeman, an arm yanked in one direction while his body was pulled in another.[54] After two hours of mass confusion, five hundred lucky souls had been ushered in and the crowd's three attempts to pierce the blockade foiled.[55] Over the next several days, however, almost ten thousand men broke through lines of officials and scrambled onto U.S. soil. This prompted the U.S. government to halt all immigration under the pretense that it lacked funds and needed further authorization from Congress.[56] President Ruiz Cortines, downplaying the seriousness of the diplomatic crisis, indicated that it could "be resolved within the norms of the good neighbor policy." He simultaneously sent Mexico's ambassador to quietly ask President Dwight D. Eisenhower to recommence negotiations, an offer the latter accepted on February 11.[57] This rapprochement, declared a victory in the Mexican press, allowed the Ruiz Cortines administration to save face at home and resolve the international imbroglio.

Even before this incident, Mexican officials had threatened to call thousands of workers home. In early June 1952, facing the vocal support of U.S. growers for a hard-line stance, they decried the unacceptably low wages paid to bracero cotton pickers. They called the stance a direct assault on their ability to negotiate a fair wage, oversee program implementation, and demand a comprehensive contract for migrant citizens.[58] The Mexican government's position, however, won no support at the 1953 U.S. congressional hearings on the program; only Representative Eugene McCarthy (D-Minn.), denounced growers' abuses. Most congressional representatives instead sided with Senator Bourke Hickenlooper (R-Iowa), who demanded an end to the entire program. He instead called on all Mexicans wanting to work to do so with no safeguards or subsidies. "Come on, boys," thundered Hickenlooper to fellow senators. "There is work here, come in under your own power and go back under your own power."[59] His was a pointed reminder of Mexico's waning diplomatic leverage and inability to protect its citizens, workers squeezed by an insatiable demand for contracts that the program was never designed to address. Mexicans, it seems, were always temporary laborers, never potential or future citizens.

In the months leading up to the 1954 border incident, U.S. negotiators had pressed for substantive changes to the agreement, and Mexican authorities had refused.[60] The political scientist Richard B. Craig attributed this refusal to three factors. First was the Mexican government's reasoning that, in a time of deteriorating bilateral relations, the United States would not adopt a unilateral approach. The second, said Craig, was Mexico's sense of political "timing" and its use of "pressure politics."[61] Last was a strong sense of dignity and self-respect, which had been on commanding display in the editorial pages of *Excélsior* and other newspapers.[62] The Mexican press heralded the impasse, calling it the result of adroit maneuvering yielding significant concessions, even as *Excélsior*, quoting "well-informed sources," asserted a conviction that the two neighbors would eventually "arrive at an agreement."[63] Newspapers had also peppered their pages with reports on development projects undertaken, factories built, and optimistic projections that food needs would be met. The same confident portrayal framed the outbreak of hoof-and-mouth disease, which brought about the closing of the border, the slaughter of thousands of Mexican cattle, and the formation of a Mexican-U.S. binational commission. This coordinated response was not a U.S. rescue mission, the newspapers said, but rather another instance of respectful treatment of Mexico by its northern neighbor.[64]

Such portrayals came at a time when the Mexican state exercised substantial influence over the media without fully controlling the message. In the 1950s newspapers wrote about the rampant misery of the majority of people in Mexico and enumerated reasons behind braceros' willingness to endure the harsh conditions of U.S. agricultural work. Article after article decried blatant corruption or the selling of program documents, chastising low-ranking police or authorities for their greediness and sins against the nation. In contrast to such sullied individuals, the state was depicted as the people's protector, the trustworthy arbiter of the family's needs and the guiding light of the revolution.[65] And yet it could not deliver on promises: men still wanted to leave. The defender of the masses found its diplomatic options impeded by those most needing its help and protection. Having cast the program and the relationship more generally as one between near equals, the Mexican state could not publicly confess diplomatic weakness or blame migrants for the lack of protection.

As the U.S. Border Patrol was helping migrants across California's southern border, other areas of the country were up in arms about the "invasion" of undocumented migrants. This outrage stemmed in part from the recession and in part from a "nativist crusade." The government reacted by rounding up those who were in the country "illegally."[66] Operation Wetback, as the policy was called, continued measures begun in 1949, when more than 250,000 persons of Mexican ancestry were repatriated. On Congress's list of recommended actions was the building of a 150-mile-long fence and having the Army work with the Border Patrol. Lieutenant General Joseph M. Swing was appointed commissioner of the Immigration and Nationalization Service to lead the efforts. No Mexico enthusiast, Swing, a former West Point classmate of President Eisenhower, had participated in General John J. Pershing's 1916 hunt for Mexican revolutionary fighter Pancho Villa.[67] Operation Wetback allowed the U.S. Border Patrol to institute military sweeps and empowered local police to stop anyone who looked Mexican and demand proof of citizenship or legal residency. In 1953 the number of repatriated reached 875,000, including many legal residents and U.S. citizens living in places such as St. Louis, Chicago, Kansas City, and Spokane. In 1954 the figure exceeded 1 million.[68] The policy angered many people across the country and elicited complaints of police-state tactics, although established Mexican American organizations, such as the League of United Latin American Citizens or American G.I. Forum, whose primarily middle-class leadership supported assimilationist policies, did not speak out against the practice.[69] Only the more radical, working-class, and short-lived Asociación Nacional México Americana supported deported Mexicans, regardless of citizenship.

By 1955 Operation Wetback was generally over, along with the recession. Although deportations continued, they now targeted those thought to be labor agitators and communists, in numbers small enough that Swing could pronounce the measure a success. He both reassured the public that the alarm was past and forced growers to end their dependence on undocumented workers, at least temporarily, and accept the better-protected braceros in their stead. Mexican officials, opposed to mass deportation, had urged their U.S. counterparts to make employing undocumented workers the punishable crime, a measure to which the United States would not consent.[70]

On some level, the policy produced the desired effect: in 1955, only thirty thousand people were apprehended for entering without a contract, while a half million braceros were hired.[71]

Realignment

The twenty-two years of the bracero program was the context for a broader realignment of diplomatic and economic power between (and within) the United States and Mexico. This realignment was impacted by three integrated changes: first, a dramatic rise in undocumented migration and a corresponding drop in the ability of Mexican officials to negotiate strong contracts; second, an intensified U.S. preoccupation with communism and a conviction that it was expanding in Mexico; and, third, the increasing concern for the safety of braceros, undocumented farmworkers, and U.S. domestic laborers. The first can be explained by the fact that, although the Mexican economy expanded significantly during the program (the time of the now-famous Mexican Miracle), the number of jobs created could never meet demand; thus, thousands of men who sought contracts actually needed jobs. In 1943, only one year after the program began, twenty thousand men lined up in Mexico City alone, surpassing the total number allotted.[72] Despite a need for contracts, the number was always set by the U.S. government in coordination with growers. Migrant hopefuls often circumvented restrictions, crossing without contracts or, as the two border incidents show, congregating at the border until they could enter. While this left the undocumented open to the kind of abuse that earlier migrants had faced, the money these workers and braceros sent home offered families economic breathing room and by the 1950s had become Mexico's third-largest source of hard currency.[73] Reluctantly migrants shifted from calling on the state to meet basic needs to meeting them on their own.

Still, increasing undocumented migration and demand for contracts constrained the Mexican government's leverage. Negotiators tried at every turn to induce the United States to impose sanctions on growers who used undocumented workers, dragging their heels, if not outright halting bargaining, until their U.S. counterparts were more accommodating. These stalling tactics backfired, redoubling demand and the lengths to which migrants would go to obtain a contract. Part of men's desire to migrate, despite sometimes horrendous working conditions, came from a perception that the Mexican state had neglected rural areas in favor of urban industrialization.[74] That is, rural folk saw themselves sacrificed in the state's industrializing push, notwithstanding a Mexican familial rhetoric of benefits for all. Demand for contracts crippled Mexico's countervailing moves to garner the reinstatement of U.S. government funding for the enforcement and monitoring of program protections, which had been cut in response to growers' pressure on local and federal officeholders and the refrain that agriculture was fundamental to California's and the nation's economy. Ultimately, Mexican officials' power to negotiate stronger protections and higher salaries was undercut by the very laborers a stronger contract was deemed to protect.

Into the discussion on the program's viability we must add a public preoccupation with communism. Some politicians, growers, and ordinary citizens saw braceros not as poor men, but as communist radicals hoping to incite a workers' revolution in the United States.[75] However, estimates that ending the program would put 315,000 braceros out of work raised attendant concerns about chaos in Mexico. Its end, warned Representative Allen Smith (R-Calif.), would make unemployed braceros more susceptible to communist rhetoric and stoke Mexican poverty and hardship. Representative Edith Green (D-Ore.) challenged his line of reasoning, arguing that the program had created bad blood between the two countries, which furthered the radicals' mission. She asked her fellow members of Congress to imagine the "tremendous harm" that might ensue "if some Mexican Fidelista took to the airwaves, and, for anti-American purposes, discussed the Bracero program, not as it might be described on the pages of some propaganda journal, but as it really exists." That the United States was "a vast market for underpaid, exploited Mexican labor," she reasoned, would certainly "do more to wreck the Alliance for Progress than all the rantings about Yanqui imperialism that emanate from Havana."[76] This fear rang true because at this moment Latin America was seen as vulnerable to communism's influence. Not only was the region's lack of modern sensibility and conveniences thought to make people susceptible to its appeal; communism was an entrenched political philosophy there, evidenced by the long tradition of radical parties in Latin American political systems. In reaction, Congress passed the McCarren-Walter Immigration Act of 1952, which made it a felony to import and harbor undocumented workers (whose numbers were growing in the years prior to Operation Wetback) and prohibited suspected communists or other radicals from immigrating. This measure allowed the government to refuse entry to known union organizers and sympathizers, and to deport on an employer's mere whim any migrant who agitated for workers' rights; it also forbade citizens from arresting undocumented workers, a tactic union activists had used to retaliate against braceros and undocumented migrants whose presence undermined organizing drives. Together, these actions hint at the depth of fear about the alleged communist threat and of the alarm about Latin America's revolutionary tendencies. This apprehension quashed or pushed underground any latent U.S. collectivist sentiments, cementing the U.S. vision of democracy and freedom as individualist and the polar opposite of communism and other collectivist trends.

Terminating the Bracero Program

In the end, the bracero program was phased out not because the Mexican government advocated its demise—it did not—but because of U.S. liberal realignments that weakened the grower consensus in favor of the program. First, the intra-agency struggle between the grower-friendly Department of Agriculture and the then more evenhanded Department of Labor for program control was temporarily settled; despite their "direct access" to and backing from the secretary of agriculture (a past American Farm Bureau Federation president during the Eisenhower administration), the DOL took steps to hold growers to the letter *and* spirit of the bilateral agreement.[77] Second, the largest original user of braceros—cotton growers—had by this time found a technological solution to their vast labor requirements.[78] Not only had DOL mandates such as a minimum wage made braceros more expensive, but growers, already helped by migrants' low wages, had amassed the capital required to invest in new technologies, such as harvesters, whose development was federally subsidized. And lastly, the public was becoming painfully aware of program's abuses; more important, it realized that large commercial growers in a few states were the main users of braceros, a realization that diminished growers' ability to portray themselves as struggling small farmers endangered without this labor source.[79] No longer could elite growers contend that they were caught in "the vagaries of weather and insects," squeezed by unions and rising prices, or that the program itself generated "international good will" and "Pan-Americanism."[80]

This temporary diminishing of grower power was part of broader institutional and societal shifts that in 1960 would bring liberals to Congress and the John Kennedy–Lyndon Johnson ticket into the White House.[81] The economy had improved in the years after 1954, lessening economic fears; in addition, the civil rights movement had caught the attention of the nation, highlighting the structural inequities facing the poor and racially disadvantaged, inequalities made glaring in the *Harvest of Shame*, Edward R. Murrow's 1960 documentary. In this new atmosphere, farm-union activists, bolstered by DOL studies, could publicize the impact of the program on both braceros *and* domestic farmhands. Although few concrete changes would be instituted to improve the lives of domestic farmworkers, Undersecretary of Labor John Hennings still labeled the importation of workers a U.S. "betrayal" of its citizens.[82]

A coalition of religious, labor, and liberal activists decried the program as unjust and immoral, in a move that began to tarnish agriculturalists' former sheen, despite deft work by their lobbyists. This coalition charged that foreign "slave labor" was a "disgrace" to the country's democratic and "Christian" values. How could a modern democracy like the United States—which had recently fought a global war and played a foundational role in establishing the United Nations in the name of freedom—support the abuse of foreign laborers whose presence, in no uncertain terms, contributed to the destitution of domestic farmhands? A House member castigated the program for using "one poverty-stricken group of men [braceros] to compete against another poverty-stricken group [domestic farmworkers] to create still more poverty. It violates the basic beliefs of our Nation."[83] Another insisted that the law establishing the program was "immoral." The use of morality as the basis for tempering growers' influence was not a strategic ploy; by then, it enabled the reframing of bracero labor as a question of and threat to the United States as a modern democracy.[84] So strong was public pressure that in 1967, prominent legislators passed an agricultural minimum wage.[85] Regardless of this temporary victory, growers' advocates had created a food production and delivery system that instantiated an economic and social gulf between U.S. rural and urban folk. Built on the backs of low-paid migrant workers—foreign and domestic—the system brought cheap food to urban and expanding suburban areas.[86]

While U.S. opposition had grown sufficiently powerful and made program termination possible, the Kennedy and Johnson administrations did not want to appear to trample on the wishes of their more circumspect southern counterparts. Both U.S. presidents realized all too well the advantages of a committed Latin American partner, and measures were instituted to minimize the threat of communism or a Soviet beachhead so close to home. To address this possibility, all the more tangible after the 1959 Cuban Revolution, Kennedy proposed the Alliance for Progress, a set of policies and programs seemingly designed to eradicate widespread hemispheric poverty. Although President Adolfo López Mateos (1958–64) acknowledged that the bracero program had always been considered temporary, he was not keen to terminate it before special provisions were made for the employment and reabsorption of returning workers. Estimates contended that an abrupt ending would leave more than two hundred thousand migrants without work or, if they stayed in the United States or continued to return there, more vulnerable to exploitation. Given the then recent paralyzing strikes by teachers and railroad workers, López Mateos and Mexican program negotiators pushed for a gradual phase-out. Still, with Mexico's economy expanding, all foresaw the economic incorporation of former braceros, accomplished in part by offering unused land in the south of the country to these now skilled farmhands.[87]

While Mexican officials agreed to defer to a U.S. decision, they presented strong reasons for the program's continuation. First, its end would not curtail outmigration, since U.S. employers still recruited Mexicans. Second, bracero labor had benefited U.S. farmers directly, and U.S. farmworkers indirectly, since braceros had proved to be an extremely productive workforce, assuaging growers' worry about the labor supply.[88] Officials, dismissing repercussions on domestic workers, argued that the agreement's provisions had set "a pattern" of U.S. farmworker benefits, a credible position since the DOL was then pushing to institute guarantees for domestic workers similar to those extended to braceros under the program.[89] Third, although the program had encountered glitches and moments of strain (most notably the two border incidents), it had established "a firm foundation for the good relations between the peoples of the two countries."[90] Not mentioned in this list of reasons was the increasing Mexican dependence on remittances, at both an individual and a national level. Such transfers were estimated in 1960 at more than $50 million, with each man's earnings supporting four persons on average. In other words, this southward flow of dollars had kept more than 750,000 Mexicans from destitution and spurred changes in rural areas in line with the program's original goals.[91] Mexico's push for a gradual end to the program delayed its shutdown by one year. In the works was the establishment of a free trade zone along the border. This move, it was said, would address Mexico's unemployment as well as those needs still unmet by the bracero program for capital, technology, and industrial (as opposed to agricultural) know-how.[92]

Conclusion

The effects of men's need and desire to migrate can be seen in the two border incidents and the international exchanges at the United Nations and
ILO I have examined in this chapter. Undocumented migrants disregarded
governmental threats of punishment and the dangers of the actual border
melee, and they likewise snubbed the proffered carrots of land and credit.
Instead they chose to cross the border at all costs, an unstemmed tide that
severely weakened negotiators' ability to insist on better compensation and
work conditions. The Mexican state attempted to link all programs to collective benefit, national unity, and sovereignty, and to position itself as the
arbiter of domestic disputes and the voice of national interests to a global
audience. Nevertheless, its inability to address these needs, made clear in
the coverage of masses congregating at the border, blunted such claims. Instead, migrant hopefuls acted in the interests of themselves and their families, weakening the state's leverage, from which they would have benefited
significantly. That is, the braceros' actions steadily wrote the state out of its
own national story.

Yet migrants were not the only ones dismissing a central role for the state.
Mexican elites, both journalists and other writers, claiming braceros for their
own, faulted the state for men's need to migrate and welcomed them back
into a new national narrative.[93] At the program's end, even those who had
initially supported it concluded that the expenditure of migrant initiative
and energy outside Mexico had weakened the nation. Working at home, they
argued, was working for the nation. Although some officials conceded that
agrarian reform policies had failed to stimulate agricultural production and
output, many, like U.N. representative Pedro de Alba, pleaded with former
braceros to employ their new agricultural knowledge at home. This decision,
he claimed, would lead individual braceros and the entire nation to prosperity. Yet the measures he imagined as necessary to invigorate rural areas and
the poor could not compete with the new reality of migration and the lure of
purchasable commodities enabled by work in the United States.

By 1964 the Mexican government had implicitly discarded small farms'
central role in its state project and tacitly encouraged land reconsolidation.
It simultaneously established the free-trade-based Border Industrialization
Program (BIP), shifting away from Import Substitution Industrialization, an
economic model that sought industrialization by fostering a manufacturing

base of formerly imported products and imposing high tariffs for imported products to redirect consumption toward domestic ones. This new BIP economic policy would draw U.S. companies, and then other foreign manufacturers, to establish assembly plants on the Mexican side of the U.S.-Mexican border. These maquiladoras did not design or manufacture products from beginning to end but instead assembled components made elsewhere into finished products. Such factories did nevertheless utilize an abundant Mexican resource: labor. In exchange for assembly jobs, the BIP exempted the economic inputs required for assembly (such as supplies, machinery, and equipment) from taxation, and products exported back to the United States would be taxed only on their value-added portion. By encouraging factories that implemented only the supposedly least skilled part of the production process, the Mexican government implicitly acknowledged that the country could not yet support full modernization. This acknowledgment also cheapened the value of the final products and the workers themselves.[94]

The contradictions that gave rise to the bracero program did not end with the pronouncement of its death. From the ashes emerged the H-2A visa, a category specifically intended for seasonal agricultural workers with fewer additional provisions than the program. Moreover, the BIP grew steadily and was, by 1969, the impetus for 147 companies employing around seventeen thousand workers. In the end, however, benefits accrued not so much to Mexico and its workers as they did to the international companies and their U.S. customers. Despite maquila workers' higher wages, the cost of living in border cities continually rose, and foreign employers hired not former braceros but young, unmarried women thought to be naturally more docile, more compliant, and less susceptible to union organizing than their male counterparts.[95] Without promised good jobs for returned braceros, undocumented migration has not just grown but exploded as Mexico's economy has worsened.

In addition, the program exposed a great many migrants to consumer products, instilling a desire for commodities that local economies could not support.[96] That is, although the program fostered the desire for modern material conveniences, Mexico's place in the global economy as the home of cheap labor has limited the realization of those desires.

In the end, we cannot see men's insistence on U.S. work as only economic. For many participants, if not the majority, the program offered something else: a response to the zeal of the antifascist fight and the lure of incorporation into the Mexican nation as recognized modern social and political actors. Yet, as this book has shown, this recognition and national incorporation was a dream deferred. It was deferred in Mexican communities that could not support braceros' return with jobs or satisfy their tastes and demands for consumer products—only a cycle of migration would do. It was deferred in the United States because, despite braceros' struggle for the rewards due modern workers, their race, nationality, and job class as farmhands ultimately remarginalized them as always already foreign, dividing them from even similarly placed domestic farmworkers. That is, they were unable to attain full incorporation in either national space. Produced, instead, were transnational subjects, a social position that demanded a movement between both nations and through which they increasingly anchored their survival and national claims.

In closing, I return to the dilemma with which I opened this book: Should we view the program as exploitation or an opportunity? Framing the program as such, I suggest, leaves little room to recognize the multiple ways that migrants acted on their own behalf and the many-sided repercussion of such actions. Nor does it capture the creativity with which they engaged the structural inequalities that gave birth to the program and that it in turn fostered. Instead, the complexity of men's actions and their multipronged effects ultimately produced these men as transnational subjects.

Epilogue

One morning in 2005, as I stared at the blinking cursor, I was distracted by the radio in the background. National Public Radio was running a story on a debate in a Washington, D.C., suburb over whether the municipality should invest in a day laborers' center to shelter immigrant men who waited outside for possible work. I was struck by the voice of Mary Barder, a white southern woman, who at a local hearing declared that "these men will never use the new facility." They "just want to gather to hang out," she claimed, instead of learning to "live like Americans." For Barder, living like Americans meant that the men should learn "to speak English," "have good hygiene," and "use appliances in their homes correctly." And "then the pride will come to them." Another town resident, Sylvia Washington, a middle-aged black woman, followed. "Not only am I repulsed—and insulted—by the derogatory comments that have been slung by some of my neighbors," she said. "If I close my eyes, it sounds like I'm back in time. . . . Only the names and the race have changed."[1]

I was still working on this book when, about eight months later (April 2006), a radically different depiction of immigrants appeared in media accounts. This time workers were not objects of derision, as in the above story, but actors. Thousands took to the streets in places like Chicago, Los Angeles, and Dallas, and even in smaller cities such as my own St. Louis. With signs, chants, flags, and pronouncements to the press, these men, women, and children, from church groups and soccer teams, hometown associations and schools, forcefully reminded onlookers, "America was built by immigrants!" They were resisting congressional moves to criminalize and deny due process to the undocumented, and to target for prosecution the clergy, health-care personnel, teachers, and social workers who supported them. The bill prioritized border enforcement and the building of a wall.² One demonstrator, Robert Martínez, told a Dallas reporter, "It's a good feeling that we are finally standing up for ourselves." Now a U.S. citizen, Martínez lamented, "For years, we never say nothing. . . . We just work hard, follow the rules, and pay taxes. And they try to make these [anti-immigrant] laws. It's time people knew how we felt." Another marcher asserted, "[We] support American values; [we] *live* the values of this country."³

Lest we think that the bracero program has been relegated to the past, or forget that braceros, too, fought for their interests, in September 2008, after years of struggle and lawsuits, the Mexican government announced it would award a one-time payment of $3,500 to approximately 250,000 former braceros—or if deceased, their spouses or heirs—if they could prove that they had been braceros least once between 1942 and 1946. The program agreement then in force had specified that 10 percent of wages would be withheld and made available on the workers' return. But most braceros never saw this money. A lawsuit was originally filed against the Mexican and U.S. governments and three program banks: Wells Fargo Bank, Union Trust Company of San Francisco, and Banco de Crédito Agrícola (Agricultural Credit Bank, which from the mid-1970s to its dissolution in 1988 was part of Banrural, itself the consolidation of several institutions). The government, acknowledging no wrongdoing, settled after Porfirio Martínez González, the leader of Alianza Braceroproa, an organization of former braceros, threatened to go public with "authentic proof" that "ex-braceros' money" had "disappeared on instructions" of a former president.⁴

This announcement sent elderly men, some in their nineties, to shoeboxes, drawers, and stacks of dusty papers. Not surprisingly, no records remain to explain what happened to the braceros' monies.⁵ Nor were most men able to take advantage of the offer. A majority misplaced their documents, lost them, or did not foresee the need to save old contracts, records of wages, and ID cards. "I saw guys ripping up their pay stubs," reflected Francisco Flores, now eighty-three, "and I said, 'Wait, save all those papers, someday it is going to be useful.'" He smiled, showing off a small black case with documents from a bygone era.⁶ Eighty-six-year-old Cirilo Pérez-Torres, typical of many former braceros, could not prove his participation because his papers had been destroyed when his home flooded several years ago. "I remember everything, the fields, the places, the crops," Pérez-Torres explained wistfully after meeting with a consular official. "But they are not accepting my memories."[7]

Former braceros sue their government, undocumented immigrants take over streets in protest, and local communities debate the merits of building a labor center for people accused of being lawbreakers, despite a tacit understanding that the center, by helping immigrants find work, would put them further outside the law. These incidents, emblematic of the struggles and transformations at the heart of this book, took place alongside others in the first decade of the new millennium: mass federal raids on businesses employing undocumented workers, separating them from their U.S. citizen children; the pressure that the economic crisis is putting on longtime U.S. residents, some now returning to Mexico; estimates that one-tenth of agricultural, food services, construction, and maintenance workers are undocumented; and the savage murders of Latinos by young white men itching to "attack a Mexican."[8] The struggles around the bracero program and the kinds of transformations these struggles elicited are of critical importance for understanding these current circumstances. They prompt the question, what has changed?

Considering Mary Barder's migrant to-do list—speaking English, having good hygiene, and knowing how to use appliances—we might likely assume, not much. Still, on closer inspection, her concerns are very telling. Migrants now live in her Washington, D.C., suburb, far beyond the large cities or bracero program sites where they generally resided. Moreover, her seemingly benign inventory of skills required for U.S. inclusion is, I suggest, a set of requirements that insists on a certain kind of transformation: to willingly discard cultures of origin and transform into Americans by readily adopting so-called American ways. This insistence speaks not only to the profound discomfort about immigrants, but to the lack of legitimate place for those not wholly engaged in assimilation—in other words, the process of becoming fully national along preset lines. Those who retain emotional connections beyond the nation provoke deep suspicion, for they expose the lie at its very heart—that people, place, and nation map onto each other perfectly.

By perfect mapping, I mean the idea that the cultural, political, economic, and social ties of citizens should correspond seamlessly with the territory that is the nation-state and that no one and no group should exceed these boundaries—that is, the belief that a nation-state comprises one people in one place. Yet no nation-state has ever met this goal. This inability has yielded substantive—and ongoing—projects to align people with place and a belief in the necessary completeness of this hypothetical alignment. In Mexico, this work is done through the formative myth of a productive racial comingling of Spanish father and indigenous mother and the concomitant downplaying (if not erasure) of the immigration, most notably, of Asian workers, escaped slaves, and Jewish and Spanish exiles. In the United States, we see it in the myths of a melting pot, a multihued quilt, or a stew, and the repetition of a popular narrative that earlier immigrants came for democracy and freedom. In all cases, immigrants undergo profound pressure to comply with the particular version of the nation-state project. Here, inclusion requires that new arrivals board the assimilation express. For those immigrating not for acceptable reasons—democracy or freedom—but for work, exclusion has been an a priori position. Despite such exclusion, immigrants do forge local connections. And in so doing, they become—and are marked as—transnational subjects.

While allegiance is not contained by borders or walls, the profound anxiety that transnational subjects provoke is at the heart of the current immigration debates and of the strategies around the earlier bracero program.[9] Yet it would be a mistake to accept a reading of migrant workers as the only transnational, and hence marked, subjects. As this book has shown, the same was true for the array of program actors. Growers acted from their position as transnational subjects when they recruited immigrant laborers, negotiated crop prices and work conditions, coordinated with those in other countries, and positioned themselves as quintessential farmers—the most patriotic of national members.[10] Union officials were transnational subjects when they, in tandem with other labor organizations, used rhetoric of class-based affinity, even as their rhetoric stressed a language of national and race-based boundaries. In the case of the U.S. and Mexican governments, the negotiating strength of the former expanded in relation to the weakening of the latter—that is, transnationally. The two nations, moreover, were—and continue to be—mutually constituted.

This is not to suggest that nation-states negotiate in global fraternal harmony; rather, my intention has been to expose the fiction of fraternity and the actuality of a hierarchical, interrelated system. There are winners who set the rules, and losers forced to negotiate within them. To see *all* actors as transnational and the centrality of this arena would expose the fiction of an entire system ostensibly organized around sovereign fraternal (coequal) nation-state actors: thus the singular focus on immigrants and on the heightened anxieties that these bodies evoke.

Part of this current anxiety came out in discussions of the immigrant rallies of April–May 2006 described above. While newspapers carried bright color photos of massive, energized demonstrations, of parents marching with children, and of protesters with signs reading "We Are America" and "America: Built by Immigrants," what stirred the most controversy were the flags some marchers waved. Besides the requisite stars and stripes, many brandished Mexican flags, as well as those of other Latin American countries. Mexican flags aroused particular fury. One angry onlooker labeled the display "disrespectful and distasteful." "If it's a Mexican flag you want to honor," said another, "then there's a country which honors that flag and perhaps that's where [you] ought to wave . . . it."[11] Even at this moment of hope and possible inclusion, talk reverted to demands for a wall.

This anger over the flying of foreign—and specifically Mexican—flags reminds us of what other scholars have argued is the conflation of Mexican with "illegal alien."[12] Moreover, it exposes the limited options open to immigrants. Their choice is assimilation or expulsion. Barder, whose comments opened this epilogue, sought a soft mandatory assimilation—the substitution of ethnicity for nationalism and a possible path to citizenship. Resentful bystanders at marches advocated swift departure—and criminal prosecution. The choice then, if this can be said to be a choice, was between becoming American along predetermined lines or going "home." Despite the concomitant celebration of pluralism, tolerance, and multiculturalism, then, there is still little public space in the U.S. nation for those whose attachments exceed national boundaries. We might see repeated appeals for a fortress-like wall and the brazen and violent attacks on immigrants as attempts to rid the national body politic of its foreign contaminants. Too much a threat, the transnational subject must literally die—or at least be expunged.

While here the (poor) transnational subject is still an indeterminate social position, south of the border there has been necessary accommodation to migration, much of it long-term, and to deep changes that this migration brings. This accommodation has grown principally out of the money that migrants remit, much of which passes through banks and into the orbit of the state. During the bracero program these remittances not only supported families and enabled local community investment, but at the program's height this money was also the third-largest source of hard currency into

Mexico, softening the state's fiscal crunch at a time when resources were funneled toward modernization projects. The government still has not freed itself of dependence on this economic source, which in 2007 totaled just under $24 billion and ranks with, and sometimes surpasses, other leading earners of foreign exchange such as direct foreign investment, petroleum, tourism, and manufactured exports.[13] Indeed, Mexican state policies—some long-standing—have encouraged the emotional bonds to family and nation on which these remittances are predicated: officials now attend formal meet-and-greet sessions with U.S.-resident migrants; they have provided the matching funds for hometown infrastructure projects; and in several recent election cycles, Mexican presidential candidates held rallies in cities like Chicago, with significant numbers of Mexican citizens and Mexican Americans attending.

This rapprochement between state and immigrant did not arise from state openness or generosity but out of a calculated response to continued pressure by migrants to reconfigure inclusion based on the economic rewards of their work. The pressure was made particularly visible on December 10, 1996, when Mexican President Ernesto Zedillo signed into law the constitutional changes allowing former Mexican nationals who are now U.S. citizens and those having a parent with Mexican citizenship to "regain" Mexican nationality. Though nonresident nationality does not bring voting rights, it does institutionalize a sense of national belonging by granting other rights, such as real estate ownership, otherwise reserved for Mexican citizens.[14] This belonging also makes more likely the remittances on which the state relies.

In sum, this book has set the struggles of migrants in relation to other state and nonstate actors not because they were the only transnational subjects, but because this focus better illuminates the entrenched practices and relationships at the core of anxiety about this subject. We should also not assume that the transnational subject is going away. Economic booms give way to busts and again to booms. Migrants come and go. Wars and terrorist incidents, too, are followed by seemingly peaceful reprieves. Yet the conditions of inequality and fictive national sovereignty that forge global movements of capital and labor do not disappear. Thus neither do the transnational subjects—or the calls for thirteen-foot walls—that these conditions produce.

Still, I do not want to imply that the men, and now women and children, who come here merely accept established terms as a Faustian bargain. As this book has shown, braceros actively negotiated the terms of attachment and belonging. Immigrants continue this negotiation to this day. In immigrants' waving of native flags and continued use of Spanish, in their self-portrayal as embodying so-called American values, and in braceros' pressure for back wages, these transnational subjects reject the parameters of the either/or options presented them in the United States or the usury relationship cultivated in Mexico. They are creating a "third way," a transnational subjectivity rooted in ongoing movement between Mexico and the United States, and in migrants' everyday acts of claiming cultural, political, and economic inclusion on *both* sides of the border. In this refusal to submit to a preset mandate, they continue to expose as myth the idea that people, place, and nation can be neatly coupled. The nation, they show us, never was only national.

Notes

Abbreviations

ACLU	American Civil Liberties Union
AGN	Archivo General de la Nación, Mexico City
AHSRE	Archivo Histórico de Secretaría de Relaciones Exteriores, Mexico City
BRBML	Beinecke Rare Book and Manuscript Library, Yale University, New Haven, Conn.
DGAHDSRE	Dirección General del Acervo Histórico Diplomático de Secretaría de Relaciones Exteriores, Mexico City
EGP	Ernesto Galarza Papers, Special Collections and University Archives, Stanford University, Stanford, Calif.
IOHUTEP	Institute for Oral History, University of Texas, El Paso
NARA	U.S. National Archives and Records Administration, Washington, D.C.
OC	Oficina de Contrataciones
PAC	Protección y Asuntos Consulares
RG	Record Group
STFU	Southern Tenant Farmers Union

Note: Unless otherwise indicated, quotations are taken from interviews I conducted and from my fieldwork. I have used pseudonyms for all individuals I interviewed, except state officials, and for interview locations. Per anthropological convention, I have not listed interviews in the bibliography. Unless otherwise indicated, all translations from the Spanish are mine.

Introduction

1. *Don* is a title of respect, social status, honor, and age used in conjunction with a man's first name.

2. Álvaro García, conversation, Santa Angélica, Durango, November 1995.

3. There was a similar shorter program to staff railroads; here I speak only of agriculture.

4. The number of participants in the program fluctuated: 38,345 in 1948, 445,197 in 1956, and 177,736 in 1964. California Assembly Committee on Agriculture, *The Bracero Program*, 4. According to Manuel García y Griego, the claim by scholars that nearly 5 million people participated reflects instead the number of contracts offered and migrant journeys taken. See García y Griego, "The Importation of Mexican Contract Laborers." Robert Michael Brown asserts that 4% of Mexico's economically active population participated as braceros. See Brown, "The Impact of Work Experience," 1.

5. I expand the definition of *transnational* by Linda Basch, Nina Glick-Schiller, and Cristina Szanton Blanc, who refer to a single "field" that spans national borders and describe migrants' "interconnected experience" of this field—that is, for Basch, Glick-Schiller, and Blanc it is a particular space that unbinds the nation-state. I move from a focus on im/migrants' space delinked from nation-state territory to one on the processes by which the space is produced, processes in which many sets of actors are caught and contribute to. The term has become extremely popular since their book's publication, now often referring to anything that transcends national borders. In using it to connote a set of processes, I build on the work of scholars such as Laura Doyle ("Toward a Philosophy of Transnationalism") and Micol Seigel ("Beyond Compare") and aim to reinvest it with some rhetorical specificity and vigor. See Basch, Glick-Shiller, and Szanton Blanc, *Nations Unbound*, 6.

6. The legal scholar Jennifer Gordon, in speaking about the contemporary situation, advocates for bringing migrant guest workers into unions prior to their departure from their home country. This idea was weakly attempted during the bracero program (chap. 6). Gordon, "Transnational Labor Citizenship."

7. The first prominent scholar to highlight migration's modernizing effects was the Mexican anthropologist Manuel Gamio. In research on earlier migration, he lauded the work habits and ethic these migrants had adopted as benefits for Mexican nation-building. See Gamio, *Mexican Immigration*.

8. I am not suggesting that each migrant left Mexico with these subjectivities, only that they were the social, economic, and cultural positions available at this historical moment.

9. I use *bracero* as a descriptive category and *transnational subject* as an analytic one. The use of *transnational subject* engages with Mae Ngai's "impossible subject," which denotes an analytical category and one of lived experience whose subject is denied a recognized position of legitimacy in the United States—the claim on rights that citizenship affords is deemed impossible because of the particular U.S. alignment of race and empire marked on these particular bodies and affixed to their

attendant social position. *Transnational subject*, in contrast, refers to a social position resulting from the demands that actors made on more than one nation, in this case, the United States and Mexico. The exercise of these demands did (and still does) provoke discomfort and anxiety for those with solely national relations. Moreover, while no bracero would likely refer to himself as a transnational subject, many did recognize and tell me of affective connections that went beyond the limits of a single nation-state. Ngai, *Impossible Subjects*.

10. The armed phase of the revolution took place from 1910 to 1917; state institutions, practices, and national myths were consolidated over the following forty years.

11. This program logic drew on a long history dating back to the second half of the nineteenth century, when elites began pondering why Mexico's development lagged behind that of the United States, France, and England. For a broader discussion of how this pertains to the bracero program, see the introduction to my "Masculine Sweat, Stoop-Labor Modernity." For additional work on Mexico's attempts at modernization, see Overmyer-Velázquez, *Visions of the Emerald City*; Wells and Joseph, *Summer of Discontent*; González Navarro, *Raza y tierra*; González Navarro, *Historia moderna de México*; González Navarro, *Sociedad y cultura*; and Vasconcelos, *The Cosmic Race*. For an earlier vision of how migration could modernize Mexico, which would then be incorporated into official state policy, see Gamio's books *Forjando patria*, *Mexican Immigration to the United States*, and *The Mexican Immigrant*. I use *peasant* to refer to an economic position, relationship, and set of priorities not automatically coextensive with a particular cultural or social worldview.

12. Anderson, *Fields of Bondage*, 73.

13. For a compelling vision of the Cold War as a struggle between two versions of modernization, one democratic and one socialist, see Westad, *The Global Cold War*. In his book on state formation in 1940s León, Mexico, Daniel Newcomer argues not only that elites failed to bring nonelites onto the modernization bandwagon but that they knew of this refusal and it provoked "major concern." This anxiety, he says, was not for modernity per se; it emerged because modernity was used as a rationale for elite governance. Newcomer, *Reconciling Modernity*, 17; Newcomer, personal communication with author.

14. In advocating this position, I build on the work of scholars who directly question the power of the Mexican state to impose its national vision and who ask when it became able to do this, if it ever did. Some advocate examining the local-state relationship as a way of seeing the unevenness of the model imposed and of the success of the imposition, while others would do away with the nation as a category. See, e.g., Van Young, "Conclusion—The State as Vampire"; Vaughan, *Cultural Politics in Revolution*; Lomnitz, *Deep Mexico*; Joseph and Nugent, *Everyday Forms of State Formation*.

15. MacKaye, "A Historical Study," 3. MacKaye draws her figures from the Farm Labor Place Office files, Sacramento, California. In 1957, the peak year for braceros, they composed 34.2% of seasonal farmworkers. In 1962, they made up almost 80% of California's tomato harvesters; for lettuce and lemons the figures were 71.4 and 81.6%, respectively. California Assembly Committee on Agriculture, *The Bracero*

Program, 5, 6. In addition, more than 60% of all braceros in 1945 went to California alone. Coalson, "Mexican Contract Labor," 231.

16. Don Mitchell, *Lie of the Land*.

17. Walsh, *Building the Borderlands*, 57. Also see Walsh, "Eugenic Acculturation"; Alonso, *Thread of Blood*; and González y González, *San José de Gracia*.

18. Walsh, *Building the Borderlands*.

19. Meyers, "Seasons of Rebellion." On integration, see Katz, *Secret War*.

20. Kitty Calavita, in *Inside the State*, shows the competing agendas of various U.S. agencies, such as the Departments of Labor and Agriculture and the Immigration and Naturalization Service, overseeing aspects of the program, and their distinction from those of growers. Calavita contends that the agencies' divergent interests arise in large part from internal contradictions in the overarching policies on immigration. See chapter 4 and conclusion. For the coalescence of the Mexican state economic project and its nationalist overtones, see Gauss, "The Politics of Economic Nationalism."

21. Gramsci, *Selections from the Prison Notebooks*.

22. Even the Smithsonian Institution's bracero program exhibit, "Bittersweet Harvest: The Bracero Program, 1942–1964," constructs the program in the same terms.

23. See, e.g., Hodes, *The Sea Captain's Wife*; Natalie Zemon Davis, *Return of Martin Guerre*; Demos, *The Unredeemed Captive*; and Rousmaniere, *Citizen Teacher*.

Chapter One

1. Editorial, "La emigración mexicana," cited in Torres Ramírez, *México en la Segunda Guerra Mundial*, 251.

2. McWilliams, "They Saved the Crops," 10. When the same thing occurred the following year, U.S. Farm Security Administration (FSA) agents recruiting workers in Mexico City pressured U.S. Ambassador George S. Messersmith to accept all of the applicants. Worried that otherwise Mexico would back out of the entire agreement, he consented. Wolff, "The Structural Development of the Bracero Program," 48. A similar number is estimated to have crossed without documents. McWilliams, "They Saved the Crops," 10.

3. Anderson, *A Harvest of Loneliness*, 7; Calavita, *Inside the State*; Martin, *Promise Unfulfilled*; McWilliams, "They Saved the Crops." Wayne Grove ("The Mexican Farm Labor Program," 309) estimates the labor surplus as closer to 5 million workers. The federal government initiated talks with Mexico in June 1942, but Texas had made overtures to Mexico as early as that February. See, e.g., Federación Regional Sociedades Mexicanas y Latinoamericanas, Estados Unidos, Texas-Houston (Emigración Mexicanos), February 14, 1942, Presidentes, Manuel Ávila Camacho, AGN, 546.6/120; and Rasmussen, *A History*, 14.

4. The FSA tried to move unemployed farmworkers to regions with jobs. See n. 6.

5. De Alba, *Siete artículos*, 41, 14.

6. Measures were instituted to transport U.S. farmworkers from places of oversupply to those of undersupply, and those transported over two hundred miles were

to be paid the same wages as the braceros. Turnier, "Public Law 45," 53; Casarrubias Ocampo, "El problema del éxodo," 21. Braceros generally made ten to fifteen times more in the United States than they did in Mexico. Stout, *Why Immigrants Come to America*, 2. The AFL-CIO economist Walter Simcich challenged the notion of a prevailing wage: "Competitive forces do not operate in an economy where an employer can create a false labor shortage by offering unacceptable wages and receive foreign workers to bring in his crops." California Senate Labor Committee, *Hearings*, January 28, 1960, 462, quoted in Gilmore and Gilmore, "The Bracero in California," 276.

7. The procedures by which the U.S. government arrived at the number of contract workers needed and where they would be sent changed over time. Early in the program, the FSA assessed local need for laborers; this assessment was later replaced by that of growers' associations, which pushed wages downward as the number of workers increased.

8. The *ejido* is a system of landholding whereby communities, as opposed to individuals, hold land. The land, which cannot be sold, is passed down to the descendents of original community members. Land is usually divided and worked as individual plots. A version of such a land system was institutionalized under President Lázaro Cárdenas (1934–40) as a component of land reform. In 1991 President Carlos Salinas removed the *ejido* provision from the Constitution in an attempt to increase agricultural output.

9. Torres Ramírez, *México en la Segunda Guerra Mundial*, 253.

10. Saunders and Leonard, *The Wetback*, quoted in Copp, "Wetbacks' and Braceros," 95. In a 1948 study Guillermo Martínez Domínguez ("Los braceros," 248) found that only 15% of braceros began as farmers, while almost 37% were workers; those chosen were, in descending order, workers, artisans, and peasants, and earning on average between two and four pesos daily.

11. Editorial, *El popular*, December 9, 1941; Torres Ramírez, *Hacia la utopía industrial*, 248–50. Parts of the country offering the lowest-paying agricultural jobs faced more shortages from internal migration as men recognized the difference in salaries between urban industrial jobs and agricultural work. Commercial and industrial groups, such as the Confederación de Cámaras Nacionales de Comercio (Confederation of National Chambers of Commerce) in northern Mexico, were opposed to the program. The government-controlled Confederación de Trabajadores Mexicanos (Mexican Workers Confederation), while not initially supportive of legalizing migration, later called for measures to protect migrants from abuse.

12. Casarrubias Ocampo, "El problema del éxodo," 19.

13. Between 1956 and 1960, the population of Mexico increased by 3.1%, while that of the United States rose 1.7%. Statistical Office of the United Nations, Department of Economic and Social Affairs, *Demographic Yearbook, 1961*; cited in Dunbar, "An Analysis," 63.

14. The percentage of those working in agriculture decreased from 1930 to 1960. Dreissig, "Working in the Fields," 15.

15. Quoted in Torres Ramírez, *México en la Segunda Guerra Mundial*, 255.

16. Anderson, *Fields of Bondage*, 23.

17. Gauss, "The Politics of Economic Nationalism," suggests that between 1948 and 1957, 97.6% of such aid went to countries outside Latin America (571).

18. Scruggs, "Texas and the Bracero Program," 257.

19. Anderson, *Fields of Bondage*, 73.

20. Of these, 54% went to California. Garcia, "Interethnic Conflict and the *Bracero Program*," 399. Carey McWilliams (*North from Mexico*, 268) claimed that braceros harvested more than $432 million (1944 dollars) worth of crops during the war. Also see U.S. President's Commission on Migratory Labor, *Migratory Labor in American Agriculture*, 45–85.

21. Jenkins, *The Politics of Insurgency*, 79. In 1943, 1956, and 1957, braceros constituted 17.4%, 34.4%, and 29.3% of California's seasonal farm labor, respectively. McCullough, "Safeguarding the Bracero Contract," 27.

22. U.S. House, Committee on Appropriations, *Hearings, Farm Labor Program, 1943*, 43, quoted in Turnier, "Public Law 45," 17.

23. Rosenberg, "Snapshots in Farm Labor," 2.

24. Runstein and Leveen, *Mechanization and Mexican Labor*, 122. Unauthorized migration increased because of worsening conditions in Mexico's rural areas toward the middle of the 1940s. See Durand, *Rostros y rastros*, 19; and Walsh, *Building the Borderlands*.

25. While the name Green Revolution was coined in 1968 by U.S. AID Director William Gaud, the program to institute these kinds of agricultural changes actually began in Mexico in the aftermath of World War II.

26. Black, "Professor Schultz and C.E.D.," 678–79.

27. This extreme labor flexibility was exactly what growers wanted, for neither they nor the surrounding communities wanted to "support" migrants and their families during seasonal fluctuations when the men did not work or in times of economic hardship. They were instead returned home, making the Mexican government, home communities, and families bear maintenance costs. A U.S. grower-government alliance, along with the latter's acquiescence to growers' desire for foreign workers, was evident prior to the program, when Mexico City hosted the Second Inter-American Conference on Agriculture, with luminaries of U.S. agriculture including Claude Wickard, U.S. secretary of agriculture; Edward O'Neal, president of the Farm Bureau Federation (who had long ties to the federal government); Eugene Aucheter, administrator of agricultural research at the U.S. Department of Agriculture; Edwin Kyle, director of Houston's Farm Credit Administration and a member of the Texas Pecan Growers Association; Knowels Pyerson, associate dean, University of California, Davis; Leslie Wheeler, director of the Office of Foreign Agricultural Relations, U.S. State Department; and Milburn Wilson, director of the U.S. Agricultural Extension Service. Cited in Turnier, "Public Law 45," 34.

28. U.S. President's Commission on Migratory Labor, *Migratory Labor in American Agriculture*, 50; Cockcroft, *Outlaws in the Promised Land*, 74. Calavita (*Inside the State*, 99–102) suggests this was only a momentary convergence of interests of growers and the Immigration and Naturalization Service (INS).

29. For a detailed explanation of Mexico's attempts to lessen discrimination, see Scruggs, "Texas and the Bracero Program," 251–64.

30. Turnier, "Public Law 45," 32.

31. "Repatriaciones de mexicanos," April 27, 1939, Repatriaciones, expediente number 20-23-52, AHSRE; "Regresarán a México muchos mexicanos arrojados del país por nuestras disidencias políticas," *El universal*, May 2, 1939; letter from Ramón Beteta to Lázaro Cárdenas, August 11, 1939, Repatriaciones, expediente number 20-23-52, AHSRE; "Dificultades para la repatriación de mexicanos," *El universal*, April 13, 1939, Repatriaciones, expediente number 27-9-164, AHSRE; "Beteta dice como se harán las repatriaciones en California," *La opinión*, July 13, 1939; and a confidential memo from Beteta to President Cárdenas, August 11, 1939, Repatriaciones, expediente number 27-9-164, AHSRE. Also see Walsh, "Demobilizing the Revolution," 5; Gamio, *Forjando patria*; and Schmidt, "Mexicans, Migrants, and Indigenous Peoples," 163–78. On Torres Bodet's concerns, see editorials in *Excélsior*, June 11, 1942; and *El nacional*, June 18, 1942.

32. Concurrent to those projects, in 1947, when cattle were being afflicted with aphthous fever (hoof and mouth disease), the Mexican government, in coordination with U.S. officials, took steps to stop the spread of the disease and prevent Mexican-raised beef from being shut out of foreign (especially U.S.) markets. Ultimately 168,000 head of cattle were slaughtered and those not yet affected vaccinated.

33. The needs of northern landowners were addressed by guaranteeing migrants' return in time for the harvest in Mexico. In fact, Mexico's Ministry of Foreign Relations tried to convince those who wanted to migrate to wait; it also shut the border, hoping that northern agriculturalists would see this as a pro-Mexico move. Editorial, *Excélsior*, August 14, 1942; Torres Ramírez, *México en la Segunda Guerra Mundial*, 253; Turnier, "Public Law 45," 36. These same sectors were protesting as late as 1952. *New York Times*, July 24, 1952.

34. The Ministry of Foreign Relations to the American Ambassador, enclosure no. 3 to dispatch no. 3153 of August 5, 1942, from the American Embassy in Mexico City, quoted in Jungmeyer, "The Bracero Program," 181–82. For other examples of the same language, see editorials in *Excelsior*, June 11, 1942; and *El nacional*, June 18, 1942.

35. Ávila Camacho, "Mensaje dirigido a los gobernadores," 24; letter from Ezequiel Padilla to Coke R. Stevenson, governor of Texas, July 20, 1943; rpt. in Stevenson and Padilla, *The Good Neighbor Policy*, 20; García Robles, "Política internacional de México," 75.

36. Galarza, "Memorándum," 48.

37. Ávila Camacho, "Mensaje dirigido a los gobernadores," 24.

38. Editorials from May 30 and June 12, 1942, editions, respectively.

39. Torres Bodet, *La victoria sin alas*.

40. Editorial, *Excélsior*, August 28, 1942; González Navarro, *Población y sociedad*, 163, 215; AGN, *Boletín*, 22–23; García y Griego, "The Importation of Mexican Contract Laborers." To some extent, this opposition continued, both on the part of large agriculturalists and those whose factories could not attract enough workers. See, e.g.,

"Los industriales no desean salgan ya braceros mexicanos para los EEUU," *El nacional*, February 13, 1946. Trade unions and organized commercial interests also argued that the exportation of men would undermine (or, at the very least, delay) Mexico's efforts toward economic modernization. See, e.g., editorials in *El popular*, December 9, 1941; and *Excélsior*, August 14, 1942; as well as Torres Ramírez, *México en la Segunda Guerra Mundial*, 248–50, 253.

41. Editorial, *El universal*, June 5, 1942. Also see Torres Ramírez, *Hacia la utopía industrial*, 251.

42. McWilliams, *North from Mexico*, 266; Dunbar, "An Analysis," 18.

43. See, e.g., the January 19, 1944, *Excélsior*. Throughout the newspaper's first section are articles discussing how the United States viewed Mexico not only as an exporter of raw materials but, because of the emerging industrialization, as a market for its products. Also see "El desarrollo industrial de México favorece a EEUU," *El nacional*, December 7, 1946.

44. Jenkins, *The Politics of Insurgency*, 78. In fact, growers, after breaking the back of farmworker resistance and the Industrial Workers of the World—through a temporary alliance with government agents, in particular, with men like Carlton Parker of the California Commission on Immigration and Housing—called for migration from Mexico to meet the demand for laborers. Don Mitchell, *Lie of the Land*, chap. 3.

45. Josefina Vázquez and Lorenzo Meyer note that Mexico's World War II military participation was small: a single squadron of three hundred men, trained in the United States. Called the 201st Squadron, it was dispatched in early 1945 to the Philippines, where it served until the war's end. They also suggest that both countries recognized that Mexico's major contributions would be not military but economic, as support to U.S. "productive apparatus." A provisional agreement signed in 1941 gave the United States access to Mexican copper, lead, zinc, graphite, and other metals; this was followed by another accord in December 1942, which "fully reopened the U.S. market to Mexican oil" and to exports of cattle minerals, silver, agricultural products, rubber, guayule, henequen, istle, chicle, salt, fish, and bananas. They claim that by 1943, 90% of Mexico's "foreign trade was with the United States" and that the European market was lost due to the war. See Vázquez and Meyer, *The United States and Mexico*, 160.

46. This restriction was moot by 1948. See Sruggs, "Texas and the Bracero Program."

47. Anderson, *A Harvest of Loneliness*, 29, 31; Hull, "The Effects of Braceros," 24; Foley, *White Scourge*; Ngai, *Impossible Subjects*.

48. In 1927 Mexicans organized themselves into the Confederation of Mexican Labor Unions. McWilliams, *Factories in the Field*, 130; Jamieson, *Labor Unionism*. James Cockcroft, in *Outlaws in the Promised Land*, claims that the AFL-CIO, like the AFL before it, "colluded with agribusiness" "through its refusal to resist . . . the actions of agribusiness sympathizers in top government positions" (71). Throughout the 1940s, however, Galarza, as a member, first, of the Pan-American Union and then the National Farmworkers' Union (later called the Agricultural Workers Organizing Committee), with its loose connections to the AFL, did attempt to publicize farmworkers' plight and help them organize unions. Galarza, *Farm Workers*

and Agri-business. On the 1930 Imperial Valley strike, see Weber, "The Organizing of Mexicano Agricultural Workers." On the El Monte berry strike (1933), see López, "The El Monte Berry Strike of 1933"; Spaulding, "The Mexican Strike at El Monte"; Jamieson, *Labor Unionism*; and McWilliams, *Factories in the Field*.

49. For an overview of agricultural organizing, see Gómez Quiñones, *Mexican American Labor*, chap. 5.

50. For the impact of crop reductions and other New Deal changes, see Foley, *White Scourge*.

51. Gómez Quiñones, *Mexican American Labor*, 108. The CROM also advocated for workers' right to migrate. Olcott, *Revolutionary Women*, introduction.

52. In the 1950s and in conjunction with Mexican unions, Galarza encouraged braceros to join a U.S. farmworker organization, for he realized that the bracero program hampered domestic organizing. See chap. 6.

53. Mexico urged passage of legislation that would make employing undocumented migrants a crime, but this was only implemented in 1986, with the Immigration Reform and Control Act.

54. Cockcroft, *Outlaws in the Promised Land*, 74. Taft-Hartley was the informal name of the Labor-Management Relations Act of 1947, which qualified or amended much of the liberal National Labor Relations (Wagner) Act of 1935.

55. California Assembly Committee, *The Bracero Program*, 3; MacKaye, "A Historical Study," 51; Lytle Hernandez, *Migra!*

56. Gamio, "Informe del doctor Manuel Gamio," 39; editorials, *El nacional*, August 7 and 8, 1942; letter, George Messersmith to Cordell Hull, August 11, 1943, Office of Labor, War Food Administration, RG 224, NARA; Scruggs, "Texas, Good Neighbor?" The contention that agriculture was good for Mexico and a permanent foundation of the economy continued the policy of Cárdenas. Aguilar Camín and Meyer, *In the Shadow*, chap. 4.

57. As late as 1947, the Mexican newspaper *El nacional* was still pushing the need for the country "to produce at minimum" what it "consume[d]." The February 18, 1947, editorial urged the "dedica[tion of] all its energies to choose seeds," "conserve the soil," and "achieve adequate . . . crop cultivation" through the use of "mechanization and technical processes."

58. Gamio, "Informe del doctor Manuel Gamio," 40.

59. Letter to Harry Truman from braceros, Camp 45, Marshall, Mich., May 15, 1945, ser. 4, subser. B, box 17, folder 9, EGP.

60. Since the 1920s, the cowboy hat was understood as synonymous with the United States and its negative influences. "Kahkis and cowboy hats of the army demonstrate the sartorial impulses from the other side of the [Rio] Bravo," said the legal scholar Eduardo Pallares. "Our national way of life is . . . being substituted by a very dubious culture and morality"; quoted in Olcott, *Revolutionary Women*, 19.

61. In the Mexican newspapers of the period, this male figure of worker is made synonymous with the nation and a project of industrialization and modernization.

62. Truman, "Inaugural Address." See also chap. 7.

63. Ibid.

64. Saldaña-Portillo, *The Revolutionary Imagination*, 24, 25.

65. Ibid., 8.

66. Westhoff, *A Fatal Drifting Apart*; Latham, *Modernization as Ideology*.

67. People exhibiting such behavior lost their chance at a program spot. "El problema que confrontan nuestros braceros al llegar a EU," ser., 4, subser. B, box 17, folder 9, EGP; Salinas, *La emigración de braceros*, 88–89.

68. Unattributed source, quoted in Olcott, *Revolutionary Women*, 37. In its antialcohol campaign, the Comité Anti-alcohólico y de Propaganda contra Todos los Vicios said that "'the only man who is happy and dignified is the one who offers his family the sustenance he has conquered by the blessed force of WORK.'" Flyer, Comité Anti-alcohólico y de Propaganda contra Todos los Vicios, Bataconcía, Río Yaqui, Sonora, November 11, 1936, quoted in Pierce, "Men Behaving Badly," 22. For masculinity in Mexico, also see Alonso, *Thread of Blood*.

69. Anderson, *A Harvest of Loneliness*, 13.

70. Memo, ser. 4, subser. B, box 17, folder 9, EGP; Meister and Loftis, *A Long Time Coming*, 73; García Téllez, *La migración de braceros*, 39.

71. I use the term *revolution* to refer not just to the battle phase, but also to the period in which the parameters of the posited and contested state project were forged.

72. For an example of this usage, see "México antes de todo," *La opinión*, April 25, 1938. Also see Welsh, "Citizenship in Crisis."

73. For Nicaragua, see Montoya del Solar, "House, Street, Collective."

74. Torres Bodet, "La obra educativa," 135, 136. Also see Corwin, "The Study and Interpretation of Mexican Labor Migration," 10; "Los sacrificios y beneficios deben ser distribuidos en forma equitativa," *El nacional*, May 28, 1946; and *With the Mexican Laborers in the United States: Address Delivered on May 13 [1945] in the City of San José, California*, quoted in Stephen Pitti, *The Devil in Silicon Valley*, 122.

75. Galarza, "Memorándum," 41.

76. Gamio, *Mexican Immigration to the United States*, 49, 67–68; Gamio, *Forjando patria*; Schmidt, "Mexicans, Migrants, and Indigenous Peoples," 170; Walsh, "Eugenic Acculturation," 119, 120. Casey Walsh, here and elsewhere, lays out the connection of migration, development, and race. See his "Demobilizing the Revolution."

77. Beatty, *Institutions and Investment*; Bortz and Haber, *The Mexican Economy*. In 1941 over a third of Mexico City did not have potable water. Ávila Camacho, *Mensaje*, 17. For U.S. statistics, see Fisher, "The Dog That Does Not Bark."

78. This same offer of land would be tried in the early 1920s and 1930s, when it was made to migrants returning from the United States. Walsh, *Building the Borderlands*, chap. 3.

79. Ibid.

80. Quoted in Walsh, *Building the Borderlands*, 56–57; his translation.

81. Ibid., chap. 3.

82. Ibid., 31–33; Olcott, *Revolutionary Women*, 127.

83. Walsh, *Building the Borderlands*, 31.

84. Meyers, "Seasons of Rebellion," 64.

85. Garloch, "Agricultural Economy of the Laguna Region," 304. The dam, being

built as Lorene Garloch was writing, was located above Torreón on the Nazas River. With a capacity of 2,430,000 acre-feet, the dam was estimated to cost 52 million pesos (or just over 6 million U.S. dollars, at the 1949 exchange rate). Ortiz, "Currency Substitution in Mexico," 175.

86. Olcott, *Revolutionary Women*, 127–28.

87. Meyers, "Seasons of Rebellion," 93.

88. Olcott, "Worthy Wives and Mothers"; Foweraker and Craig, *Popular Movements*, 74.

89. Olcott, "Worthy Wives and Mothers," 106–7. This reorientation, says Jocelyn Olcott, remained strong under Cárdenas's successors, Manuel Ávila Camacho (1940–46) and Miguel Alemán (1946–52).

90. Walsh, *Building the Borderlands*, 46–47. *Ejidos*, in comparison, would produce food for national consumption.

91. Gamio, quoted in ibid., 55; Walsh's translation.

92. Nye, *Electrifying America*, 384; Milham and Ossiander, "Historical Evidence."

93. McWilliams, *Ill Fares the Land*, 30; Rajendra, "Hopeless Struggle," 14; Foley, *White Scourge*; Ngai, *Impossible Subjects*; Ngai, "Braceros"; Olmstead and Rhode, "The Evolution of California Agriculture," 9. Agricultural workers would only become covered by an agricultural minimum wage, lower than that for other workers, in 1967. Grove, "The Mexican Farm Labor Program," 318.

94. Ngai, "Braceros," 210; Ngai, *Impossible Subjects*, 131.

95. Grove, "Cotton on the Federal Road," 281; Cockcroft, *Outlaws in the Promised Land*, 68.

96. Grove, "Cotton on the Federal Road."

97. J. Craig Jenkins argues that Japanese and Japanese Americans, who by 1920 were more than thirty thousand strong in the fields and praised by growers for their skill and willingness to work long hours, mobilized "strong kinship ties" to position themselves as the "highest paid farmworkers." They "pooled" money to purchase successful farms that encroached on large holdings. Jenkins, *The Politics of Insurgency*, 76; Davis, "The Demise of Braceros," ii.

98. Grove, "Cotton on the Federal Road," 277; and Jack Kirby, quoted in ibid., 274; Runstein and Leveen, *Mechanization and Mexican Labor*, 45. Senator James Kem (R-Mo.) expressed the view of many members of Congress when he said that the program "subject[ed] the small-scale American farmer who works with his hands to unfair competition by granting to the employers of foreign contract labor a subsidy not granted to others." U.S. Congress, *Congressional Record*, 80th Cong., 1st sess., 1947, 3202; Murphy, "American Opposition," 34, 64.

99. Dislocated, primarily female farmhands of color were redirected into the expanding end of the agricultural industry, food processing, at wages lower than in other factories.

100. U.S. Congress, *Congressional Record*, 87th Cong., 1st sess., 1961, 18792; Murphy, "American Opposition," 75.

101. U.S. Senate, Committee on Agriculture, Nutrition, and Forestry, "Chapter 5."

102. Rounds, *The Impossible Land*, 19, 21.

103. Ibid., 23.

104. Lawson, "The Bracero in California's Imperial Valley," 1; MacKaye, "A Historical Study," 11, 12.

105. County of Imperial, Calif., "Welcome to the County of Imperial."

106. Martin, "Handling and Marketing Durango Cotton," 2; McLachlan, "Community Production of Durango Cotton in the Imperial Valley," 1; O'Donnell, "Selling California Cotton," 293.

107. Martin, "Handling and Marketing Durango Cotton," 3–4.

108. Gilmore and Gilmore, "The Bracero in California," 265.

109. Lawson, "The Bracero in California's Imperial Valley," 2. James Rooney reports that for the neighboring San Joaquin Valley, concentration had already begun such that by 1954, of the 5,437 farms, almost 70% had fewer than fifty acres, totaling a mere 7.7% of the region's total acreage; farms between fifty and 1,000 acres were about 40% of farms and nearly 48% of the land mass; and 2.5% of farms were more than 1,000 acres, totaling 44.5% of the acreage. While I could not locate an estimate for Imperial Valley, I expect that it had the same level of concentration. Rooney, "The Effects of Imported Mexican Farm Labor," 513.

110. A partial list of strikes goes as follows: cantaloupe and lettuce in the Imperial Valley, 1928 and 1930, respectively; cotton in the San Joaquin Valley, 1933; strawberries in El Monte, California, 1933; and lemons and other farm and packing shed work strikes 1934–36 and 1941. Cockcroft writes, "The El Monte berry strike obtained the support of the Mexican consulate, unified Mexican and Japanese workers, and led directly to the grower's recognition of the union and the formation of California's 10,000-member Confederation of Mexican Peasants and Workers in 1934. All these strikes . . . received the support of communists and other radicals, leading to constant Red-baiting and frequent attacks by goon squads in the pay of employers" (*Outlaws in the Promised Land*, 60).

111. MacKaye, "A Historical Study," 15–16. For more information on early 1930s strikes, see Weber, *Dark Sweat*.

112. Garcia, "Cain contra Abel," 183.

113. Cockcroft, *Outlaws in the Promised Land*, 70, 78.

114. For the role of the Industrial Workers of the World, see Foner, *History of the Labor Movement*, 258–60; Veblen, *Farm Labor and the IWW*; and Federal Workers Project, "Unionization of Migratory Labor." On CIO efforts, see Selvin, *Sky Full of Storm*. On the AFL response, see Taft, *Labor Politics American Style*, 112–14. For other U.S. efforts, see McWilliams, *Factories in the Field*; Chaffee, "A History of the C&AWIU"; California Fact-Finding Committee, *Mexicans in California*; Gómez Quiñones, *Mexican American Labor*, 136–37.

115. For how the Mexican Revolution restructured the economy and larger social relations, see, among others, Hamilton, *The Limits of Autonomy*; Knight, *Counterrevolution and Reconstruction*; Katz, *The Secret War*; Vaughan, *Cultural Politics in Revolution*; Joseph and Nugent, *Everyday Forms of State Formation*; Boyer, *Becoming Campesinos*; Sanders, "Gender, Welfare, and the 'Mexican Miracle'"; Stephanie

Smith, *Gender and the Mexican Revolution*; Rubenstein, *Bad Language*; Gauss, "Working Class Masculinity"; and Pierce, "Men Behaving Badly."

116. Olcott, *Revolutionary Women*, 12. Women gained the vote fully in 1953.

117. Ibid.

118. Ibid.

119. The 1917 Constitution, Article 34, quoted in Olcott, *Revolutionary Women*, 11. See also Alonzo, *Thread of Blood*.

120. Olcott, *Revolutionary Women*, 11–12, 19, 37.

121. Hedrick, *Mestizo Modernism*.

122. Letter from Juan N. Uzeta to Ruiz Cortines, Presidentes, Ruiz Cortines, AGN, 546.6/55.

123. Jacobson, *Whiteness of a Different Color*. See also social visibility in chap. 4.

124. Ngai, *Impossible Subjects*, chap. 1.

125. Gómez, *Manifest Destinies*.

126. Ngai, *Impossible Subjects*, chap. 1; Luibhéid, *Entry Denied*; Foley, "Partly Colored."

127. Other scholars, such as Alicia Schmidt Camacho and Shirley Lim, also argue that becoming modern is a central requirement for U.S. national membership. Those whose bodies do not bear the dominant racial signs of national belonging—e.g., Latinos and Asian Americans—are required to substantiate a claim to the modern in order to be admitted to cultural citizenship. "Narratives of belonging and citizenship," says Lim, "are frequently renegotiated through acts of modernity." Put another way, being modern was seen to attenuate other factors—namely, race—that in the United States could undercut the exercise of formal citizenship. Lim, *A Feeling of Belonging*, 9; Schmidt Camacho, *Migrant Imaginaries*.

Chapter Two

1. U.S. House of Representatives, *Mexican Farm Labor Program* (1955), 113.

2. The same is true today. An American Farm Families Association commercial, aired on a Sunday morning news show in January 2010, speaks to its continued resonance. See epilogue, n. 10.

3. Hardin, "Farm Political Power," 1652–53.

4. Lewthwaite, "Race, Paternalism, and 'California Pastoral,'" 2.

5. Writings on grower narratives include Sackman, *Orange Empire*; Lewthwaite, "Race, Paternalism, and 'California Pastoral'"; Martín, "Mechanization and 'Mexicanization'"; Starr, *Americans and the California Dream*; Starr, *The Dream Endures*; and Don Mitchell, *Lie of the Land*.

6. I use the terms "American" and "America" not as synonyms for "U.S." and "United States" but to point to the particular nationalist and imperialist overtones often grounding their usage. A caveat: when used by migrants, the terms imply no such overtones but are merely the correct translations.

7. See Don Mitchell, *Lie of the Land*, for how California was produced as a certain kind of imagined space. My analysis of grower narratives builds on and extends his reading.

8. A joint congressional resolution established the National Agricultural Jefferson Bicentenary Committee, which brought together the U.S. Department of Agriculture and representatives from land-grant colleges. For more information, see Griswold, "The Agrarian Democracy of Thomas Jefferson," 658; Wilson, *Proceedings of the American Philosophical Society*; and Edwards, "The National Agricultural Jefferson Bicentenary Committee."

9. Moore, *The Slaves We Rent*, 71.

10. No Californian held one of these positions, however. Internal division emerged between the Midwest and Northeast, on the one hand, and the South, on the other, as well as between commodities. Hardin, "Farm Political Power," 1648, 1650 (emphasis in original); Edward Higbee, quoted in Truman Moore, *The Slaves We Rent*, 69.

11. Grubbs, "Prelude to Chavez," 454–55.

12. Quoted in House of Representatives, *Mexican Farm Labor Program* (1962), 11 (emphasis mine). Ironically, the machinery Langenegger claimed small U.S. farmers could not afford was the same equipment the Mexican state envisioned braceros' purchasing with their earnings.

13. David Wyatt, quoted in Don Mitchell, *Lie of the Land*, 23.

14. Sackman, *Orange Empire*, 128; Don Mitchell, *Lie of the Land*, 41.

15. McWilliams, *Factories in the Fields*.

16. Sackman, *Orange Empire*, 128; *California Farmer*, May 25, 1854, cited in ibid., 127.

17. Moore, *The Slaves We Rent*, 82–83.

18. Teague, *Fifty Years a Rancher*, 141.

19. Garcia, *A World of Its Own*.

20. Teague, *Fifty Years a Rancher*, 141, 143–44; Sackman, *Orange Empire*, 128.

21. Proceedings of the Seventh Western Divisional Meeting, Chamber of Commerce of USA, quoted in Sackman, *Orange Empire*, 129–30; 128; Almaguer, *Racial Fault Lines*.

22. Sackman, *Orange Empire*, 9, 126–31; Meister and Loftis, *A Long Time Coming*, 87–88.

23. House of Representatives, *Mexican Farm Labor Program* (1962), 14, 24–37.

24. Ibid.

25. Teague, *Fifty Years a Rancher*, 161, 162.

26. Ibid., 112, 113, v, 147–49.

27. Ibid., 147–49.

28. Olmstead and Rhode, "The Evolution of California Agriculture," 2; John Deere, "Our Company"; Grove, "Cotton on the Federal Road"; Grove, "The Mexican Farm Labor Program."

29. Rooney, "The Effects of Imported Mexican Farm Labor," 513; Growing a Nation, "A History of American Agriculture"; Olmstead and Rhode, "The Evolution of California Agriculture," 7.

30. "Jap Ban"; Schwartz, "Farm Labor Policy," 692, 698. As far as I know, no work has examined the timing of agricultural expansion in California and President Roosevelt's decision to intern Japanese and Japanese Americans or the pressure to carry out this policy.

31. McWilliams, "They Saved the Crops," 14.

32. Meister and Loftis, *A Long Time Coming*, 87.

33. Anonymous interviewee, December 18, 1956, quoted in Anderson, *The Bracero Program*, 217.

34. Anonymous interviewee, January 2, 1957, quoted in ibid., 216.

35. Anonymous interviewee, May 8, 1957, quoted in ibid., 218; Sackman, *Orange Empire*, 128.

36. Teague, *Fifty Years a Rancher*, 141; anonymous interviewee, May 8, 1957, quoted in Anderson, *The Bracero Program*, 218; Sackman, *Orange Empire*, 128.

37. Quoted in Carney, "Postwar Mexican Migration," 152–55; Lawson, "The Bracero in California's Imperial Valley," 12; Grove, "Cotton on the Federal Road," 274.

38. U.S. House of Representatives, *Mexican Farm Labor Program* (1962), 13.

39. Ibid., 14; 18–19.

40. Shindo, *Dust Bowl Migrants*.

41. Jenkins, *The Politics of Insurgency*, 79.

42. The 10% of braceros' wages held in escrow to be made available on their return to Mexico was explicitly designed for the purchase of agricultural equipment such as tractors. See the introduction and chap. 1.

43. Anderson, *Fields of Bondage*, 73.

44. Meister and Loftis, *A Long Time Coming*, 87; U.S. House of Representatives, Committee on Agriculture, *Hearings on Mexican Farm Labor Program*, 88th Cong., 1st sess., 1963, 166, quoted in Hull, "The Effects of Braceros," 92.

45. Quoted in U.S. House of Representatives, *Mexican Farm Labor Program* (1955), 123.

46. Ibid.

47. Murrow, *CBS Reports: Harvest of Shame*.

48. U.S. House of Representatives, *Mexican Farm Labor Program* (1955), 114; "The Wetbacks, McCarran's Immigrants," *Nation*, August 22, 1953, 177.

49. Teague, *Fifty Years a Rancher*, 144.

50. Grove, "Cotton on the Federal Road"; Grove, "The Mexican Farm Labor Program."

51. Grove, "The Mexican Farm Labor Program."

52. "Farm Economy Evolution in State to Have Wide Effect," *Los Angeles Times*, March 19, 1961; "Farm Workers' Lot Held Worsening in Southland," *Los Angeles Times*, November 27, 1962; rpt. in Salazar, *Border Correspondent*, 75–76.

53. "Farm Economy Evolution in State to Have Wide Effect," *Los Angeles Times*, March 19, 1961.

54. Ibid.; "Farmers Compete with Industry for Talent," *Los Angeles Times*, March 22, 1961; "One Location Farming, Crating Typical Today," *Los Angeles Times*, March 20, 1961.

55. "Plights of Americans and Braceros Compared," *Los Angeles Times*, Mar 21, 1961.

56. "Farm Workers' Lot Held Worsening in Southland," *Los Angeles Times*, November 27, 1962; rpt. in Salazar, *Border Correspondent*, 76.

57. "Brown Aims to Mediate Farm Strike," *Los Angeles Times*, March 7, 1961 (ellipses in original).

58. Quoted in McWilliams, "They Saved the Crops," 14.

59. "Farms in State Hit by Strikes," *Los Angeles Times*, June 9, 1960.

60. "Farm Economy Evolution in State to Have Wide Effect," *Los Angeles Times*, March 19, 1961; "One Location Farming, Crating Typical Today," *Los Angeles Times*, March 20, 1961.

61. "One Location Farming, Crating Typical Today," *Los Angeles Times*, March 20, 1961 (emphasis mine).

62. "Plight of Americans and Braceros Compared," *Los Angeles Times*, March 21, 1961.

63. "Farmers Compete with Industry for Talent," *Los Angeles Times*, March 22, 1961; "Farm Economy Evolution in State to Have Wide Effect," *Los Angeles Times*, March 19, 1961.

64. At times, braceros' living conditions were portrayed as being equally dismal as those of domestic workers. For example, one article described how "at one camp . . . 'four men and a kerosene stove are squeezed into each . . . ten by twelve . . . hut. . . . [Since t]he door . . . c[ould]n't be closed . . . chickens invade and leave their droppings on the floor. Crushed wooly worms . . . garbage . . . [and] filth are also very much in evidence inside the huts.'" "Plight of Americans and Braceros Compared," *Los Angeles Times*, March 21, 1961.

65. Ibid.

Chapter Three

1. Quezada, "El mexicano," 23.

2. Ramón Avitia, conversation, Santa Angélica, Durango, October 1995; Álvaro Garcia, conversation, Santa Angélica, Durango, October 1995. William Form and Julius Rivera ("Work Contacts and International Evaluations," 339) and Daniel Martinez ("The Impact of the Bracero Program," 46) found similar expectations.

3. Massey, *Space, Place, and Gender*.

4. In constituting men as specifically gendered beings as opposed to the stand-in for a universal, I engage with the literature of men's studies. Among these, see Chris Beasley ("Gender/Masculinity Studies"), Timothy Beneke (*Proving Manhood*), R. W. Connell (*Masculinities* and "Masculinities, Change and Conflict in Global Society"), R. W. Connell and James Messerschmidt ("Hegemonic Masculinity"), S. Connor ("The Shame of Being a Man"), Don Conway-Long ("Gender, Power and Social Change in Morocco" and *Violence in the Fields*), Michael Kimmel ("Invisible Masculinity" and *The History of Men*), Michael Messner ("Men Studying Masculinity" and "White Guy Habitus in the Classroom"), and Alfredo Mirande (*Hombres y Machos*).

5. Ochoa, "La geografía e historia de Durango," 346. Despite its abundant natural resources and physical size, the state has historically possessed one of the lowest state populations. Durango's land area makes up 6% of the national territory, but its residents were less than 3% of national population in 1930. As late as 1960, while the state's overall population grew slightly, the proportion of people working in the primary sector did not change and those working in the industrial sector actually declined, meaning that state authorities had little incentive to provide additional educational resources, public services, or economic opportunities to the majority of communities.

6. Suinaga Luján, *Viente años de legislación mexicana*, 1312; Raigosa Reyna, "La industria siderúrica y el ferrocarril," 193. A great overall source is still Coatsworth, *Growth against Development*.

7. I surveyed a number of communities and selected two for in-depth analysis, oral history, and ethnographic research. For scholars of Durango or Mexico as a whole, Santa Angélica was organized around small plots of land, while San Andrés was an *ejido*. As mentioned earlier, per convention, I have adopted pseudonyms for my two field sites and the men I interviewed, indicated in footnotes.

8. Durango has been used as the location in many movies, both Mexican and Hollywood, beginning in 1898 with *Train Hour in Durango*. Paul Newman's *Fat Man and Little Boy* (1989) and John Wayne's *True Grit* (1969) were filmed there, and John Candy died making his last film in Durango.

9. Durán y Martínez, *Cuatro haciendas de Durango*; Rouaix, *Diccionario*. According to census records, in 1900 there were 817 males and 799 females, for a total of 1,616; in 1910 the figures were 1,011 males, 998 women, for a total of 2,009 (figures from personal communication with Patricia Fernández de Castro). El Casco and Santa Catalina, the hacienda from which San Andrés was founded, were efficient enterprises, both raising cattle and growing produce.

10. Rouaix, *Diccionario*, 401.

11. I converted the original figure, 444,000 hectares, to acres. Original figure in ibid., 411.

12. Letter from Juan Pescador Polanco to Adolfo Ruiz Cortines, September 7, 1953, AGN, Presidentes, Ruiz Cortines, 546.6/55.

13. Moncayo, "El proceso de urbanización," 130.

14. Casarrubias Ocampo, "El problema del éxodo," 64.

15. Lira López, Fernández y Fernández, and Olazcoaga, *La pobreza rural*, 56.

16. Dreissig, "Working in the Fields," 14.

17. Casarrubias Ocampo, "El problema del éxodo," 63, 64.

18. See, e.g., "American Slackers Head Mexican Reds; Organize Soviet, with I.W.W., and Preach Anarchy Openly in Mexico City. Say They Are Protected They Claim Several Friends in the Administration—Cabinet Divided on Expulsion," *New York Times*, July 14, 1920.

19. Meyers, "Seasons of Rebellion," 64.

20. Vaughan, *Cultural Politics in Revolution*, 11.

21. Also see Snodgrass, "Coming Home to Jalisco," 16.

22. *El heraldo*, April 28, 1944, quoted in Alanis Enciso, "La contratación de braceros," 54; Moore, "El problema de la emigración," 37. By 1963 a mere 2% of men were rejected in Mexico.

23. Letter to López Mateos from Juan Soria V. and Jesús León Tórrez, February 2, 1959, Presidentes, López Mateos, AGN, 546.6/55, no. 5230.

24. Alonso, *Thread of Blood*, 168.

25. Letters themselves did not use the term *proper man*; however, the array of characteristics, attitudes, and judgments that I fold into this term were outlined in letters; this array was also referenced in newspaper articles and other documents from the period, conveyed in conversations with former braceros, and expressed in interactions with others whom I saw in my fieldwork. I thus use it as shorthand for this broad set of cultural values.

26. Hershfield, "Screening the Nation," 273–74.

27. Ibid.

28. See, e.g., letter from Antonio López G. to the president, February 7, 1959, Presidentes, López Mateos, AGN, 546.6/74, no. 5774.

29. See Domingo and Sieder, *Rule of Law*; and Scardaville, "Los procesos judiciales."

30. See, e.g., letter from Juan N. Uzeta to Ruiz Cortines, October 6, 1953, Presidentes, Ruiz Cortines, AGN, 546.6/55, no. 37558.

31. Pierce, "Men Behaving Badly," 22.

32. Letters to President Miguel Alemán from Rodrigo Gómez, June 13, 1950, Presidentes, Miguel Alemán, AGN, 671/974, nos. 17896 and 14731.

33. Letter to López Mateos from Juan Soria V. and Jesús León Tórrez, December 1958, Presidentes, López Mateos, AGN, 546.6/55, no. 5230.

34. Letter to President Miguel Alemán from General de Obreros y Campesinos de México, National Executive Committee, Agustín Guzmán, secretary general, Vicente Padilla, secretary of peasant matters, April 4, 1951, AGN, Presidentes, Alemán, 671/974, no. 11257.

35. These petitions are housed in the Archivo Histórico del Estado de Durango, Durango City.

36. Jaime Simón, conversation, Santa Angélica, Durango, February 1996.

37. Paco Martínez, conversation, Santa Angélica, Durango, September 1995.

38. This notion of adventure was complicated for, like other patriarchal privileges, it was also a constituent component of adult manhood. When men were asked why they wanted to head north and what they expected from their journeys, many, like David Camacho Iracheta and Jesús Esquivel, replied that they sought adventure or "to have better experiences." *El heraldo*, April 28, 1944, quoted in Alanis Enciso, "La contratación de braceros," 56.

39. Mexican officials told me that only men who wanted adventure would cross the border without documents, denying the state's culpability or its inability to meet citizens' needs.

40. Letter to President Ruiz Cortines from Pedro Iturralde Aguilar, Cerro Prieto, Durango, May 3, 1958, Presidentes, Ruiz Cortines, AGN, 548.1/236, no. 17540.

41. Letter from Juan Uzeta to Ruiz Cortines, October 6, 1953, Presidentes, Ruiz Cortines, AGN, 546.6/55, no. 37558.

42. Letter from Margarito Contreras to Ruiz Cortines, July 19, 1958, Presidentes, Ruiz Cortines, AGN, 548.1/678, no. 12314.

43. Ibid.

44. Letter from Guadalupe Granados to Miguel Alemán, October 3, 1951, Presidentes, Miguel Alemán, AGN, 546.6/1-2.

45. In Durango the literacy figures were 49.9%, 67.8%, and 75.2% for the years 1940, 1950, and 1960, respectively. This compares to rates of 74.0%, 81.4%, and 83.4% for Mexico City for the same years. See Greer, "An Analysis of Mexican Literacy," 468.

46. Literacy, said Jaime Torres Bodet, head of the campaign, enabled justice and liberty, for it brought "knowledge," "independence of the soul," and "the domination of misery by work." "The best citizen of a just people," Torres Bodet claimed, "is and will be the man [sic] most honest." The possibility of creating such an honest citizen and, in the process, liberating the countryside of its belief in nonmodern superstitions, the government argued, could only be realized through a massive rural and urban literacy program for children and adults. President Ávila Camacho, in announcing the literacy program on August 21, 1944, said that "in the years of war, defense cannot be reduced to the material coordination of military measures and . . . nothing will truly substitute for the . . . resistance that intellectual, spiritual, and moral preparation of a nation anxious to conserve the legacy [patrimonio] of liberties represents." Torres Bodet, "La obra educativa," 134–36.

47. Vaughan, Cultural Politics in Revolution; Lacy, "Literacy Policies and Programs," 21–22.

48. Letter from Enrique Rodríguez Cano to Margarito Morales and Juan Morales de Jesús, Pino Suarez 407, Hotel Nacional, Durango City, September 26, 1952, Presidentes, Ruiz Cortines, AGN, no document number.

49. Letter from José T. Rocha, head of the Office of Emigrant Workers, to Simón Corona L. and Zenón Salas V., president and secretary of the Civil Union of Workers without Work from the State of Durango, Independencia y Allende, Gómez Palacio, Durango, April 3, 1954, Presidentes, Ruiz Cortines, AGN, 548.1/69, no. 000128.

50. Ibid.

51. Letter from Rafael Elizalde, Ejido Los Charcos de Oriente, El Naranjo, Municipio de Ciudad del Maiz, San Luis Potosí, to Licenciado Mariano Piña Olaya, March 20, 1959, Presidentes, López Mateos, AGN, 546.6/73, no. 5618.

52. Letter to President Alemán from the Federation of Mexican Workers and Peasants, Rafael Ortega C., secretary general; Maurilio Luna, secretary of organization and propaganda, and Pablo H. Silva, secretary of labor, January 23, 1951, Presidentes, Alemán, AGN, 671/974, 0/000(1,32)51, no. 2013.

53. Letter to President Alemán from Unión General de Obreros y Campesinos de México, National Executive Committee, Agustín Guzmán, secretary general, Vicente Padilla, secretary of peasant matters, April 4, 1951, Presidentes, Alemán, AGN, 671/974, no. 11257.

54. Letter to President Ruiz Cortines from Irineo González Esparza, June 5, 1955, Presidentes, Ruiz Cortines, AGN, 548.1/344, no. 16485; letter from Margarito Contreras to President Ruiz Cortines, June 19, 1958, Presidentes, Ruiz Cortines, AGN, 548.1/678, no. 12314.

55. Letter to Ruiz Cortines from Grupo San Luis, Union of Residents from the state of Baja California, November 6, 1956, Presidentes, Ruiz Cortines, AGN, 548.1/124, no. 26515.

56. Summary of a letter to the president from Deputy Adolfo Omaña, February 5, 1951, Presidentes, Miguel Alemán, AGN, 546.6/1–2; letter from Angel Muñoz Gónzalez and María Guadalupe G. de Muñoz to the president, October 3, 1951, Presidentes, Miguel Alemán, AGN, 671/974, no. 23801; letter from Antonio López G. to the president, February 7, 1959, Presidentes, López Mateos, AGN, 546.6/74, no. 5774.

Chapter Four

1. Álvaro García and Ramón Avitia, conversation, Santa Angélica, Durango, February 1996.

2. Letter from Erasmo Bolívar to Miguel Alemán, June 23, 1950, Presidentes, Miguel Alemán, AGN, 546.6/1–2.

3. Quoted in Domínguez López, "El programa bracero," 76, 78.

4. Jesús Amerzquita Ulloa, quoted in Snodgrass, "Coming Home to Jalisco," 17.

5. *El heraldo*, April 28, 1944, quoted in Alanis Enciso, "La contratación de braceros," 56; Romero Loaíziga, interview, San Andrés, Durango, November 1995; Deborah Cohen, "Sex and Betrayal," unpublished ms.

6. Álvaro García, conversation, Santa Angélica, Durango, November 1995.

7. See also Labastida Rojas, "El traque," 40; Escalante, "An Oral History," 40.

8. Roldán Herrera, "Mientras llega la chamba," 47.

9. Contract length varied from three months in the beginning, forty-five days in the mid-1950s, and eighteen months near the program's close. Álvaro García, conversation, Santa Angélica, Durango, October 1995; Paco Zermeño, interview, San Andrés, Durango, October 1995; letter from Rafael Elizalde to Licenciado Mariano Piña Olaya, March 20, 1959, Presidentes, López Mateos, AGN, 546.6/73, no. 5618.

10. Jesús Saucedo, quoted in Hernandez, "The Bracero Program," 2 (in English in original).

11. Labastida Rojas, "El traque," 40; Escalante, "An Oral History," 40.

12. Francisco Avenilla, conversation, Santa Angélica, Durango, December 1995. *El heraldo*, May 10, 1944, quoted in Alanis Enciso, "La contratación de braceros," 50.

13. Hancock, *The Role of the Bracero*, 66–72.

14. Quoted in Cockcroft, *Outlaws in the Promised Land*, 33.

15. Paco Zermeño, conversation, Santa Angélica, Durango, January 1996.

16. Alanís Enciso, "La contratación de braceros."

17. Escalante, "An Oral History," 40; Madrazo, *La verdad en el "caso" de los braceros*, 6–7.

18. Mize, "Workplace Identities," 136, 138 (emphasis in original); Anderson, *A Har-*

vest of Loneliness, 140–42; American G.I. Forum, *What Price Wetbacks?*, 5; Cockcroft, *Outlaws in the Promised Land*, 81; Lawson, "The Bracero in California's Imperial Valley," 23, 24. Ernesto Galarza (*Strangers in Our Fields*, 36) claims that more than 75% of all braceros paid a fee. Richard Hancock (*The Role of the Bracero*, 11) claims that men paid over 90 million pesos in bribes annually to go north.

19. Hancock, *The Role of the Bracero*, 66–72.

20. Lic. Antonio Paredes (program director, Durango, 1963–67), interview, Durango City, October 1995.

21. Alanis Enciso, "La contratación de braceros," 51.

22. Lic. Antonio Paredes, interview, Durango City, October 1995. For the first call for braceros in Mexico City, deputies (akin to members of the U.S. House of Representatives) were invited to participate. Madrazo, *La verdad en el "caso" de los braceros*, esp. 15–17.

23. Ernesto Galarza, quoted in Mize, "Workplace Identities," 145.

24. "Alemán es gran hombre," *El nacional*, December 1, 1946. This notion of braceros as grassroots ambassadors and the face of Mexico was not only a Mexican portrayal but also a descriptor north of the border. For example, Ignacio López, an activist and part-owner of *El espectador*, a California newspaper directed at the ethnic Mexican community, referred to braceros as "ambassadors in overalls." Ignacio López, quoted in Garcia, *A World of Its Own*, 181.

25. The last names of both an applicant's father and mother had to match what was on the official list, and men whose names had been written incorrectly were not allowed to enter. On the use of a loudspeaker system, see Salinas, *La emigración de braceros*, 83.

26. Moore, "El problema de la emigración," 25.

27. Paco Zermeño, conversation, Santa Angélica, Durango, October 1995; Aníbal Bañales, conversation, Santa Angélica, Durango, February 1996.

28. Álvaro García, conversation, Santa Angélica, Durango, September 1995.

29. Picture IDs were instituted in 1953. Their three-peso cost was borne by each bracero and went directly to the photographer. Salinas, *La emigración de braceros*, 85.

30. Men often had to wait for days or even weeks after their selection until buses or trains became available. When chosen, they were given a document with a departure date, which they sometimes "erased, putting an earlier one in its place." Ibid., 77.

31. I define citizenship as more than nationality (the gender-based rights conferred on someone born within the nation's territorial borders) and less than social visibility. Amy Brandzel ("Queer Citizenship?" 174) outlines Linda Bosniak's conception of citizenship as "a collection of 'strands.'" Brandzel lists four: "citizenship as legal recognition by an organized political community; citizenship as either the enjoyment of or the possession of rights in the political and/or social communities; citizenship as the practice of political and social engagement, activity, and/or organization; and citizenship as identity and the collective experience of belonging to a community," which Brandzel suggests "are always already entangled." Legal recognition is not the same as social recognition, nor is it an acknowledgment of those rights and privileges, which bring inclusion. The latter is how I define social visibility.

32. Gallo, *Mexican Modernity*, 202, 27, 203.

33. Ozouf, *Festivals*, 128.

34. Ibid.

35. Torres Bodet, "La obra educativa," 136.

36. Gallo, *Mexican Modernity*, 212. The other possible venue was a local church or cathedral, but neither the state nor the church would have permitted this. Church authorities had fought against the program, fearing a loss of influence over men traveling to the protestant United States. The government would not sanctify the church as official arbiter of Mexico's political life. Moreover, it had identified the church as antimodern and antidemocratic for promoting a relationship not of equals but of subject to omnipotent, not of scientific knowledge and reason but of faith and superstition. For the state, the church was the antithesis of modern values, symbolizing the feminine to the state's masculine. See Curley, "Sociólogos peregrinos." U.S. Southern Baptists saw the influx of "pagan souls" as a godsend. "God has given Evangelicals an opportunity to strike at the very heart of Roman Catholic power in Mexico," for "its great numbers have come to our very doors. No wonder the Catholic hierarchy wants to stop the bracero program." Jack Taylor, *God's Messengers*, 15.

37. Men who carried the requisite *mica* but whose names did not appear on the official list could not proceed. I suspect that if a bracero in this circumstance offered a bribe, his name would be added to the list.

38. The lack of shoes and the wearing of *huaraches* (a style of sandal) were signs of poverty and indigeneity. Many letters to presidents cited a father's need to buy school shoes for children as a reason he needed to migrate. "Altos jefes militares son acusados de explotar a los braceros," *Excélsior*, January 6, 1944. Also see "Mordían de lo lindo a los braceros," *Excélsior*, January 4, 1944.

39. By the 1950s, the standard bribe was three hundred pesos. "Sigue inicua la explotación de los braceros," *Excélsior*, May 7, 1944; "Explotación inicua de braceros," *Excélsior*, March 10, 1944; *El sol de Durango*, April 12, 1954; *Excélsior*, October 11, 1957, and October 13, 1957.

40. *El heraldo*, May 7, 1944, quoted in Alanis Enciso, "La contratación de braceros," 60.

41. Diego Hernández, quoted in Hernandez, "The Bracero Program," 11.

42. This bracero paid all his expenses himself, going into debt. See Anderson, *A Harvest of Loneliness*, 226.

43. Jesús Saucedo, quoted in Hernandez, "The Bracero Program," 3.

44. Rutilio González-Sánchez, quoted in Jacobo, *Los Braceros*, 77.

45. Álvaro García, conversation, Santa Angélica, Durango, October 1995.

46. Gerardo Huerta, conversation, Santa Angélica, Durango, May 1996.

47. Saúl Navarro, interview, San Andrés, Durango, February 1996.

48. Francisco Aguilar, interview, San Andrés, Durango, October 1995.

49. Álvaro García, conversation, Santa Angélica, Durango, October 1995.

50. Anonymous program official, interviewed May 11, 1958, quoted in Anderson, *A Harvest of Loneliness*, 261.

51. Ibid., 262.

52. Anonymous interviewees, interviewed July 24, 1957, and April 12, 1957, respectively, quoted in ibid.

53. Rodríguez López, "La bracereada," 34.

54. Salinas, *La emigración de braceros*, 85; anonymous interview, June 22, 1957, quoted in Anderson, *A Harvest of Loneliness*, 64.

55. Mitchell labeled the women screeners Mexican, even though the process occurred in the United States; I assume that he was referring to Mexican Americans. James Mitchell, *Farm Labor Fact Book*, 170.

56. Quezada, "El mexicano," 23. A man could be rejected for gonorrhea, leprosy, and syphilis, eye maladies, a hernia, heart defects, varicose veins, and amputations of fingers or other body parts.

57. Moore, "El problema de la emigración," 26.

58. Álvaro García, conversation, Santa Angélica, Durango, March 1996.

59. Rigoberto García, quoted in Bacon, "Fast Track."

60. Quezada, "El mexicano," 23–24.

61. Aníbal Bañales, conversation, Santa Angélica, Durango, January 1996.

62. Gerardo Huerta, conversation, Santa Angélica, Durango, May 1996.

63. Álvaro García, conversation, Santa Angélica, Durango, March 1996.

64. Foley, *The White Scourge*; Montejano, *Anglos and Mexicans*; Shah, *Contagious Divides*; Ngai, *Impossible Subjects*.

65. Rigoberto García, quoted in Bacon, "Fast Track."

66. Anderson, *Fields of Bondage*, 26–27.

67. Ibid., 53.

68. Anonymous interviewee, September 2, 1958, quoted in Anderson, *The Bracero Program*, 49–50.

69. Anderson, *Fields of Bondage*, 30.

70. Ibid., 27–28.

71. LeBerthon, "At the Prevailing Rate," 123; Murphy, "American Opposition," 100.

72. Mass bathing and delousing were a regular part of the inspection process facing Mexicans coming over the border, even at earlier moments. See Sánchez, *Becoming Mexican American*; and Stern, "Buildings, Boundaries, and Blood."

73. Anonymous interviewee, May 8, 1958, quoted in Anderson, *A Harvest of Loneliness*, 263.

74. While contracts were written in Spanish, high illiteracy rates meant that many workers might still not understand the farm owners' responsibilities or their own rights.

75. Anonymous interviewee, July 16, 1958, quoted in Anderson, *A Harvest of Loneliness*, 263.

76. *New York Times*, October 8, 1951, quoted in Dreissig, "Working in the Fields," 77.

77. Letter to Ernesto Galarza from Henry Anderson, May 9, 1958, ser. 4, subser. A, box 17, folder 3, EGP.

78. Ibid.

79. Supplement, Mexican Migrant Labor Program, Reports of Glenn Kaufman,

CPA, state financial examiner III, Office of the Attorney General, December 1959, ser. 4, subser. C, box 20, folder 7, 100, EGP.

80. Anonymous interviewee, May 12, 1960, quoted in Anderson, *The Bracero Program*, 19.

81. Anderson, *Fields of Bondage*, 23.

82. Paco Zermeño, conversation, Santa Angélica, Durango, March 1996.

83. *Tiempo*, January 15, 1943, 33, quoted in Torres Ramírez, *México en la Segunda Guerra Mundial*, 236.

84. McWilliams, "They Saved the Crops," 12.

85. See, e.g., Shah, *Contagious Divides*; Mize, "The Invisible Workers."

86. Aníbal Bañales, conversation, Santa Angélica, Durango, May 1996.

87. Álvaro García, conversation, Santa Angélica, Durango, May 1996.

88. Félix Ávalos, conversation, Santa Angélica, Durango, May 1996.

89. Ibid., September 1995.

90. Anonymous source, quoted in Anderson, *The Bracero Program*, 25.

91. Anderson, *A Harvest of Loneliness*, 209.

92. Emiliano Corral, conversation with author, May 2000.

93. Álvaro García, conversation, Santa Angélica, Durango, October 1995.

94. *Curanderos* and *curanderas* are seen to possess knowledge, not special powers.

95. Aníbal Bañales, conversation, Santa Angélica, Durango, March 1996.

96. Meyers, "Seasons of Rebellion"; Snodgrass, *Deference and Defiance*.

97. Sánchez Soto, "Por ahí anduve," 59.

98. Ibid.

99. Field notes, ser. 4, subser. B, box 18, folder 3, EGP.

100. "Farm Labor Has History of Broken Rules," *Santa Rosa (Calif.) Press Democrat*, June 28, 1987, quoted in Lawrence, "The Heart of an Industry," 90.

101. Field notes, ser. 4, subser. B, box 18, folder 3, EGP.

102. Anonymous interviewee, May 16, 1958, quoted in Anderson, *A Harvest of Loneliness*, 63.

103. Quoted in Cockcroft, *Outlaws in the Promised Land*, 24.

104. Among the most notable, see Ngai, *Impossible Subjects*; Molina, *Fit to Be Citizens?*; Gómez, *Manifest Destinies*; de Genova, *Working the Boundaries*; Benton-Cohen, *Borderline Americans*; and Schmidt Camacho, *Migrant Imaginaries*. In *Walls and Mirrors*, David Gutiérrez, by contrast, uses the term "ethnic Mexicans" to refer to both U.S. citizens of Mexican descent and Mexican citizens. One can only assume that he did not see this as a racialized category.

Chapter Five

1. Mauricio Herrera, interview, San Andrés, Durango, September 1995.

2. This information is drawn from oral interviews with former braceros, ethnographic fieldwork, records from the U.S. Departments of State, Public Health, and Agriculture, Mexican presidential papers, newspapers, and papers from activists and unions.

3. Olcott, *Revolutionary Women*, 11. Briefly, by "social visibility," I mean the recognition of an individual as a member of the nation with the ability to impact its sociocultural boundaries and reap its rewards. For further explanation, see chap. 4.

4. Torres Ramírez, *México en la Segunda Guerra Mundial*, 253; Saunders and Leonard, *The Wetback*; Copp, "'Wetbacks' and *Braceros*," 95; Martínez Domínguez "Los braceros mexicanos en los Estados Unidos"; Sedgwick, *Epistemology of the Closet*.

5. Mexican and U.S. officials struggled over the placement of the reception centers, due both to cost and practicality. Mexican negotiators sought to put centers in the interior of their country as a way of transferring to the U.S. government as much of the program's cost as possible. They also believed that centers in the interior made undocumented outmigration easier to monitor and control. For the U.S. government, the concerns were reversed; it benefited by minimizing the distance over which it would have to pay for transportation of workers and food; and its negotiators—and definitely growers—believed that a large pool of laborers at the border might impel Mexico to capitulate to demands. Mexico, whose bargaining position weakened over the life of the program, was forced to concede on this issue (see chap. 8).

6. There were numerous accidents during travel between labor camps and fields. The most notable occurred on September 18, 1963, when a makeshift truck carrying braceros collided with a speeding train; 28 men were killed and 35 more were injured. This is called the Chualar accident.

7. Quezada, "El mexicano," 24.

8. Gerardo Huerta, conversation, Santa Angélica, Durango, May 1996.

9. Mauricio Herrera, interview, San Andrés, Durango, September 1995.

10. Andrés Morales, interview, San Andrés, Durango, October 1995; Samuel Carrillo, conversation, Santa Angélica, Durango, January 1996.

11. Alejandro Medina, conversation, Santa Angélica, Durango, November 1995.

12. Dreissig, "Working in the Fields," 77.

13. Diego Hernández, quoted in Hernandez, "The Bracero Program," 13 (in English in original).

14. Jesús Saucedo, quoted in ibid., 2 (in English in original).

15. *Houston Post*, August 20, 1953, quoted in Anderson, *A Harvest of Loneliness*, 265.

16. Pitti, *The Devil in Silicon Valley*.

17. *San José Mercury News*, June 5, August 10, August 21, 1944, quoted in ibid., 123; Lutz and Collins, "Color of Sex."

18. McWilliams, "They Saved the Crops," 14.

19. "Braceros mexicanos en Dakota del Norte EUA," August 16, 1944, Braceros, III-716-13, AHSRE. The abundant talk of victory in Mexico labeled state policies as antifascist and signs of the country's place in the community of democracies. Torres Bodet, *La victoria sin alas*.

20. "Braceros mexicanos en Dakota del Norte EUA," August 16, 1944, Braceros, III-716-13, AHSRE.

21. Ibid.

22. "Fiestas patrias de septiembre en México: 1945, Informe," September 15, 1945, Fiestas, III-736-32, AHSRE.

23. Ibid. This was not the first time that a Mexican official had toured the United States to draw those who had come previously and stayed back to Mexico. In the late 1930s, Mario Ramón Beteta, undersecretary of the Ministry of Foreign Relations, traveled to various cities and centers with large Mexican populations and offered land to those then working as agricultural laborers, with financial assistance to defray the cost of repatriation. See, e.g., documents 20-23-52, August 11, 1939, and 27-9-164, April 18, 1939, Repatriaciones, AHSRE.

24. Documents 20-23-52, August 11, 1939, and 27-9-164, April 18, 1939, Repatriaciones, AHSRE. In addition, in the 1930s and 1940s, Germany had a project to establish relations with German immigrant communities, especially those in the Americas, based on a concept of homeland. In other words, modern imperial states were competing for immigrant souls. See Widenthal, *German Women for Empire*.

25. *La mujer abnegada*, the long-suffering woman, was a salient image in Mexico, describing both a woman's place and what was expected of her.

26. García y Griego, "The Importation of Mexican Contract Laborers."

27. Braceros' living and eating conditions varied as they occupied housing structures previously used by domestic migrant workers. While facilities were minimally upgraded to meet standards detailed in the contract, over the life of the program these standards, too, deteriorated.

28. Samuel Carrillo, conversation, Santa Angélica, Durango, January 1996.

29. Dreissig, "Working in the Fields," 90; Anderson, *The Bracero Program*, 66–68.

30. Agricultural Workers Organizing Committee, "Braceros' Sit-Down Strike"; Diego Hernández, quoted in Hernandez, "The Bracero Program," 13 (in English in original).

31. Anonymous interviewee, August 10, 1957, quoted in Anderson, *The Bracero Program*, 77.

32. Anonymous interviewee, January 7, 1957, quoted in ibid., 76.

33. Anonymous interviewee, August 10, 1957, quoted in ibid., 221.

34. LeBerthon, "At the Prevailing Rate," 123; Murphy, "American Opposition," 100.

35. The production of the bracero as a social position is comparable to Ngai's "illegal alien," *Impossible Subjects*. See also de Genova, *Working the Boundaries*.

36. *Worldover Press*, "The World from Washington," Sept 26, 1945, ser. 4, subser. B, box 17, folder 9, 4, EGP.

37. LeBerthon, "At the Prevailing Rate," 124; Murphy, "American Opposition," 98.

38. Galarza, "Memorándum," 42.

39. Anonymous interviewee, January 7, 1957, quoted in Anderson, *A Harvest of Loneliness*, 283.

40. Anonymous interviewee, June 21, 1957, quoted in ibid., 283 (emphasis mine).

41. Brute physical labor and modernist labor regime are not antithetical. See Mark Smith, *Mastered by the Clock*; and Trouillot, *Silencing the Past*.

42. Ramón Avitia, conversation, Santa Angélica, Durango, November 1995.

43. Álvaro García, conversation, Santa Angélica, Durango, November 1995.

44. Archer Audio Archives. Joy Hayes (*Radio Nation*, 6 n. 2) contends that although

battery operated radios were available in Mexico, the cost was prohibitive, and affordable ones required electricity. While she says that many homes with limited wattage reduced the use of lamps in order to power radios, most men I spoke with commented on their pueblo's lack of consistent electricity.

45. Miller, *Red, White, and Green*, 1. I found a small book dedicated to teaching migrants basic English phrases and particular farming terms in English, with Spanish equivalents for growers: Skaggs and Skaggs, *Manual práctico de inglés para los braceros*.

46. Hayes, *Radio Nation*, 50, 8; Miller, *Red, White, and Green*.

47. The same logic is used today to argue for increased border enforcement and worksite inspection. Both measures, it is suggested, will decrease the number of undocumented workers, forcing the invention of machines and/or an increase in wages such that domestic workers will engage in such work. See *The Diane Rehm Show*, National Public Radio, November 29, 2005.

48. Runstein and Leveen, *Mechanization and Mexican Labor*.

49. Galarza, "Memorándum," 44.

50. Anderson, *A Harvest of Loneliness*, 284. Gamboa, "Under the Thumb of Agriculture," 131.

51. Article 23, Standard Work Contract, U.S.-Mexico Agreement.

52. Anonymous interviewee, January 7, 1957, quoted in Anderson, *A Harvest of Loneliness*, 299.

53. Catholic priest, interviewed January 3, 1957, quoted in ibid., 298.

54. Anonymous interviewee, July 13, 1957, quoted in ibid., 57.

55. Quoted in ibid., 299.

56. Martinez, "The Impact of the Bracero Program," 56–57.

57. U.S. House of Representatives, *Hearing before a Subcommittee of the Committee on Agriculture*, 1958, 443; Gina Marie Pitti, "A Ghastly International Racket," n. 67.

58. Martinez, "The Impact of the Bracero Program," 56–57.

59. Clark, *Health in the Mexican-American Culture*, 79; Dunbar, "An Analysis," 79.

60. Clark, *Health in the Mexican-American Culture*, 16–17.

61. McWilliams, "They Saved the Crops," 14.

62. Anonymous interviewee, August 15, 1957, quoted in Anderson, *A Harvest of Loneliness*, 189; Diego Hernández, quoted in Hernandez, "The Bracero Program," 13.

63. Quoted in Varrelman, "Fraud in the Fields," 17.

64. Gamio, "Informe del doctor Manuel Gamio," 39.

65. Quoted in Anderson, *A Harvest of Loneliness*, 189.

66. Aníbal Bañales, conversation, Santa Angélica, Durango, January 1996.

67. Anderson (*A Harvest of Loneliness*, 206) calls tortillas, chiles, and beans "the rod and staff of life to most Mexicans of the poorer classes."

68. Aníbal Bañales, conversation, Santa Angélica, Durango, January 1996.

69. Álvaro García, conversation, Santa Angélica, Durango, December 1995.

70. Andrés Morales, interview, San Andrés, Durango, October 1995.

71. Anderson, *A Harvest of Loneliness*, 206–7.

72. "Imported Mexican War Emergency Workers and the Community," a Community Service Bulletin of the American Federation of International Institutes, New York, July 1945, ser. 4, subser. B, box 17, folder 9, EGP.

73. For more on the connection between food and Mexican national identity, see Pilcher, ¡Qué Vivan los Tamales!

74. Federico Garciniega, interview, San Andrés, Durango, November 1995.

75. See Alonso, Thread of Blood, for more about gender and sexuality in Mexico.

76. Sandra Deutsch, "Gender and Sociopolitical Change," 267–68.

77. Martínez Domínguez, "Los braceros mexicanos."

78. Quoted in Anderson, Harvest of Loneliness, 188–90.

79. Galarza, Strangers in Our Fields, 44.

80. Anderson, Fields of Bondage, 37.

81. Letter to Minister of Foreign Relations from Antonio Salazar, August 16, 1951, OC, PAC-247-26, DGAHDSRE.

82. Anderson, Fields of Bondage, 37, 52.

83. Tiempo, January 15, 1943, 33, quoted in Torres Ramírez, México en la Segunda Guerra Mundial, 256.

84. Andrés Morales, interview, San Andrés, October 1995.

85. "Imported Mexican War Emergency Workers and the Community," a Community Service Bulletin of the American Federation of International Institutes, New York, July 1945, ser. 4, subser. B, box 17, folder 9, EGP.

86. Corridos recount everyday experiences and are sung by people who are not famous. Paredes, With a Pistol in His Hand; Avitia Hernández, Corridos de Durango; Herrera-Sobek, Northward Bound and The Mexican Corrido. Joy Hayes (Radio Nation) and Marco Velázquez and Mary Kay Vaughan ("Mestizaje and Musical Nationalism in Mexico") suggest that the consolidation and identification of a particular type of music as Mexican was well underway by the moment of the program. Hayes argues that radio played a central role in connecting disparate communities and cities, and uniting them under the banner of Mexican. Velázquez and Vaughan argue that, through the development of radio and the recording industry, music was used to unite and make the nation.

87. "Alemán es gran hombre," El nacional, December 1, 1946, sec. 1, p. 13; speech from North Dakota Governor John Moses to arriving braceros, August 16, 1944, OC, III-716-13, DGAHDSRE.

88. Antonio Ramírez, interview, San Andrés, Durango, September 1995.

89. José Moreno, interview, San Andrés, Durango, March 1996.

90. Ibid.

91. "Natividad Bejarano Bustillos, informes sobre muerte," 1952, OC, PAC T14-7, DGAHDSRE.

92. For various work on this, see chap. 4, n. 104.

93. Ana Alonso (Thread of Blood) and Christian Krohn-Hansen ("Masculinity and the Political") found a similar tension in northern Mexico and the Dominican Republic, respectively.

94. Samuel Carrillo, conversation, Santa Angélica, Durango, January 1996.

95. Alejandro Medina, conversation, Santa Angélica, Durango, November 1995.

96. Paco Zermeño, conversation, Santa Angélica, Durango, November 1995.

97. Félix Ávalos, conversation, Santa Angélica, Durango, October 1995.

98. Aníbal Bañales, conversation, Santa Angélica, Durango, February 1996.

99. Álvaro García, conversation, Santa Angélica, Durango, October 1995.

100. Martinez, "The Impact of the Bracero Program," 57–59.

101. Anonymous interviewee, May 20, 1957, quoted in Anderson, *The Bracero Program*, 174.

102. Deborah Cohen, "Sex and Betrayal," unpublished ms; MacKaye, "A Historical Study," 71–73; Dunbar, "An Analysis," 59.

103. Daniel Martinez ("The Impact of the Bracero Program," 57) drew the same conclusion.

104. "Memorandum on Migratory Labor in the Americas for the CIO," Jan 3, 1947, ser. B, subser. 4, box 17, folder 10, EGP; Quezada, "El mexicano," 27.

105. Mauricio Herrera, interview, San Andrés, Durango, September 1995.

106. Diego Hernández, quoted in Hernandez, "The Bracero Program," 14.

107. Reynaldo López R., interviewer, Oscar J. Martinez, July 27, 1981, no. 566, 442–54, IOHUTEP.

108. Unnamed former bracero, no. 1, quoted in *Seasonal Farm Laborers Program*, director's translation.

109. Unnamed former bracero, no. 2, quoted in ibid.

110. Quoted in ibid.

111. Andrés Morales, interview, San Andrés, Durango, September 1995.

112. Mauricio Herrera, interview, San Andrés, Durango, September 1995. Numerous instruction manuals offered tips on how to do various jobs. See, e.g., "Records of the Bureau of Training, Records of Training with Industry Service," Records of the Office of Associate Director, Records Relating to the Job Instruction Program, 1942–1945, RG 211, Entry 233, box 4, File Instructor Manuals, NARA.

113. Ignacio Ochoa Perdomo, quoted in *Seasonal Farm Laborers Program*; Galarza, *Strangers in Our Fields*, 66.

114. Ramón Avitia, conversation, Santa Angélica, Durango, March 1996.

115. Álvaro García, conversation, Santa Angélica, Durango, March 1996.

116. Ibid., September 1995.

117. Jesús Saucedo, quoted in Hernandez, "The Bracero Program," 4 (in English in original).

118. Ramón Serrano, interview, San Andrés, Durango, February 1996.

119. Juan Luis Martínez, interview, San Andrés, Durango, January 1996.

120. Quoted in Dunbar, "An Analysis," 77.

121. "Imported Mexican War Emergency Workers and the Community," a Community Service Bulletin of the American Federation of International Institutes, New York, July 1945, ser. 4, subser. B, box 17, folder 9, EGP.

122. Félix Ávalos, conversation, Santa Angélica, Durango, November 1995.

123. Cockcroft, *Outlaws in the Promised Land*, 22.

124. Ramón Avitia, conversation, Santa Angélica, Durango, January 1996.

125. Álvaro García, conversation, Santa Angélica, Durango, October 1995.

126. In the program selection process, Mexican officials scrutinized men's hands for evidence of hard labor, work which men saw as making hands men's hands (chap. 4).

127. "Mexican Laborers, Worker Complains to Ambassador of Bad Treatment, Withheld Pay," *San Francisco Chronicle*, September 11, 1952, 11, ser. B, subser. 4, box 18, folder 4, EGP.

128. Agricultural Workers Organizing Committee, "Braceros' Sit-Down Strike."

129. Ngai, *Impossible Subjects*, 146.

130. Agricultural Workers Organizing Committee, "Braceros' Sit-Down Strike."

131. This framing of unionizing and nonunion farmworkers as brethren calls attention to an unresolved struggle. American G.I. Forum (*What Price Wetbacks?*, 56) wrote, "Over 80 percent of [1953] national migratory farm labor force is made up of American citizens of Mexican descent." While some organizations sought immigration restriction, labeling braceros and undocumented workers as *the* problem confronting Mexican American (especially agricultural) laborers, other groups realized that the issue was not Mexican laborers' presence but their position as nonunion and thus more exploitable workers.

132. Ngai, *Impossible Subjects*; Foley, *White Scourge*. Braceros then constituted around 95% of all those harvesting tomatoes; for lettuce and citrus crops the figures were 90% and 80%, respectively. We can deduce as much from the near exclusive use of braceros in various markets: they dominated the melon crop in Arizona (95%), pickle cucumbers in Michigan (75%), and cotton in New Mexico (90%). See Williamson, "Labor in the California Citrus Industry," quoted in González, *Guest Workers or Colonized Labor?* 54.

133. See PAC documents, OC, DGAHDSRE. By 1959 more than 75% of braceros went to those two states. Rosenberg, "Snapshots in Farm Labor," 2.

134. Galarza and Goodwin, *Reply to Mr. Robert C. Goodwin's Letter*, 9.

135. Quoted in Murphy, "American Opposition," 99.

136. Galarza, *Strangers in Our Fields*, 66.

137. Ibid.

138. In 1956, the minimum daily wage in Mexico was less than six pesos; U.S. farmers offered a minimum of seventy pesos. Marcell, "Bracero Program Hurt Domestic Farm Workers."

Chapter Six

1. Ramón Avitia, conversation, Santa Angélica, Durango, April 1996.

2. Quoted in Galarza, *Strangers in Our Fields*, 1, 75.

3. While Stephen Pitti (*The Devil in Silicon Valley*, 138–45) suggests that rank and file increasingly recognized their class attachment to braceros, which they expressed through a pan-Mexicanness, I see this recognition in the 1940s and 1950s as sporadic and largely union-leader (specifically Galarza) driven. See n. 104.

4. Cherny, Issel, and Taylor, introduction to *American Labor and the Cold War*, 1;

Lorence, *The Suppression of "Salt of the Earth"*; Stromquist, *Labor's Cold War*; Bell, *The Liberal State on Trial*.

5. Cherny, Issel, and Taylor, introduction to *American Labor and the Cold War*, 2.

6. Grubbs, "Prelude to Chavez," 454–55.

7. For a detailed discussion of the strike, see Street, "Poverty in the Valley of Plenty"; and Grubbs, "Prelude to Chavez."

8. "Farm Economy Evolution in State to Have Wide Effect," *Los Angeles Times*, March 19, 1961, D1, 17.

9. Street, "Poverty in the Valley of Plenty," 28.

10. Grubbs, "Prelude to Chavez," 458; Weedpatch Camp, "DiGiorgio Farms Packing Shed."

11. Quoted in H. L. Mitchell, *Mean Things Happening*, 258. The closed shop, the requirement that everyone who worked at a particular site had to join the union, was removed with the passage of the Taft-Harley Act.

12. Victor Riesel, "Inside Labor," February 27, 1948, quoted in *DiGiorgio Strike Bulletin*, no. 18, March 7, 1948, 1, Curt Hyans Papers, box: National Farm Labor Union and the DiGiorgio Strike, 1947, Walter Reuther Library, Wayne State University.

13. Lockwood, "The DiGiorgio Strike," 1. *Fortune Magazine*, August 1946, 97, quoted in Galarza, *Spiders in the House*, 14, 13 (emphasis mine).

14. Grubbs, "Prelude to Chavez," 456–57.

15. "Support of DiGiorgio Strikers Voted by Federation Executive Council," *Weekly News Letter from California State Federation of Labor*, October 29, 1947, 1, quoted in Rajendra, "Hopeless Struggle," 2, 24. Galarza, *Spiders in the House*, 16; 17; letter/report from Curt Hyans to C. J. Haggerty, California State Federation of Labor, November 4, 1947, Curt Hyans Papers, box: National Farm Labor Union and the DiGiorgio Strike, 1947, Walter Reuther Library, Wayne State University, 1. Estimate for DiGiorgio's water usage comes from McClendon, "Power and Protest in the Valley of Plenty," 83.

16. Galarza, *Spiders in the House*; 23; Joseph DiGiorgio, quoted in ibid., 1, 22.

17. Letter/report from Curt Hyans to C. J. Haggerty, California State Federation of Labor, November 4, 1947, Curt Hyans Papers, box: National Farm Labor Union and the DiGiorgio Strike, 1947, Walter Reuther Library, Wayne State University, 1. "U.S. Bans Farm Strike by Mexicans," *San Francisco Chronicle*, October 3, 1947, quoted in Lockwood, "The DiGiorgio Strike," 7.

18. McClendon, "Power and Protest in the Valley of Plenty," 39.

19. Galarza (*Farmworkers and Agri-business*, 103–4) contends that Mexican consuls pushed workers to back down. Meister and Loftis, *A Long Time Coming*, 75; Moore, *The Slaves We Rent*, 156. "U.S. Charged as Di Giorgio Strikebreaker," *Bakersfield Californian*, October 3, 1947, quoted in Lockwood, "The DiGiorgio Strike," 7.

20. "DiGiorgio Mexicans Will Be Sent Home," *San Francisco Chronicle*, November 12, 1947, quoted in Lockwood, "The DiGiorgio Strike," 14.

21. "Mexican Workers Not in Dispute, Representative Elliot Says," *Bakersfield Californian*, October 10, 1947, quoted in Lockwood, "The DiGiorgio Strike," 9–10.

22. Street, "Poverty in the Valley of Plenty," 26; "Mexican Workers Not in Dispute, Representative Elliot Says," *Bakersfield Californian*, October 10, 1947, quoted in Lockwood, "The DiGiorgio Strike," 9–10.

23. Galarza, *Farmworkers and Agri-business*, 103–4; Meister and Loftis, *A Long Time Coming*, 75; Moore, *The Slaves We Rent*, 156.

24. H. L. Mitchell, *Mean Things Happening*, 259; H. L. Mitchell, *Roll the Union On*.

25. Richard Combs, quoted in *DiGiorgio Strike Bulletin*, no. 18, March 7, 1948, 1, Curt Hyans Papers, box: National Farm Labor Union and the DiGiorgio Strike, 1947, Walter Reuther Library, Wayne State University.

26. U.S. House of Representatives, "Memorandum," November 12, 1949, 12, 24, 25; *The Farm*, November 14, 1947, and *Los Angeles Herald-Express*, February 9, 1948, ser. 4, subser. F, box 35, folder 14, EGP.

27. Special Citizens Committee Investigating DiGiorgio Farms, *A Community Aroused*, 2, 6–8. "DiGiorgio Mexicans Will Be Sent Home," *San Francisco Chronicle*, November 12, 1947, quoted in Lockwood, "The DiGiorgio Strike," 14.

28. *Bakersfield Californian*, November 13, 1949, quoted in Galarza, *Spiders in the House*, 25 (emphasis mine).

29. As but one example, a *San Francisco Chronicle* article published nine months after pickers walked off the job announced that the federal government had finally "stepped in." Implied in this wording is that government officials had heretofore remained neutral. See "U.S. Is Seeking Injunction in DiGiorgio Strike," *San Francisco Chronicle*, June 18, 1948, quoted in Lockwood, "The DiGiorgio Strike," 26.

30. "The Value of Music in IWW Meetings," *Industrial Union Bulletin*, May 16, 1908, quoted in Street, *Beast of the Field*, 603 n. 20.

31. H. L. Mitchell, *Roll the Union On*, 91.

32. Graduate School of Information and Library Science, "20th-Century American Bestsellers."

33. Street, "Poverty in the Valley of Plenty," 31.

34. Kosek, *Understories*.

35. Paul Thompson, "Agrarianism," 3; Tarla Rai Peterson, "Jefferson's Yeoman Farmer," 14.

36. Lewthwaite, "Race, Paternalism, and 'California Pastoral,'" 2.

37. Pateman, "The Fraternal Social Contract."

38. A *Colliers* reporter, quoted in Street, "Poverty in the Valley of Plenty," 29.

39. Louis Stark, "Farm Union Head Demands Benefits," *New York Times*, October 13, 1946; Rajendra, "Hopeless Struggle," 31.

40. Hollywood Film Council, *Poverty in the Valley of Plenty*; Galarza, *Spiders in the House*, 30; Street, "Poverty in the Valley of Plenty," 31.

41. Street, "Poverty in the Valley of Plenty," 31.

42. Galarza, *Spiders in the House*, 30.

43. Ibid. *Thomas v. Collins* 323 U.S. 516 (1945), quoted in Acuña, *Occupied America*, 265.

44. Acuña, *Occupied America*, 265.

45. *DiGiorgio Fruit Corp. v. AFL-CIO* (1963) 215 CA2d 560; cited in Galarza, *Spiders in the House*, 30.

46. Street, "Poverty in the Valley of Plenty," 27.

47. In this case, the limitation concerns Taft-Hartley's provision against second- ary boycotts and Wagner's guarantee of the right to organize a union. Thus, though farmworkers were officially exempted from Wagner, the NFLU was held responsible when other unions attempted to boycott DiGiorgio products.

48. H. L. Mitchell, *Mean Things Happening*, 261.

49. Special Citizens Committee Investigating DiGiorgio Farms, *A Community Aroused*, 6–8. See also n. 27.

50. In rejecting a susceptibility to communism, workers implicitly rejected the idea that Mexico (indeed, all Latin America) was vulnerable to its deception. See, e.g., *New York Times Magazine*, January 11, 1948; and *Life* 30 (May 21, 1951): 21.

51. Lizabeth Cohen, *A Consumer's Republic*; Westhoff, *A Fatal Drifting Apart*, chap. 4.

52. H. L. Mitchell, *Mean Things Happening*, 261.

53. "Caravan Will Help DiGiorgio Strikers," *San Francisco Chronicle*, January 28, 1948; "500-Car Cavalade Due Today," *Kern County (Calif.) Union Labor Journal*, Feb- ruary 6, 1948; "Italian Swiss Winery Closed Second Day," *San Francisco Chronicle*, February 29, 1948, "Winery Workers," *San Francisco Chronicle*, March 3, 1948; all quoted in Lockwood, "The DiGiorgio Strike," 20, 21, 22. The boycott was illegal be- cause Taft-Hartley had made it against the law for unions not directly involved in the strike to boycott a particular company's products.

54. NFLU Report to the Subcommittee, February 3, 1948; cited in Lockwood, "The DiGiorgio Strike," 20.

55. "Caravan Will Help DiGiorgio Strikers," *San Francisco Chronicle*, January 28, 1948; cited in Lockwood, "The DiGiorgio Strike," 20. Not only did local stores take DiGiorgio products off shelves, the retail clerks, winery workers, and carpenters unions refused to move DiGiorgio products during the strike. Street, "Poverty in the Valley of Plenty," 30.

56. LeBerthon, "At the Prevailing Rate," 123; Murphy, "American Opposition," 99. Evidence suggests that the Mexican consuls who campaigned to protect braceros were those, such as Arkansas and Mississippi, whose connections had begun with the program. See PAC 1942–64, OC, DGAHDSRE.

57. Galarza, "The Mexican American," 28; Ngai, *Impossible Subjects*; Foley, *White Scourge*. I am referring to the Wagner Act.

58. Sommer, *Foundational Fictions*. I suggest that this immigrant narrative, a U.S. foundational fiction, structured the ways in which farmworkers' claims were under- stood and negated.

59. Quoted in Watson, "Testing U.S. Farm Labor Policy," 3.

60. *Imperial Valley (Calif.) Press*, October 30, 1960, and January 1, 1961, quoted in ibid., 2.

61. "Violence in the Oasis," *Time*, February 17, 1961, ⟨http://www.time.com/time/ magazine/article/0,9171,826851-1,00.html⟩ (May 29, 2008).

62. Ibid. Not all local growers were affected.

63. "Farmers Seen Unhurt by Labor Activities," *Los Angeles Times*, September 7, 1960; "Farm Economy Evolution in State to Have Wide Effect," *Los Angeles Times*, March 19, 1961.

64. Watson, "Testing U.S. Farm Labor Policy," 2.

65. Ibid., 2.

66. "Unions Claim U.S. to Send Braceros Back," *Los Angeles Times*, January 17, 1961.

67. "U.S. Upholds Withdrawal of Braceros," *Los Angeles Times*, March 5, 1961; "Farmers Seen Unhurt by Labor Activities," *Los Angeles Times*, September 17, 1961; "Unions Claim U.S. to Send Braceros Back," *Los Angeles Times*, January 17, 1961 (emphasis mine).

68. "Unions Claim U.S. to Send Braceros Back," *Los Angeles Times*, January 17, 1961.

69. Watson, "Testing U.S. Farm Labor Policy," 3.

70. "Violence in the Oasis," *Time*, February 17, 1961, ⟨http://www.time.com/time/magazine/article/0,9171,826851-1,00.html⟩ (May 29, 2008).

71. "Farms in State Hit by Strikes," *Los Angeles Times*, June 9, 1960.

72. "U.S. Upholds Withdrawal of Braceros," *Los Angeles Times*, March 5, 1961.

73. "Unions Claim U.S. to Send Braceros Back," *Los Angeles Times*, January 17, 1961.

74. "Brown Aims to Mediate Farm Strike," *Los Angeles Times*, March 7, 1961.

75. Ibid.

76. "U.S. Upholds Withdrawal of Braceros," *Los Angeles Times*, March 5, 1961, A1.

77. "Lettuce Strike 'Lost,' Unions Blame Goldberg," *Los Angeles Times*, March 18, 1961. The ruling decreed that a grower only lose the number of braceros working the very field in which the strike began. Watson, "Testing U.S. Farm Labor Policy," 3.

78. Quoted in Watson, "Testing U.S. Farm Labor Policy," 8–9.

79. Letter to Galarza from Henry Anderson, Washington, April 14, 1961, box 17, folder 3, EGP. Vales, "Machine Politics in California Agriculture," attributes this to growers' collusion with the Immigration and Naturalization Service, and to the AWOC's inability to organize nonwhite workers (211).

80. "U.S. Upholds Withdrawal of Braceros," *Los Angeles Times*, March 5, 1961, A1; "Brown Aims to Mediate Farm Strike," *Los Angeles Times*, March 7, 1961, B1, 6.

81. Galarza, "Letter to the Editor," *Stockton (Calif.) Record*, June 15, 1960.

82. Ibid.

83. "Unions Map New Drive for Organizing Farms," *Los Angeles Times*, April 23, 1961; *Bakersfield Californian*, November 13, 1949, quoted in Galarza, *Spiders in the House*, 25 (emphasis mine).

84. "Unions Map New Drive for Organizing Farms," *Los Angeles Times*, April 23, 1961.

85. Gina Marie Pitti, "A Ghastly International Racket," 3. The Baptist Church, however, would not willingly be left out of the "opportunity." The "challenge" for this church, the Baptist minister Jack Taylor commented, was how to convert a "per-

son without true Christian foundations." According to him, "the challenge [wa]s not to help [the bracero] materially. The Bracero Program itself [wa]s doing more for him materially than the churches could ever hope to do." Rather, at issue was the "spiritual[ity]" of men who were seen to rely on a mixture of "Christo-pagan and Roman Catholic . . . forms, ceremonies, rites and idols." Jack Taylor, *God's Messengers*, 1, 15, 21–22.

86. Bishops' Committee for Migrant Workers, *Newsletter* 1, no. 3 (December 1960): 2, quoted in McBride, "A History of the Bracero Program," 56.

87. Jack Taylor, *God's Messengers*, 21–22; Gina Marie Pitti, "A Ghastly International Racket," 2.

88. *Jubilee*, 41, quoted in McBride, "A History of the Bracero Program," 50, 51.

89. "Churches and the Braceros," *America* 104 (March 25, 1961): 811.

90. "Farm Groups Protest Minimum Wage Rule," *Los Angeles Times*, February 2, 1961; "Churches and the Braceros," 811.

91. *Catholic Worker* 24, no. 3 (October 1957): 1, 7.

92. "S.F. Migrants' Plan Is Example for U.S.," *Monitor*, October 31, 1952, quoted in Gina Marie Pitti, "A Ghastly International Racket," 13, 16.

93. "Professional Migrant Is Big Problem in California Agriculture," *Monitor*, March 18, 1955, quoted in ibid., 13.

94. Anonymous interviewee, January 3, 1957, quoted in Anderson, *The Bracero Program*, 163.

95. "S.F. Migrants' Plan Is Example for U.S.," *Monitor*, October 31, 1952, quoted in Pitti, "A Ghastly International Racket," 13, 16.

96. "Bracero Program Denounced," *Monitor*, April 25, 1958: 1–2, and Most Reverend Robert E. Lucey, Report to American Hierarchy, November 18, 1959, quoted in Pitti, "A Ghastly International Racket," 14, 15.

97. For how this claim opened spaces for African Americans to push for their civil rights, see (most notably) Dudziak, *Cold War Civil Rights*; Bortelsmann, *The Cold War and the Color Line*; Plummer, *Rising Wind*; Plummer, *Window on Freedom*; and Von Eschon, *Race against Empire*. Regarding discrimination against Mexican Americans, Zamora argues that Mexico pushed "the United States to make discrimination a central issue in wartime relations." See Zamora, "Mexico's Wartime Intervention"; Ngai, *Illegal Subjects*; Ngai, "Braceros"; and Guglielmo, "Fighting for Caucasian Rights." This also continued a New Deal focus on all male camps as the site of unseemly behavior. See Canaday, *The Straight State*, chap. 3.

98. Gina Marie Pitti, "A Ghastly International Racket," 16, 11.

99. Al Antczak, "Migrants' Lot Held 'Disgrace' of Agriculture," *Monitor*, April 29, 1955, quoted in ibid., 7.

100. Anonymous interviewee, January 3, 1957, quoted in Anderson, *The Bracero Program*, 163.

101. "Bracero Union Cooperation," March 8, 1951, ser. 3, subser. A, box 9, folder 6, EGP.

102. Mimeo extract from report, "Unrest of Domestic Workers," ser. 4, subser. B, box 18, folder 3, EGP.

103. Box 36, folder 12: DiGiorgio Fruit transcripts of forum and radio program, 1949, STFU Papers, Reel 32.

104. Quoted in Stephen Pitti, *The Devil in Silicon Valley*, 143. While he reads the song and other measures as signs of the rank and file's "common cause" with braceros, members of the transnational working class see this orientation as largely confined to Galarza, Mitchell, and a few other labor leaders.

105. Anonymous interviewee, August 7, 1957, quoted in Anderson, *The Bracero Program*, 159; oral history of Jose Roman, MD, El Paso physician, interviewer Olivia Roman, April 4–6, 1976, transcript, no. 219, 5, IOHUTEP.

106. "El bracero y la pachuca" tells the story of a bracero who tries to woo a *pachuca* (a young Mexican American woman who is part of a Mexican American youth subculture that emerged during the 1930s and 1940s). When the *pachuca* responds to his wooing, she answers in a slang he cannot understand. Thus, the song suggests the futility of this kind of union. The song was written by Miguel Salas and recorded in Los Angeles by Dueto Taxco and Mariachi Los Caporales del Norte.

107. Anonymous interviewee, August 7, 1957, quoted in Anderson, *The Bracero Program*, 159.

108. According to John Hart ("Revolutionary Syndicalism in Mexico"), during the first thirty years of the twentieth century, conditions in Mexico had produced "the largest and most revolutionary syndicalist movement ever known in the Americas," the results of which were later enshrined in Mexico's constitution. For work on Durango and northern Mexico, also see Snodgrass, *Deference and Defiance*; Carr, *Marxism and Communism*; Olcott, *Postrevolutionary Women*; Katz, *The Secret War*; Raat, *Revoltosos*; and Gigi Peterson, "Grassroots Good Neighbors."

109. "Union Organization of Braceros," A. J. Clark, secretary of Central Labor Union of Monterey, Calif., ser. 4, subser. A, box 19, folder 6, EGP.

110. Memo, ser. 4, subser. H, box 45, folder 2, EGP; H. L. Mitchell, oral history transcript, 1956–57, 163–64, 169–70, ser. 3, subser. A, box 8, folder 6, EGP.

111. Joint United States–Mexico Trade Union Committee, "Declaration of Brownsville-Matamoros," 1.

112. H. L. Mitchell, oral history transcript, 1956–57, 163–64, 169–70, ser. 3, subser. A, box 8, folder 6, EGP.

113. Letter to Honorable James P. Mitchell, secretary of labor, from Frank L. Noakes, chairman, Joint U.S.-Mexico Trade Union Committee, January 28, 1958, 2–3, ser. 4, subser. C, box 21, folder 9, EGP.

114. Ibid.; press release, March 14, 1951, ser. 4, subser. C, box 19, folder 6, EGP. Also see mention in chap. 5.

115. Ibid.

116. Letter from H. L. Mitchell, president of NFLU in the Imperial Valley of California, to George Rundquist, ACLU (New York), re: agreement with Mexicali Farm Labor Union, April 5, 1951, ser. 4, subser. C, box 19, folder 6, EGP.

117. Jenkins and Perrow, "Insurgency of the Powerless," 252; Dudziak, *Cold War Civil Rights*.

118. Chafe, "American since 1945," 161.

119. Galarza, "The Mexican American," 29.

120. "The Migrants and Organized Labor," Lewis Hines, AFL-CIO staff (Washington, D.C.), ser. 4, subser. C, box 21, folder 5, EGP.

121. U.S. President's Commission on Migratory Labor, *Migratory Labor in American Agriculture*, 178.

122. Schwartz, "Farm Labor Policy," 700.

123. U.S. President's Commission on Migratory Labor, *Migratory Labor in American Agriculture*, 3.

124. Galarza, "Memorándum," 43; LeBerthon, "Exchange on Farm Workers from Mexico," 354; Murphy, "American Opposition," 100.

125. Martín, "Mechanization and Mexicanization," 312–13.

126. Murrow, *Harvest of Shame*.

127. Jenkins and Perrow, "Insurgency of the Powerless," 259, 260.

128. Ibid.; McWilliams, "What We Did about Racial Minorities," quoted in Goodman, *While You Were Gone*, 94.

129. Jerry Cohen, taped interview with Rich Lyness of KUOP-FM, Stockton, Calif., August 28, 1973, quoted in Grubbs, "Prelude to Chavez," 458.

130. "Farmers Seen Unhurt by Labor Activities," *Los Angeles Times*, September 7, 1960.

131. Although this quote appears in English, it was most likely a translation from Spanish. In Spanish, the expression "ser gallina" has similar implications of cowardice as does "to be chicken." Also of note, the user of the expression "like a chicken in another rooster's yard" could have referred to the 1952 Mexican movie of a similar title, *Gallo en corral ajeno* (Rooster in a foreign pen). Used in this way *gallo*, itself not automatically pejorative, suggests feminization or emasculation. Alejandro Mejías-López, personal communication, April 2008.

Chapter Seven

1. Raúl Molina, conversation, Santa Angélica, Durango, January 1996.

2. Diaz Herrera, "The Bracero Experience," 103–4.

3. Beginning in the twentieth century, agricultural laborers in California and Texas became part of a rural proletariat forced to follow crops from field to field. This divide between forced movement and mobility reinstantiated the racial division built on slave labor as black and free labor as white. This coding framed the public understanding of agricultural labor into which braceros would come and its racializing effects, with all stoop laborers of Mexican descent made foreigners regardless of citizenship. Their "foreignness" "located them . . . [as] seemingly biologically perfect immigrants [and] rendered this labor 'cheap,'" that is, devalued and backward. David Roediger, quoted in Ngai, "Braceros," 210, 211. According to Roediger (*Wages of Whiteness*), this coding blocked poorly paid and ill-treated white workers from seeing the class connections they had with black workers and instead reoriented them toward a (national) racial payoff.

4. Ramón Montoya ("El cura y los braceros," 85) also found the trading of sombreros for Stetsons.

5. Luis Camarena, interview, San Andrés, Durango, November 1995.

6. Conversation, Santa Angélica, Durango, March 1996.

7. On the success of the nation-building project, see Vaughan, *Cultural Politics in Revolution*; Olcott, *Postrevolutionary Women*; Schell, *Church and State Education*; Mitchell and Schell, *The Women's Revolution in Mexico*; Bliss, *Compromised Positions*; Wood, *On the Border*; Sanders, "Gender, Welfare and the 'Mexican Miracle'"; Newcomer, *Reconciling Modernity*; Snodgrass, *Deference and Defiance*; and Becker, *Setting the Virgin on Fire*. For a look at the different kind of affective ties required to make various Chilean political projects possible and competition to institute those state projects, see Frazier, *Salt in the Sand*. For an analysis of how the particular economic vision became consolidated as part of the state's revolutionary political project, see Gauss, "The Politics of Economic Nationalism."

8. Editorial, *Excélsior*, May 12, 1942.

9. In Spanish there are two terms for godfather: *compadre*, godfather vis-à-vis the biological parents or other godparents, and *padrino*, godfather vis-à-vis the child. In this sense *compadre* is also a lateral connection.

10. Quoted in "Que son tratados como bestias los braceros deportados," *El heraldo*, May 3, 1957, Presidentes, Ruiz Cortines, AGN, 546.6/55. For further "la familia mexicana" references, see, e.g., the following *Excélsior* articles published in the first three months of 1944: "Cultural obliga," January 5, 1944; "Corresponde a los intelectuales la tarea de formar un México grande," January 5, 1944; "Continuidad histórica," January 31, 1944; "Gobernar es prever," January 10, 1944; "Doloroso contraste," March 8, 1944; "Nuestro país puede tener un mejor nivel de vida," March 12, 1944; "Defensa del patrimonio cultural," March 13, 1944; "Coordinación de esfuerzos," March 24, 1944; and "Casa y dignidad," March 29, 1944.

11. "Que son tratados como bestias," *El heraldo*, May 3, 1957, Presidentes, Ruiz Cortines, AGN, 546.6/55 (emphasis mine). When this article was written, Chihuahua was experiencing mass return of undocumented workers and mass outmigration. Mexican negotiators were calling for sanctions on employers using undocumented laborers, a provision that it wanted incorporated into the bracero agreement. U.S. counterparts, although refusing the provision, tried to appease Mexico by deporting men instead of "drying out" "wetback" workers and awarding them contracts as usually done.

12. Ibid. (emphasis mine).

13. Miller, *Rise and Fall of the Cosmic Race*, 2.

14. Vaughan, *Cultural Politics in Revolution*; Olcott, *Revolutionary Women*; Katz, *The Secret War of Mexico*; Alonso, *Thread of Blood*; Nugent, *Spent Cartridges*.

15. According to the historian Susan Gauss (communication with author, July 15, 2008), after a major overhaul in 1930, tariffs tended to be higher on consumer goods and lower on intermediate and capital inputs (as a means to encourage manufacturing). In the post-1947 period, the Alemán administration moved beyond tariffs to import controls (licensing that actually blocked the movement of goods rather than

just tariffs to deter it). She notes that Monterrey industrialists complained quite a bit about contraband (illegally produced or distributed products such as clothing moving through the area to and from the border). The consumer products with which braceros returned could be the very items that these industrialists flagged as contraband.

16. For the guards and other Mexicans who did not migrate, the desire for U.S. commodities was no doubt further stimulated by the Mexican tourist industry, which was then growing rapidly. The Mexican state saw tourism as part of constructing a new economy. Citizens catering to tourists, state planners foresaw, would be exposed to U.S. comforts, boosting local demand. As in the bracero program, the state saw tourism as another opportunity to foment desire for commodities. See Berger, *The Development of Mexico's Tourism Industry*.

17. García Robles, "Política internacional de México," 75; Quintana, "La acción presidencial," 250.

18. See, e.g., Coronil, *The Magical State*.

19. Unnamed source, quoted in American G.I. Forum, *What Price Wetbacks?*, 34.

20. Guillermo Viveros, interview, San Andrés, Durango, December 1995.

21. "Bracero Program Aids Both U.S. and Mexico, Imported Workers Took Back $35 Million to Improve Living Standards Last Year," *Los Angeles Times*, August 27, 1959; ser. 4, subser. B, box 18, folder 1, EGP.

22. Anderson, *The Bracero Program*, 160.

23. While this camp manager would invoke men's backwardness as a reason for protection, in 1963 the California legislature said that the program afforded migrants the hands-on experience of the modern in the place of the modern.

24. Montoya, "El cura y los braceros," 90.

25. Ibid. U.S. Catholic and mainline Protestant churches said that the program "depress[ed] farm wages, offer[ed] unfair competition to American workers and disrupt[ed] the family and community life, not only of the itinerant Mexicans, but of our own farm workers." See "Churches and Braceros," *America*, March 25, 1961, 810; Gina Marie Pitti, "A Ghastly International Racket." I also found influence of English on the language of former migrants. A young man who had driven with family to visit Durango relatives for Christmas described how the water on the road "se puso frizada" (had become frozen), Hispanicizing the English word *to freeze*.

26. Cockcroft, *Outlaws in the Promised Land*, 30.

27. Lic. Mario Valero Salas, administrator of Durango's program, 1962–67, interview with author, September 21, 1995, Durango City (emphasis mine).

28. Félix Ávalos, conversation, Santa Angélica, Durango, September 1995. Ramón Montoya ("El cura y los braceros," 90) similarly found that braceros recognized and repaid the favor of getting a bracero contract.

29. Álvaro García, conversation, Santa Angélica, Durango, September 1995.

30. The program itself generated ways that men could reposition themselves at home in relation to others less fortunate than they. Occasionally braceros could become "specials," a program designation handed out by U.S. foremen to particularly trusted workers, which enabled men to do work normally off-limits to braceros, re-

ceive higher wages, and avoid much of the red tape required for readmission to the program. Most important, being a special allowed a man to stay longer and return to a single worksite and employer. While this aspect of the program was beneficial to employers, specials also gained, for employers often urged specials to bring friends with them when they returned. That is, these specials now wielded some power. With jobs to offer, these lucky few now became the ones from whom others asked favors, financial support, and knowledge about a world beyond their community. For more on specials and this cost, see Rosas, "Flexible Families"; and Salinas, *La emigración de braceros*, 79–82.

31. Anonymous interview, August 1, 1958, quoted in Anderson, *The Bracero Program*, 23.

32. Quezada, "El mexicano," 28.

33. Félix Ávalos, conversation, Santa Angélica, Durango, December 1995. In *The Making of the English Working Class*, E. P. Thompson also talks about time as crucial in turning peasants into workers.

34. Félix Ávalos, conversation, Santa Angélica, Durango, December 1995.

35. Álvaro García, conversation, Santa Angélica, Durango, March 1996.

36. Gerardo Huerta, conversation, Santa Angélica, Durango, March 1996.

37. Álvaro García, conversation, Santa Angélica, Durango, March 1996.

38. Rodríguez López, "La bracereada," 35.

39. Diaz Herrera, "The Bracero Experience," 103–4.

40. Juan Pablo Renato Ruiz de Vásquez, Chicago, June, 1991.

41. In research on El Salvador, Sarah Mahler found an understanding of men's sexuality similar to what I found for Mexican migrants. She uses the word *need* to talk about how women understood male sexuality. Wives she spoke with often confided to her that "'they knew' their migrant husbands were being unfaithful, if for no other reason than the length of time they had been away and the 'needs' men have." Mahler, "Transnational Relationships," 607. For other work on sexual practice and migration, see Hirsch, *A Courtship after Marriage*; Gonzalez-Lopez, *Erotic Journeys*; Cantú, Naples, and Vidal-Ortiz, *The Sexuality of Migration*; and, in a different way, Luibhéid, *Entry Denied*; and Canaday, *The Straight State*.

42. This household arrangement was written into law. The Civil Code of Marriage for Durango, dated January 29, 1948, stipulates obligations and privileges coming from marriage. It states that married men have to live with wives, an exception made only if they have migrated out of their home state (chap. 3, art. 158); in addition a man "must provide food to his wife and make expenditures to sustain household" (chap. 3, art. 159). Interestingly, chapter 3, article 162 of this same civil code states that "husband and wife will, at home, have equal authority and consideration . . . [even] regarding education and residence of children, and over administration of goods that belong to them. . . . In the case the husband and wife are not in agreement . . . , it falls to a judge in Civil Court to . . . allocate these in the [best] interests of children." Article 163 assigns to the wife "the heading and care of household work," while article 164 states that she may work outside the home, provided that her work "does not get in the way of mission as laid out in previous article." The archive contains

petitions from both wives and husbands imploring the courts to require that their wayward spouse comply with the mandated duties. Women wanted the courts to order husbands to "complir sus deberes" (fulfill their obligations) and support them, while husbands use a similar language to demand that women "cumplir los deberes de su sexo" (fulfill the duties of their sex) and maintain the household and raise the children.

43. See chap. 1.

44. Roldán Herrera, "Mientras llega la chamba," 52.

45. "Bracero Called Good Salesman for U.S. Ideals," *New York Times*, October 1, 1961; Sánchez Soto, "Por ahí anduve," 64–65.

46. Anonymous interviewee, August 1, 1958, quoted in Anderson, *The Bracero Program*, 23.

47. Gauss, "The Politics of Economic Nationalism," 571.

48. See Vaughan, *Cultural Politics in Revolution*; and Miller, *Red, White, and Green*.

49. Hirsch, *A Courtship after Marriage*.

50. Saldaña-Portillo, *The Revolutionary Imagination*, 25 (emphasis in original).

51. Lic. Miguel Bermúdez Cisneros, Durango's director of the Secretaría de Trabajo y Previsión Social, interview with author, Durango City, September 21, 1995.

52. Martín, "Mechanization and Mexicanization," 314.

53. See, e.g., Hondagneu-Sotelo and Ávila, "'I'm Here, but I'm There.'"

Chapter Eight

1. Ramón Avitia, Álvaro García, and Felipe Castañeda, conversation, Santa Angélica, Durango, April 1996. Another man also said the money he had earned "cost" him. See chap. 7.

2. This limited availability of contracts was built into the program. Mexican negotiators wanted to use the supply of men as a bargaining chip for stronger provisions, while growers saw the availability of Mexican labors—both braceros and undocumented workers—as a means to exert downward pressure on the price of farm labor and control union activity (chap. 1).

3. By 1952 Mexican government officials were used to migrant remittances, which had already topped $30 million. In 1952, 204,000 braceros were contracted and earned $67 million. By then, remittances were Mexico's third-largest source of income. *Excelsior*, May 1, 1953, and *Las últimas noticias*, March 5, 1953, respectively; cited in American G.I. Forum, *What Price Wetbacks?*, 33.

4. Corwin and Cardoso, "Vamos al Norte," 54. The Spanish-language Los Angeles daily *La opinión* claimed that braceros' U.S. earnings were approximately eleven times greater than pay for equivalent work in Mexico and that wages had continued going up, while in Mexico they had fallen steadily. "Braceros, miseria," *La opinión*, March 3, 1954. The Pan American (labor) Union found that retail prices increased during the 1939 and the beginning of 1940 as a result of the war. It estimated that by December 1939 "the cost of clothing had risen by fifty percent" over 1935 prices. See Pan American Union, *Labor Trends and Social Welfare*, 54.

5. "Serio problema de los braceros," *El nacional*, October 3, 1948; "Braceros, miseria," *La opinión*, March 3, 1954.

6. "Serio problema de los braceros," *El nacional*, October 3, 1948 (emphasis mine). Also see Galarza, *Merchants of Labor*, 63; and García y Griego, "The Importation of Mexican Contract Laborers," 54.

7. See "Repercusiones en relación con el fraude a braceros," *El nacional*, July 11, 1946.

8. "Amplia documentación relativa a la ilícita entrada de braceros a EEUU," *El nacional*, October 18, 1948.

9. "Contratación de braceros in Mexicali, Baja California," *La opinión*, September 28, 1948; "Monterrey invadido por los que pretenden trabajar en los EEUU," *La opinión*, October 3, 1948; Huelga de hambre de los braceros," *La opinión*, October 9, 1948; Galarza, *Merchants of Labor*, 49; Kirstein, *Anglo over Bracero*. For a different perspective see "Ilegalmente hay en México 15,000 guatemaltecos," *La opinión*, October 26, 1948.

10. "Amplia documentación relativa a la ilícita entrada de braceros a EEUU," *El nacional*, October 18, 1948. For another reading, see "Más elogios recibe México aun por su patriótica actitud ante EU de A," *La opinión*, October 26, 1948.

11. "Pasaron 6,000 braceros a EU en un sólo día," *La opinión*, October 17, 1948; "Quedó derogado el acuerdo entre ambos países, para la contratación de braceros," *El nacional*, October 19, 1948. See Kirstein, *Anglo over Bracero*.

12. Report from the National Advisory Committee on Farm Labor, "Farm Labor Organizing, 1905–1967," quoted in Meister and Loftis, *A Long Time Coming*, 81. For another reading, see "La cuestión de los 'braceros,'" *La opinión*, October 25, 1948.

13. Across the country states were battling each other for braceros. See "Dos estados en pugna: Ambos quieren braceros," *La opinión*, September 22, 1948; "Otro conflicto por los braceros," *La opinión*, September 29, 1948; "Denuncian graves violaciones," *La opinión*, October 18, 1948; "Que castigue a los culpables de la entrada ilegal de braceros," *La opinión*, October 27, 1948; "Ecos mexicanos de la actitud estadounidense sobre los braceros," *La opinión*, October 23, 1948; "Llamado a braceros," *La opinión*, October 20, 1948; "EU regresará a México todos los braceros ilegales," *La opinión*, October 26, 1948. For further information, see Kirstein, *Anglo over Bracero*; Craig, *The Bracero Program*; Galarza, *Merchants of Labor*; García y Griego, "The Importation of Mexican Contract Laborers"; and Tomasek, "The Political and Economic Implications," 232–35.

14. Meister and Loftis, *A Long Time Coming*, 81. Also see "Empleados mexicanos acusados," *La opinión*, September 22, 1948; and "Protesta de 7000 braceros ante Ruiz Cortines," *La opinión*, September 17, 1948.

15. "Hermano bracero," *La opinión*, October 30, 1948; "La demanda de garantías," *La opinión*, October 28, 1948.

16. "La demanda de garantías," *La opinión*, October 28, 1948.

17. "Protesta de 7000 braceros ante Ruiz Cortines," *La opinión*, September 17, 1948; "Huelga de hambre de los braceros," *La opinión*, October 9, 1948; "La demanda de guarantías," *La opinión*, October 28, 1948; "Más de 1000 son las solicitudes de los

obreros," *La opinión*, October 26, 1948; "Ecos de la actitud mexicana por los braceros," *La opinión*, October 22, 1948; "Colonización de mexicanos antes que extranjeros," *La opinión*, October 15, 1948; "Monterrey invadido por los que pretenden trabajar en los EEUU," *La opinión*, October 3, 1948; "Otro conflicto por los braceros," *La opinión*, September 28, 1948; "Contratación de braceros en Mexicali, Baja California," *La opinión*, September 28, 1948.

18. From the Mexican government's perspective, the location of final inspections sites close to or at the border only enhanced the likelihood that men not winning contracts would be lured north. This undercut diplomats' ability to negotiate strong agreement protections and limited authorities' ability to accrue or repay huge political favors and establish or firm up alliances through the distribution of reception centers. Shopkeepers and ambulant merchants near selection sites garnered revenue, hacienda owners were stocked with pickers and harvesters when locals did not leave, and small-time politicos reaped cash and favors for the contracts they awarded. Not surprisingly, the U.S. government preferred a border location, which made transportation easier, cheaper, and shorter, and growers benefited from the increased number of undocumented workers that border locations generated. In the end, as Mexican authorities' negotiating clout vis-à-vis their U.S. counterparts was weakened by the greater pressure from hopeful migrants, reception centers, like the men themselves, edged north. See Craig, *The Bracero Program*; García y Griego, "The Importation of Mexican Contract Laborers"; Kiser and Kiser, *Mexican Workers in the United States*; and Scruggs, *Braceros*.

19. During the initial phase of the program, the main reception centers were located in Mexico City, Guadalajara, and Irapuato (Guanajuato). These not-so gradually shifted northward, to Monterrey, Chihuahua City, Zacatecas, Hermosillo, and Mexicali; by 1955, some braceros were processed at the Mexican-U.S. border. García y Griego, "The Importation of Mexican Contract Laborers," 67; Galarza, *Merchants of Labor*, 77; González Navarro, *Población y sociedad*, 248; García, *Operation Wetback*, 39.

20. According to Otey Scruggs ("Texas and the Bracero," 263), the ban was gradually though not publicly removed after 1947. By then, undocumented workers made it all but irrelevant.

21. De Alba, *Siete artículos*, 31. This section relies heavily on his book, 31–36.

22. Ibid., 31–36.

23. Hawley, "The Mexican Labor Issue," 159 n. 9.

24. Record of Proceedings, 38th Session, International Labor Organization Conference, Geneva, 1955, 95, quoted in James Mitchell, *Farm Labor Fact Book*, 164.

25. Ibid.

26. García y Greigo, "Mexican Contract Laborers," 65.

27. "Continuarán trayendo braceros mexicanos a EU," *La opinión*, January 2, 1954.

28. "Estados Unidos quiere braceros 'a como de lugar,'" *La opinión*, January 13, 1954; "Otro programa para traer braceros," *La opinión*, January 16, 1954; "Fondos para los braceros en el presupuesto," *La opinión*, January 23, 1954; "México suspende el envío de braceros," *La opinión*, January 17, 1954; "Los partidos aprobaron el acuerdo del gobierno sobre braceros," *La opinión*, January 19, 1954.

29. "Medidas para evitar que vengan braceros," *La opinión*, January 20, 1954; "Se cumplió el plazo a los braceros," *La opinión*, February 27, 1954; "EU y México en un acuerdo sobre braceros," *La opinión*, February 28, 1954. Also see Craig, *The Bracero Program*, 105–6; García y Griego, "Mexican Contract Laborers," 65; and García y Griego, "The Bracero Policy Experiment," 622.

30. Anonymous interviewee, December 1956, quoted in Anderson, *The Bracero Program*, 39.

31. "Medidas para evitar que vengan braceros," *La opinión*, January 20, 1954; "Tropas mexicanas evitan la salida de braceros," *La opinión*, January 24, 1954; "Los Estados Unidos piden tropas mexicanas para vigilar la frontera," *La opinión*, January 2, 1954. Kelly Lytle Hernandez, in her study of the U.S. border patrol, shows "how Mexican officials actively participated in the imagination and implementation of policing unsanctioned [Mexican] migration [north and] . . . Mexico's domestic interests in regulating the international mobility of Mexican laborers." See Lytle Hernandez, "The Crimes and Consequences," 2; and Lytle Hernandez, *Migra!*

32. "Estados Unidos quiere braceros 'a como de lugar,'" *La opinión*, January 13, 1954; editorial, *Excelsior*, January 17, 1954.

33. Sydney Gruson, "Mexico Reassures U.S. On Farm Labor," *New York Times*, December 22, 1953; *New York Times (1857–Current File)*, 22 Dec. 1953, ProQuest Historical Newspapers, The New York Times (1851–2006), ProQuest (July 24, 2008).

34. "México sólo negociará si se suspende la libre contratación de los braceros," *La opinión*, January 23, 1954; "Dos aspectos de un problema," editorial, *La opinión*, January 26, 1954; "2,211 braceros cruzaron la frontera," *La opinión*, January 27, 1954.

35. "2,211 braceros cruzaron la frontera," *La opinión*, January 27, 1954.

36. Editorials, *Excélsior*, January 21, 1954; January 23, 1954.

37. García y Griego, "The Importation of Mexican Contract Laborers," 66.

38. "Se agrava el problema de los braceros," *La opinión*, January 26, 1954.

39. "Evitarán la emigración de braceros a EU con amplios créditos y trabajo," *La opinión*, January 25, 1954.

40. "Se arremolinan en la frontera los braceros," *La opinión*, January 29, 1954; "Se agrava el problema de los braceros," *La opinión*, January 26, 1954; editorial, *New York Times*, January 16, 1954.

41. "Se arremolinan en la frontera los braceros," *La opinión*, January 29, 1954.

42. See editorials in *Excelsior*, January 24, 27, 28, 29, and February 2, 1954, along with the *El Paso Times* for complete description of events.

43. García y Griego, "The Importation of Mexican Contract Laborers."

44. Craig, *The Bracero Program*, 113.

45. Allsup, *American G.I. Forum*, 103–4.

46. "2,211 braceros cruzaron la frontera," *La opinión*, January 27, 1954; "A pesar de la excitativa oficial, empezó la fuga de braceros," *Excélsior*, January 23, 1954.

47. "Una gran multitud de braceros se lanza sobre la línea," *La opinión*, January 28, 1954.

48. "Los braceros se desesperan," *La opinión*, January 29, 1954.

49. "Una gran multitud de braceros se lanza sobre la línea," *La opinión*, January 28, 1954.

50. "Podrán ya salir los braceros," *La opinión*, January 30, 1954; "Teme un nuevo motín de braceros," *La opinión*, January 31, 1954.

51. "Otro túmulo de braceros en Mexicali," *La opinión*, February 2, 1954; "Una gran multitud de braceros se lanza sobre la línea," *La opinión*, January 28, 1954.

52. "La avalancha braceril," *La opinión*, February 2, 1954.

53. "Otro túmulo de braceros en Mexicali," *La opinión*, February 2, 1954.

54. *Hispanic American Report* 7, no. 1 (January 1954), 1; Craig, *The Bracero Program*, 112–13.

55. "Otro túmulo de braceros en Mexicali," *La opinión*, February 2, 1954.

56. "9,000 asaltaron la frontera con EEUU," *La opinión*, February 3, 1954; "EU detiene la contratación," *La opinión*, February 5, 1954.

57. Ruiz Cortines, quoted in Tomasek, "The Political and Economic Implications," 260–61; Craig, *The Bracero Program*, 117; García y Griego, "The Importation of Mexican Contract Laborers," 66.

58. "Medidas para evitar que vengan braceros," *La opinión*, January 20, 1954.

59. U.S. Senate, Committee on Agriculture and Forestry, *Extension of the Mexican Farm Labor Program*, 24, 26.

60. "Medidas para evitar que vengan braceros," *La opinión*, January 20, 1954.

61. Craig, *The Bracero Program*, 107.

62. See *Excelsior*'s editorial pages during the week January 15–24, 1954.

63. Editorial, *Excelsior*, January 15, 1954; García y Griego, "The Bracero Policy Experiment," 625, 627.

64. Torres Ramírez, *Hacia la utopía industrial*.

65. See, e.g., editorial from *Excelsior*, January 22, 1954; "Los braceros y la verdad mexicana," *Excelsior*, February 1, 1954; "La cuestión de los braceros," *Excelsior*, February 5, 1954. See also chap. 3.

66. U.S. President's Commission on Migratory Labor, *Migratory Labor in American Agriculture*, 69–88.

67. Navarro, *Mexicano Political Experience*, 246, 248–49.

68. García y Griego ("The Bracero Policy Experiment," 624) puts the 1953 figure at more than 1 million apprehended. See also Navarro, *Mexicano Political Experience*, 248–49.

69. LULAC, established in Texas in 1929, was initially largely a middle-class organization that advocated policies that pitted Mexican Americans against lower-class Mexican migrants. Still, it was the lead plaintiff in *Hernandez v. Texas*, the Supreme Court case, decided in favor of Hernandez, that guaranteed Mexican Americans equal protection under the Fourteenth Amendment. American G.I. Forum grew out of a disagreement that Héctor P. García had with the Corpus Christi, Texas, Naval Air station, which refused to accept Mexican American war veterans. It came to national prominence because of the "Félix Longoria Affair," when the only funeral parlor in Corpus Christi refused to prepare and bury the body of this Mexican American fallen

soldier. In the end, then-Senator Lyndon Johnson stepped in and Longoria was buried at Arlington Cemetery in Washington, D.C., and given full military honors. Like LULAC, the American G.I. Forum tended to favor the extension of civil rights based on U.S. citizenship.

70. Lawson, "The Bracero in California's Imperial Valley," 19.

71. Ibid., 20.

72. Sánchez Soto and Roldán Herrera, "Introducción a la primera parte," 18.

73. Braceros sent home $30 million in 1954, an average of $73 per bracero. González, *Guest Workers or Colonized Labor?*, 36.

74. García y Griego, "The Bracero Experiment," 209.

75. The United Packinghouse Workers of America, a Congress of Industrial Organizations (CIO) union, was accused of "coordinating with Mexican Communists," in particular, labor leader Vicente Lombardo Toledano, to "infiltrate[e] the bracero stream." See Watson, "Mixed Melody," 62.

76. U.S. Congress, *Congressional Record*, 87th Cong., 1st sess., 1961, 7708, 7719; Murphy, "American Opposition," 71.

77. After the 1960 election of John Kennedy, the administration took on the pro-bracero position exhibited by the DOL. Craig, *The Bracero Program*, 163. See his chap. 5 for an in-depth assessment of the struggle between labor and agriculture. Wright, "The Bracero Question," chap. 2; Hawley, "The Politics of the Mexican Labor Issue."

78. By 1959, more than 98% of the country's commercial growers received no braceros at all. Hawley, "The Politics of the Mexican Labor Issue," n. 19, 157, 163.

79. Craig, *The Bracero Program*, 161.

80. Elite growers at 305 associations, with a membership of over 43,000, relied on braceros, whereas only 8,100 individual growers did. See Hawley, "The Politics of the Mexican Labor Issue," n. 19, 163, 157.

81. Ibid., 172.

82. Craig, *The Bracero Program*, 189.

83. U.S. House of Representatives, *One-Year Extension of Mexican Farm Labor Program*, 34; Craig, *The Bracero Program*, 193.

84. Hawley, "The Politics of the Mexican Labor Issue," 169, 171, 170, 173. I came to this assessment of the centrality of the use of morality independent of Hawley.

85. Grove, "The Mexican Farm Labor Program," 318.

86. Runstein and Leveen, *Mechanization and Mexican Labor*, 122.

87. *El universal*, May 31, 1963; June 2, 1963; June 4, 1963; Craig, *The Bracero Program*, 185–86.

88. Grove, "The Mexican Farm Labor Program," suggests that while growers could hire cheap undocumented workers, those workers faced "a perpetual threat of deportation," while "the Mexican guest-worker program institutionalized commercial grower access to the productive, reliable supplementary labor force required by [large] commercial growers" and "allowed for its corporate management" (317).

89. Craig, *The Bracero Program*, 187.

90. Ibid., 188.

91. Ibid., 187.

92. Alan Riding, "U.S. Rejects Mexico's Proposal to Renew Migrant Agreement: Successful Entries Pack Revoked in 1964," *New York Times*, August 8, 1974; *New York Times (1857–Current File)*, 8 Aug. 1974, ProQuest Historical Newspapers The New York Times (1851–2006), ProQuest. Web. 8 July 2008.

93. Deborah Cohen, "Claiming Braceros as Our Own."

94. Wright, *Disposable Women*.

95. Two of the best of an expanding list of works on this topic are Salzinger, *Gender under Production*; and Wright, *Disposable Women*.

96. Grove, "The Mexican Farm Labor Program," 318.

Epilogue

1. Luden, "Day-Labor Centers Spark Immigration Debate."

2. I am referring to the "Border Protection, Anti-terrorism, and Illegal Immigration Control Act of 2005," or Sensenbrenner Bill (HR 4437), named for its sponsor, Representative James Sensenbrenner (R-Wisc.); it was not passed.

3. Quoted in McFadden, "Across the U.S., Growing Rallies for Immigration," *New York Times*, April 10, 2006 (emphasis mine).

4. Claudia Aguilar, "Alianza Braceroproa tiene pruebas de 'dónde quedó el dinero que envió EU': Representante," *La jornada Michoacán*, May 19, 2008, ⟨http://www. lajornadamichoacan.com.mx/2008/05/19/index.php?section=politica&article=003 n2pol⟩ (December 2, 2008).

5. Randal C. Archibold, "Owed Back Pay, Guest Workers Comb the Past," *New York Times*, November 23, 2008, ⟨http://www.nytimes.com/2008/11/24/us/24braceros. html?_r=1&scp=1&sq=Owed%20Back%20Pay,%20Guest%20Workers%20 Comb%20the%20Past&st=cse⟩ (December 6, 2008).

6. Quoted in ibid.

7. Ibid.

8. Kareem Fahim and Karen Zraick, "Killing Haunts Ecuadoreans' Rise in New York," *New York Times*, December 14, 2008, ⟨http://www.nytimes.com/2008/12/15/ nyregion/15ecuador.html?scp=1&sq=ecuadoran%20immigrants&st=cse⟩ (December 14, 2008); "Death in Patchogue," editorial, *New York Times*; November 11, 2008, ⟨http://www.nytimes.com/2008/11/11/opinion/11tue3.html?scp=2&sq=murder%20 of%20immigrant&st=cse⟩ (December 19, 2008). Pew Hispanic Center, "The Labor Force Status of Short-Term Unauthorized Workers," quoted in Ilias, Fennelly, and Federico, "American Attitudes toward Guest Worker Policies," 741.

9. A poll published in a March 30, 2006, study by the Pew Hispanic Center, *No Consensus on Immigration Problem*, generally found that U.S. citizens had more positive attitudes toward immigrants as the length of acquaintance with them increased.

10. Monsanto, the world's largest producer of genetically modified seeds, recognizes just how salient the image of the small farmer still is. Its new campaign, "America's Farmers," has a website urging visitors to "thank a farmer" and an emotionally resonant set of commercials. The commercials, first aired on network television in

early January 2010, are replete with images of small-town diners, laughing children, and rows of growing wheat, accompanied by touching music. One begins by asking, "Who grows our economy?"; another, "Who cares for the land?" The answer in both is the same: "America's farm families." "As farming grows, so does our quality of life. We're all connected through agriculture. . . . America's farmers grow America." ⟨http://www.monsanto.com/americasfarmers/⟩ (January 19, 2010).

11. Quoted in Hiram Soto, "Mexican Flag Kindles Passions Pro and Con," *San Diego Union-Tribune*, April 8, 2006, ⟨http://legacy.signonsandiego.com/union-trib/20060408/news_7m8mexflag.html⟩ (December 11, 2008). Also see Pineda and Sowards, "Flag Waving as Visual Argument."

12. Ngai, *Impossible Subjects*; de Genova, *Working the Boundaries*. This is not to say that Guatemalans and Salvadorans, for example, do not face rage for being undocumented, but rather that despite the increasing immigration from Guatemala, El Salvador, and Ecuador, illegal aliens are still emblematically "Mexican." As the *New York Times* article reports, while Ecuadorans were attacked, the men were out looking for Mexicans. Fahim and Zraick, "Killing Haunts Ecuadoreans' Rise in New York," *New York Times*, December 14, 2008.

13. The exact ranking is subject to fluctuations. Remittances have dropped due to the recession in construction and in the rest of the U.S. economy. Elisabeth Malkin, "Mexicans Barely Increased Remittances in '07," *New York Times*, February 26, 2008, ⟨http://www.nytimes.com/2008/02/26/business/worldbusiness/26mexico.html⟩ (December 6, 2008). Yet even as these emotional bonds are fostered, steps have been taken to increase the state's access to migrant remittances by taxing a portion of them. Part of a packet of fiscal reforms passed in October 2007, the tax in question, the *Impuesto a los Depósitos en Efectivo* (IDEO or the Tax on Cash Deposits) places a 2% tax on all bank deposits in a single month that surpass 25,000 pesos, which at the current exchange rate equals just over 1,800 U.S. dollars. Even though the IDEO might be seen as an attack on the millions of dollars in drug money that pass through Mexican banks, many immigrants will still pay a fee. Sandra Nichols, "Technology Transfer through Mexican Migration," *Grassroots Development* (2004), ⟨http://geocommunities.org/metaPage/lib/IAF-2004-TechTransf-Eng.pdf⟩ (December 3, 2008).

14. The Mexican constitution differentiates between citizenship and nationality, with nationality understood as the sense of belonging individuals feel toward country and citizenship affording particular rights, such as voting.

Bibliography

Primary Sources

Manuscript Collections

Durango, City
    Archivo Histórico del Estado de Durango
El Paso, Texas
    Institute for Oral History, University of Texas, El Paso
Mexico City
    Archivo General de la Nación, Mexico City
        Galería 3: Presidentes
            Miguel Alemán Valdés
            Manuel Ávila Camacho
            Adolfo López Mateos
            Adolfo Ruiz Cortines
        Secretaría de Relaciones Exteriores
            Archivo Histórico
                Braceros
                Fiestas
                Repatriaciones
            Dirección General del Acervo Histórico Diplomático
                Fondos Documentales
                    Protección y Asuntos Consulares, 1942–1964
Stanford, Calif.
    Special Collections and University Archives, Stanford University
        Ernesto Galarza Papers
        Annie Loftis Papers
Upland, Calif.
    Upland Public Library
        Dundas, Frederick Winn. Transcript of oral history. Conducted by
            Betty Maxie, November 23, 1976. Transcribed by Myrna Eidson.
            Tapes nos. 38 and 39.

Sandoval, Baudelio. Transcript of oral history. Conducted by Carlos Arturo
Castañeda, May 24, 1975. Transcribed by Aurora Alemán. Tape nos. 13 and 14.
Vásquez, Enrique. Transcript of oral history. Conducted by Carlos Arturo
Castañeda, March 3, 1978. Transcribed by Aurora Alemán. Tape no. 64.
Whitney, George H. Transcript of oral history. Conducted by Betty Maxie,
October 9, 1981. Transcribed by Myrna Eidson. Tape no. 205.
Washington, D.C.
U.S. National Archives and Records Administration
RG 16, Records of the Office of the Secretary of Agriculture
RG 90, Records of the Public Health Service, 1912–1968
RG 96, Records of the Farmers Home Administration
RG 174, General Records of the Department of Labor
RG 211, Records of the War Manpower Commission
RG 224, Records of the Office of Labor (War Food Administration)
Records of the Department of State relating to internal affairs of Mexico,
1940–1949; 1950–1959 (Decimal File 812)

Newspapers and Magazines

Bakersfield Californian
Catholic Worker
Excélsior (Mexico City)
The Farm
El heraldo (Chihuahua City)
Imperial Valley (Calif.) Press
La jornada (Mexico City)
Kern County (Calif.) Union
Labor Journal
Los Angeles Herald-Express
Los Angeles Times
Monitor (McAllen, Texas)
El nacional (Mexico City)

Nation
New York Times
New York Times Magazine
La opinión (Los Angeles)
El popular (Mexico City)
San Diego Union-Tribune
San Francisco Chronicle
Santa Rosa (Calif.) Press Democrat
El sol de Durango (Durango City)
Tiempo
Time
Las últimas noticias
El universal (Mexico City)

Oral Interviews

Lic. Bermúdez Cisneros, director, Secretaría de Trabajo y Previsión for Durango.
Interview with author. Durango City, September 21, 1995.
Lic. Mario Valero Salas, administrator of Durango's program, 1962–67. Interview
with author. Durango City, September 21, 1995.

Published Primary Sources

Agricultural Workers Organizing Committee. "Braceros' Sit-Down Strike at
Growers Association." Press release, October 6, 1961. Beinecke Rare Book
and Manuscript Library, Yale University, New Haven, Conn.

Aleman, Marco. "The Mexicans Keep 'Em Rolling." *Inter-American* 4 (October 1945): 20–23, 36.

American G.I. Forum of Texas and Texas State Federation of Labor. *What Price Wetbacks?* Austin: Texas State Federation of Labor, 1953.

Anderson, Henry P. *The Bracero Program in California.* Berkeley: University of California Press, 1961.

———. *Fields of Bondage: The Mexican Labor System in Industrialized Agriculture.* Berkeley, Calif.: Henry P. Anderson, 1963.

———. *A Harvest of Loneliness: An Inquiry into a Social Problem.* Berkeley, Calif.: Citizens for Farm Labor, 1964.

Ávila Camacho, Manuel. *Mensaje de año nuevo al pueblo mexicano para 1942.* Mexico City: Secretaría de Gobernación, 1941.

Black, John D. "Professor Schultz and C.E.D. on Agriculture in 1945." *Journal of Farm Economics* 28, no. 3 (August 1946): 669–86.

California Assembly Committee on Agriculture. Legislative Reference Service. *The Bracero Program and Its Aftermath: An Historical Summary.* Sacramento, 1965. ⟨http://are150.ucdavis.edu/class/cid_330/are150_chapter-2_braceros-ca-assem-1965.pdf⟩ (June 4, 2008).

California Fact-Finding Committee. *Mexicans in California: Report of Governor C. C. Young's Mexican Fact-Finding Committee.* Sacramento: California State Printing Office, 1930.

Carney, John Phillip "Postwar Mexican Migration: 1945–1955, with Particular Reference to the Policies and Practices of the United States Concerning Its Control." PhD diss., University of Southern California, 1957.

Casarrubias Ocampo, Daniel. "El problema del éxodo de braceros en México y sus consecuencias." Mexico City: Injumex (Instituto Nacional de la Juventud Mexicana), vol. 15, Universidad Nacional Autónoma de México, Facultad de Jurisprudencia, 1956.

Chaffee, Porter M. *A History of the C&AWIU.* WPA, Federal Writers Project, Oakland, Calif., 1938.

"Churches and the Braceros." *America* 104 (March 25, 1961): 810–11.

Clark, Margaret. *Health in the Mexican-American Culture: A Community Study.* Berkeley: University of California Press, 1959.

Coalson, George. "Mexican Contract Labor in American Agriculture." *Southwestern Social Science Quarterly* 33 (September 1952) 228–38.

Copp, Nelson G. "'Wetbacks' and *Braceros*: Mexican Migrant Laborers and American Immigration Policy, 1930–1960." PhD diss., Boston University, 1963.

County of Imperial, Calif. "Welcome to the County of Imperial." ⟨http://www.co.imperial.ca.us/⟩ (September 12, 2008).

Davis, Kenneth A. "The Demise of Braceros and Mechanization of California's Canning Tomato Industry." MA thesis, California State University, Sacramento, 1969.

de Alba, Pedro. *Siete artículos sobre el problema de los braceros.* Mexico City: n.p., 1954.

Dunbar, Robert LaFrance. "An Analysis of the Effects of Importing Farm Workers from Mexico." MA thesis, University of the Pacific, 1963.

Edwards, Everett E. "The National Agricultural Jefferson Bicentenary Committee: Its Activities and Recommendations." *Agricultural History* 19, no. 3 (July 1945): 167–85.

Escalante, Madga Elena. "An Oral History of Magdaleno Escalante, with an Emphasis on His Experiences in the Bracero Program from 1957 to 1962." MA thesis, California State University, Northridge, 2006.

Federal Workers Project. "Unionization of Migratory Labor, 1903–1930." Bancroft Library, Berkeley: University of California Press, n.d.

Foreign Relations of the United States, Diplomatic Papers. Vol. 6. Washington, D.C.: U.S. Government Printing Office, 1962 [1942].

Form, William H., and Julius Rivera. "Work Contracts and International Evaluations: The Case of a Mexican Border Village." *Social Forces* 37, no. 7 (May 1959): 334–38.

Galarza, Ernesto. *Farm Workers and Agri-business in California, 1947–1960.* Notre Dame, Ind.: University of Notre Dame Press, 1977.

———. "Letter to the Editor, *Stockton Record*, Stockton, California: Dear Sir, on May 16, 1960, the Record Published an Account of Statements Made by Mr. A. R. Duarte, Manager of the San Joaquin Farm Production Association." San Jose, Calif.: n.p., June 15, 1960.

———. "Memorándum acerca de los trabajadores mexicanos contratados en Estados Unidos." In Manuel Gamio, Ernesto Galarza, and Carlos E. Castañeda, "Tres estudios especializados acerca de los braceros." *Boletín del archivo general de la nación* ser. 3, no. 4 (1980): 41–49.

———. *Merchants of Labor: The Mexican Bracero Story.* Charlotte, N.C.: NcNally and Loftin, 1964.

———. "The Mexican American: A National Concern, Program for Action." *Common Ground* 9 (Summer 1949).

———. *Reply to Mr. Robert C. Goodwin's Letter on "Strangers in Our Fields."* n.p., October 22, 1956.

———. *Spiders in the House and Workers in the Field.* Notre Dame, Ind.: University of Notre Dame Press, 1971.

———. *Strangers in Our Fields: Based on a Report Regarding Compliance with the Contractual, Legal and Civil Rights of Mexican Agricultural Contract Labor in the United States Made Possible through a Grant-in-Aid from the Fund for the Republic,* 2nd ed. Washington, D.C.: U.S. Section, Joint United States–Mexico Trade Union Committee, 1956.

Gamio, Manuel. *Forjando patria.* Mexico City: Porrúa Hermanos, 1916.

———. "Informe del Doctor Manuel Gamio al Presidente de la República Mexicana, General Manuel Ávila Camacho." In Manuel Gamio, Ernesto Galarza, and Carlos E. Castañeda, "Tres estudios especializados acerca de los braceros." *Boletín del archivo general de la nación* ser. 3, no. 4 (1980): 38–40.

———. *The Mexican Immigrant: His Life Story.* New York: Arno, 1969 [1931].

———. *Mexican Immigration to the United States: A Study of Human Migration and Adjustment.* Chicago: University of Chicago Press, 1930.

García Robles, Alfonso. "Política internacional de México." In *Seis años de actividad nacional*, edited by Secretaría de Gobernación; introduction by Primo Villa Michel, 41–79. Mexico City: Talleres Gráficos de la Nación, 1946.

García Téllez, Ignacio. *La migración de braceros a los Estados Unidos de Norteamérica.* Mexico City: n.p., 1955.

Garloch, Lorene A. "Agricultural Economy of the Laguna Region." *Economic Geography* 20, no. 4 (October 1944): 296–304.

———. "Development of the Laguna Region." *Economic Geography* 20, no. 3 (July 1944): 221–27.

Gilmore, N. Ray, and Gladys Gilmore. "The Bracero in California." *Pacific Historical Review* 32, no. 3 (1963): 265–82.

Goodman, Jack. *While You Were Gone: A Report on Wartime Life in the United States.* New York: Da Capo, 1946.

Goott, Daniel. "Employment of Foreign Workers in United States Agriculture." *Department of State Bulletin* 21 (July 4, 1949).

Greer, Thomas V. "An Analysis of Mexican Literacy." *Journal of Inter-American Studies* 11, no. 3 (July 1969): 466–76.

Griswold, A. Whitney. "The Agrarian Democracy of Thomas Jefferson." *American Political Science Review* 40, no. 4 (August 1946): 657–81.

Hancock, Richard. *The Role of the Bracero in the Economic and Cultural Dynamics of Mexico.* Stanford, Calif.: Stanford University Press, 1959.

Hardin, Charles M. "Farm Political Power and the U.S. Governmental Crisis." "Proceedings of the Joint Annual Meeting," special issue of *Journal of Farm Economics* 40, no. 5 (December 1958): 1646–59.

Hawley, Ellis W. "The Politics of the Mexican Labor Issue, 1950–1965." *Agricultural History* 40, no. 3 (July 1966): 159–76.

Hispanic American Report 7, no. 1 (January 1954).

Hollywood Film Council (AFL). *Poverty in the Valley of Plenty.* Narrated by Harry W. Flannery. 1948. Rereleased by California Federation of Teachers, Oakland, 1995. Videocassette, 21 mins.

Jacobo, José Rodolfo. *Los Braceros: Memories of Bracero Workers, 1942–1964.* San Diego: Southern Border, 2004.

Jacobs, Paul. "The Forgotten People." *Reporter*, January 22, 1959, 13–20.

Jamieson, Stuart Marshall. *Labor Unionism in American Agriculture.* U.S. Bureau of Labor Statistics, Bulletin Number 836. Washington, D.C.: U.S. Government Printing Office, 1945.

"Jap Ban to Force Farm Adjustments." *San Francisco News*, March 4, 1942. Virtual Museum of the City of San Francisco. ⟨http://www.sfmuseum.org/hist8/land3.html⟩ (July 24, 2008).

John Deere. "Our Company: Timeline, 1940–1959." ⟨http://www.deere.com/en_US/compinfo/student/timeline_1940.html⟩ (June 5, 2006).

Joint United States–Mexico Trade Union Committee. "Declaration of Brownsville-Matamoros on the Bracero Program." Sixth International Conference of the Joint United States–Mexico Trade Union Committee, n.p., 1960.

Jones, Robert C. *Mexican War Workers in the United States: The Mexico–United States Manpower Recruiting Program and Operation, 1942–1944, Inclusive.* Washington, D.C.: Pan American Union, Division of Labor and Social Information, 1945.

Kibbe, Pauline. "The American Standard for All Americans." *Common Ground* 10 (Fall 1949): 19–27.

Labastida Rojas, Carlos. "El traque: Historia oral de don José Assaf." In *Rostros y rastros: Entrevistas a trabajadores migrantes en Estados Unidos,* edited by Jorge Durand, 39–44. San Luis Potosí: Colegio de San Luis, 2002.

Lawson, Luther William. "The Bracero in California's Imperial Valley." MA thesis, University of Southern California, 1965.

Leary, Mary Ellen. "As the Braceros Leave." *Reporter,* January 28, 1965, 43–45.

LeBerthon, Ted. "At the Prevailing Rate." *Commonweal,* November 1, 1957, 122–25.

———. "Exchange on Farm Workers from Mexico." *Commonweal,* July 4, 1958, 341–42.

Lira López, Salvador, Ramón Fernández y Fernández, and Quintín Olazcoaga. *La pobreza rural en Mexico.* Mexico City: n.p., 1945.

Lockwood, Robert Wayne. "The DiGiorgio Strike." Student paper for Economics 252A, University of California, Berkeley, 1950.

Luden, Jennifer. "Day-Labor Centers Spark Immigration Debate." *Morning Edition,* National Public Radio. August 19, 2005. ⟨http://www.npr.org/templates/story/story.php?storyId=4806486⟩ (August 20, 2005).

Lyon, Richard Martin. "The Legal Status of American and Mexican Migratory Farm Labor: An Analysis of U.S. Farm-Labor Legislation, Policy and Administration." PhD diss., Cornell University, 1954.

MacKaye, Margaret Breed. "A Historical Study of the Development of the Bracero Program, with Special Emphasis on the Coachella and Imperial Valleys." MA thesis, University of the Pacific, 1958.

Madrazo, Carlos. *La verdad en el "caso" de los braceros: Origen de esta injusticia y nombre de los verdaderos responsables.* Mexico City: Secretaría de Trabajo y Previsión Social, 1945.

Martin, J. G. "Handling and Marketing Durango Cotton in the Imperial Valley." *United States Department of Agriculture Bulletin* 458 (March 31, 1917).

Martinez, Daniel. "The Impact of the Bracero Program on Southern California Mexican American Community: A Field Study of Cucamonga, California." MA thesis, Claremont Graduate School, 1958.

Martínez Domínguez, Guillermo. "Los braceros: Experiencias que deben aprovecharse." *Revista mexicana de sociología* (IIS: UNAM) 10, no. 2 (1948): 177–96. Reprinted in *Braceros: Las miradas mexicana y estadounidense,* edited by Jorge Durand, 231–49. Mexico City: Miguel Angel Porrúa/Universidad Autónoma de Zacatecas, 2007.

McBride, Sister Mary Anne Patrick. "A History of the Bracero Program in California." MA thesis, Department of History, University of Notre Dame, 1965.

McCullough, Rev. Thomas. "Safeguarding the Bracero Contract." *Ninth Regional Conference Catholic Council for the Spanish Speaking.* San Antonio, April 15–17, 1958.

McLachlan, Argyle. "Community Production of Durango Cotton in the Imperial Valley." *United States Department of Agriculture Bulletin* 324 (December 22, 1915).

McWilliams, Carey. *Factories in the Field: The Story of Migratory Farm Labor in California.* Berkeley: University of California Press, 1982.

——. *Ill Fares the Land: Migrants and Migratory Labor in the United States.* Boston: Little, Brown, 1942.

——. *North from Mexico: The Spanish-Speaking People of the United States.* Philadelphia: J. B. Lippincott, 1948.

——. "They Saved the Crops." *Inter-American* 2 (August 1943): 10–14.

Mexico. Secretaría de Relaciones Exteriores. *Memoria de la Secretaría de Relaciones Exteriores, septiembre de 1951 a agosto de 1952.* Mexico City: Talleres Gráficos de la Nación, 1952.

——. *Memoria de la Secretaría de Relaciones Exteriores, septiembre de 1952 a diciembre de 1953.* Mexico City: Talleres Gráficos de la Nación, 1953.

Mexico. Secretaría del Trabajo y Previsión Social. *Los braceros.* Mexico City: Secretaría del Trabajo y Previsión Social, Dirección de Previsión Social, 1946.

Mitchell, H. L. *Mean Things Happening in This Land: The Life and Times of H. L. Mitchell, Co-founder of the Southern Tenant Farmers Union.* Montclair, N.J.: Allanheld, Osmun, 1979.

——. *Roll the Union On: A Pictorial History of the Southern Tenant Farmers' Union, as Told by Its Co-founder HL Mitchell.* Chicago: Charles H. Kerr, 1987.

Mitchell, James P., Secretary, U.S. Department of Labor. *Farm Labor Fact Book.* Washington, D.C.: U.S. Government Printing Office, 1959.

Moore, Truman. *The Slaves We Rent: An Explosive Report about the Shame of America—Two Million Migrant Men, Women and Children.* New York: Random House, 1965.

Moore, Woodrow. "El problema de la emigración de los braceros mexicanos." MA thesis, Universidad Nacional Autónoma de México, 1961.

Murphy, Willie Mae. "American Opposition to the Bracero Program." MA thesis, Lamar State College of Technology, 1970.

Murrow, Edward R. *CBS Reports: Harvest of Shame,* producer, David Lowe; editor, John Schultz; executive producer, Fred W. Friendly. Aired November 25, 1960.

National Advisory Committee on Farm Labor. *The Case for the Domestic Farm Worker.* New York: National Advisory Committee on Farm Labor, 1965.

——. *Poverty on the Land in a Land of Plenty.* New York: National Advisory Committee on Farm Labor, 1965.

O'Donnell, Cyril. "Selling California Cotton, 1944–1948." *Southern Economic Journal* 17, no. 3 (January 1951): 288–301.

Pan American Union. *Labor Trends and Social Welfare in Latin America, 1939–1940*. Washington, D.C.: Pan American Union, Division of Labor and Social Information, 1941.

Quezada, Claudia. "El mexicano, nomás que le pongan para que el agarre: Historia oral de don Carlos Quezada." In *Rostros y rastros: Entrevistas a trabajadores migrantes en Estados Unidos*, edited by Jorge Durand, 21–30. San Luis Potosí: Colegio de San Luis, 2002.

Quintana, Miguel A. "La acción presidencial en favor de los trabajadores." In *Seis años de actividad nacional*, edited by Secretaría de Gobernación, 221–60. Introduction by Primo Villa Michel. Mexico City: Talleres Gráficos de la Nación, 1946.

Rasmussen, Wayne D. *A History of the Emergency Farm Labor Supply Program, 1943–1947*. Washington, D.C.: U.S. Department of Agriculture: Agriculture Monograph 13 (September 15, 1951).

Reilly, Sister de Prague. "The Role of the Churches in the Bracero Program in California." MA thesis, University of Southern California, 1969.

Rodríguez López, María del Pilar. "La bracereada: Historia oral con Gonzalo Salazar." In *Rostros y rastros: Entrevistas a trabajadores migrantes en Estados Unidos*, edited by Jorge Durand, 31–38. San Luis Potosí: Colegio de San Luis, 2002.

Roldán Herrera, Francisco Javier. "Mientras llega la chamba: Historia oral de don Manuel Rodríguez Silva." In *Rostros y rastros: Entrevistas a trabajadores migrantes en Estados Unidos*, edited by Jorge Durand, 45–52. San Luis Potosí: Colegio de San Luis, 2002.

Rooney, James. "The Effects of Imported Mexican Farm Labor in a California County." *American Journal of Economics and Sociology* 20, no. 5 (October 1961): 513–21.

Rouaix, Pastor. *Diccionario geográfico, histórico, y biográfico del Estado de Durango*. Mexico City: Instituto Panamericano de Geografía e Historia, 1946.

Salazar, Ruben. *Border Correspondent: Selected Writings, 1955–1970*. Edited and with an introduction by Mario T. García. Berkeley: University of California Press, 1995.

Salinas, José Lázaro. *La emigración de braceros: Visión objetiva de un problema mexicano*. Mexico City: José Lázaro Salinas, 1955.

Sánchez Soto, Gabriela. "Por ahí anduve, ni pa' morirme: Historia oral de don Catarino Hernández Ramos." In *Rostros y rastros: Entrevistas a trabajadores migrantes en Estados Unidos*, edited by Jorge Durand, 53–65. San Luis Potosí: Colegio de San Luis, 2002.

Saunders, Lyle, and Olen E. Leonard. *The Wetback in the Lower Rio Grande Valley of Texas*. Austin: University of Texas Press, 1951.

Schwartz, Harry. "Farm Labor Adjustments after World War I." *Journal of Farm Economics* 25, no. 1 (February 1943): 269–77.

———. "Farm Labor Policy, 1942–1943." *Journal of Farm Economics* 25, no. 3 (August 1943): 691–701.

Seasonal Farm Laborers Program: Sad Recollections. Directed by Jorge Luis Vázquez. 26 mins. Mexico City: Motor Films, 2002.

Spaulding, Charles B. "The Mexican Strike at El Monte, California." *Sociology and Social Research* 18 (July 1934): 571–80.

Special Citizens Committee Investigating DiGiorgio Farms. *A Community Aroused.* Bakersfield, Calif.: s.n., 1947.

Stevenson, Coke, and Ezequiel Padilla. *The Good Neighbor Policy and Mexicans in Texas.* National and International Problems Series. Mexico City: Cooperativa Talleres Gráficos de la Nación, 1943.

Suinaga Luján, Pedro R. *Veinte años de legislación mexicana, 1931–1951.* Vol. 3. Durango: Stylo, 1951.

Taylor, Jack E. *God's Messengers to Mexico's Masses: A Study of the Religious Significance of Braceros.* Eugene, Ore.: Institute of Church Growth, 1962.

Taylor, Paul S. *Imperial Valley.* Vol. 1, no. 1, of *Mexican Labor in the United States.* University of California Publications in Economics. Berkeley: University of California Press, 1928.

Teague, Charles Collins. *Fifty Years a Rancher.* Los Angeles: Ward Richie, 1944.

Tomasek, Robert D. "The Political and Economic Implications of Mexican Labor in the United States under the Non-quota System, Contract Labor Program, and Wetback Movement." PhD diss., University of Michigan, 1957.

Torres Bodet, Jaime. "La obra educativa." In *Seis años de actividad nacional,* edited by Secretaría de Gobernación, 103–42. Introduction by Primo Villa Michel. Mexico City: Talleres Gráficos de la Nación, 1946.

———. *La victoria sin alas: Memorias.* Mexico City: Porrua, 1970.

Truman, Harry S. "Inaugural Addresses of Harry S. Truman." ⟨http://avalon.law .yale.edu/20th_century/truman.asp⟩ (November 5, 2009).

Turnier, Maria F. V. "Public Law 45, 'Braceros' and West Indians, Their Impact on Native American Farm Laborers, 1942–1946." MA thesis, Pennsylvania State University, 1969.

U.S. Congress. *Congressional Record.* 80th Cong., 1st sess., 1947.

———. *Congressional Record.* 87th Cong., 1st sess., 1961.

———. *Congressional Record.* 88th Cong., 1st sess., 1964.

U.S. Department of Health, Education, and Welfare. *Braceros, Mexico, and Foreign Trade.* Washington, D.C.: Farm Labor Developments, 1966.

U.S. House of Representatives. *One-Year Extension of Mexican Farm Labor Program.* Report Number 722. 88th Cong., 1st sess. Washington, D.C.: U.S. Government Printing Office, September 6, 1963.

U.S. House of Representatives, Subcommittee of the Committee on Agriculture. *Hearing before a Subcommittee of the Committee on Agriculture, House Resolution 7028.* 85th Cong., 2nd sess., 1958. Washington, D.C.: U.S. Government Printing Office, 1958.

U.S. House of Representatives, Subcommittee of the House Labor Committee. *Memorandum—Brief on the DiGiorgio Strike and Conditions among the Agricultural*

Workers of California, Presented to the Sub-committee of the House Labor Committee by the NFLU-AFL, Bakersfield, Cal. 80th Cong., 1st sess., November 12, 1949. Washington, D.C.: U.S. Government Printing Office, 1949.

U.S. House of Representatives, Subcommittee on Equipment, Supplies, and Manpower of the Committee on Agriculture. *Mexican Farm Labor Program: Hearings before the Subcommittee on Equipment, Supplies, and Manpower of the Committee on Agriculture.* 84th Cong., 1st sess., 1955. Washington, D.C.: U.S. Government Printing Office, 1955.

U.S. House of Representatives, Subcommittee on Equipment, Supplies, and Manpower of the Committee on Agriculture. *Mexican Farm Labor Program: Hearing before the Subcommittee on Equipment, Supplies, and Manpower of the Committee on Agriculture.* 87th Cong., 2nd sess., 1962. Washington, D.C.: U.S. Government Printing Office, 1962.

U.S. President's Commission on Migratory Labor. *Migratory Labor in American Agriculture.* Washington, D.C.: U.S. Government Printing Office, 1951.

U.S. Senate, Committee on Agriculture. *Nutrition and Forestry, 1825–1998: Members, Jurisdiction, and History, S. Doc. 105–24.* ⟨http://www.access.gpo.gov/congress/senate/sen_agriculture/ch5.html⟩ (January 23, 2004).

U.S. Senate, Committee on Agriculture and Forestry. *Extension of the Mexican Farm Labor Program, Hearing on S. 1207.* 83rd Cong., 1st sess., March 24, 25, and 26, 1953. Washington, D.C.: U.S. Government Printing Office, 1953.

U.S. Senate, Committee on Agriculture, Nutrition, and Forestry. "Chapter 5: War, Peace, and Prosperity, 1940–1959." ⟨http://www.access.gpo.gov/congress/senate/sen_agriculture/ch5.html⟩ (January 23, 2004).

Vasconcelos, José. *The Cosmic Race: A Bilingual Edition.* Translated and annotated by Didier T. Jaén, afterword by Joseba Gabilondo. Baltimore: Johns Hopkins University Press, 1979.

Veblen, Thorstein. "An Unpublished Paper, Using the I.W.W. to Harvest Grain." *Journal of Political Economy* 40 (December 1932 [1918]): 797–807.

———. "Unionization of Migratory Labor, 1903–1930." Federal Workers Project, Bancroft Library. Berkeley: University of California Press, n.d.

Weedpatch Camp (Arvin Federal Camp): Personal Reminiscences. "1930: DiGiorgio Farms Packing Shed Largest of Its Kind in the World." *Arvin Tiller/ Lamont Reporter Supplement*, October 8, 1997, ⟨http://www.weedpatchcamp.com/Reminiscences/DiGiorgio%20Farms.htm⟩ (May 30, 2008).

Wilson, M. L. *Proceedings of the American Philosophical Society*, July 14, 1943, 216–22.

Wolff, William George. "The Structural Development of the Bracero Program, 1942–1947." MA thesis, Southern Illinois University, 1967.

Wright, Linda Chapple. "The Bracero Question, 1942–1964: Congress, the Nation, and Texas." MA thesis, Southwest Texas University, 1980.

Zorrilla, Luis G. *La emigración de braceros a los Estados Unidos de América.* Mexico City: n.p., 1964.

Secondary Sources

Acuña, Rodolfo. *Occupied America: A History of Chicanos*. 6th ed. New York: Longman, 2006.

Aguilar Camín, Héctor, and Lorenzo Meyer. *In the Shadow of the Mexican Revolution: Contemporary Mexican History, 1910–1989*. Translated by Luis Alberto Fierro. Austin: University of Texas Press, 1993 [1989].

Alanis Enciso, Fernando Saúl. "La contratación de braceros en San Luis Potosí." In *La emigración de San Luis Potosí a Estados Unidos pasado y presente*, edited by Fernando Saúl Alanis Enciso, 41–74. San Luis Potosí: Colegio de San Luis, 2001.

Allsup, Carl Vernon. *The American G.I. Forum: Origins and Evolution*. Austin: Center for Mexican American Studies, University of Texas, 1982.

Almaguer, Tomas. *Racial Fault Lines: The Historical Origins of White Supremacy in California*. Berkeley: University of California Press, 1994.

Alonso, Ana. *Thread of Blood: Colonialism, Revolution and Gender on Mexico's Northern Frontier*. Tucson: University of Arizona Press, 1995.

———. "Work and Gusto: Gender and Re-creation in a North Mexican Pueblo." In *Workers' Expressions: Beyond Accommodation and Resistance*, edited by John Calagione, Doris Francis, and Daniel Nugent, 164–85. Albany: State University of New York Press, 1992.

Archer Audio Archives. ⟨http://www.archer2000.net/1940.html⟩ (July 23, 2009).

Avitia Hernández, Antonio. *Corridos de Durango*. Mexico City: Instituto Nacional de Antropología e Historia, Colección Divulgación, 1989.

Bacon, David. "Fast Track to the Past: Is a New Bracero Program in Our Future? (And What Was Life Like under the Old One?)." ⟨http://dbacon.igc.org/Imgrants/17FastPast.htm⟩ (June 8, 2008).

Basch, Linda, Nina Glick-Schiller, and Cristina Szanton Blanc. *Nations Unbound: Transnational Projects, Postcolonial Predicaments, and Deterritorialized Nation-States*. London: Routledge, 2003.

Beasley, Chris. *Gender and Sexuality: Critical Theories, Critical Thinkers*. London: Sage, 2005.

Beatty, Edward. *Institutions and Investment: The Political Basis of Industrialization in Mexico before 1911*. Stanford, Calif.: Stanford University Press, 2001.

Becker, Marjorie. *Setting the Virgin on Fire: Lázaro Cárdenas, Michoacán Peasants, and the Redemption of the Mexican Revolution*. Berkeley: University of California Press, 1996.

Bell, Jonathan. *The Liberal State on Trial: Cold War and American Politics in the Truman Years*. New York: Columbia University Press, 2004.

Beneke, Timothy. *Proving Manhood: Reflections on Men and Sexism*. Berkeley: University of California Press, 1997.

Benton-Cohen, Katherine. *Borderline Americans: Racial Divisions and Labor War in the Arizona Borderlands*. Cambridge: Harvard University Press, 2009.

Berger, Dina. *The Development of Mexico's Tourism Industry: Pyramids by Day, Martinis by Night.* New York: Palgrave, 2006.

Bliss, Katherine E. *Compromised Positions: Prostitution, Public Health, and Gender Politics in Revolutionary Mexico City.* University Park: Pennsylvania State University, 2002.

Bortelsmann, Thomas. *The Cold War and the Color Line: American Race Relations in a Global Arena.* Cambridge: Harvard University Press, 2003.

Bortz, Jeffrey, and Stephen Haber, eds. *The Mexican Economy, 1870–1930: Essays on the Economic History of Institutions, Revolution, and Growth.* Stanford, Calif.: Stanford University Press, 2002.

Boyer, Christopher R. *Becoming Campesinos: Politics, Identity, and Agrarian Struggle in Postrevolutionary Michoacán, 1920–1935.* Stanford, Calif.: Stanford University Press, 2003.

Brandzel, Amy. "Queer Citizenship? Same-Sex Marriage and the State." *GLQ: A Journal of Lesbian and Gay Studies* 11, no. 2 (2005): 171–204.

Brown, Robert Michael. "The Impact of U.S. Work Experience on Mexican Agricultural Workers: A Case Study in the Village of Jacona, Michoacán, Mexico." PhD diss., University of Colorado, 1975.

Calavita, Kitty. *Inside the State: The Bracero Program, Immigration, and the I.N.S. After the Law.* New York: Routledge, 1992.

Campbell, James. "Personhood and the Land." *Agriculture and Human Values* 7, no. 1 (Winter 1990): 39–43.

Canaday, Margot. *The Straight State: Sexuality and Citizenship in Twentieth-Century America.* Politics and Society in Twentieth-Century America. Princeton, N.J.: Princeton University Press, 2009.

Cantú, Lionel, Nancy A. Naples, and Salvador Vidal-Ortiz. *The Sexuality of Migration: Border Crossings and Mexican Immigrant Men.* Intersections: Transdisciplinary Perspectives on Genders and Sexualities. New York: New York University Press, 2009.

Carr, Berry. *Marxism and Communism in Twentieth-Century Mexico.* Lincoln: University of Nebraska Press, 1992.

Chafe, William H. "American since 1945." In *The New American History*, edited by Eric Foner. Critical Perspectives on the Past. Philadelphia: Temple University Press, 1997.

Cherny, Robert, William Issel, and Keiran Walsh Taylor. Introduction to *American Labor and the Cold War: Grassroots Politics and Post-war Political Culture*, edited by Robert Cherny, William Issel, and Keiran Walsh Taylor, 1–6. Piscataway, N.J.: Rutgers University Press, 2004.

Coatsworth, John H. *Growth against Development: The Economic Impact of Railroads in Porfirian Mexico.* DeKalb: Northern Illinois University Press, 1981.

Cockcroft, James D. *Outlaws in the Promised Land: Mexican Immigrant Workers and America's Future.* New York: Grove, 1986.

Cohen, Deborah. "Claiming Braceros as Our Own: Elite Visions of the Nation during the Bracero Program." Unpublished ms.

———. "Masculine Sweat, Stoop-Labor Modernity: Gender, Race, and Nation in Mexico and the United States." PhD diss., University of Chicago, 2001.

———. "Sex and Betrayal: Migration, Sentiment, and Citizenship." Unpublished ms.

Cohen, Lizabeth. *A Consumer's Republic: The Politics of Mass Consumption in Postwar America*. New York: Knopf, 2003.

Connell, R. W. *Masculinities*. St. Leonard's, Australia: Allen and Unwin, 1995.

———. "Masculinities, Change and Conflict in Global Society: Thinking about the Future of Men's Studies." *Journal of Men's Studies* 11, no. 3 (2003): 249–67.

Connell, R. W., and James W. Messerschmidt. "Hegemonic Masculinity: Rethinking the Concept." *Gender and Society* 19, no. 6 (December 2005): 829–59.

Connor, S. "The Shame of Being a Man." *Textual Practice* 15, no. 2 (2001): 211–30.

Conway-Long, Don. *Gender, Power and Social Change in Morocco*. In *Islamic Masculinities*, edited by Lahoucine Ouzgane. London: Zed, 2006.

———. "Violence in the Fields: Masculinities, Social Sciences, and Terrorisms." Keynote speech. 3rd annual SIUE Colloquium: Talking about Masculinity. Southern Illinois University–Edwardsville, April 6, 2005.

Coronil, Fernando. *The Magical State: Nature, Money, and Modernity in Venezuela*. Chicago: University of Chicago Press, 1997.

Corwin, Arthur F. "The Study and Interpretation of Mexican Labor Migration: An Introduction." In *Immigrants and Immigrants: Perspectives on Mexican Labor Migration to the United States*, edited by Arthur Corwin, 3–24. Contributions in Economics and Economic History, no. 17. Westport, Conn.: Greenwood, 1978.

Corwin, Arthur F., and Lawrence Cardoso. "'Vamos al Norte': Causes of Mass Mexican Migration to the United States." In *Immigrants and Immigrants: Perspectives on Mexican Labor Migration to the United States*, edited by Arthur F. Corwin, 38–66. Contributions in Economics and Economic History, no. 17. Westport, Conn.: Greenwood, 1978.

Craig, Richard B. "Interest Groups and the Foreign Policy Process: A Case Study of the Bracero Program." PhD diss., University of Missouri–Columbia, 1970.

———. *The Bracero Program: Interest Groups and Foreign Policy*. Austin: University of Texas Press, 1971.

Curley, Robert. "Sociólogos peregrinos: Teoría social católica en el fin-de-régimen porfiriano." In *Catolicismo social en México*, vol. 1, *Teoría, fuentes e historiografía*, edited by Manuel Ceballos Ramírez and Alejandro Garza Rangel, 195–237. Monterrey: Academia de Investigación Humanística, 2000.

Davis, Natalie Zemon. *Return of Martin Guerre*. Cambridge: Harvard University Press, 1983.

Demos, John. *The Unredeemed Captive: A Family Story from Early America*. New York: Vintage, 1995.

de Genova, Nicholas. *Working the Boundaries: Race, Space, and "Illegality" in Mexican Chicago*. Durham, N.C.: Duke University Press, 2005.

Deutsch, Sandra McGee. "Gender and Sociopolitical Change in Twentieth-Century Latin America." *Hispanic American Historical Review* 71, no. 2 (1991): 259–306.

Deutsch, Sarah. "Being American in Boley, Oklahoma." In *Beyond Black and White:*

Race, Ethnicity, and Gender in the United States South and Southwest, edited by Stephanie Cole and Alison M. Parker, introduction by Nancy A. Hewitt, 97–122. Waiter Prescott Webb Memorial Lectures, no. 35. College Station: Texas A&M University Press for the University of Texas, Arlington, 2004.

Diaz Herrera, Maria. "The Bracero Experience: In Life and Fiction." MA thesis, University of California, Los Angeles, 1971.

Domingo, Pilar, and Rachel Sieder. *The Rule of Law in Latin America: The International Promotion of Judicial Reform*. London: University of London, Institute of Latin American Studies, 2001.

Domínguez López, Emelia Violeta. "El programa bracero, 1942–1947: Un acercamiento a través de los testimonios de sus trabajadores." BA thesis: Universidad Nacional Autónoma de México, 2001.

Doyle, Laura. "Toward a Philosophy of Transnationalism." *Journal of Transnational American Studies* 1, no. 1 (2009). ⟨http://www.escholarship.org/uc/item/9vr1k8hk⟩ (August 14, 2009).

Dreissig, Mathias. "Working in the Fields: The Bracero Program and Labor Relations in American Agriculture, 1942–1965." MA thesis, University of Cincinnati, 1987.

Dudziak, Mary L. *Cold War Rights: Race and the Age of American Democracy*. Princeton, N.J.: Princeton University Press, 2002.

Durand, Jorge. "Presentación." In *Rostros y rastros: Entrevistas a trabajadores migrantes en Estados Unidos*, edited by Jorge Durand, 9–14. San Luis Potosí: Colegio de San Luis, 2002.

Durán y Martínez, Francisco. *Cuatro haciendas de Durango: La Concepción, El Casco, La Naicha y San Antonio Padres*. Mexico City: Sistema Estatal de Educación, 1997.

Edwards, Everett E. "The National Agricultural Jefferson Bicentenary Committee: Its Activities and Recommendations." *Agricultural History* 19, no. 3 (1945): 167–85.

Escobar, Edward J. *Race, Police, and the Making of a Political Identity: Mexican Americans and the Los Angeles Police Department, 1900–1945*. Berkeley: University of California Press, 1999.

Fein, Seth. "Myths of Cultural Imperialism and Nationalism in Golden Age Mexican Cinema." In *Fragments of a Golden Age: The Politics of Culture in Mexico since 1940*, edited by Gilbert Joseph, Anne Rubenstein, and Eric Zolov, 159–98. American Encounters/Global Interactions. Durham, N.C.: Duke University Press, 2001.

Fisher, Richard. "The Dog That Does Not Bark but Packs a Big Bite: Services in the U.S. Economy." Remarks before the U.S.–China Business Council, the Coalition of Service Industries, and the American Council of Life Insurers. Washington, D.C., May 14, 2007. ⟨http://www.dallasfed.org/news/speeches/fisher/2007/fs070514.cfm⟩ (July 24, 2009).

Foley, Neil. "Partly Colored or Other White: Mexican Americans and Their Problem with the Color Line." In *Beyond Black and White: Race, Ethnicity, and Gender in the U.S. South and Southwest*, edited by Stephanie Cole and Alison

M. Parker, introduction by Nancy A. Hewitt, 341–55. Waiter Prescott Webb Memorial Lectures, no. 35. College Station: Texas A&M University Press for the University of Texas, Arlington, 2004.

———. *The White Scourge: Mexicans, Blacks, and Poor Whites in Texas Cotton Culture.* Berkeley: University of California Press, 1997.

Foner, Philip. *History of the Labor Movement in the United States*, vol. 6, *The Industrial Workers of the World, 1905–1917.* New York: International, 1975.

Foweraker, Joe, and Ann L. Craig. *Popular Movements and Political Change in Mexico.* (Boulder, Colo.: Lynne Rienner, 1990.

Frazier, Lessie Jo. *Salt in the Sand: Memory, Violence and the Chilean Nation-State, 1890–Present.* Politics, History, and Culture. Durham, N.C.: Duke University Press, 2007.

Gallo, Rubén. *Mexican Modernity: The Avant-Garde and the Technological Revolution.* Cambridge: Massachusetts Institute of Technology Press, 2005.

Gamboa, Erasmo. "Under the Thumb of Agriculture: Bracero and Mexican American Workers in the Pacific Northwest." PhD diss., University of Washington, 1984.

García, Juan Ramón. *Operation Wetback: The Mass Deportation of Mexican Undocumented Workers in 1954.* Westport, Conn.: Greenwood Press, 1980.

Garcia, Matt. "Cain contra Abel: Courtship, Masculinities, and Citizenship in Southern California Farming Communities." In *Race, Nation, and Empire in American History*, edited by James T. Campbell, Matthew Pratt Guterl, and Robert G. Lee, 180–200. Chapel Hill: University of North Carolina Press, 2007.

———. "Interethnic Conflict and the *Bracero* Program." In *American Dreaming, Global Realities: Rethinking U.S. Immigration History*, edited by Donna Gabaccia and Vicki L. Ruiz, 399–410. Statue of Liberty–Ellis Island Centennial Series. Urbana: University of Illinois Press, 2006.

———. *A World of Its Own: Race, Labor, and Citrus in the Making of Greater Los Angeles, 1900–1970.* Chapel Hill: University of North Carolina, 2002.

García y Griego, Manuel. "The Bracero Policy Experiment: U.S.-Mexican Responses to Mexican Labor Migration, 1942–1955." PhD diss., University of California, Los Angeles, 1988.

———. "The Importation of Mexican Contract Laborers to the United States, 1942–1964." In *The Border That Joins: Mexican Migrants and U.S. Responsibility*, edited by Peter G. Brown and Henry Shue. Totowa, N.J.: Rowman and Littlefield, 1983.

Gauss, Susan. "The Politics of Economic Nationalism in Postrevolutionary Mexico." *History Compass* 4, no. 3 (2006): 567–77.

———. "Working-Class Masculinity and the Rationalized Sex: Gender and Industrialized Modernization in the Textile Industry in Postrevolutionary Puebla." In *Sex in Revolution: Gender, Politics, and Power in Modern Mexico*, edited by Jocelyn Olcott, Mary Kay Vaughan, and Gabriela Cano, 181–98. Durham, N.C.: Duke University Press, 2006.

Gómez, Laura E. *Manifest Destinies: The Making of the Mexican American Race.* New York: New York University Press, 2007.

Gómez Quiñones, Juan. *Mexican American Labor, 1790–1990*. Albuquerque: University of New Mexico Press, 1994.

Gonzalez, Gilbert. *Guest Workers or Colonized Labor? Mexican Labor Migrants to the United States*. Boulder, Colo.: Paradigm Publishers, 2007.

Gonzalez-Lopez, Gloria. *Erotic Journeys: Mexican Immigrants and Their Sex Lives*. Berkeley: University of California Press, 2005.

González Navarro, Moisés. *Historia moderna de México—El porfiriato: La vida política interior*, 2nd part. Mexico City: Hermes, 1972.

———. *Población y sociedad en México, 1900–1970*, 2 vols. Estudios, no. 42. Mexico City: Universidad Nacional Autónoma de México, Facultad de Ciencias Políticas y Sociales, 1974.

———. *Raza y tierra: La guerra de castas y el henequín*. Mexico City: Colegio de México, 1970.

———. *Sociedad y cultura en el porfiriato*. Mexico City: Consejo Nacional para la Cultura y las Artes, 1994.

González y González, Luis. *San José de Gracia: Mexican Village in Transition*. Translated by John Upton. Austin: University of Texas Press, 1974.

Gordon, Jennifer. "Transnational Labor Citizenship." *Southern California Law Review* 80, no. 3 (March 2007): 503–87.

Graduate School of Information and Library Science, University of Illinois. "20th-Century American Bestsellers." ⟨http://www3.isrl.uiuc.edu/~unsworth/courses/bestsellers/search.cgi?title=The+Grapes+of+Wrath⟩ (July 9, 2008).

Gramsci, Antonio. *Selections from the Prison Notebooks*. New York: International, 1971.

Grove, Wayne. "Cotton on the Federal Road to Economic Development: Technology and Labor Policies following World War II." *Agricultural History* 74, no. 2 (Spring 2000): 272–92.

———. "The Mexican Farm Labor Program, 1942–1964: Government-Administered Labor Market Insurance for Farmers." *Agricultural History* 70, no. 2 (Spring 1996): 302–20.

Growing a Nation: The Story of American Agriculture. "A History of American Agriculture, Farmers and the Land." ⟨http://www.agclassroom.org/gan/timeline/farmers_land.htm⟩ (July 10, 2008).

Grubbs, Donald H. "Prelude to Chavez: The National Labor Union in California." *Labour History* 19, no. 6 (1975): 453–69.

Guglielmo, Thomas. "Fighting for Caucasian Rights: Mexicans, Mexican Americans, and the Transnational Struggle for Civil Rights in World War II Texas." *Journal of American History* 92, no. 4 (March 2006): 1212–37.

Gutiérrez, David Gregory. *Walls and Mirrors: Mexican Americans, Mexican Immigrants, and the Politics of Ethnicity*. Berkeley: University of California Press, 1995.

Hamilton, Nora. *The Limits of Autonomy: Post-revolutionary Mexico*. Princeton, N.J.: Princeton University Press, 1982.

Hart, John Mason. "Revolutionary Syndicalism in Mexico." In *Revolutionary Syndicalism: An International Perspective*, edited by Marcel van der Linden and

Wayne Thorpe. London: Scolar, 1990. ⟨http://libcom.org/library/revolutionary-syndicalism-mexico-john-m-hart⟩ (July 26, 2009).

Hayes, Joy Elizabeth. *Radio Nation: Communication, Popular Culture, and Nationalism in Mexico, 1920–1950*. Tucson: University of Arizona Press, 2000.

Hedrick, Tace. *Mestizo Modernism: Race, Nation, and Identity in Latin American Culture, 1900–1940*. New Brunswick, N.J.: Rutgers University Press, 2003.

Hernandez, Jose. "The Bracero Program of 1951–1964." BA thesis, History Department, California Polytechnic State University, San Luis Obispo, 1996.

Herrera-Sobek, Maria. *The Mexican Corrido: A Feminist Analysis*. Bloomington: Indiana University Press, 1990.

———. *Northward Bound: The Mexican Immigrant Experiences in Ballad and Song*. Bloomington: Indiana University Press, 1993.

Hershfield, Joanne. "Screening the Nation." In *The Eagle and the Virgin: Nation and Cultural Revolution in Mexico, 1920–1940*, edited by Mary Kay Vaughan and Stephen E. Lewis, 259–79. Durham, N.C.: Duke University Press, 2006.

Hirsch, Jennifer S. *A Courtship after Marriage: Sexuality and Love in Mexican Transnational Families*. Berkeley: University of California Press, 2003.

Hodes, Martha. *The Sea Captain's Wife: A True Story of Love, Race, and War in the Nineteenth Century*. New York: W. W. Norton, 2006.

Hondagneu-Sotelo, Pierrette, and Ernestine Avila. "'I'm Here, but I'm There': The Meanings of Latina Transnational Motherhood." In *Women and Migration in the U.S.-Mexico Borderlands: A Reader*, edited by Denise A. Segura and Patricia Zavella, 388–412. Durham, N.C.: Duke University Press, 2007.

Hull, Frank Leroy. "The Effects of Braceros on the Agricultural Labor Market in California, 1950–1970: Public Law 78 and Its Aftermath." PhD diss., University of Illinois, 1973.

Ilias, Shayerah, Katherine Fennelly, and Christopher M. Federico. "American Attitudes toward Guest Worker Policies." *International Migration Review* 42, no. 4 (Winter 2008): 741–66.

Jacobson, Matthew Frye. *Whiteness of a Different Color: European Immigrants and the Alchemy of Race*. Cambridge: Harvard University Press, 1995.

Jenkins, J. Craig. *The Politics of Insurgency: The Farm Worker Movement in the 1960s*. New York: Columbia University Press, 1985.

Jenkins, J. Craig, and Charles Perrow. "Insurgency of the Powerless: Farm Worker Movements, 1946–1972." *American Sociological Review* 42 (April 1977): 249–68.

Johnson, Benjamin Heber. *Revolution in Texas: How a Forgotten Rebellion and Its Bloody Suppression Turned Mexicans into Americans*. New Haven, Conn.: Yale University Press, 2003.

Joseph, Gilbert M., and Daniel Nugent, eds. *Everyday Forms of State Formation: Revolution and the Negotiation of Rule in Modern Mexico*. Durham, N.C.: Duke University Press, 1994.

Jungmeyer, Roger L. "The Bracero Program, 1942–1951: Mexican Contract Labor in the United States." PhD diss., University of Missouri, Columbia, 1988.

Katz, Friedrich. *The Secret War in Mexico: Europe, the United States, and the Mexican Revolution*. Chicago: University of Chicago Press, 1981.

Kim, Joon. "The Political Economy of the Mexican Farm Labor Program, 1942–1964." *Aztlan* 29, no. 2 (Fall 2004): 13–53.

Kimmel, Michael. *The History of Men: Essays on the History of American and British Masculinities*. Albany: State University of New York Press, 2005.

———. "Invisible Masculinity." *Society* 30, no. 6 (September–October 1993): 28–35.

Kirstein, Peter N. *Anglo over Bracero: A History of the Mexican Worker in the United States from Roosevelt to Nixon*. San Francisco: R and E Associates, 1977.

Kiser, George C., and Martha Woody Kiser, eds. *Mexican Workers in the United States: Historical and Political Perspectives*. Albuquerque: University of New Mexico Press, 1979.

Knight, Alan. *Counter-revolution and Reconstruction*. Vol. 2 of *Mexican Revolution*. Lincoln: University of Nebraska Press, 1990.

Kosek, Jake. *Understories: The Political Life of Forests in Northern New Mexico*. Durham, N.C.: Duke University Press, 2006.

Krohn-Hansen, Christian. "Masculinity and the Political among Dominicans: 'The Dominican Tiger.'" In *Machos, Mistresses, Madonnas: Contesting the Power of Latin American Gender Imagery*, edited by Marit Melhuus and Kristi Anne Stolen, 108–34. London: Verso, 1996.

Lacy, Elaine Cantrell. "Literacy Politics and Programs in Mexico, 1920–1958." PhD diss., Arizona State University, 1991.

Latham, Michael E. *Modernization as Ideology: American Social Science and "Nation Building" in the Kennedy Era*. Chapel Hill: University of North Carolina Press, 2005.

Lawrence, Zachary A. "The Heart of an Industry: The Role of the Bracero Program in the Growth of Viticulture in Sonoma and Napa Counties." MA thesis, Sonoma State University, 2005.

Lewthwaite, Stephanie. "Race, Paternalism, and 'California Pastoral': Rural Rehabilitation and Mexican Labor in Greater Los Angeles." *Agricultural History* 81 (2007): 1–35.

Lim, Shirley Jennifer. *A Feeling of Belonging: Asian American Women's Public Culture, 1930–1960*. New York: New York University Press, 2006.

Lomnitz, Claudio. *Deep Mexico, Silent Mexico: An Anthropology of Nationalism*. Public Worlds Series. Minneapolis: University of Minnesota Press, 2001.

López, Ronald W. "The El Monte Berry Strike of 1933." *Aztlan* 1, no. 1 (Spring 1970): 101–14.

Lorence, James. *The Suppression of "Salt of the Earth": How Hollywood, Big Labor, and Politicians Blacklisted a Movie in the American Cold War*. Albuquerque: University of New Mexico Press, 1999.

Luibhéid, Eithne. *Entry Denied: Controlling Sexuality at the Border*. Minneapolis: University of Minnesota, 2002.

Lutz, Catherine A., and Jane L. Collins. "The Color of Sex: Postwar Photographic

Histories of Race and Gender in National Geographic." In *The Gender Sexuality Reader: Culture, History, Political Economy*, edited by Roger N. Lancaster and Micaela Di Leonardo, 291–309. New York: Routledge, 1997.

Lytle Hernandez, Kelly. "The Crimes and Consequences of Illegal Immigration: A Cross-Border Examination of Operation Wetback, 1943–1954." Paper presented at the Organization of American Historians Conference, April 19, 2006.

——. *Migra! A History of the U.S. Border Patrol*. Berkeley: University of California Press, 2010.

Mahler, Sarah J. "Constructing International Relations: The Role of Transnational Migrants and Other Non-state Actors." *Identities* 7, no. 2 (June 2000): 197–233.

——. "Transnational Relationships: The Struggle to Communicate across Borders." *Identities* 7, no. 4 (January 2001): 583–620.

Maldonado Ochoa, Mariano. "La geografía e historiade Durango." In *Memoria No. 2, Primer Congreso de Historiadores Duranguenses, 1985*, 343–52. Durango City: Universidad Juárez del Estado de Durango, Instituto de Investigaciones Históricas, 1990.

Marcell, Ronald O. "Bracero Program Hurt Domestic Farm Workers." *Borderlands: An El Paso Community College Local History Project* 12 (1994). ⟨http://www.epcc .edu/nwlibrary/borderlands/12_bracero_program.htm⟩ (July 25, 2009).

Martín, Carlos E. "Mechanization and 'Mexicanization': Racializing California's Agricultural Technology." *Science as Culture* 10, no. 3 (2001): 310–26.

Martin, Phillip. *Promise Unfulfilled: Unions, Immigration, and Farm Worker*. Ithaca, N.Y.: Cornell University Press, 2003.

Massey, Doreen. *Space, Place, and Gender*. Minneapolis: University of Minnesota Press, 1994.

McClendon, V. Jolice. "Power and Protest in the Valley of Plenty: The DiGiorgio Strike of 1947–1950—A Union Interpretation." MA thesis, Midwestern State University, 1987.

Meister, Dick, and Anne Loftis. *A Long Time Coming: The Struggle to Unionize America's Farm Workers*. New York: Collier MacMillan, 1977.

Messner, Michael. "Men Studying Masculinity: Some Epistemological Issues in Sport Sociology." *Sociology of Sport Journal* 7, no. 2 (June 1990): 136–53.

——. "White Guy Habitus in the Classroom: Challenging the Reproduction of Privilege." *Men and Masculinities* 2, no. 4 (April 2000): 457–69.

Meyers, William K. "Seasons of Rebellion: Nature, Organization of Cotton Production, and the Dynamics of Revolution in La Laguna, Mexico, 1910–1916." *Journal of Latin American Studies* 30, no. 1 (February 1998): 63–94.

Milham, S., and E. M. Ossiander. "Historical Evidence That Residential Electrification Caused the Emergence of the Childhood Leukemia Peak." *Medical Hypotheses* 56, no. 3 (2001): 290–95.

Miller, Marilyn Grace. *Rise and Fall of the Cosmic Race: The Cult of Mestizaje in Latin America*. Berkeley: University of California Press, 1996.

Miller, Michael Nelson. *Red, White, and Green: The Maturing of Mexicanidad, 1940–1946*. El Paso: Texas Western Press, 1998.

Mirande, Alfredo. *Hombres y Machos: Masculinity and Latino Culture*. Boulder, Colo.: Westview, 1997.

Mitchell, Don. *Lie of the Land: Migrant Workers and the California Landscape*. Minneapolis: University of Minnesota, 1996.

Mitchell, Stephanie, and Patience Schell, eds. *The Women's Revolution in Mexico, 1910–1953*. Latin American Silhouettes. Lanham, Md.: Rowman and Littlefield, 2007.

Mize, Ronald L. "The Invisible Workers: Articulations of Race and Class in the Life Histories of Braceros." PhD diss., University of Wisconsin, Madison, 2000.

———. "Workplace Identities and Collective Memory: Living and Remembering the Effects of the Bracero Total Institution." In *Immigrant Life in the U.S.: Multi-disciplinary Perspectives*, edited by Donna R. Gabaccia and Colin Wayne Leach, 133–51. London: Routledge, 2003.

Molina, Natalia. *Fit to Be Citizens? Public Health and Race in Los Angeles, 1879–1930*. American Crossroads. Berkeley: University of California Press, 2006.

Montejano, David. *Anglos and Mexicans in the Making of Texas, 1836–1986*. Austin: University of Texas Press, 1987.

Montoya, Ramón Alejandro. "El cura y los braceros: La administración de la fe y la migración de mano de obra en Cerritos, San Luis Potosí, durante el programa bracero." In *La emigración de San Luis Potosí a Estados Unidos, pasado y presente*, edited by Fernando Saúl Alanis Enciso, 75–94. San Luis Potosí: Colegio de San Luis, 2001.

Montoya del Solar, Rosario A. "House, Street, Collective: Revolutionary Geographies and Gender Transformation in Nicaragua, 1979–99." *Latin American Research Review* 38, no. 2 (2003): 61–93.

Navarro, Armando. *Mexicano Political Experience in Occupied Aztlán: Struggles and Change*. Walnut Creek, Calif.: AltaMira, 2005.

Newcomer, Daniel. *Reconciling Modernity: Urban State Formation in 1940s León, Mexico*. Lincoln: University of Nebraska Press, 2007.

Ngai, Mae M. "Braceros, 'Wetbacks,' and the National Boundaries of Class." In *Repositioning North American Migration History: New Directions in Modern Continental Migration, Citizenship, and Community*, edited by Marc S. Rodriguez, 206–64. Studies in Comparative History. Rochester, N.Y.: University of Rochester, 2004.

———. *Impossible Subjects: Illegal Aliens and the Making of Modern America*. Princeton, N.J.: Princeton University Press, 2003.

Nichols, Sandra. "Technology Transfer through Mexican Migration." *Grassroots Development* (2004). ⟨http://geocommunities.org/MetaPage/lib/IAF-2004-TechTransf-Eng.pdf⟩ (June 12, 2009).

Nugent, Daniel. *Spent Cartridges: An Anthropological History of Namiquipa, Chihuahua*. Chicago: University of Chicago Press, 1993.

Nye, Don Edward. *Electrifying America: Social Meanings of New Technology, 1880–1940*. Boston: Massachusetts Institute of Technology Press, 1990.

Olcott, Jocelyn. *Revolutionary Women in Postrevolutionary Mexico*. Durham, N.C.: Duke University Press, 2005.

———. "'Worthy Wives and Mothers': State-Sponsored Women's Organizing in Postrevolutionary Mexico." *Journal of Women's History* 13, no. 4 (2002): 106–31.

Olmstead, Alan L., and Paul R. Rhode. "The Evolution of California Agriculture, 1850–2000." In *California Agriculture: Dimensions and Issues*, edited by Jerome B. Siebert, 1–28. Berkeley: Giannini Foundation, University of California, 2004 ⟨http://giannini.ucop.edu/CalAgBook/Chap1.pdf⟩ (July 12, 2006).

Ortiz, Guillermo. "Currency Substitution in Mexico: The Dollarization Problem." *Journal of Money, Credit, and Banking* 15, no. 2 (1983): 174–85.

Overmyer-Velázquez, Mark. *Visions of the Emerald City: Modernity, Tradition, and the Formation of Porfirian Mexico*. Durham, N.C.: Duke University Press, 2006.

Ozouf, Mona. *Festivals and French Revolution*. Translated by Alan Sheridan. Cambridge: Harvard University Press, 1988.

Palacios Moncayo, Miguel. "El proceso de urbanización en Durango." In *Memoria no. 2, primer congreso de historiadores Duranguenses, 1985*, 123–29. Durango City: Universidad Juárez del Estado de Durango, Instituto de Investigaciones Históricas, 1990.

Paredes, Américo. *With a Pistol in His Hand: A Border Ballad and Its Hero*. Austin: University of Texas Press, 1971.

Pateman, Carole. "The Fraternal Social Contract." In *Civil Society and the State: New European Perspectives*, edited by John Keane, 101–28. London: Verso, 1988.

Peterson, Gigi Annette. "Grassroots Good Neighbors: Connections between Mexican and U.S. Labor and Civil Rights Activists, 1936–1945." PhD diss., University of Washington, 1998.

Peterson, Tarla Rai. "Jefferson's Yeoman Farmer as Frontier Hero: A Self-Defeating Mythic Structure." *Agriculture and Human Values* 7, no. 1 (Winter 1990): 9–19.

Pew Hispanic Center. *No Consensus on Immigration Problem or Proposed Fixes: America's Immigration Quandary*. ⟨http://people-press.org/reports/pdf/274.pdf⟩ (December 29, 2008).

Pierce, Gretchen. "Men Behaving Badly: Mexico's Anti-alcohol Campaign and the Reconstruction of Working-Class Masculinity, 1929–1940." Paper presented at Rocky Mountain Council for Latin American Studies conference, Tucson, Ariz., April 1, 2005.

Pilcher, Jeffrey M. *¡Qué Vivan los Tamales! Food and Mexican Identity*. Albuquerque: University of New Mexico Press, 1998.

Pineda, Richard D., and Stacey K. Sowards. "Flag Waving as Visual Argument: 2006 Immigration Demonstrations and Cultural Citizenship." *Argumentation and Advocacy* (Winter–Spring 2007), ⟨http://findarticles.com/p/articles/mi_hb6699/is_3-4_43/ai_n29413446⟩ (December 11, 2008).

Pitti, Gina Marie. "'A Ghastly International Racket': The Catholic Church and the Bracero Program in California, 1942–1964." CUSHWA Center for the Study of American Catholicism, University of Notre Dame, 2001.

Pitti, Stephen J. *The Devil in Silicon Valley: Northern California, Race, and Mexican Americans*. Princeton, N.J.: Princeton University Press, 2002.

Plummer, Brenda Gayle. *Rising Wind: Black Americans and U.S. Foreign Affairs, 1935–1960*. Chapel Hill: University of North Carolina Press, 2003.

———, ed. *Window on Freedom: Race, Civil Rights, and Foreign Affairs, 1945–1988*. Chapel Hill: University of North Carolina Press, 2003.

Raat, Dirk. *Revoltosos: Mexico's Rebels in the United States, 1903–1923*. College Station: Texas A&M University Press, 1981.

Raigosa Reyna, Pedro. "La industria siderúrica y el ferrocarril en el Durango del siglo XIX." In *La nostalgia y la modernidad: Empresarios y empresas regionales de México*, edited by María Guadalupe Rodríguez López, 185–96. Durango City: Instituto de Investigaciones Históricas de la Universidad Juárez del Estado de Durango, 2005.

Rajendra, Raphael. "Hopeless Struggle: The National Farm Labor Union's Attempt to Organize Farm Workers in California." BA thesis, Columbia University, 2003.

Roediger, David. *Wages of Whiteness: Race and the Making of the American Working Class*. Expanded and revised ed. New York: Verso, 2007.

Rosas, Ana E. "Flexible Families: Bracero Families' Lives across Cultures, Communities, and Countries, 1942–1964." PhD diss., University of Southern California, 2006.

Rosenberg, Howard R. "Snapshots in Farm Labor." *Labor Management Decisions* 3 (Winter–Spring 1993): 1–7.

Rounds, Phillip H. *The Impossible Land: Story and Place in California's Imperial Valley*. Albuquerque: University of New Mexico Press, 2008.

Rousmaniere, Kate. *Citizen Teacher: The Life and Leadership of Margaret Haley*. Albany: State University of New York Press, 2005.

Rubenstein, Anne. *Bad Language, Naked Ladies, and Other Threats to the Nation: A Political History of Comic Books in Mexico*. Durham, N.C.: Duke University Press, 1998.

Runstein, David, and Phillip Leveen. *Mechanization and Mexican Labor in California Agriculture*. Monographs in U.S.-Mexican Studies 6. La Jolla, Calif.: Center for U.S.-Mexican Studies, 1981.

Sackman, Douglas Cazaux. *Orange Empire: California and the Fruits of Eden*. Berkeley: University of California Press, 2005.

Saldaña-Portillo, María Josefina. *The Revolutionary Imagination in the Americas and the Age of Development*. Durham, N.C.: Duke University Press, 2003.

Salzinger, Leslie. *Gender under Production: Making Workers in Mexico's Global Factories*. Berkeley: University of California Press, 2003.

Sánchez, George J. *Becoming Mexican American: Ethnicity, Culture, and Identity in Chicano Los Angeles, 1900–1945*. Oxford: Oxford University Press, 1995.

Sánchez Soto, Gabriela, and Roldán Herrera. "Introducción a la primera parte." In *Rostros y rastros: Entrevistas a trabajadores migrantes en Estados Unidos*, edited by Jorge Durand, 17–20. San Luis Potosí: Colegio de San Luis, 2002.

Sanders, Nichole. "Gender, Welfare, and the 'Mexican Miracle': The Politics of Modernization in Postrevolutionary Mexico, 1937–1958." Unpublished ms.

Scardaville, Michael. "Los procesos judiciales y la autoridad del estado." In *Poder y legitimidad en México en el siglo XIX: Instituciones y cultura política*, edited by Brian F. Connaughton, 379–428. Mexico City: Universidad Autónoma Metropolitana-Iztapalapa, 2003.

Schell, Patience A. *Church and State Education in Revolutionary Mexico City.* Tucson: University of Arizona Press, 2003.

Schmidt, Arthur. "Making It Real Compared to What? Reconceptualizing Mexican History since 1940." In *Fragments of a Golden Age: The Politics of Culture in Mexico since 1940*, edited by Gilbert Joseph, Anne Rubenstein, and Eric Zolov, 23–69. American Encounters/Global Interactions. Durham, N.C.: Duke University Press, 2001.

———. "Mexicans, Migrants, and Indigenous Peoples: The Work of Manuel Gamio in the United States, 1925–1927." In *Strange Pilgrimages: Exile, Travel, and National Identity in Latin America*, edited by Ingrid E. Fey and Karen Racine, 263–78. Wilmington, Del.: Scholarly Resources, 2000.

Schmidt Camacho, Alicia. *Migrant Imaginaries: Latino Cultural Politics in the U.S.-Mexico Borderlands.* Nation of Newcomers. New York: New York University Press, 2008.

Scruggs, Otey M. "The Bracero Program under the Farm Security Administration." *Labor History* 3, no. 2 (March 1962): 149–68.

———. *Braceros, "Wetbacks" and the Farm Labor Program: Mexican Agricultural Labor in the United States, 1942–1954.* New York: Garland, 1988.

———. "Texas and the Bracero Program, 1942–1947." *Pacific Historical Review* 32, no. 3 (August 1963): 251–64.

———. "Texas, Good Neighbor?" *Southwestern Social Science Quarterly* 43, no. 2 (September 1963): 118–25.

Sedgwick, Eve Kosofsky. *Epistemology of the Closet.* 2nd ed. Berkeley: University of California Press, 2008.

Seigel, Micol. "Beyond Compare: Comparative Method after the Transnational Turn." *Radical History Review* 91 (Winter 2005): 62–90.

Selvin, David F. *Sky Full of Storm: A Brief History of California Labor.* Berkeley, Calif.: Center for Labor Research, 1966.

Shah, Nayan. *Contagious Divides: Epidemics and Race in San Francisco's Chinatown.* American Crossroads. Berkeley: University of California Press, 2001.

Shindo, Charle J. *Dust Bowl Migrants in the American Imagination.* Lawrence: University of Kansas Press, 1997.

Skaggs, Samuel R., and Amelia Montes Skaggs. *Manual práctico de inglés para los braceros: Spanish for Farmers.* 3rd ed. Las Cruces, N.M.: Las Cruces Citizen Publishing, 1956.

Smith, Mark M. *Mastered by the Clock: Time, Slavery, and Freedom in the American South.* Fred W. Morrison Series in Southern Studies. Chapel Hill: University of North Carolina Press, 1997.

Smith, Stephanie J. *Gender and the Mexican Revolution: Yucatán Women and the Realities of Patriarchy*. Chapel Hill: University of North Carolina Press, 2009.

Smithsonian Institution. "Bittersweet Harvest: The Bracero Program, 1942–1964." ⟨http://americanhistory.si.edu/theme/story.51.5.html⟩ (December 26, 2009).

Snodgrass, Michael. "Coming Home to Jalisco: Emigration and Return Migrations in Post-revolutionary Mexico." Paper presented at Seventeenth International Congress of the Latin American Studies Association, 2007.

———. *Deference and Defiance in Monterrey: Workers, Paternalism and Revolution in Mexico, 1890–1950*. Cambridge: Cambridge University Press, 2003.

Sommer, Doris. *Foundational Fictions: The National Romances of Latin America*. Berkeley: University of California Press, 1993.

Starr, Kevin. *Americans and the California Dream, 1850–1915*. New York: Oxford University Press, 1973.

———. *The Dream Endures: California Enters the 1940s*. New York: Oxford University Press, 1997.

Stern, Alexandra Minna. "Buildings, Boundaries, and Blood: Medicalization and Nation-Building on the U.S.-Mexico Border, 1910–1930." In *Hispanic American Historical Review* 79, no. 1 (February 1999): 41–81.

Stout, Robert Joe. *Why Immigrants Come to America: Braceros, Indocumentados, and the Migra*. Westport, Conn.: Praeger, 2008.

Street, Richard. *Beast of the Field: A Narrative History of California Farmworkers, 1769–1913*. Stanford, Calif.: Stanford University Press, 2004.

———. "Poverty in the Valley of Plenty: The National Farm Labor Union, DiGiorgio Farms, and Suppression of Documentary Photography in California, 1947–66." *Labor History* 48, no. 1 (February 2007): 25–48.

Stromquist, Shelton. *Labor's Cold War: Local Politics in a Global Context*. Urbana: University of Illinois Press, 2008.

Taft, Philip. *Labor Politics American Style*. Cambridge: Harvard University Press, 1968.

Thompson, E. P. *The Making of the English Working Class*. New York: Vintage, 1966 [1963].

Thompson, Paul. "Agrarianism and the American Philosophical Tradition." *Agriculture and Human Values* 7, no. 1 (Winter 1990): 3–8.

Torres Ramírez, Blanca. *Hacia la utopía industrial: Período 1940–1952*. Vol. 20 of *Historia de la revolución mexicana*. Mexico City: Colegio de México, 1979.

———. *México en la Segunda Guerra Mundial: Período 1940–1952*. Vol. 19 of *Historia de la revolución mexicana*. Mexico City: Colegio de México, 1979.

Trouillot, Michel-Rolph. *Silencing the Past: Power and the Production of History*. New York: Beacon, 1997.

Turner, Victor. *The Ritual Process: Structure and Anti-structure*. Ithaca, N.Y.: Cornell University Press, 1995 [1969].

Valdés, Dennis Nodin. "Machine Politics in California Agriculture, 1945–1990s." *Pacific Historical Review* 63, no. 2 (May 1994): 203–24.

Van Young, Eric. "Conclusion—The State as Vampire: Hegemonic Projects, Popular

Rituals, and Popular Culture in Mexico, 1600–1900." In *Rituals of Rule, Rituals of Resistance: Public Celebrations and Popular Culture in Mexico*, edited by William H. Beezley, Cheryl English Martin, and William E. French, 343–74. Wilmington, Del.: Scholarly Resources, 1994.

Varrelman, Stephanie N. "Fraud in the Fields: The Collapse of the Bracero Program." MA thesis, California State University, Sacramento, 2006.

Vaughan, Mary Kay. *Cultural Politics in Revolution: Teachers, Peasants, and Schools in Mexico, 1930–1940.* Tucson: University of Arizona Press, 1997.

Vázquez, Josefina Zoraida, and Lorenzo Meyer. *The United States and Mexico.* Chicago: University of Chicago Press, 1985.

Velázquez, Marco, and Mary Kay Vaughan. "*Mestizaje* and Musical Nationalism in Mexico." In *The Eagle and the Virgin: Nation and Cultural Revolution in Mexico, 1920–1940*, edited by Mary Kay Vaughan and Stephen E. Lewis, 95–118. Durham, N.C.: Duke University Press, 2006.

Von Eschon, Penny. *Race against Empire: Black Americans and Anticolonialism, 1937–1957.* Ithaca, N.Y.: Cornell University Press, 1997.

Walsh, Casey. *Building the Borderlands: A Transnational History of Irrigated Cotton on the Mexico-Texas Border.* College Station: Texas A&M University Press, 2008.

———. "Demobilizing the Revolution: Migration, Repatriation, and Colonization in Mexico, 1911–1940." Center for Comparative Immigration Studies, University of California, San Diego; Working Paper 26, November 2000.

———. "Eugenic Acculturation: Manuel Gamio, Migration Studies, and the Anthropology of Development in Mexico, 1910–1940." *Latin American Perspectives* 31, no. 5 (2004): 118–45.

Watson, Don. "Mixed Melody: Anticommunism and the United Packinghouse Workers in California Agriculture, 1954–1961." In *American Labor and the Cold War: Grassroots Politics and Postwar Political Culture*, edited by Robert W. Cherny, William Issel, and Kieran Walsh Taylor, 58–71. New Brunswick, N.J.: Rutgers University Press, 2004.

———. "Testing U.S. Farm Labor Policy: The 1961 Imperial Lettuce Strike." Paper presented at Southwest Labor Studies Conference, 2000.

Weber, Devra Anne. *Dark Sweat, White Gold: California Farm Workers, Cotton, and the New Deal.* Berkeley: University of California Press, 1996.

———. "The Organizing of Mexicano Agricultural Workers: Imperial Valley and Los Angeles, 1928–34, an Oral History Approach." *Aztlan* 3, no. 2 (Fall 1972): 307–50.

Wells, Allen, and Gilbert M. Joseph. *Summer of Discontent, Seasons of Upheaval: Elite Politics and Rural Insurgency in Yucatán, 1876–1915.* Stanford, Calif.: Stanford University Press, 1996.

Welsh, Martin Larson. "Citizenship in Crisis: Oil, Banks, and the Public Sphere, 1938 and 1982." Paper presented to the Latin American History Workshop, University of Chicago, January 19, 1999.

Westad, Odd Arne. *The Global Cold War: Third World Interventions and the Making of Our Times.* Cambridge: Cambridge University Press, 2005.

Westhoff, Laura M. *A Fatal Drifting Apart: Democratic Social Knowledge and Chicago Reform*. Urban Life and Urban Landscape. Columbus: Ohio State University Press, 2007.

Widenthal, Lora. *German Women for Empire, 1884–1945*. Durham, N.C.: Duke University Press, 2001.

Wilson, M. L. "Thomas Jefferson—Farmer." *Proceedings of the American Philosophical Society* 87, no. 3 (July 1943): 216–22.

Wood, Andrew Grant. *On the Border: Society and Culture between the United States and Mexico*. Latin American Silhouettes. Wilmington, Del.: Scholarly Resources, 2004.

Wright, Melissa W. *Disposable Women and Other Myths of Global Capitalism*. Perspectives on Gender. New York: Routledge, 2006.

Zamora, Emilio. "Mexico's Wartime Intervention on Behalf of Mexicans in the United States." In *Mexican Americans and World War II*, edited by Maggie Rivas-Rodriguez, 211–44. Austin: University of Texas Press, 2005.

Acknowledgments/Agradecimientos

Finishing a book is akin to training for and running a marathon (in my case, it was a half marathon). You recognize you owe it to a wealth of support along the way, from those hardy souls cheering on the sidelines and friends waiting to congratulate you at the finish, to those running alongside you or who turned a grueling training schedule into a social activity. I have been extremely fortunate to have had scream teams always at my side.

Part of this backing has been financial, for few historians complete a book without travel to archives and dedicated writing time. I was the beneficiary of generous support from the Center for Latin American Studies, the Department of History, and the Division of Social Sciences at the University of Chicago; the Clements Center for Southwest Studies at Southern Methodist University; the Wenner Gren, Andrew E. Mellon, and Hewlett Foundations; the Institute for the Study of Man; a Mount Holyoke College travel grant; the Mexico-North Research Network; the Department of American Studies at Indiana University; the Research Board of the University of Missouri system; and the Department of History, the Center for International Studies, and the Institute for Women's and Gender Studies at the University of Missouri–St. Louis. I also extend my sincere thanks to the hardworking staffs at the archives and libraries I visited and consulted, most notably the Archivo Histórico del Estado de Durango (Durango City); Archivo General de la Nación (Mexico City); Archivo Histórico and Dirección General del Acervo Histórico Diplomático, Secretaría de Relaciones Exteriores (Mexico City); Biblioteca Pública del Estado de Durango (Durango City); Interlibrary Loan at Thomas Jefferson Library, University of Missouri–St. Louis; National Archives and Records Administration (Washington, D.C.); and Special Collections and University Archives, Stanford University.

A unique debt of gratitude goes to my editor at the University of North Carolina Press, Charles Grench, who expressed a sincere interest in this project when it was still in a rough form. Through long-running discussions over the book's title, he has been a joy to work with, nothing but a constant and reliable source of encouragement and assistance. Thanks also go to Paula Wald and Alex Martin, who polished this book as they expertly shepherded me through the production process. Nonpress technical support was provided by Jeanne Barker-Nunn, Kathryn Hurley, Ryan Jones, Kathryn Litherland, Valerie Manzano, Luimil Negrón Pérez, and Antonio Reyes Valdez, who found forgotten cites, corrected inconsistencies in logic, constructed my map, helped with the translation of the acknowledgments, and redacted my prose.

My quest to finish this book has taken me from Chicago to Durango, Mexico City, Columbia (South Carolina), Ithaca (New York), South Hadley (Massachusetts), Bowling Green/Toledo (Ohio), Dallas, and now St. Louis. At the University of Chicago, I owe an intellectual debt to Leora Auslander, John Coatsworth, Friedrich Katz, Mae Ngai, and Leslie Salzinger, each of whom, as members of my dissertation committee, contributed in a multitude of ways to this finished product. Most transformations, intellectual and otherwise, are bumpy, and mine was no exception. I was skillfully guided, both *around* obstacles and *into* them, by this incredible crew of scholars, among the profession's finest minds. Others at Chicago due untold thanks for encouragement and scholarly prodding include Jovita Baber, Jeremy Baskes, Christopher Boyer, Emiliano Corral, Robert Curley, Nicholas de Genova, Robin Lauren Derby, Jill Dupont, Ben Fallaw, Sarah Gualtieri, Luin Goldring, Eleanor Hannah, María-Elena Martínez, Sigfrido Reyes, Richard Turits, Charles Walker, and Eric Zolov. My wish for all graduate students is that they find—and treasure—the kind of dynamic environment and smart peers I had.

After Chicago, I spent several years as an academic migrant. At the University of South Carolina and then Cornell University, I benefited from discussions with Laura Ahearn, Pamela Barnett, Kenneth Clemments, Jefferson Cowie, and Maria Cristina Garcia; at Mount Holyoke College, I enjoyed the support of permanent and migrant faculty: Daniel Czitron, Manali Desai, Lowell Gudmundson, Holly Hanson, Marion Katz, Jeremy King, Jonathon Lipman, Mary Renda, and Robert Schwartz; and during the subsequent summer, Sonya Michel graciously opened her home when I needed a place to stay and has continued to give encouragement. At Bowling Green State University, Vibha Bhalla, Eithne Luibéid, Michael Martin, Sridevi Menen, and Susana Peña welcomed me into their tight-knit circle and urged me on as I wrote and looked for a job. A fellowship at the Clements Center for Southwest Studies at Southern Methodist University gave me additional writing time. David Weber, Sherry Smith, Andrea Boardman, and Ruth Ann Elmore helped me settle in and join an established academic community. I benefited immeasurably from lively interchanges with Suzanne Bost, Crista Deluzio, Alexis McCrossen, John Mears, Marc Rodriguez, and Kathleen Wellman. Ana Alonso, David Gutiérrez, and George Sanchez read and commented thoroughly on an early version of the manuscript at my workshop; they, along with John Chávez, Manuel García y Griego, J. Gabriel Martínez-Serna, and the others at SMU, helped move the manuscript in perspicacious directions. At the University of Missouri–St. Louis, I have learned from an array of wonderful students and have grown through the tremendous backing of my colleagues, in particular Susan Brownell, Mark Burkholder, Priscilla Dowden-White, Andrew Hurley, Jody Miller, and Ronald Yasbin. They, more than any others, extended a sure hand at a time when I sorely needed it.

I have presented chapters and portions of chapters at various conferences and have called on friends and acquaintances to read multiple parts of this book and some in its entirety. For these critical interventions I would like to thank Josef Barton, Eileen Boris, Laura Briggs, Robert Buffington, Gabriela Cano, Elaine Carey, Dorothy Sue Cobble, Raymond Craib, Susan Deeds, Sarah Deutsch, Patricia Fernández de Castro, Leon Fink, John French, Tami Friedman, Donna Gabaccia, Matt Garcia, Susan Gauss, Jeff Gould, James N. Green, Thomas Guglielmo, Matthew Guterl, Ramón Gutiérrez, Vicky Hattam, Scott Heath, Sarah Hill, Andrew Hoberek, Joel Jennings, Benjamin Johnson, Elaine Lacy, Stephanie Lewthwaite, George Lipsitz, Kelly Lytle Hernandez, Alejandro Mejías-López, William Meyer, Ronald Mize, Khalil Mohammed, Michelle Nickerson, John Nieto-Phillips, Jocelyn Olcott, Stephen Pitti, Margaret Power, David Roediger, Michael Scardaville, Arthur Schmidt, Micol Siegel, Michael Snodgrass, Michael Ugarte, Mary Kay Vaughan, Pamela Voekel, Casey Walsh, and Elliott Young. They will see the results of their astute critiques.

Another debt of gratitude goes to Oscar Salazar. Without his friendship, I would have never chosen to work on Durango or befriended another set of wonderful people: sisters María Elena, Liliana, and Angélica; parents Joaquín and Juana Salazar; Manuel Torres Alba and Lucina Benavente Ramírez; Alejandro Palacios and the de la Hoya family, especially Joel. I also had the good fortune to meet and work with many incredible people at the Instituto de Investigaciones Históricas de la Universidad Juárez del Estado de Durango, my primary intellectual home and stomping ground in Durango. Then-director Miguel Vallebueno gave me an office and orientation to the array of local archives. This project took shape through scholarly, social, and educational exchanges with institute researchers and personnel: Antonio Arreola, Jesus Carreón, Manuel Estrada Escalera, Elvira Hernández Hernández, Norma Alicia Hernández Soto, Gabino Martínez Guzmán, Guadalupe Rodríguez López, and Mauricio Yen Fernández. A note of thanks goes to the Wallenders, Alejandro and Mayte, for nourishment of a different kind.

Throughout this process and as I moved from place to place, I have built up an extraordinary group of friends, academic and otherwise: Gloria Cano Cooley, Patricia Chu, John Furlong, Peter Guardino, Minsoo Kang, Kecia LiCausi, Theresa Mah, Antonia Martínez Estrada, Reyna Martínez Estrada, Greg Rieger, José Luis Robles Maldonado, Hannah Rosen, Michael Sacco, Silvana Siddali, and Ellen Stoecker. Some have schooled me—repeatedly—in Durango's delicacies of mescal and *gorditas*, sat through episodes of *Alondra* and *Nada Personal*, snacked on *bollilos falsos*, and labeled me *lachicuela*, a nickname that stuck. With others I have struggled with feminist theory, done dinner and a movie, cried over life's unfortunate turns, laughed over glasses of wine, conspired for world peace (among other things), walked dogs and fed cats, exchanged (unrequested) advice, logged those critical miles, and rejoiced in festive occasions. And one friend always urged me to "remember the workers." In word and deed, these incredible people reminded me to put in the miles and time, and always—always—run as if the wind were at my back.

In spite of my hard work and the patience of my friends, UNC Press would have had nothing to publish if not for members of my writing groups: Flannery Burke, Andrea Friedman, Emily Maguire, Rosario Montoya, and Ellen Moodie. Smart, creative scholars in their own right, these women read drafts of chapters, often with little lead time and many more than once. They were patient at times, were short with me when needed, and celebrated each step as if it were a milestone. Despite bouts of resistance on my part, they helped me think through what I was merely hinting and transform a thread of ideas into a coherent whole, all while trying out various coffee shops. Special recognition goes to Laura Westhoff, my colleague at UM–St. Louis, writing group member, and part of the infamous Learned Sisters Club. From the moment we spoke, I knew that I would find in her a great friend and tremendous source of support.

No list of acknowledgments would be complete without thanking my family, real and fictive. My real sisters, Sheri and Barbara, always expressed their belief in me and in the undertaking I had set out for myself; I hope they share in the joy of its completion. To my fictive sister, Joan Bernstein, who I met the first week of high school, I offer a humble thank you for the wonders and sustenance of a friendship over half a life long. To family members Arnold Craine, Lori Dru, and Beverly and Seymour Schpoont who kept asking, "What about the book?" the need for accountability helped keep me focused on the task at hand. Please do not yet ask about the next one.

I save the last thank you for the one most due acknowledgment: Lessie Jo Frazier. Throughout our friendship and collaboration, now more than twenty years, she has never ceased to amaze me, and her intellectual creativity, passion, curiosity, and fun side have guided me through the writing of this book. She pushed me to think more deeply, analytically, and theoretically when I could not see the implications of my ideas or material, and she reminded me of what drew me to the life of the mind when I became frustrated or unsure. Whatever its flaws and omissions, this book would (probably) not exist without her unwavering encouragement and prodding. She is implicit in its pages.

To my mother, Elayne Diamond Cohen, who died when I was an adolescent, and to my paternal grandfather, Ira "Izzie" Cohen, who did not live to see the project to its fruition: Your love and unwavering faith gave me the courage and fortitude to choose a path most do not dare to travel and a goal that too many told me was unreachable. To the many former braceros who shared with me the hopes of younger men: thank you for your openness and honesty about tender moments long past. I dedicate this book to them, all critical in my life but unknown in history.

* * *

Terminar un libro es como entrenar y correr un maratón (en mi caso fue medio maratón). Reconoces en el camino una deuda por el apoyo que los amigos y esas almas fuertes te dan desde la barrera a lo largo del camino, esperando felicitarte al final y también con aquellos que corren a tu lado o quienes convierten los entrenamientos extenuantes en una actividad entre amigos. Yo he sido extremadamente afortunada en tener un gran equipo siempre a mi lado echándome apoyo.

Parte de este respaldo ha sido financiero, ya que pocos historiadores terminan un libro sin viajar a los archivos y dedicarse de tiempo completo escribir. En mi caso tuve la fortuna de ser beneficiaria del generoso apoyo del centro de estudios latinoamericanos, la facultad de historia y la división de ciencias sociales de la universidad de Chicago; el centro Clements para estudios del Suroeste en universidad Southern Methodist; las fundaciones Wenner Gren, Andrew E. Mellon y Hewlett; el instituto para el estudio del hombre; una beca de viaje del colegio Mount Holyoke; la red de investigación México-Norte; la facultad de estudios americanos de la universidad Indiana; el Research Board (consejo de investigaciones) del sistema de la universidad de Missouri; y de la facultad de historia, el centro de estudios internacionales y el instituto para los estudios de la mujer y el género en la universidad de Missouri–San Luis. Asimismo, extiendo mi más sincero agradecimiento al personal que trabaja arduamente en los archivos y bibliotecas que visité y consulté, principalmente en el Archivo de Histórico del Estado de Durango (ciudad de Durango); Archivo General de la Nación (ciudad de México); Archivo Histórico y Dirección General Del Acervo Histórico Diplomático, Secretaría de Relaciones Exteriores (ciudad de México); Biblioteca Pública del Estado de Durango (ciudad de Durango); el préstamo inter-bibliotecario de la biblioteca Thomas Jefferson en la universidad de Missouri–San Luis; Archivos Nacionales y Registros de la Administración (Washington, D.C.); el Fondo Reservado y el Archivo Universitario, en Stanford University.

Siento una deuda y gratitud especial hacia mi editor en la universidad de la prensa de Carolina del Norte, Charles Grench, quien manifestó un interés sincero por este proyecto desde su inicio cuando no era más que un borrador. A través de largas discusiones sobre el título del libro ha sido un verdadero placer trabajar con él, siempre sirviendo como una fuente confiable y constante de ánimo y apoyo. Agradezco también a Paula Wald y Alex Martin, quienes pulieron este libro mientras me guiaban con gran experiencia a través del proceso de producción. El apoyo técnico, no editorial, se lo agradezco a Jeanne Barker-Nunn, Kathryn Hurley, Ryan Jones, Kathryn Litherland, Valerie Manzano, Luimil Negrón Pérez y Antonio Reyes Valdez, que encontraron las citas olvidadas, corrigieron inconsistencias lógicas, diseñaron mi mapa, ayudaron con esta traducción y corrigieron mi prosa.

Mi búsqueda por terminar este libro me llevó de Chicago a Durango, Distrito Federal de México, Columbia (Carolina del Sur), Ithaca (Nueva York),

South Hadley (Massachusetts), Bowling Green/Toledo (Ohio), Dallas y ahora, a San Luis (Missouri). En la universidad de Chicago tengo una deuda intelectual con Leora Auslander, John Coatsworth, Friedrich Katz, Mae Ngai y Leslie Salzinger. Cada uno de ellos, como miembros del comité en la defensa de mi tesis de doctorado, contribuyó de múltiples maneras a la creación del producto final. La mayoría de las transformaciones, intelectuales y de otro tipo, son accidentados y las mías no fueron la excepción. En este proceso fui hábilmente guiada, tanto alrededor de los obstáculos como dentro de ellos, por este gran grupo de académicos que incluye a algunas de las mentes más brillantes del gremio. En Chicago muchas personas más merecen infinitos agradecimientos por animarme y "arrearme" académicamente, entre ellos Jovita Baber, Jeremy Baskes, Christopher Boyer, Emiliano Corral, Robert Curley, Nicholas de Genova, Robin Lauren Derby, Jill Dupont, Ben Fallaw, Sarah Gualtieri, Luin Goldring, Eleanor Hannah, María-Elena Martínez, Sigfrido Reyes, Richard Turits, Charles Walker y Eric Zolov. Mi deseo para todos los estudiantes de posgrado es que encuentren—y aprecien—un ambiente dinámico y compañeros tan inteligentes como yo los tuve.

Después de estar en Chicago, pasé muchos años como migrante académica. En la universidad de Carolina del Sur y la universidad Cornell, me beneficié de las discusiones con Laura Ahearn, Pamela Barnett, Kenneth Clemments, Jefferson Cowie y Maria Cristina Garcia; en el colegio Mount Holyoke disfruté el apoyo de un grupo permanente y otro fluctuante de académicos: Daniel Czitron, Manali Desai, Lowell Gudmundson, Holly Hanson, Marion Katz, Jeremy King, Jonathon Lipman, Mary Renda y Robert Schwartz; durante el verano subsecuente, Sonya Michel amablemente me abrió las puertas de su casa cuando necesité de un lugar para quedarme y desde entonces he gozado de su apoyo moral. En Bowling Green State University, Vibha Bhalla, Eithne Luibéid, Michael Martin, Sridevi Menen y Susana Peña me recibieron en su muy selecto y unido grupo que me alentó para escribir al mismo tiempo que emprender la búsqueda de empleo. Una beca del centro Clements para estudios del Suroeste de la universidad Southern Methodist me dio tiempo adicional para escribir. David Weber, Sherry Smith, Andrea Boardman y Ruth Ann Elmore me auxiliaron para integrarme a una comunidad académica ya consolidada. Me beneficié de forma inconmensurable de las discusiones energéticas con Suzanne Bost, Crista Deluzio, Alexis McCrossen, John Mears, Marc Rodriguez y Kathleen Wellman. Ana Alonso, David Gutiérrez y George Sánchez leyeron y comentaron desde las primeras versiones del manuscrito en mi taller; ellos, junto con John Chávez, Manuel

García y Griego, J. Gabriel Martínez-Serna y otros más de SMU, ayudaron a dirigirme en direcciones perspicaces. En la universidad de Missouri–San Luis, he aprendido mucho de una colección de estudiantes increíbles y me he formado con el apoyo tremendo de mis colegas, en particular Susan Brownell, Mark Burkholder, Priscilla Dowden-White, Andrew Hurley, Jody Miller y Ronald Yasbin. Ellos, más que todos, extendieron una mano segura cuando más la necesitaba.

He presentado capítulos y parte de ellos en varios foros donde algunos amigos y conocidos hicieron comentarios muy útiles. Por esas críticas observaciones quisiera agradecer a Josef Barton, Eileen Boris, Laura Briggs, Robert Buffington, Gabriela Cano, Elaine Carey, Dorothy Sue Cobble, Raymond Craib, Susan Deeds, Sarah Deutsch, Patricia Fernández de Castro, Leon Fink, John French, Tami Friedman, Donna Gabaccia, Matt Garcia, Susan Gauss, Jeff Gould, James N. Green, Thomas Guglielmo, Matthew Guterl, Ramón Gutiérrez, Vicky Hattam, Scott Heath, Sarah Hill, Andrew Hoberek, Joel Jennings, Benjamin Johnson, Elaine Lacy, Stephanie Lewthwaite, George Lipsitz, Kelly Lytle Hernandez, Alejandro Mejías-López, William Meyer, Ronald Mize, Khalil Mohammed, Michelle Nickerson, John Nieto-Phillips, Jocelyn Olcott, Stephen Pitti, Margaret Power, David Roediger, Michael Scardaville, Arthur Schmidt, Micol Siegel, Michael Snodgrass, Michael Ugarte, Mary Kay Vaughan, Pamela Voekel, Casey Walsh y Elliott Young. Todos verán el resultado de sus astutas críticas.

Una deuda más de gratitud la tengo con Oscar Salazar. Sin su amistad nunca hubiera escogido trabajar en Durango ni tener la amistad de otro grupo de personas maravillosas: las hermanas María Elena, Liliana y Angélica; sus padres Joaquín y Juana Salazar; Manuel Torres Alba y su esposa Lucina Benavente Ramírez; Alejandro Palacios y la familia de la Hoya, principalmente a Joel; también he tenido la buena fortuna de conocer y trabajar con gente increíble del Instituto de Investigaciones Históricas de la Universidad Juárez del Estado de Durango, mi principal casa y territorio intelectual en Durango. Su entonces director, Miguel Vallebueno, me dio una oficina para trabajar y me orientó en la selección de los archivos locales. Este proyecto tomó forma a través de intercambios sociales, académicos y educativos con los investigadores y todo el personal del instituto: Antonio Arreola, Jesús Carreón, Manuel Estrada Escalera, Elvira Hernández Hernández, Norma Alicia Hernández Soto, Gabino Martínez Guzmán, Guadalupe Rodríguez López y Mauricio Yen Fernández. Tengo un agradecimiento especial para Alejandro y Mayte Wallender por alimentación de otra índole.

A través de este proceso, de un lugar a otro, he construido un extraordinario grupo de amigos: Gloria Cano Cooley, Patricia Chu, John Furlong, Peter Guardino, Minsoo Kang, Kecia LiCausi, Theresa Mah, Antonia Martínez Estrada, Reyna Martínez Estrada, Greg Rieger, José Luis Robles Maldonado, Hannah Rosen, Michael Sacco, Silvana Siddali y Ellen Stoecker. Algunos me instruyeron—repetidamente—sobre las delicias duranguenñas como el mezcal y las gorditas, compartimos episodios de *Alondra* y *Nada Personal*, comiendo bolillos falsos y me apodaron "la chicuela." Con otros he debatido sobre teoría feminista, ido a cenar o al cine, llorado acerca de las vueltas infortunadas de la vida, reído con vasos de vino, conspirado por la paz mundial (entre otras cosas), paseado perros y alimentado gatos, intercambiado consejos (no siempre solicitados), navegando una larga e importante distancia y regocijándonos en las ocasiones que lo ameritaban. Uno de estos amigos me insistió repetidamente "recordar a los trabajadores." En dichos y en hechos, estas magníficas personas me recordaron la importancia de invertir el tiempo y la distancia y siempre, como dice el proverbio irlandés, desear que el viento sople siempre a mis espaldas.

A pesar de mi duro trabajo y la paciencia de mis amigos, la prensa de UNC no tendría nada que publicar si no fuera por los miembros de mis grupos de redacción: Flannery Burke, Andrea Friedman, Emily Maguire, Rosario Montoya y Ellen Moodie. Académicas inteligentes y creativas por derecho propio, estas mujeres leyeron versiones de los capítulos, más de una vez, frecuentemente con poco tiempo y anticipación. Ellas fueron pacientes conmigo, me llamaron la atención cuando lo necesitaba y celebraron cada paso como si fuera un gran éxito. A pesar de los ataques de resistencia de mi parte, me ayudaron a transformar lo que en ese entonces eran sólo insinuaciones y un continuo de ideas en algo coherente, mientras probábamos distintas cafeterías. Un especial reconocimiento va para Laura Westhoff, mi colega en la universidad de Missouri–San Luis, parte de los grupos de redacción y compañera del notorio club Learned Sisters. Desde la primera vez que hablamos, supe que encontraría en ella una gran amiga y una tremenda fuente de apoyo.

Ninguna lista de agradecimientos podría estar completa sin agradecer a mi familia, real y "postiza." Mis verdaderas hermanas Sheri y Barbara, siempre expresaron su confianza en mí y el camino que emprendí; espero que compartan la alegría de su culminación. Para mi hermana espiritual, Joan Bernstein, a quien conocí la primera semana de secundaria, le ofrezco un humilde agradecimiento por su maravillosa y sostenida amistad durante más de la mitad de una vida. A otros miembros de la familia, Arnold Craine, Lori Dru y Beverly y Seymour Schpoont, quienes siempre preguntaron ¿y qué hay del libro?, sus exigencias me ayudaron a mantenerme enfocada a la tarea que tenía en mis manos. Por favor no pregunten acerca del siguiente.

Me reservo el último agradecimiento para la persona con la que tengo la mayor deuda de gratitud: Lessie Jo Frazier. A través de nuestra amistad y colaboración, ahora de más de veinte años, nunca dejó de asombrarme, y su creatividad intelectual, pasión, curiosidad me guiaron de forma divertida a través de la escritura de este libro. Me empujó a pensar más profunda, analítica y teóricamente cuando yo no podía ver las implicaciones de mis ideas o de mi material, y me recordó que la vida intelectual fue lo que me atrajo cada vez que me frustraba o sentía insegura. Cualquiera que sean los defectos u omisiones de este libro, (probablemente) éste no existiría sin su inquebrantable ánimo y apoyo. Ella está implícita en estas páginas.

Para mi madre, Elayne Diamond Cohen, quien murió cuando yo era una adolescente, y para mi abuelo paterno, Ira "Izzie" Cohen, quien no vivió para realizar los frutos del proyecto: su amor y férrea confianza me dio la valentía y la fortaleza para escoger un camino que no tomarían la mayoría y una meta que muchos me dijeron era inalcanzable. A todos los ex-braceros que compartieron conmigo las esperanzas de hombres más jóvenes: gracias por su sinceridad sobre esos tiernos momentos de su pasado lejano. Les dedico este libro a todos ellos, todos importantes a mi vida pero no conocidos por la historia.

Index

Glendora Lemon Growers Association, 55
Globalization, 8
Goldberg, Arthur (U.S. secretary of labor), 168
Golden Shears, 135
Good Neighbor policy, 4, 28, 203
Goodwin, Robert G., 168
Grapes of Wrath, 61, 151–55
Green, Edith (D-Ore.), 215
Green Revolution, 25, 236 (n. 25)
Grievances/grievance procedures, 14, 142, 147
Grove, Wayne, 39, 40
Growers, 7, 14, 28, 29, 30, 47, 53–58, 147, 154, 155, 159, 168, 169, 217; alliance with U.S. government officials, 4, 7, 39, 40, 236 (n. 27), 238 (n. 44); control over agriculture, 145; as modern business owners, 47–48, 59–65; narratives, 47–65, 144, 154, 159, 160; narratives as racial ideology, 47–65; narratives of braceros, 61–62; narratives of domestic farmworkers, 29, 48, 50–52, 53–54, 57–59, 61–65; narratives of self, 47–65; as small (yeoman) farmers, 15, 47–50, 53–59, 240 (n. 2), 277–78 (n. 10)
Guillermo, 13, 113, 129
Guitars. *See* Music/musicians

Haciendas, 36, 37, 38, 70, 71, 80, 91, 204; El Casco, 70; Santa Catalina del Álamo, 70
Hands, 52, 56, 93, 98, 101, 105, 108, 111, 118, 119, 120, 138, 181, 188, 241 (n. 98), 260 (n. 126)
Handschin, Robert, 24
Hardin, Charles, 47, 49
Harvest of Shame, 24, 58, 169, 217, 245 (n. 47), 267 (n. 126)
Hats, 31, 89, 101, 109, 115, 117, 120, 175, 176, 195, 239 (n. 60), 268 (n. 4)
Havana, 147, 215

Hayes, Edward, 148, 156, 159
Health, 71, 84, 93, 101, 105, 106, 109, 119, 160, 162
Hennings, John, 217
Heraldo, El, 178
Hermanos de raza (blood brothers), 178, 179, 181. *See also* Silos, Juan
Hernández, Catarino, 193
Hernández, Diego, 96, 115, 118
Hernández Cano, Francisco, 139–40
Herrera, Mauricio, 13, 113, 115, 134, 135
Hickenlooper, Bourke (R-Iowa), 211
Higbee, Edward, 49
Historical practice, 11–14
Hollywood Film Council. See *Poverty in the Valley of Plenty*
Homosociality, 113, 114, 128, 133, 139
Honor, 74, 75, 78, 84, 110, 177, 232 (n. 1). *See also* Gender; Growers: narratives of self; Manhood
Houston Post, 115
H-2A visa, 220
Huerta, Gerardo, 188

Immigration and Naturalization Service (INS), 100, 103, 140, 209, 234 (n. 20), 236 (n. 2), 264 (n. 79)
Imperial Valley, x, 7, 8, 40–42, 56, 111, 139, 146, 156, 157, 164, 242 (nn. 109, 110). *See also* California
Imperial Valley Farmers Association (IVFA), 156
Imperial Valley Lettuce Growers and Shippers Association, 62
Import Substitution Industrialization, 32, 219
Indians, 44–45, 70, 94, 100, 101, 109, 115, 124, 178. *See also* Mestizos; Mexico: racial system in
Industrial Workers of the World (IWW), 72, 150
Instituto de Investigaciones Históricas (Institute for Historical Research), 12
International Harvester, 31, 39

International Labor Organization (ILO), 207, 219

Italian prisoners of war, 119

Jacobson, Matthew Frye, 45

Jalisco, 68

Japan, 28, 194

Japanese, 40, 50, 51, 52, 55, 241 (n. 97), 242 (n. 110)

Japanese Americans, 40, 55. *See also* Japanese

Jefferson, Thomas (U.S. president, 1801–9), 49, 244 (n. 8); Jeffersonians, 15, 47, 50. *See also* Growers: as small (yeoman) farmers; Yeomen

Jessup, Bruce, 61

Joad, Tom, 152

John Deer, 39

Johnson, Lyndon, 166, 216, 217, 276 (n. 69)

Johnson-Reed Act (1924), 45

Juárez, Benito (Mexican president, 1858–61), 81

Kansas City, 213

Kennedy, John F. (U.S. president, 1961–63), 158, 166, 168, 216, 217, 276 (n. 77)

Kern County. *See* California: Kern County

Kern County Central Labor Council, 147

Keynes, John Maynard, 195

Kieser, Rev. Julian, 161

Knowledge, 3, 6, 35, 60, 81, 98, 106, 107, 116, 136, 139, 152, 182–86, 189, 192, 195, 198, 249 (n. 46), 252 (n. 36), 254 (n. 94), 270 (n. 30). *See also* Agriculture: agricultural knowledge

Korean War, 23

Labastia, Carlos, 90

Labor, 3, 5, 6, 12, 21, 24, 26, 27, 31, 43, 50, 51, 59, 64, 74, 78, 97, 99, 103, 104, 109, 113, 114, 118, 120, 124, 128, 131, 141, 143, 144, 176, 180, 181, 186, 187, 188–89, 194, 196, 208, 213, 216, 217, 218, 225, 234 (n. 3), 235 (nn. 6, 7), 236 (nn. 21, 27), 238 (n. 44), 256 (n. 41), 260 (n. 126), 276 (n. 77); and bosses and foremen, 2, 5, 10, 11, 14, 57, 58, 62, 63, 67, 76, 90, 91, 93, 100, 101, 109, 111, 115, 119, 130, 136, 137, 139, 140, 142, 150, 168, 177, 180, 183, 187, 188, 191, 269 (n. 30); labor activists, labor movement, and labor organizing, 2, 3, 10, 11, 14, 22, 27, 29, 30, 42, 48, 54, 100, 108, 141, 145–71, 177, 204, 217, 226, 239 (nn. 49, 52), 266 (n. 104), 276 (n. 75); labor regimes, 8, 9, 23, 26, 28, 29, 36, 37, 38, 41, 50–65, 72, 107, 108, 109, 120, 134, 137, 145–71, 174, 188–89, 205–7, 218; and legislation, 39, 57, 146, 156, 217, 239 (n. 53); Ministry of Labor and Social Welfare (Mexico), 21, 23, 196. *See also* Bracero program: and barracks; Braceros; Farmworkers/workers; Growers: narratives; Unions; United States: Farm Security Administration

Laguna (Comarca Lagunera). *See* Durango: Laguna (Comarca Lagunera)

Lange, Dorothea, 39, 41, 49, 50

Langenegger, Bill, 49, 50

Latinos, 225, 243 (n. 127)

League of United Latin American Citizens (LULAC), 213, 275–76 (n. 69)

Leave It to Beaver, 9

LeBerthon, Yed, 168

Lederer, Robert. *See* American Association of Nurserymen

Lee, Russell, 41

Leisure, 15, 120, 132, 134, 143, 188

Lepper, Norman, 148

Letters, 14, 31, 72–86, 89, 91, 92, 108, 147, 159, 165, 248 (n. 25), 252 (n. 38)

Mississippi, 128

Mitchell, H. L., 151, 153, 154, 164, 165, 171

Mitchell, James P. (U.S. secretary of labor), 168, 253 (n. 55), 266 (n. 104)

Mobility, 36, 152, 174, 189, 268 (n. 3), 273 (n. 31); versus movement, 152, 173, 174. *See also* Class; Movement

Modern, the, 14, 77, 105, 106, 107, 113, 192, 196, 215; benefits of, 110, 197; as border, 7, 46, 169, 170, 183, 184, 186, 188, 195–98; definition of, 3, 4, 7; desire for, 10, 15, 35–36, 106, 108, 109, 110, 113, 122, 180, 182, 189, 191, 192, 194, 195, 196, 220; as ideological package or worldview, 2, 3, 4, 6, 11, 173, 195–96; modern subjects, 16, 32, 33, 43, 46, 64, 72–86, 104, 111, 112, 114, 116, 119, 137, 171, 174, 176, 194, 195; multiple versions of, 192–93, 194; as national belonging, 46, 114, 167, 169, 173, 174, 181, 182; as progress, 1, 3, 10, 82, 108; relation to national identity, 243 (n. 127); as transformational, 4. *See also* Citizens/ citizenship

Modernization, 3, 4, 5, 9, 32, 35–42, 43, 44, 52, 67, 73, 179, 180, 195; definition of, 3, 4, 7, 32; as foreign policy, 4, 5, 32; in Mexico through migration, 2, 4, 10, 171, 202, 232 (n. 7), 233 (n. 11), 238 (n. 40), 269 (n. 23); modernization projects, 24, 25, 26, 72, 205, 228, 233 (n. 13), 239 (n. 61), 249 (n. 46), 256 (n. 41); modernization theory, 3, 4, 32–33; relation to eugenics, 3, 4, 32. *See also* Modern, the: as ideological package or worldview

Molina, Raúl, 173

Monitor, The, 161

Monroe Doctrine, 4

Moore, Truman, 49, 50

Morales, Andrés, 125, 128, 135

Morales de Jesús, Juan, 82

Morality, 34, 35, 91, 122, 123, 133, 161, 162, 163, 181, 207, 239 (n. 60), 249 (n. 46), 276 (n. 84); agriculture as immoral, 160, 162–63, 170, 217

Moreno, José, 130–31

Movement, 15, 21, 29, 71, 72, 89, 104, 123, 152, 167, 173, 174, 187, 190, 191, 198, 202, 221, 228, 229, 266 (n. 108), 267 (n. 3), 268 (n. 15); movement as freedom, 33, 72, 144, 152, 170, 216. *See also* Labor: labor activists, labor movement, and labor organizing; Manhood; Mobility; Modernization: modernization theory

Murphy, George (R-Calif.), 56

Murrow, Edward R. See *Harvest of Shame*

Music/musicians, 1, 13, 92, 115, 120, 121, 122, 129–31, 135, 150–51, 160, 177, 256 (n. 86), 277–78 (n. 10). See also *Corridos*

Nacional, El, 203

Nation/nation-state, 2, 3, 4, 5, 6, 7, 8, 10, 15, 16, 17, 26, 27, 29, 31, 32, 34, 35, 36, 37, 41, 42, 43, 44, 45, 46, 47–65, 67, 70, 72, 73, 75, 77, 79, 80, 82, 83, 84, 85, 89, 90, 91, 93, 94, 95, 101, 104, 108, 110, 111, 112, 114, 116, 117, 118, 121, 127, 128, 129, 130, 131, 134, 137, 141, 142, 143, 144, 145, 146, 151, 153, 154, 155, 156, 157, 160, 162, 164, 166, 167, 168, 170, 171, 174, 175, 176, 177, 178, 179, 180, 181, 182, 183, 191, 192, 193, 194, 195, 201, 204, 210, 212, 215, 217, 218, 219, 220, 221, 225, 226, 227, 228, 229. *See also* Citizens/citizenship; Growers: narratives

National Alliance of Braceros from Mexico (Alianza Nacional de Braceros de México), 164, 165

National Catholic Rural Life Conference, 122, 161

National Farmers Union, 25

National Farm Labor Union (NFLU),
146, 149, 150, 151, 153, 154, 157, 163,
164, 165, 166, 263 (n. 47); Local 218,
146, 149, 155, 164
National Geographic magazine, 115
Nationality: versus citizenship, 228
National Labor Relations Act (1935), 39
National Public Radio, 223
National subjects, 5, 6, 15, 16, 31, 32, 33,
43, 44, 46, 75, 85, 94, 104, 110, 111,
119, 127, 128, 129–31, 134, 137, 144,
170, 173–82, 192, 195. *See also* Mod-
ern, the: modern subjects; Trans-
national subjects/subjectivity
Nature, 151–52, 153
Nayarit, 68
New Deal, 39, 164
New York City, 147
New York Times, 102
Ngai, Mae M. 45
1948 Incident. *See* El Paso Incident
1954 Incident, 208–14, 218, 219
Nixon, Richard M. (U.S. president,
1969–74), 154

Ochoa Perdomo, Ignacio, 135
Oklahoma, 39, 57
Operation Wetback, 42, 208, 213, 215
Opinión, La, 203, 209, 210, 211, 271 (n. 4)
Opportunity, 1, 3, 10, 21, 32, 34, 46, 48,
54, 65, 67, 110, 116, 129, 174, 175, 193,
201, 202, 221; versus exploitation, 11,
16, 201, 221, 252 (n. 36), 264 (n. 85),
269 (n. 16). *See also* Exploitation

Pacific Ocean, 153
Padilla, Ezequiel (Mexican minister of
foreign relations), 26, 34
Padrino (godfather). See *Compadre*
Pan-Americanism, 216
Pan-American Union, 238 (n. 48), 241
(n. 98), 271 (n. 4)
Patria, 117
Patriarchy, 16, 34, 73, 75, 81, 82, 85, 91,

106, 110, 114, 127, 128, 131, 132, 133,
134, 139, 142, 143, 171, 173–92, 248
(n. 38); modernization of, 73. *See also*
Gender; Manhood
Pérez-Torres, Cirilio, 224–25
Perluss, Irving, 170
Pescador Polanco, Juan, 70–71
Phelps-Dodge mine, 72
Pitti, Gina Marie, 162
Poverty in the Valley of Plenty, 153
Practices of border, 90, 101, 102, 111,
114, 119, 136, 144, 171, 173, 174, 183,
184, 194
Premodern, the. *See* Modern, the
Progress, 1, 2, 3, 10, 11, 27, 32, 33, 34, 35,
37, 38, 51, 53, 62, 81, 82, 85, 89, 95,
104, 118, 156. *See also* Exploitation;
Modern, the; Opportunity
Proper patriarch. *See* Patriarchy
Public Law 45, 23
Public Law 78, 61

Queso. See Cheese

Race, 4, 6, 8, 11, 14, 15, 16, 29, 33, 35, 37,
39, 44, 45, 47, 48, 51, 52, 53, 57, 58,
61, 65, 75, 90, 94, 99, 101, 102, 104,
105, 108, 111, 112, 113, 114, 116, 119,
127, 130, 131, 134, 142, 144, 145, 147,
152, 160, 163, 166, 168, 171, 174, 175,
178, 179, 182, 186, 191, 192, 194, 206,
217, 221, 226, 232 (n. 9), 240 (n. 76),
243 (nn. 126, 127), 254 (n. 104), 267
(n. 3). *See also* Indians; Mestizos;
Mexico: racial system in; United
States: racial system/ideology in
Radio(s), 72, 121, 144
Ramírez, Antonio, 13, 129–30
Reception centers, 95, 96, 97, 98, 100,
102, 103, 104, 106, 112, 143, 168, 203,
204, 273, 255 (n. 5), 273 (nn. 18, 19);
El Centro reception center, 96, 102,
103. *See also* Contracting centers;
Migratory stations

Tractors, 2, 31, 57, 121, 148, 180, 198, 245 (n. 42)

Traditional, the. *See* Modern, the

Trains, 27, 28, 37, 68, 69, 71, 94, 97, 98, 114, 115, 119, 144, 178, 218, 232 (n. 3), 251 (n. 30), 255 (n. 6)

Transnational, the, 3, 4, 5, 6, 7, 8, 9, 14, 15, 16, 17, 60, 65, 72, 104, 127, 128, 142, 143, 144, 160, 170, 173, 189, 197, 226; definition of trans-, 7

Transnational subjects/subjectivity, 3, 4, 5, 6, 7, 8, 9, 13, 14, 15, 16, 17, 48, 68, 86, 90, 108, 111, 112, 119, 127, 128, 129–31, 134, 137, 139, 142, 144, 145, 170, 173–82, 192, 195, 221, 226, 227, 228, 229; definition of, 5, 68

Transnational system/space/world, 3, 5, 6, 7, 8, 11, 14, 16, 17, 112, 120, 174, 185, 186, 189, 198; definition of, 3

Triggs, Matt. *See* American Farm Bureau

Trucks, 57, 69, 114, 125, 164, 203, 255 (n. 6)

Truman, Harry S. (U.S. president, 1945–53), 31, 166, 195, 207; Commission on Migratory Labor (1951), 167; narrative of progress, 32–33; Point Four program, 32

Tuberculosis, 98, 103, 105, 193

Undocumented workers, 25, 29, 30, 71, 112, 141, 161, 164, 165, 202–21, 223, 225, 239 (n. 53), 255 (n. 5), 257 (n. 47), 260 (n. 131), 268 (n. 11), 271 (n. 3), 273 (nn. 18, 20), 276 (n. 88), 278 (n. 12). *See also* Farmworkers/ workers

Unión de Trabajadores Agrícolas del Valle de Mexicali (Mexicali Valley Farmworkers Union), 165

Unión de Trabajadores del Valle Imperial (Imperial Valley Workers Union), 42

Unions, 2, 14, 21, 24, 26, 27, 28, 29, 30, 35, 38, 40, 41, 42, 47, 52, 54, 57, 62, 63, 108, 141, 146–71, 205, 215, 216, 217, 220, 226, 232 (n. 6), 238 (n. 40), 239 (n. 52), 242 (n. 110), 260 (nn. 131, 3), 261 (n. 11), 263 (nn. 47, 53, 55), 271 (n. 2), 276 (n. 75). *See also* Farmworkers/workers; Labor: labor activists, labor movement, and labor organizing

Union Trust Company of San Francisco, 224

United Farm Workers. *See* Chávez, César

United Kingdom, 206

United Nations (UN), 217, 219; Fifth General Assembly, 205, 207

United States: border patrol, 10, 30, 42, 202–5, 208–14; boycott of Mexican oil, 28; Chamber of Commerce, 51; Congress, 30, 39, 50, 52, 57, 58, 123, 149, 154, 156, 169, 211, 213, 215, 216, 223, 241 (n. 98), 244 (n. 8); *Congressional Record*, 153; Department of Agriculture (DOA), 41, 54, 148, 160, 216, 234 (n. 20), 236 (n. 27), 244 (n. 8); Department of Justice (DOJ), 208; Department of Labor (DOL), 22, 56, 98, 100, 118, 142, 158, 161, 168, 208, 216, 217, 218, 275 (n. 77); Department of Public Health, 98, 100; Department of State, 208; Farm Security Administration (FSA), 22, 39, 41, 42, 55, 234 (nn. 2, 4), 235 (n. 7); House Committee on Education and Labor, 153; language of citizenship, 45–46, 166–67; and parity, 47, 52, 59; racial system/ideology in, 6, 11, 16, 29, 39, 45–47, 51–53, 58, 61, 90, 99, 101, 102, 104, 108, 111, 119, 127, 131, 134, 142, 144, 145–71, 174, 175, 186, 194, 206, 217, 243 (n. 127), 267 (n. 3); relations with Mexico, 16, 21, 23, 27–28, 30, 201–21; support for growers, 40

CPSIA information can be obtained at www.ICGtesting.com
Printed in the USA
LVOW10s0138120816

500012LV00003B/182/P